Dario Fo
and
Franca Rame

By the same author

Dario Fo and Franca Rame:
Harlequins of the Revolution

Leonardo Sciascia

Sicily: A Cultural History

Non è tempo di nostalgia with Franca Rame

La mia vita, le mie battaglie with Dacia Maraini

Robert Louis Stevenson in Samoa

Dario Fo and Franca Rame

Theatre, Politics, Life

Joseph Farrell

Methuen

First published by Methuen
2019

1

Methuen
Orchard House
Railway Street
Slingsby
York YO62 4AN

Copyright © Joseph Farrell 2019

A CIP catalogue record for this book is available
from the British Library

ISBN: 978 0 413 77712 3

Typeset by SX Composing DTP, Rayleigh, Essex.
Printed and bound in Great Britain by Clays Ltd, Elcograf S.p.A.

www.methuen.co.uk

Contents

Introduction

The output of Dario Fo and Franca Rame, jointly or singly, is vast and as such creates problems for the conscientious critic or biographer. Even if modern publishers afforded authors the Victorian luxury of the three-volume work, it would still be a daunting task to contain everything in one book. At times, it seemed they had simply done too much, written too much, spoken too much, given too many interviews, made too many television programmes, supervised too many workshops, been involved in too many controversies, appeared too often on stage, performed in too many countries and have had too many plays translated into too many languages for any one book to provide a complete record of their lives and achievements. Not even Dario Fo can have read all that has been written by Dario Fo, let alone about Dario Fo. Franca certainly facilitated the biographer's task, since she has shown herself to be an astonishing archivist who has collected everything written about them in every language of every country they have visited since they first worked together, so the mass of material is impressive, but overwhelming.

In addition, they have been observers of, and participants in, many of the great events which have shaped modern Italy, which means they have been in equal measure supported and opposed, loved and hated, admired and vilified, revered and persecuted. The fact that in the course of their lives they were assaulted in Argentina, that the American

1

government twice found it necessary to refuse them visas, that the Vatican attacked them, that Soviet authorities refused to license their plays for performance, that bombs were placed near their homes and theatres, that Franca was kidnapped and raped with the connivance of the police forces and that they faced prosecution on many occasions in Italy is proof, however desperate the expression of that proof, of their national and international status as spokespersons for causes unpopular with those who wield power.

Now that both are dead, this is the moment to attempt to chronicle and assess their achievements, not only in theatre. They are known in Italy and abroad as actor-authors, and their political campaigning has been widely reported. Franca, even if she was uncomfortable with the label 'feminist,' was a leading figure in the women's movement, but the range of their interests and activities was much wider. Dario can be regarded as one of those artist-creators who flourished in later life, especially after the award of the Nobel Prize in 1997 gave him enhanced prestige. From his earliest youth, he was also an artist, but took to painting with renewed vigour in his later years, producing such a volume of work that the Italian government established a gallery in Verona exclusively devoted to him. He also dedicated himself, in books and television programmes, to the criticism and popularising of the great masters of Italian art; he became a spokesman on issues associated with ecological and green politics, being particularly outspoken on questions of bio-engineering and cloning; at the age of 88, he produced his first novel, going on to produce six, two co-authored. Both he and Franca entered the arena of active politics, Franca as a Senator in Italy's parliament and Dario as candidate for mayor of Milan and then as active supporter of the 5 Star Movement founded by the ex-comedian Beppe Grillo.

The present volume attempts to cover their life and work as completely as is feasible. The first part is a comprehensive revision of my earlier biography - *Dario Fo and Franca Rame: Harlequins of the Revolution* (London, Methuen, 2001), which ended approximately with the award of the Nobel Prize. An Italian translation was published as *Dario e Franca: la biografia della coppia Fo/Rame attraverso la storia italiana* (Milan,

INTRODUCTION

Ledizioni, 2014), and I took advantage of the publication of that edition to revise the original work and to update up to the death of Franca Rame in May 2013. The new chapters were published in English in a separate pamphlet in Milan by the same publisher, but not distributed in the UK. These too have been rewritten and the work extended up to the death of Dario. This is now a complete biography of Dario Fo and Franca Rame.

There are many people to whom I am indebted. My principal debt is to Franca Rame for her patience and willingness to spend time with me answering questions. I mourn her passing and regret that she will not see the result. I am grateful to Dario Fo for many enjoyable, stimulating and informative conversations. I would also like to express gratitude for assistance at various times to Walter Valeri, Bianca Fo Garambois, Ron Jenkins, Piero Sciotto, Paolo Puppa, Vittorio Franceschi, Tony Mitchell, Antonio Scuderi, Tom Baldwin, Ed Emery, Mario Pirovano, Jacopo Fo, Felice Cappa, Jessica Borroni, Chiara Porro, and Mariateresa Pizza. I owe a debt too to some who are no longer with us, Emilio Tadini, Flavia Tolnay, Chris Cairns and Nanni Ricordi, and others who preferred not to be named. I cannot quantify my debt to my wife, Maureen.

Joseph Farrell
Glasgow
1 February 2019

CHAPTER 1

Childhood and War

Dario Fo was born in the village of San Giano near Lake Maggiore on 24 March 1926, four years after Mussolini's march on Rome. The stout anti-fascism of his immediate family left an enduring mark, but the centuries-old culture of his birthplace made a deeper, more lasting impact. In his whimsical, and not always reliable, memoir, *My First Seven Years*, he quotes the psychologist Bruno Bettelheim as stating that for the formation of the mind and character of an individual 'all you have to give me is the first seven years of life.'[1] On another occasion, Dario wrote: 'I am quite certain that everything has its origins in the place you are born. For my part, I was born in a . . . village of smugglers and poachers, two trades for which you need, in addition to a generous helping of courage, a great deal of imagination. It is well known that anyone who uses imagination to break the law will always have a lot left over for his own enjoyment and that of his closest friends.'[2]

His father, Felice Fo, was a stationmaster, and his mother, Pina Rota, a woman of peasant stock, neither of them given to law-breaking, but on his mother's side Dario found an abundance of that whimsical imagination and creative flair he regarded as his principal inheritance from his boyhood on the lake. The Rotas had lived in Monferrato in Piedmont until Dario's great-grandfather, Giuseppe, moved the family to Sartirana, in southern Lombardy. Only one aspect of Giuseppe's talents has lingered in the family memory: he could read and write in an

4

age of mass illiteracy, and used these skills to compose commemorative eulogies or optimistic madrigals at funerals or weddings. The payment helped keep bread on the table. Sartirana was the chosen destination because it lay in the heart of Italy's rice-growing area, and the Rotas were peasants who had to go where work could be found. Rice-growing was crippling, back-breaking work, requiring the mainly female employees to work bent double, with water up to their knees, but at least it offered some form of guaranteed income. The plight of the rice workers was memorably dramatised in the 1949 neo-realist film, *Riso amaro*. The title is ambiguous: the second word means bitter and the first has the double meaning of 'laughter' or 'rice'. Any laughter was bitter indeed, and the image of Silvana Mangano standing, unbroken and uncowed, in the paddy fields remained as an icon of defiance long after conditions had altered. Dario's grandmother, Maria, born in 1876, experienced such conditions. She was required to leave home each day before dawn to walk three hours to the fields. It was thankless labour, and any woman who straightened up to relieve the pressure on her spine was liable to feel the supervisor's rod on her back, 'the same as they did with cows or oxen'. By the time Pina started work in the same fields, the rod was no longer in use but the women were still treated like beasts. 'I used to work ten to twelve hours a day when I was only ten,' she wrote, 'bending down in water that came up over my knees, with leeches clinging to my legs.'[3]

The family prospered, after a fashion, thanks to Pina's father, who was given the name Luigi at baptism but was invariably known as Bristin. He was born in 1860, and his hard work and ingenuity enabled him to rise to the status of *perdapè*, a dialect word which translates, approximately if unhelpfully, as 'lost foot'. To make a living from the land, a *perdapè* laboured 'from the stars to the stars', every day of the week, even on Sundays, with such exertion that his feet risked taking root in the soil. In the complex hierarchy of peasant life, he occupied an intermediate position between the normally absentee landowner from whom he rented his land, and the casual workers who were taken on when needed. The various grades of peasant lived cheek by jowl on a *cascina*, a collective farmstead. Houses, stables, barns, pigsties and stalls for sheep, goats and cattle were huddled one alongside the other, while the central space was occupied by a compost heap and drinking trough. There were around one hundred people in the *cascina* inhabited by Dario's grandparents. Bristin and his wife Maria had seven children who survived infancy, with Pina, Dario's mother, born in 1903, the sixth. She was a sickly child, prone to all the illnesses that periodically struck the children of the area, so she derived little benefit from the garlic necklace she was made to wear to ward off disease.

It is Bristin who emerges as the dominant figure in her recollections of her girlhood, and as the central influence on Dario as a boy. A man of superabundant energy and initiative who combined the peasant's down to earth competence with an irrepressible imagination of his own, he made his mark on all who met him. The traditional methods of agriculture and the modesty of subsistence farming were not for him. He expanded his smallholding and experimented with systems for grafting and cross-planting apples and pears, or plums and apricots in an attempt to produce new varieties of fruit. The results were sufficiently impressive to cause the university botanists in Padua to invite him, a mere peasant, to share the results of his research with them.

These achievements drew the respect of his contemporaries, but his real fame among them was due to his quixotic imagination, his malicious wit, his biting sarcasm, his ability as teller of tales and taste for rumbustious fun. The nickname 'Bristin', a local term for pepper seed, the part of the plant which burns and stings the tongue, was conferred in recognition of these qualities. 'When my father told stories about his own family, he put on the story-teller voice, which was solemn, with breaks for comic comments. We listened to him in astonishment,' wrote Pina. These monologues were acted rather than recounted but what impressed her, and later Dario, was his ability to change key, to instil in his listeners a sense of fear or awe and then deftly switch the mood to deflating or liberating humour. Pina was especially impressed by the gruesome tale of the monks of Monferrato, a community of holy men who disapproved of the late night drinking habits of the townsfolk but who instead of limiting themselves to exhortations and sermons took to frightening revellers by climbing up the belfry and projecting weird, ghost-like shadows onto the walls of the village houses. The terrified drinkers assumed their village was viewed by God as a new Sodom and Gomorrah and fearing a visitation by the Almighty, resolved to stay at home after nightfall. Business at the inns suffered until a tavern-owner discovered that the shadows were not signs of divine displeasure but of vengeful malice by the monks. The enraged population marched on the monastery, locked the monks in the belfry and set fire to it, leaving them to roast. The story had a happy ending, since the frantic ringing of the bells brought rescuers from nearby, but thereafter the roistering and revelling resumed, while the monks were left to their chanting in the cloister. Bristin was an atheist, who took delight in anti-clerical jibes, and doubtless this added spice to the tale.[4]

He had no shame over being a peasant, even if he displayed his caste's ambiguous relationship with the land. For him, peasants were the dispossessed of the earth and working the land meant 'spitting sweat and blood', but he also believed that 'the real gold was land' and that there was a dignity and rightness to such labours. He was enraged when his sons and sons-in-law one after the other left the country for the city. Pina was anxious to follow them. Dario later wrote that his mother described Sartirana as a paradise, adding that he too remembered it that way, and perhaps he did, but the view of the *cascina* and the village she expressed in her autobiographical *The Country of the Frogs* is decidedly disenchanted. The reference to the frogs is double edged. Frogs were one of the plagues of ancient Egypt and she complained, unsurprisingly, of having to live surrounded by the croaking of frogs which even invaded the houses, but frogs were also a delicacy for those who could not afford meat. Chicken was the food of the masters.

The first meeting of Dario's parents is enveloped in a pleasing air of Latin romance. Pina's eldest sister, Clementina, was engaged to one Luigi, a member of the extended Fo clan, and the guests at the wedding included Luigi's cousin, Felice Fo. As in the best love stories, Pina and Felice were immediately attracted to each other, but there was an obstacle on true love's smooth path: Pina was already engaged. It was not acceptable for young ladies to break promises of marriage, and when she announced her new love the ex-fiancé reacted as was expected of a man whose honour had been offended. He turned up in the *cascina* with a gun, demanding satisfaction and firing in all directions. Pina managed to hide and the man was calmed down before blood was spilled. Felice and Pina were married in 1925.

By coincidence, the Fos too could trace their ancestry back to Monferrato, although family historians speculate that the name was originally Genoese. Fo is not a particularly common name in any part of Italy and indeed Dario's sister, Bianca, claimed that they can always trace some family link with any other Fo they come across. It is also a dialect word for beech tree, and later in life Dario enjoyed the comparison with the strength and straightness of the wood. Felice's father, Luigi, led the family migration from Piedmont to Lombardy in the late nineteenth century, with one branch settling in Sartirana and the rest moving up towards Lake Maggiore. They were more open to new technologies than the Rotas, and Luigi found employment with the Italian railways. He married Teresa Barzaghini, and they had three daughters and two sons, of whom Felice, born in 1898, was the youngest. Felice followed his father into railways, although at the more elevated level of stationmaster.

Employment as a stationmaster was highly desirable in pre-war Italy. D H Lawrence, who lived for a time in the village of Gargnano on the nearby Lake Garda, wrote that life for an Italian stationmaster was one long conversation interrupted by a telephone call, but Felice took his job with greater seriousness. 'Our degree of poverty can be established in relation to the activity of my father, a stationmaster with the National Railways,' Dario wrote. The family was able to live comfortably, experiencing neither wealth nor poverty. Felice seems not to have possessed any outdoor clothes apart from his railway uniform, a striking red jacket and dark trousers which Pina cleaned every night, but in that he cut an imposing figure. Some pundits have been tempted to read a great deal into the fact that he performed with amateur dramatic societies. While still very young, Dario remembered being taken to see his father on stage in 'a cruel Ibsen play' featuring parents out to rid themselves of their child. His main reaction was dismay at seeing another child using his rocking horse on stage. Felice was also given to going around the house declaiming in a loud, resonant voice verses from Giosuè Carducci, Italy's nineteenth-century Nobel prize winning poet, and from the *Divine Comedy*.

The marriage was a happy one, but the two were very different personalities. 'My mother,' wrote Dario, 'was full of fantasy and irony. My father less so, because he worked very hard and studied. He was self-taught.'[5] Pina was plainly a woman of spirit, of open affections, wide-ranging imagination and boundless creativity. She had little formal education, but shared with Bristin a restless curiosity. She inherited her father's nickname and many of his talents, including a flair for story-telling. Felice, on the other hand, was a man of serious manners and serious mind, and showed his gravitas by a tendency to wear his worries on his sleeve. The world was to be made aware that the problems of bringing up a young family were burdensome, especially on an inadequate income. For Bianca, he was a gentle, amiable man, but Dario remembers a harsher side to his nature. In his memoir, he admits he was somewhat afraid of his father,[6] and in an interview he went further:

> My father was severe, a bit like the overbearing fathers described in the tear-jerking novels of other times. Like my grandfather he was capable of extraordinary openness with his grandchildren, but he was very hard on his own children. He shouted a lot and at times raised his hands, even if he did regret it ten seconds later. I can still see one scene where my father slapped and kicked my brother because he had gone to steal fruit in the countryside.[7]

Such experiences, and recollections of friends turning up at school covered with bruises or a broken nose left Dario with an abiding horror of all forms of physical brutality. In the same interview, he said he 'had never lifted a finger on his son,' since he and Franca Rame had agreed that no form of physical punishment would ever be employed at home.

Felice was a socialist, although not an active party member, and the family are still convinced that the Fascist apparatchiks made him pay by denying him a fixed posting. The family were forced to live a nomadic existence in Lombardy as Felice was moved first to San Giano, where Dario was born, then to Luino, where Fulvio was born in 1928 and Bianca in 1931, then to Voghera, then Oleggio and finally, in 1936, to Porto Valtravaglia, on the shores of Lake Maggiore. Although Dario was already ten years old when they arrived there, this is the village which he regarded as his childhood home.

Porto Valtravaglia, a small town of around 2000 souls, lies halfway up Lake Maggiore on the eastern side, not far from the Swiss border. Nestling between the mountains and the waters, it was and is an idyllic spot which became a fabled place in Dario's private mythology. The lake was the heart of the world for him as a boy. In spring, the landscape is bright and lively, and in autumn grave and peaceful. Dario never became a writer who excelled in poetic descriptive prose, but the colours and atmosphere of the landscape around Lake Maggiore appear in many of his paintings. Already in his boyhood, he demonstrated that ease with the paintbrush which never deserted him. In his earliest canvases, he depicted valleys, villages and farms of his native region with astonishing vividness and precision.

In the town, Felice rented an art nouveau villa, known locally as the *palazzetto*, which was surrounded by a garden stretching down to the lake. Grapes, apples, plums and other fruits and vegetables grew there, but workmen helped with the cultivation of the plants, so the children did not experience the grinding toil which was the lot of the peasant children in the neighbourhood. Near their house, stood the villas of the *signori* from Milan, who came there in the summer to escape the heat of the city. Already as a boy, Dario displayed spirit and imagination. Anecdotes abound. One summer he built a boat, summoned the children of the neighbourhood for a ceremonial launch and turned up in a white uniform. Regrettably, the naval architecture was not of the required standard, for the craft capsized on its first outing. The *palazzetto* had a little tower, with a window opening onto the garden, and in summer Dario, Fulvio and Bianca converted the tower into a puppet theatre. Dario carved by himself the puppets which represented devils, Russian princes or Pulcinella. The three children set up chairs in the garden and asked the infant spectators to make a payment towards the purchase of materials for future enterprises. The inspiration for such shows came partly from the touring puppet theatres which did the rounds of the villages on the lake. Dario and Fulvio went along as frequently as they could and learned by heart several of the standard dialogues. The circus was another occasional visitor. The children would be blacked up by the circus owners and sent round the village dressed in mock-African outfits to drum up interest. Bianca used one incident for a children's story she later published, with illustrations by Dario. In it, Dario disappeared when the circus arrived in town, but turned up in the Big Top that evening on an elephant's back, in the guise of an African boy.

Political events cast a shadow, but not one of sufficient strength to darken their lives. The opposition of Felice and Bristin to Mussolini and the Fascist regime was purely private. 'Capitalism, Vatican and Fascism – there's the great secret of the Trinity revealed,' was one of Bristin's slogans,[8] but Fascism and anti-Fascism intruded comparatively little into domestic life. The parents did what was necessary to keep peace, for example, sending the children to the Fascist youth organisation, the *balilla*. When he was sixteen, Dario won an art prize from the youth organisation for a portrait of Fulvio.[9] Bianca once came rushing home from school in fear after listening to a denunciation in the classroom of the terrible creatures who were called socialists, and being subjected to mockery in the yard by other children who claimed her father was such a one. Felice diplomatically denied it.

'I had a happy childhood,' said Dario, 'even not counting the fact that I lived in a splendid place, on Lake Maggiore. I used to go to school on skis, just imagine what a joy that was. In spring, I walked there through fields of flowers.'[10] Any amateur psychologist hoping to locate in Dario or his brother and sister some trauma or wound arising from family circumstances or relationships will be disappointed. The nearest approach to any such feeling is the mild annoyance expressed by Bianca over favoured treatment accorded by Pina towards Dario. Pina encouraged his youthful creativity and fostered the talents she believed he had, but she also may have been more protective towards him because of an already evident tendency towards absent-mindedness. In another story, Bianca retold a favourite family tale of Dario being sent out to buy butter and returning much later without the butter but with the body of a lizard whose colours had caught his imagination. 'He had always a pencil or a brush in his hand,' recalled Bianca, 'always sketching out some face, figure, tree or house.' His mother's pride was strained when Dario's distracted artistic bent led him to use a nail to scratch wild scenes on the wooden bedstead.

Porto Valtravaglia was unlike the other communities which lined Lake Maggiore. Like them, the principal legal occupation was fishing and the main illegal source of income was smuggling, but Porto Valtravaglia also boasted a glass-works, an industry which gave this small town an unexpectedly cosmopolitan stamp. The owners of the factory had recruited their workers from all over Europe, from Flanders, France, Germany and Slovenia, so Dario's school friends had a range of exotic names and something of a dual culture. 'It was an absurd, paradoxical place,' he wrote, 'which came to life by night, so much so that the nickname of the inhabitants was "half-mouse," in other words "bat." Many of the men had to do night-shifts, so the town was alive, with its bars and restaurants always full of people going to and coming from work.' He made the strange boast that Porto Valtravaglia had the highest proportion of madmen in Italy. 'They had a special ambulance to transport people from the town to the asylum,' he recalled, bizarrely.

Their grandmother, Maria, died in 1938, too early to leave the children anything other than a vague memory of a quiet woman with a soft voice, but Bristin continued to enthrall them. After the death of his wife, he sold up but resisted all attempts to have him leave the land. When the Fo children went to visit him in Sartirana, he joined boisterously in their games, and more than once constructed precarious rafts on which, to Pina's consternation, he took them cruising on the region's small canals. Before his retirement, Dario often accompanied him on his rounds to sell his produce to the nearby villages and farmsteads, where his arrival would cause outbursts of excited expectation. Bristin publicised his wares with his extemporised tales and extravagant flights of fancy, but also spread local news and peddled outrageous gossip, illustrating sexual exploits and misdemeanours with leeks and courgettes to show the activities in question and the size of the organs involved. 'Tragedy in Sarzana', was one typical opening gambit. 'He came out onto the balcony in his underwear, dragging his naked wife behind him. "She's a whore, he announced to the crowd". Meanwhile her faithless friend was racing down the side stairs, but he slipped and broke his leg. You can find him in hospital at Carrara, room 32. Bring him flowers, he deserves them'.[11] Dario later paid Bristin the highest compliment in his repertory by referring to him as 'the first Ruzzante' he had known, associating him with the sixteenth-century actor-author who was to become Dario's supreme theatrical model and inspiration.

Bristin was typical of the *fabulatore,* or story-teller, a familiar figure in Porto Valtravaglia and the one who made the deepest contribution to Dario's development. Years later in his official speech to the Royal Academy in Stockholm on the award of the Nobel prize, Dario recalled his debt to the men who had fashioned from their own experience, or from their own fantasy, stories they retold for fun or for profit. There were still travelling, professional story-tellers in the region, but the *fabulatori* who particularly fascinated Dario were the local fishermen who spun their yarns as they repaired their nets, or the glassworkers who recounted their narratives while blowing glass.

These stories had no savour of humdrum realism. They were hyperbolic tales spiced with whimsy, in which the grotesque and the absurd, observation and surreal wit, mordant satire and resigned nonchalance mingled together. They transported the audience into a fantasy dimension which somehow overlapped with the world inhabited by the narrator and the listener. Although seemingly a retelling of real events, the list of improbable characters included an enthusiastic fisherman who cast his line so far it fell on the opposite bank of the lake, causing him to haul in a church and congregation; giant snails which terrified their hunters; and women who got drunk in the taverns and returned home to beat up their husbands. There was one long tale, retold during the Nobel prize speech in Stockholm, dealing with the pig-headed villagers of Caldè. The village was liable to subsidence and began sliding towards the lake. Experts came from the city to advise the villagers to get out before it was too late, but they were too stubborn to admit what was happening before their eyes and rejected all warnings until they went under with the village. In their obstinacy, they still refused to recognize reality and carried on life under water as though they were exposed to nothing more than a general dampening of the climate. Stories from the Bible or from mythology could be adapted and turned on their head. At night, when the three children were in their bedroom, Dario retold these stories to his brother and sister, with improvised additions and comment of his own. Like the Brontë sisters in Yorkshire, the Fo children inhabited their own private fantasy land, peopled by extravagant villagers from far-off places and by lakeside monsters, by creatures of the air and princelings from the east.

The experience of listening to these men left an enduring mark. 'Having grown up in a village where every man is a character, where every character is in search of a tale to tell, I was able to enter the theatre with a baggage which was unusual and, even more, alive, up-to-date and true. True in the way that stories invented by true men are true'.[12] The teller of tales provided him with his first model in theatre, and the art of the *fabulatore* even lay behind mature works such as *Mistero buffo* or *Story of a Tiger.* It also provided him with instances of what, following Gramsci, he would define as popular culture. Whimsy had its limits, since Fo believed that the fantasy of the *fabulatore* often concealed a vein of anger. 'Simplicity was their keynote . . . but beneath these absurd tales their bitterness was concealed. It was the bitterness, which perhaps few picked up, of a disappointed people, expressed in an acid satire aimed at the official world. I suddenly discovered both a new, genuine culture and the creative force of those who have always been defined as "simpletons" or "ignorant". They have always been the pariahs of official culture.'[13] Dario was to remain a teller of tales, imbued with the popular approach. The technique of tempering grotesque whimsy with the acid of irony was not the least of his gifts from Porto Valtravaglia.

At that time, Italian children were only required by law to attend primary school, but in 1940, when he was fourteen, the family decided Dario was showing unusual promise and should be enabled to continue his education. The decision meant a daily departure at five o'clock and a round trip of five hours to Milan. The daily commute by train gave him unexpected opportunities as it was there he found his first audience for his story-telling abilities. The school chosen was the Brera *liceo*, part of the renowned educational-artistic complex which includes the National Library, the famous art gallery and the Academy where he would later enrol as an art student. From this point, even if his writing would never be of a sort which would make him a Milanese writer in the way Dickens was a London writer or Balzac a Parisian writer, Dario's growth and development have been inextricably linked with the history of the city.

If 1940 was important in Dario's personal development, it was also the year when Italy entered the war. Detachments of the Italian army served on the Russian front, as well as in Greece, Albania and North Africa but in the early stages, for the inhabitants of Lombardy, it was a phoney war, fought in far-off lands of which they knew little. This situation changed with the Allied Landing in Sicily in July 1943 and the subsequent overthrow of Mussolini by the Grand Council in Rome. The *Duce* was briefly imprisoned before being freed by a German detachment, while General Badoglio assumed power in Rome. The advance of the British and American armies up the Italian peninsula split the country in two, with the South under Allied control and the North ruled, at least in principle, by the Repubblica Sociale Italiana (RSI) headed by Mussolini. The RSI, with its capital at Salò on Lake Garda, was theoretically autonomous with its own military and bureaucratic apparatus, but was de facto a Nazi satellite state. Fascism continued to have its sympathisers, while armed Resistance groups, whose targets were both the Nazi invader and the Fascist militia, sprang up all over the North. The situation became more complex when Badoglio declared an Armistice on 8 September 1943, thereby releasing the army from any obligation to continue the fight against the Allied forces. The divided country was now in a state of civil war. The first actions of the Resistance were organised by members of the Italian army, but various partisan groups, of differing political orientation, some overtly Communist, others more centrist, began to be formed. The area around Lake Maggiore became the front line.

Historians are now divided in their interpretations of this period of Allied invasion, Nazi occupation, Resistance and Liberation. In the immediate post-war period, it was an article of faith that the Resistance units were composed of idealistic knights, while the RSI militia were mobs of killers and thugs, but the efforts of revisionist historians and of right-wing politicians in recent times have compelled substantial rethinking. Bad memory, bad faith, guilty conscience, ideological preconceptions and sheer opportunism have helped blur distinctions. Some historians suggest that there were three kinds of war underway at the one time: a war of national liberation, a civil war and a class war. A necessary balance in the polemical discussions was given by Italo Calvino, who fought with the partisans but who later refused to have his choice seen as dictated by principled idealism. In his novel, *The Path to the Spiders' Nests*, the greatest work of fiction on that period, he dismissed all talk of heroism and highlighted the confusion and uncertainty of the protagonists, both in fiction and in history. In spite of the praise bestowed on it on first publication in 1947, Calvino was dissatisfied with his novel, and for the 1964 edition he wrote a new introduction in which he discussed not only the nature of neo-realism but also the impulses behind individual decisions to join the Resistance: 'For many of my contemporaries, it had been solely a question of luck which determined which side they should fight on: for many of them, the sides suddenly changed over, so that soldiers on Mussolini's Fascist Republic became partisans and vice versa. They shot or were shot at on either side; only death signalled an end to their choices.'[14]

Inevitably, Dario Fo became caught up in these complex political and moral debates, as in his youth he was entangled in the anarchy of those confused and bloody times. His family were convinced anti-Fascists, but Lombardy, including both Sartirana and Lake Maggiore, was in territory ruled from Salò and became one of the main arenas of civil war. Bombardments by the Allies were frequent, although Porto Valtravaglia itself was never struck. The glassworks were converted into a barracks for the Seventh Infantry regiment, while the Fo house was requisitioned by the RSI army. Bianca had to be moved from her room to make way for a colonel who was billeted with them. Other members of the family faced dangers of their own. Beniamino, Dario's uncle, was in uniform in the Air Force, which he had joined before the war out of an interest in aviation engineering. After the Armistice, he was one of some 600,000 Italian soldiers arrested and deported to Germany. (Franca Rame's brother suffered the same fate.) While in Germany, Beniamino's expertise in engineering, which was useful to the German war effort, saved him.

The rest of the family was engaged in support for partisan groups. Bristin, a sprightly eighty-three year old in 1943, was now living with his daughter, Tina, whose house was near the woods along the Po river where many escaped Allied POWs were in hiding. He and his son, Nino, brought them food and Nino helped organise escape parties to Switzerland. When the Fascists came to arrest Nino, Bristin caused a diversion which allowed him to make his escape across the rooftops.[15] Felice was one of the leading lights in the local CLN – Committee for National Liberation – and he too guided parties of escaped British and American prisoners of wars across the border into Switzerland. In spite of the presence of the Fascist militia, the garden of the Fo house in Porto Valtravaglia was used by the partisans to conceal fuel. This could have created mayhem, but the stocks were never discovered.

Dario's life changed when, aged seventeen, he received call-up papers from the RSI. He was too young for military service, but was required to present himself for civilian service, which might have taken him to Germany. Even had he remained in Italy, the North was under Allied bombardment, and large sections of Milan were devastated. After discussions with his father, he decided to enrol with the Anti-Aircraft Artillery detachment in Varese. There has been considerable mystery and confusion over Dario's movements and activities in those chaotic, muddled and murderous months, not helped by the varying and incomplete accounts he has given at different times. The decisions he took returned, fairly or unfairly, to dog him all his life, and smears by opponents who suggested that he had supported Fascism were invariably met by libel actions from him, notably to a case for slander in 1978. He was on many occasions questioned by interviewers over his decision to join up 'voluntarily', and wrote various accounts on the dilemmas facing him, including two personal aides-mémoire.[16] In addition, four chapters of My First Seven Years are devoted to his experiences in the closing years of the war.

In his view, his options at that moment were stark: to join up as ordered, to become a member of the partisans or to flee into Switzerland. Each course of action carried its own risk, as he explained to Chiara Valentini, a journalist who followed his career closely and who is author of a biography of his early life:

> Going with the partisans was not easy because at that time the groups in the zone were collapsing because of the continual round-ups carried out by the Germans. Fleeing to Switzerland had become very complicated. I prefered to choose a waiting position and try to dodge the call-up with trickery.[17]

The problem with this explanation is that in his *First Seven Years* memoir, he gives accounts of his father's activities in helping escaped British, American and South African POWs to escape to Switzerland, including one hilarious episode where Dario helped a large, unshaven, red-haired Scotsman implausibly disguised as a woman. The train they were on was stopped, but by chance the guards did not reach their compartment.[18] The undoubted fact is that Dario did not, unlike such writers as Elio Vittorini or Italo Calvino, join the partisans or take any direct part in the Resistance. He was not alone in this lack of crispness, and even those who took what was later judged the most acceptable course agonised in the post-war period over their motivations. As he wrote in one of the *aides-memoire,* on the dilemmas facing him: 'There was no possibility of joining the partisan groups. All the groups existing in the zone had been destroyed in recent round-ups, or had withdrawn across the border into Switzerland'. Even those most reluctant to pass judgement on an eighteen year old boy must find the explanation puzzling. Guerrilla war was raging around him, and he tells us his own father was fully committed. When interviewed in November 2000 by the *Corriere della Sera* on the publication of a work by Roberto Vivarelli, who had joined the Salò forces out of conviction, Dario said that, unlike Vivarelli, his hope was simply 'to hide away, to come home with my skin intact.'[19] Perhaps that is the final truth, but he also highlighted to Valentini his father's close involvement with escape groups as making it impossible for him to flee lest he implicate his father. He has also suggested that his decision to join was determined by a request from the partisans for inside information. Had he failed to present himself for military service as required, the family house would have been, at the very least, searched and the operations of his father and the group he was leading put in jeopardy. The consequences could have been much worse. The penalty for anyone trying to escape the draft was death, and during this brutal period of the war in Italy, summary execution, mass slaughter and deportation were commonplace.

The trickery, delaying tactics, of enlisting in Varese was based on the belief that 'this division did not have so much as one cannon, so that immediately after enlisting, these boys were given a month's leave and returned home'. The ruse did not work for him. When he reported to Varese, he discovered that the story about the lack of equipment was a bluff and the new recruits were due to be posted to Germany. The company was moved in cattle trucks to Mestre, where they were issued with German uniforms, then to Monza where they were kept in a compound while awaiting transfer. Here they were harangued by Mussolini in person, who told them of their good fortune in being chosen for a glorious destiny. Allied bombing raids increased in number and intensity, with Mestre reduced to rubble. Typically when writing about these events, Dario chose to give a comic account of the destruction of a brothel, from which the women and their clients managed to escape but the first woman out gave Dario a generous kiss.[20]

The position of the new recruits was dire. They understood they were to take up anti-aircraft operations inside Germany, since the Reich's own manpower had been reduced by the RAF bombing campaign. The news got back to his home in Porto Valtravaglia, where Bianca remembers their frantic mother screaming that she had to go to Monza to see her son before he was dispatched abroad. Dario managed to get a reassuring message to his family, carried to the village by a blind man. The scribbled note read – 'Calma mamma! Nobody's leaving'.

In the unpromising surroundings of his barracks, Dario managed to perform some comic monologues and even to put on his first farce. Unsurprisingly, not a scrap of it has remained except in the second-hand recollections of his mother, who was told that it dealt with a servant who drove his master mad, only to be driven to insanity in his turn by the same master. Pina received, by some means, a photograph of the event, with Dario in the part of the servant.

Shortly afterwards, Dario deserted and spent some time in hiding, initially in the mountains. He had with him forged identity papers, so felt able to move into Milan. In Piazzale Loreto, the very square where a few months later the corpses of Mussolini and Clara Petacci would be strung up, he was stopped by Fascist officers carrying out a routine check. The false papers duped the guards, and Dario was allowed to go, but the experience left him terrified. In the meantime, Felice had been arrested, and Dario, in his own account, was anxious to avoid any action which might imperil him. He decided to re-enlist. On the 10 November 1944, he joined the Folgore parachute division, one of the most notorious of all Fascist forces, in Tradate, not far from his home village. On this occasion, he says he was acting on advice from the local partisan force who requested information about the activities of this division. Fo mentions in particular the request made by Leo Wachter, a Jewish activist who had found refuge in the Fo home.[21] A pen portrait of Wachter by Fo is now on the opening section of the Fo-Rame archive in the section headed "Cases, Trials or Reports by or against Dario Fo and Franca Rame."

He was employed in the printing section of the barracks, and never took part in the increasingly brutal 'hunt and destroy' missions which the Fascist militia were mounting against the partisans. This fact was accepted by the court in the 1979 legal action he brought against a writer who asserted that he had been involved in such actions. After two months on the base, he deserted once again. On this occasion, he said he attempted to make contact with the Lazzarini group, a powerful guerrilla force, but was unsuccessful. For a time, he holed up in various spots in the valleys and mountain caves near his own home, but later found refuge 'in the attic of a colleague of my father, a retired station-master'. On more than one occasion, he narrowly escaped capture so his final judgement that that period was 'an appalling adventure, seven months of fear and horror that seemed as long as seven years' is unsurprising. His overall view is similar to Calvino's: 'we were permanent deserters, terrified, disoriented young men. Men in flight, enlisted by deceit, trapped by violence. The greater part of the Salò army was made up of people like us, with no banner, concerned with one thing only: to survive.'[22] The war in Italy ended on 25 April 1945.

Even if he had been in danger of his life, Fo had not fought in the ranks of the Resistance, as did many others of his generation. He had not been a combatant. Photographs produced during the 1980 libel case show him not in the company of partisans but in the uniform of Mussolini's RSI. The Resistance, however, became for him the great myth of liberation, featuring in several plays, particularly those written in the sixties and seventies after his break with commercial theatre. Dario subscribed fully to the idea, widely held on the Left, that the Resistance and the Liberation represented not only victory over dictatorship but the betrayed revolution, the unfulfilled dream of realising the Italian road to socialism, the denial of the one opportunity Italy gave itself for renewal and purification. Remember and relive the Resistance, was the slogan that would ring out in his post-1968 theatre. One of his best and most moving songs, *Six Minutes to Dawn*, depicts the last moments of a partisan about to face the firing squad. The guards and the priest arrive, but when an officer offers a cigarette, the condemned man initially refuses then accepts only because of the hurt expression on the face of the officer who is about to carry out the execution.

> On the eighth of September I fled
> I ended my time as a soldier
> To my village I returned
> Where they called me deserter
> Loaded on a train
> I fled once more
> I went to the mountains, but yesterday
> They seized me as a rebel.[23]

Dario had to endure a whispering campaign about his failure to fight with the partisans in the closing months of the war, and particularly by the unqualified description of him as a *repubblichino*, that is, an adherent of the 'Little Republic' of Salò. The historian and ex-Fascist, Giorgio Pisanò, who became a member of Parliament with the neo-fascist MSI, Italian Social Movement, published in the mid 1960s several volumes entitled *Histories of the Civil War in Italy*, in which he took a polemical look at the story of Dario's tangled involvement with the Salò forces. Many influential people had interests in discrediting him, so the suggestion in the book that Dario had skeletons in his cupboard was enthusiastically taken up and questions were asked in Parliament. His outraged self-defence then and later was weakened in the eyes of some by the fact that he had not chosen to speak of the matter spontaneously, but had stayed silent until the matter was revealed by hostile critics.

If his involvement in the Resistance had been marginal, Dario shared in all the exhilaration and unrestrained optimism of the Liberation. Italians are fond of depicting themselves as being, by virtue of a culture which combines a Catholic sense of the imperfections of humankind with direct experience of much of the worst history can offer, immune to the waves of hope which affect other nations. In reality, few peoples are so prone to bouts of collective optimism or so ready to place their hopes in clay-footed messiahs as Italians. It was Dario's fortune to live through several such waves of public enthusiasm, and to have emerged from the disappointment which succeeded them with his appetite for life undiminished, and his utopianism – his most fundamental trait – unimpaired. No man has ever believed less in original sin.

Italy itself had no sense of being a defeated country, nor even a country liberated by outsiders, but viewed itself as a land freed by its own sacrifices and struggles. In spite of material privations, there was a sense of elation and determination at large, particularly among those who were young, resourceful, plucky, self-confident, or merely conceited and anxious to seize the day. Primo Levi, on returning to Turin from Auschwitz, was astounded at the 'extreme vitality' shown by his fellow citizens, and regretted that he could not share it since 'they were victorious, and I was not'.[24] That sense of being victorious in war and capable of constructing an equally victorious peace was especially strong in Milan and the North, where those who had participated in the Resistance were clustered. The established habits of previous times had been shown to be inadequate, indeed the cause of national disaster and humiliation, so the young found themselves facing not merely the challenge of rebuilding cities but the invigorating task of creating a civilisation afresh. Laws were to be redrafted, political institutions reformed, industry rebuilt, economic relations rethought, the relations between classes reshaped and the pillars of a new civil society erected. As Carlo Levi wrote at the time, 'something deeper has changed in men's souls, something which it is difficult to define, but which is expressed unconsciously in every act, every word, every gesture: the very vision of the world, the sense of the relationship of people with one another, with things, with society'.[25]

Dario responded to that mood. In 1945, still only nineteen, he put on his first art exhibition in Bergamo. The paintings are realist in style, and some of the more notable feature a landscape with unmoving trees picked out against hills, the drawing of a boy pulling on football boots and a self-portrait of a brooding, unsmiling Fo looking defiantly at the spectator. There was a remarkable maturity and confidence to the works displayed, and certainly no sign of any gloom or self-doubt.

He resumed commuting to Milan, now accompanied by Fulvio, who was studying accountancy at the Bocconi University, and Bianca, who was attending the Brera *liceo*. Dario himself was in attendance at two institutions. Unsure of his future, he enrolled at the Accademia Brera as an art student and at the Politecnico to study architecture. He never did study theatre. To while away the time during the lengthy toing and froing, the three Fos took to performing recitals and monologues on the train. Dario was eclectic in his tastes, and seemingly drew an appreciative audience. Some of the material was written by himself, but he also performed sketches by the humourist Achille Campanile, or by the Neapolitan comic actor Totò, whose work he had always loved and on whom, much later, he wrote an admiring essay. This high-spirited display on a train was not yet a sign of some systematic interest in theatre or ambition to be an actor or playwright. The reopened theatres in Milan commanded the attention of the bohemian young, but painting was still Dario's principal passion.

In 1949, Pina decided that this daily travelling was unduly stressful, and moved to Milan to set up home there. The family found a little house on the outskirts of a city still recovering from the devastation of war. At the back of their house lay the rubble of houses destroyed in the air-raids, while the front looked onto new, nine-storey blocks being thrown up to replace them. Money continued to be a problem. Felice retired from the railway, but stayed on in Porto Valtravaglia where he opened a little business to supplement his pension and help support the family. The rest pitched in as best they could. Pina took in some work as a seamstress. Ever thrifty and inventive, she managed to make from the one blanket a reversible overcoat which could be a male garment for Fulvio or, turned inside out, a more feminine item which Bianca could wear. Dario earned some cash by designing stalls and executing frescos at the Milan Fiera. He sold some canvases, accepted commissions to decorate different kinds of structures which included family tombs and, more eccentrically, made extra cash by sketching cadavers for the theses of medical students. Felice came down to Milan twice a week to visit the new house. The family lived in happy disorder, but felt obliged to rush around replacing door handles, repairing wiring and adjusting carpets each time he was due.

The previous occupants had left a piano, and perhaps by itself this was sufficient to ensure that the Fo house became the favoured meeting place for friends and acquaintances. Jazz had been declared unwholesome by the Fascist regime, but was accepted joyously by the new Italy. Fulvio learned to play some numbers on the piano, and Dario imitated the most popular blues and jazz singers. As described by Bianca, the home is reminiscent of the artists' attic in *La Bohème*, with her in the part of Mimì. 'Little by little our house became the meeting place of all our friends, and there were many of them, painters, poets, actors. We would sit around the sawdust-fired stove, which gave off more smoke than heat, and there were endless discussions about this or that painter, about new forms of theatre or cinema. They spoke of Sartre and existentialism. Emilio Tadini declaimed Garcia Lorca, while every evening Dario would reinvent history and recount stories of poor Cain, or of Samson and Delilah. I was always silent, listening rapt. I could not speak like them.'[26]

For the intelligentsia in that climate, to be communist was merely a matter of good manners and *bon ton*. They took Antonio Gramsci to their hearts. Mussolini had imprisoned Gramsci, Italy's leading Marxist philosopher, and banned his writings but his *Prison Notebooks* now became available. Any attempt to put flesh on the cultural beliefs and poetics of Dario Fo must begin with Gramsci, whose main contribution was to switch the emphasis of Marxist theory away from economics to culture itself. The building of socialism was not a matter for political activity alone, indeed could only be attempted once civil society was reformed. This assertion amounted to a root and branch review of classical Marxism, in which cultural activities were no more than a projection onto a 'superstructure' of tensions and contradictions which existed on the basic, that is, economic, substructure of society. Gramsci included culture in his analysis of the power structures, since for him it was a means by which privileged élites maintained their authority. In Gramscian terms, culture is a pre-rational complex of ideas, values and assumptions, or a dimension of consciousness which shapes human life as powerfully as any physical or economic force. Dario's early familiarity with Gramscian theories caused him to see cultural change, which could be worked by theatre, as an indispensable tool for the decolonisation of the mind, of the will, of the imagination.

One other aspect of Gramsci's thought was of decisive importance to him. In Gramsci's analysis, a popular culture reflecting the experiences of the subaltern classes existed side by side with the high, aesthetic culture of the patrician and educated classes. It had, however, been the fate of popular culture to be systematically ignored and derided or, when it showed some vitality, annexed to the higher culture. In calling for a re-evaluation of popular culture, Gramsci set the intellectual parameters within which Fo later worked. Gramsci's beliefs gave him justification for giving higher priority to the theatrical forms, principally farce, to which he was drawn by innate talent, and for jettisoning the hierarchy which awarded pride of place to tragedy and comedy. In addition, Gramsci called on intellectuals to create not only a new future but also a new past. 'The past is a complex thing, a mixture of dead and alive, in which the choice cannot be made arbitrarily, *a priori*, by an individual or by a political tendency,' as Gramsci wrote. The past had to be claimed, or reclaimed, as Fo would do with his plays.

These and other topics occasioned rowdy debates among the student body in places like the Bar Giamaica, where they congregated. Dario's circle of friends included future painters, like Emilio Tadini, who later became president of the Brera, sculptors like Alik Cavaliere, musicians like Fiorenzo Carpi, who worked with Fo on many shows, as well as future actors and writers. Fo met up with De Chirico, the futurist Carlo Carrà, as well as the new generation of film-makers including Gillo Pontecorvo, Vittorio De Sica, Carlo Lizzani and Federico Fellini. *Politecnico*, the review edited by the novelist Elio Vittorini, another habitué of the Bar Giamaica, was both an encyclopedia which updated Italians on new thinking in other countries, and the main forum for left-wing intellectual debate. Unlike many others in his circle, Dario did not join the Communist Party, but his ideas were in line with theirs. 'Everybody found their way to the Brera; we were all in favour of general change, in art as in politics. We paid no heed to the party who told us to stick to being artists and to stay in our own place. Today it is hard to imagine what Milan was in those days and how a painter, as I wanted to be, felt himself involved in all forms of expression, from stories which appeared in *Politecnico* to neo-realist cinema.' Almost as an afterthought, he added, 'I gave little thought to the theatre, but theatre pulled us all in.'[27]

It was only gradually that the pull of theatre became irresistible. 'My principal interest was painting. I wanted to be a painter,' he repeated.[28] He continued to pick up prizes. In 1946, he won a prize at the Brera, and used the money to go with Tadini to Paris for the first time and familiarise himself with the work of Ferdinand Léger. In 1949, a Still Life took first prize at the Triennale in Melzo. For all their protestations of poverty, the group had sufficient means to allow them some mobility, and could, on an impulse, go to Venice or Turin to see an important exhibition.

The Young Turks had no doubts that history was on their side and that the future was theirs to reshape as they wished. The old forms of thought and performance, controlled by a hostile, alien force called the 'bourgeoisie' needed, they were convinced, to be swept away. Baiting the bourgeoisie had the advantage over other forms of political activity that it required no training and overlapped with the expression of youthful high spirits. Paolo Grassi, who was to be one of the founders of Milan's Piccolo theatre, organised groups to visit theatres, but not to study established masters. The members unabashedly called themselves 'whistlers', although the Italian *fischiatori* also suggests 'booers' or 'jeerers'. Dario enlisted with alacrity. They travelled to venues where plays by old-guard authors, or featuring actors or directors compromised by association with the Fascist regime, were in performance. At sensitive moments, the 'whistlers' rose from their seats and hurled abuse at stalls and stage. Grassi wrote of a particularly lively evening at the Teatro Nuovo in Milan during the romantic comedy, *Twelve Red Roses* by Aldo de Benedetti, who was judged to have shown undue tolerance towards the *bien pensant*, 'let sleeping dogs lie' mentality which Fascism encouraged in drama. One actress, believed to have been the mistress of a high-ranking Fascist official, was a target for special abuse. That same evening, Vittorio Gassman, later to star both in Italian theatre and in Hollywood cinema, leapt on to a chair declaiming that theatre must mature or die. In the ensuing mêlée, Grassi was heard to denounce the then respected actor Renzo Ricci as 'a worthless old ham'. At a later society soirée, Emilio Tadini concealed himself in a large plant-pot and jumped out as the canapés were being served, screaming, 'Bourgeois! We will bury you.'

Pranks and stunts of the sort tolerated, or endured, in university towns all over Europe for centuries acquired for that generation political overtones. Dario was Puckish mischief-maker in chief. One winter, there was an unusually heavy fall of snow, forcing the City Council to take on extra staff. A certain salary was agreed and Dario and his friends were among those employed. The teams spent the morning clearing the roads, only to discover that the Council intended reneging on the agreed payment. In protest, the team spent the afternoon replacing the snow on the roads. Alik Cavaliere was the inspiration for another stunt. To make a few lire, an unemployed man had set himself up as guardian of bicycles near the Brera. One day, Cavaliere saw him being booked by the police, who demanded that the bicycles be removed forthwith. Dario and Cavaliere went to his aid. The Brera was being restored at that time, allowing the two to clamber up an extemporised scaffolding bridge between two buildings. From there they hauled the bicycles up by rope, one by one, leaving them dangling in an elaborate pattern across the face of the Academy.

The group's most celebrated escapade involved spreading word that Pablo Picasso himself was about to visit Milan. They persuaded friendly journalists to carry the story in their papers, and tickets were sold for a reception to welcome the great artist to Milan. A janitor from the Brera, who apparently had some resemblance to Picasso, was put on the Paris express a couple of stations up the line and was met in Milan's central station by a crowd, including both false and genuine photographers. He was showered with bouquets by Fo's group but, complaining of exhaustion, refused to say anything to the waiting journalists. That evening, substantial numbers of ticket holders turned up for the soirée. 'Picasso' failed to arrive at the appointed time, and the festivities continued with a motor bike circulating among the tables and the arrival of a stretcher carrying the injured body of a critic supposedly hostile to Picasso. Dario and his friends moved among the guests, stopping to debate trends in art with painters whose work was fashionable with Milan society, and to tell them how far behind the times they were. Somewhere along the way, what began as an elaborate hoax was transformed into a futurist act of anti-bourgeois scorn, whose object was not enjoyment but exposure of pretension and conformism.

In the midst of this extra-curricular activity, Dario was employed by an architect's studio to help with various projects, including the construction of a condominium on land for which no planning permission had been granted. He believed he was doing his employers a favour by pointing this out, but they smirked at his naivety in not realizing that permission could be had if the appropriate hands in the City Hall were greased. He left in disgust, claiming that for him this realization of corruption was 'like a blow on the back of the head'.[29] There would be many such blows in the coming years. His infinitely tolerant parents continued to support him. He had gained substantial experience in architects' studios and on building sites, but the path architects were following bored and repelled him. His tolerance of the humdrum was never to be high, and on this occasion his impatience was mingled with disgust at the neo-brutalist, high-rise architecture commissioned by the municipal authorities and with the mis-spending of the millions made available for post-war reconstruction. Minimum cost and maximum profit were the order of the day. Such poverty of vision and such a willingness to cram people into little boxes were a far cry from the dreams for the future he had sketched out in debates in the Bar Giamaica. Dario fell into a nervous depression, was subject to vomiting fits until a friendly doctor diagnosed 'a crisis of the brain', and advised him to follow his own interests.

He nonetheless never regretted his study of architecture which, like his knowledge of art, enriched his perspective on theatre. In 1984, he wrote: 'Even today when I plan a project, when I write, I think in terms of 'plane and elevation', two fundamental architectural terms, two dimensions often used in reference to painting as well: that which is viewed from above and in front of us, as well as the 'opening' and perspective. When I write a play, even before I think of the lines, I imagine the physical space, the space where the actors and audience are situated. In completing a work, it is unusual for me to be uncertain over where the actors enter or exit, or to have to think about it afterwards.'[30] Whatever he believed at the time, his study of art and architecture were to have their real value for his work in theatre, which was beginning to command his attention.

CHAPTER 2

First Ventures in Theatre

Sheer exuberance of personality rather than some radical dissatisfaction with current conditions was the impulse which carried Dario towards theatre. Whether travelling on the train or painting in the Brera, there was no way of stemming the flow of fantastic tales. In the autobiographical work, he gave an account of tales he created by overturning ancient mythology and says the train became his 'stage, with the stalls always sold out and appreciative!'[1] Of particular interest was his chance encounter with Professor Civolla, a historian and anthropologist, who told Dario he was, spontaneously, performing in the narrative tradition of writers and story-tellers, even of ancient times, who parodied rather than reproduced heroic tales.

With his companions at the Brera, he improvised scenes and sketches which were played around the academy, and with his brother and sister he put on small sketches in village halls. In 1948, he created a longer, satirical work – *The Tresa Divides Us* – presented in Luino in the aftermath of the Left's electoral defeat in April that year. Borges used to say that Europe could be divided between those who believed Waterloo was a victory and those for whom it was a defeat. For the Left, April 1948 was a defeat which brought to an end the exhilarated optimism of the Liberation. The issue in *The Tresa Divides Us* is the ownership of milk produced by a cow which wanders between two communities, one 'red,' or Communist, and the other 'white', or Christian Democrat.

The cow belongs to the people on one side of the river but feeds on the grass on the other. The action, in a foretaste of those elements of rumbustious fantasy which were always to enliven Dario's work, was brightened by a Garibaldi encased in plaster, a motorcycle which careered around the audience, and by an angel, played by Dario Fo, who descended from a tower to denounce bigotry.

This buccaneering dilettantism constituted a cheerful apprenticeship, but Dario's friends encouraged him to make moves towards professional theatre. There were others in Milan whose ideas on the role of theatre in the construction of the new order were much more developed than Dario's. 'If we are not mistaken', and the suggestion that they could be mistaken was self evidently laughable, 'every civilisation develops by a process of bringing one group, in all its variety and multiplicity, close to another and integrating them', ran the manifesto of the theatrical company, established by Giorgio Strehler and Paolo Grassi, which became the Piccolo Teatro. In January 1947, the Milan City Council allocated an ex-cinema, used as a torture chamber by the Gestapo during the German occupation, to the new group for use as a theatre. The Piccolo was Italy's first *teatro stabile*, or fixed theatre, where *stabile* served to distinguish it from the touring companies which ever since *commedia dell'arte* had been the backbone of theatrical life in Italy. In the jargon imported from France, theatre was to be viewed as a 'public service', on a par with transport or education. Theatre was indispensable to the well-being of the body politic.

Grassi took charge of the administration, and Strehler of artistic policy. Strehler's position at the Piccolo was of enormous importance to the development of Italian theatre, not merely because of the quality of his productions over succeeding decades, but because it guaranteed the pre-eminence of the theatrical director, still resented by many as a late and unnecessary foreign intrusion into Italian ways where the actor was dominant. The objective of the new company was to play not to an exclusive élite but to a group who would be the vanguard of new, more informed mass audiences of the future. 'The theatre will remain what it has always been in the deepest intentions of its founders – a place where a community, freely gathered together, reveals itself to itself, where the

31

community listens to words which it will accept or reject.' The emerging Christian Democrat regime was not slow to react. The first scheduled production, Machiavelli's *La Mandragola*, was banned on the grounds that it featured the violation of the secrecy of the confessional and was replaced by Gorki's *Lower Depths*. The choice of a communist work was deliberately provocative, and it is curious that the Council raised no objection. The production, and the official veto, secured the Piccolo's position as rallying point for the new, left-leaning intelligentsia.

Strehler was Dario's first master. Over coming decades the two men, while always expressing admiration for each other's achievements, would frequently veer apart and hurl public execrations at each other, but at this time Dario attended the Piccolo frequently, watching from the wings both during performance and rehearsal. Strehler provided him with an introduction to the craft and profession of theatre-making, but Dario had no wish to develop in the image and likeness of Strehler or of the Piccolo. Strehler and Grassi were dedicated to providing a radical reinterpretation of the classics but Dario, while he had no precisely formulated aesthetic starting point, had an instinctive, albeit still unformed, view of his own talents and of the direction he wished to follow. He knew he was a story teller at home in the rough and tumble of the popular tradition, and sought out those who produced the same style of theatre. His decisive break came when, in the town of Intra in 1950 he went to meet Franco Parenti, then at the height of his fame as stage actor and radio performer with sketches featuring the character, Anacleto the Gasman. Anacleto was something of a rebel, an outsider with an anarchic outlook perpetually at odds with the society he inhabited. Parenti was plainly endowed with unusual generosity of spirit. He must have been accustomed to dealing with hosts of hopefuls turning up with armfuls of scripts, but when Dario arrived at his house asking to be given a chance to show his mettle, he readily agreed. When he saw Dario in action at the microphone, he was impressed both by the surreal inventiveness of the tales and by the freshness and conviction of his performance style. He wrote that however raw Dario was, 'he had an already formed personality . . . with a definite way of seeing things, of understanding, of delivering judgements'.[2] On the evening of their first meeting, the two went along the lakeside for a stroll both would recall many times later. For Dario, it was his introduction to the world he wished to inhabit, while for Parenti the meeting was an encounter with a talent which would enrich his own professional life. Dario recounted to him other tales from his repertory, and Parenti promised to use his influence to introduce him to others who would help him.

Parenti took him on tour to theatres and halls around Milan, sometimes run by unscrupulous managements and frequented by an audience who made few concessions to performers, young or old, who did not meet their standards. He also secured him an audition with radio producers. Dario was brought in cold to an audition room where the producers were seated, bored and unsmiling, almost defying the candidates to make them laugh. His first instinct was to turn tail, but he persisted and was encouraged when he detected the outlines of a smile on the face of one of the panel.[3] He was given a commission for a series of twelve humorous monologues, to be broadcast over the 1950-1 season. The monologues were collected under the title *Poer nano*, and staged at the Odeon in Milan in 1952 as part of a Variety show.

Poer nano is a dialect expression common in Lombardy, corresponding approximately to 'poor sod'. While there is little advantage in subjecting juvenilia to over-interpretation, all the distinguishing marks of Fo's work are already present. Tragic figures are viewed through the prism of a comic vision that sees the heroic in the commonplace and the commonplace in the heroic. The tales as a whole display a taste which Dario would never lose for the grotesque, the absurd, the satirical, the paradoxical and the ironic. The view of the world from the perspective of the underdog would become a staple of his theatre. Performance and writing were combined from the outset. Then as later, he had little interest in publication. When *Poer nano* was eventually published in 1976, it was in a revised, comic strip form, prepared by his son, Jacopo, who did the drawings.

The 'poor sod' is closely related to Chaplin's tramp in his mixture of pathos and wile. The hero is the underling, the downtrodden victim of misfortune or oppression. Dario here gives the first glimpse of his basic comic technique, which is the overturning of conventions, expectations and roles; the character receiving pity is the one who had been conventionally seen as villain or tyrant. The Biblical Cain, who would always be a favourite of Fo's, appears not as a murderous bully but as a good-hearted, goofy, ill-at-ease adolescent overshadowed by Abel, his dazzlingly talented and good-looking brother. Samson is transformed into a conceited cretin who stands in front of his mirror every morning asking who is the strongest in the kingdom, Noah into a benign but weak father-figure with too much fondness for wine and even God emerges as an absent-minded old buffer. The story of Goliath, a lonely giant who is forced by politics to fight David, his only friend, is brought up to date to incorporate jibes against war, especially 'short wars which then last a decade'.

Three of the tales, *Hamlet*, *Othello* and *Romeo and Juliet* were based on Shakespeare, with the tragedy transformed into comedy. This Hamlet could not care less about his late father. The events in Elsinore are recounted by a friend who is surprised when he ends up in a place called a theatre, where a group of vulgar voyeurs gawk at Hamlet and Ophelia who are only interested in finding a bit of privacy to conduct their love affair. To the dismay of the narrator, these unwelcome onlookers refuse to get out of their seats to stop the fighting and brawling. Juliet, who has a preference for 'difficult loves,' causes problems for both sets of parents with her offensive manner. Her attitude becomes too much for Romeo's father, who gives her such a severe slap that she dies, causing poor Romeo to kill himself. Othello makes his entrance singing a blues number, and complaining of the lack of black faces among the angels on the altarpieces of Venice. This Othello is childish, prone to tantrums and so given to tears that he ends up with a collection of handkerchiefs. He kills Desdemona out of pique because she had not kept his things in order, only to discover later that the guilty party had been Iago.

Christopher Columbus, later to feature in *Isabella, Three Caravels and a Con-Man* and *Johan Padan*, makes his first appearance here as a spoiled brat who annoys his parents and neighbours by his demands for a hundred lire to enable him to go to America. In his home village he played tricks with eggs, but it all goes wrong when he uses an egg to explain a point to Queen Isabella, lets it fall, stains the queen's dress and is chased from the royal presence. Another monologue features Rigoletto, who, although still recognisable as Verdi's hero, is the first example of that central figure in Dario's work, the *giullare*, or jester. Already this key character faces the dilemma of being either court entertainer, and hence the plaything of authority, or the voice of the people.

The success of these works on radio might have led to an extended contract, but instead Dario found himself fired. The management of RAI detected, rightly, a subversive streak in them and objected to his habit of making the character normally viewed as villain into the hero. They suspected that there was a political agenda behind this work, and declined to give Dario a platform on national radio. However discouraging this development was to Dario at the time, the managers' judgement was shrewd. In any case, Dario was establishing a name in the business and was invited to appear in cabaret and reviews. In 1951, he took part in *Seven Days in Milan*, a summer review. During the run, he met Franca Rame, also appearing in the same bill. The subsequent personal and professional lives of the two are inseparable.

Franca was born into a family which produced as a matter of routine the popular theatre which Dario was later to write and perform as a matter of intellectual conviction. The Rame family were a company of performers, originally puppeteers and later actors, who toured in Northern Italy, who could trace their ancestry back to the seventeenth century, and who performed a style of improvised drama which had its roots in the *commedia dell'arte*.[4] They created the entire paraphernalia of their trade, and some items belonging to the company are now on display in the La Scala museum. Since they lived on their daily takings, they had to be attentive to the signs of the times, and in the early twentieth century, the menace came from the encroachment onto their territory of the new invention called cinema. At a family council around 1920, the family decided that the popularity of moving pictures represented a switch in public taste it would be futile to oppose or ignore. Other family troupes attempted to incorporate short films into their shows, while others again viewed the new technology as a passing fad. Grandfather Pio Rame was of that mind, but his sons Tommaso and Domenico, the father of Franca, were resolute modernisers.

The family moved into what they termed *teatro di persona*, people rather than puppet theatre. It was a bold move, but they decided to stay as close to their previous area of expertise as possible. They transferred all the devices, tricks of the trade and even plotlines they had accumulated in more than a century of glove and string puppet-theatre into their new craft. People rather than puppets would take the stage. The scenery had to be modified, costumes prepared and with that the family considered themselves equipped. They had a friend, a scene painter at La Scala, who managed to acquire for them costumes no longer needed for Opera. It was their boast that, unlike other troupes of strolling players, they were not mere charlatans who turned up in a town, set up an extemporised stage in the main square, took the money and moved on. They converted some public hall or cinema and set about fitting it out it with a stage, scenery, props and backcloth so that their audiences would not be short-changed. The backdrops were their pride and joy, and on more than one occasion Franca had the experience of being a guest in the houses of the affluent bourgeoisie of Milan and seeing hanging on the wall a tapestry which had started life as a prop in their shows.

On switching from puppetry to acting, they did not consider retraining, but then they had never trained. The family drew on inherited skills, on instinct and observation, on an apprenticeship which began at birth. Stanislavsky, who wrote that actors required to make the performing space their home, would have envied their ease and confidence on stage, but he might not have approved of their relaxed relationship to character and their nonchalance over identifying motive or understanding the wells of action. Much later, Franca would scandalise an audience of actors in Scandinavia who asked how she prepared for a part. 'I read it through and go on stage', she replied. Rame theatre was theatre of improvisation, which did not mean free invention day by day. The family members consigned to memory a range of dialogues and exchanges relating to situations which might arise in several different plays. Round the table at dinner one evening, Dario coaxed the family to play variations on the boy-meets-girl theme, such as, 'she's in love but is too proud to say so', 'he is enamoured of her but is tongue-tied', 'the two meet but are conscious of being watched'. Each individual took on the required role then and there. The appropriate lines were thrown back and forth during the meal, each seemingly fresh and spontaneous but ready for use when the need arose on stage.

On other occasions, different improvisational skills were needed. When the run of six performances from the established repertoire was completed but the family felt there was sufficient interest to allow them to prolong their stay in a particular place, Domenico would summon them to a meeting and explain the plot of a book he had been reading. Alternatively, especially in a town they had not visited before, they would inquire about local legends, miracles associated with the patron saint or episodes in the history of the area. Domenico would then allocate parts, explain to each member of the family-cum-company exactly what was expected of them, prepare an outline plot detailing the essential action and giving all the various entrances and exits. The outline was pinned up in the wings, and the family would take their cue from it between entries and exits. Rehearsals were kept to a bare minimum, because a troupe like theirs could not afford the luxury of unprofitable time. The adaptation unfolded spontaneously on stage.

Such companies were not unknown in other countries, but whereas elsewhere they were a pleasing sideline, in Italy they were the quintessence of the national tradition. Many historians of theatre have puzzled over why the Italian tradition, in spite of its great vibrancy, should have produced so few playwrights. Only Goldoni and Pirandello have an undisputed place in the classical European repertoire, with De Filippo and Fo claiming a place among the moderns. The explanation of this scarcity is surely that companies who operated like the Rame family were actor-centred, not author-centred. The writer was a redundant figure, and the director simply unknown. Domenico Rame could stand as representative man of Italian theatre. He was a performer-organiser who could have played with the Andreini family in the sixteenth century at the birth of *commedia dell'arte*, who could have appeared with the *Comédie Italienne* in Paris in the days of Molière, who would

37

have undergone a period of crisis in the eighteenth century when Carlo Goldoni introduced his reforms.

The Rame family, not Strehler or the *teatro stabile*, provided the model Dario would follow in the late sixties. Art did not figure in their outlook. The family were professionals, as sure of their place in a community as the bakers or butchers. Franca followed the family profession instinctively, saying that 'if my father's job had been shoe-making, I would have set out to make shoes'.[5] In meeting Franca and her family, Dario had his first encounter with much of what would characterise his own theatre, especially post-1968. For him, as for Domenico Rame, the actor would be the central figure in the process of theatre creation. Unlike Domenico, Dario was also a writer whose plays could be performed by others, but his scripts were conceived for that evening's performance, not for posterity. He had no truck with the effete conceit that he was writing only to please himself. The only standard of success he would recognise was audience approval.

When the Rame family did use established scripts, they cheerfully modified them for their own purposes, in accordance with the tastes of the community for whom they played. One of the most popular items in their repertoire was a version of *Romeo and Juliet*. They knew their audiences would not cope with a straight translation of Shakespeare's verse, so they produced their own adaptation, refashioning the plot without parody, making it accessible and emphasising narrative momentum. They played tear-jerking melodrama and knockabout farce, but also produced lives of Galileo or Giordano Bruno, adapted stories from the Bible (as Dario had heard the *fabulatori* do) and staged versions of Chekhov, Ibsen and even of modern authors like Gabriele D'Annunzio. Popular culture, as Dario would later grudgingly admit, was intricately bound up with the official culture. They were both islands in the same sea, washed by the same tides and obliged to cope with the same flotsam and jetsam swept up on their beaches. The Rame family acted as mediators between two slants of mind but for them popular culture was not the downstairs, philistine version of concepts elaborated by its upstairs counterpart. They exploited high culture, even if they also scoffed at it.

Anyone who married into the family was expected to learn the trade. Franca's mother, Emilia Baldini, came from a family who were not exactly well off, but who regarded themselves as being a cut above itinerant players. Her father was an engineer in Bobbio, a town in Lombardy on the Rame circuit. At eighteen, Emilia was already at work as a primary school teacher when she met up with Domenico, twenty years her senior. Initially he was unsure of this girl from a different world, his doubts which were more than shared by her parents who were not pleased at the prospect of their daughter marrying an actor. Emilia was a young lady of spirit, and would brook no resistance. She and Domenico were married in 1924 and Emilia threw herself into her new life. As Franca would later do, she became the company administrator, learned to sew, helped mend costumes and prepare scenery. Even more remarkably, she became the company's leading actress, taking on the roles of Juliet or Tosca as well as of various more melodramatic parts according to the requirements of the touring programme.

In spite of the objections raised by Franca's parents, the Rame family were not rootless bohemians living in caravans. Their regular touring schedule took them no further afield than Lombardy and Piedmont, and normally they performed only from Sunday until Thursday, when they returned to their home in Varese. When they were away for longer periods, they rented a house as a base, and travelled from there to the communities in the vicinity. On Sunday, the company would split into two, and would do a total of four performances, usually with the assistance of other professional actors, or amateur members of local drama clubs. Both the families of Domenico and of his brother Tommaso lived on the earnings of the company. Emilia and Domenico were able to purchase for themselves a house on the coast, as well as a flat in Milan.

Franca, the youngest of a family of three girls and one boy, was born on 18 July 1929, in Parabiago, in the Province of Milan, where the family happened to be performing. She made her first appearance on stage eight days later in the part of Genevieve of Brabant, a child of the woods. From then on, she did the parts which were appropriate to her age. Being the youngest, she had the advantage of watching her sisters play the same roles, but it was her mother who took it upon herself to teach the parts. When she was three, her mother decided she should start acting, and taught her the lines 'mouth to mouth', as the expression was. This apprenticeship made her an actress almost unique in the profession. For her, improvisation was natural and undemanding. She spoke witheringly of actors who were incapable of thinking on stage, who listened only to the rhythms of speech of fellow actors while waiting for their prompt, and who were incapable of adjusting if something went wrong. Dario learned improvisation from her. She was delighted at the panic she saw in his eyes when, during a performance of *He Had Two Pistols and White and Black Eyes*, she forgot her lines and began to improvise. The stage hands began making frantic signals that they would pull down the curtains, but she continued until she chanced on the right word and was able to carry on. She was quite bereft of the nerves and fears which even seasoned actors feel before their first entrance. One awed colleague said that he noticed that every actor standing in the wings would feel their hands either freeze or turn clammy with perspiration, and that several of them had developed a superstitious rite of touching Franca's hands, which were always at their normal temperature, before going onstage.

Being on stage with members of the family playing parts foreign to their nature could be a confusing experience for a child. Franca recalled one such event:

> My mother, who always took the important decisions, decided that I should take the part of the second angel, supporting my sister Pia who was the first angel, in the Passion of Our Lord, Act V, Garden of Gethsemane. 'Repent, Judas, you traitor. You have sold your Lord for thirty pieces of silver. Repent, Repent', I was to shout from time to time. The part was not long, and my mother made me repeat it over and over again as she peeled potatoes. There was no rehearsal. I only knew that I had to follow my sister on stage and that at an agreed signal from my mother I was to scream 'Repent, Judas' and so on. What I did not know was that Judas was played by Uncle Tommaso, a man whom I had always seen

as calm, smiling, who told me beautiful stories, and was always great fun. To see him there with a nasty black wig on his head, shouting out in despair – 'May the crows tear out my innards, may the eagles pull out my eyes!' had a terrible effect on me. I swear I could have spoken, but it did not seem right to make things worse for him. What was going on? In little steps, the way angels do, I went up to him, put my arm round his neck and hugged him. My sister fell silent and from the wings my mother was making signs which held promise of nothing good. Uncle Tommaso lost the place for no more than three seconds, before beginning – 'God, thou art good! To this dreadful sinner you send the final comfort, a little angel . . .' With a scream he rushed off stage in search of a tree to hang himself. I do not know if it was a fear of being told off or a sense of duty which urged me on, but I shouted out – 'He is hanging himself. He has not repented!' From then on, there were always two angels in the Passion of the Lord, one of whom gave Judas a hug to demonstrate the greatness of God. And to send the audience home in tears.

The German occupation of Italy created difficulties for travelling players. At the age of fifteen, Franca underwent the terrifying experience of being hauled from the classroom to answer questions about her first boyfriend, who had disappeared. The guards suspected, rightly, that she knew he had left to join the partisans, but her air of innocence convinced them otherwise. On another occasion, after a performance in Masnago, the family, together with others who happened to be on the street at the wrong time, was rounded up by the SS and kept all night in custody in a courtyard. Only later did they discover that they had been held as hostage against the success of a Nazi raid. If the raid had gone badly, they would have been shot.

When Franca was eighteen, her father had a stroke which left him paralysed on one side. It was impossible to continue as the family had done for generations, but the main concern was not the abandonment of tradition but what to do with Franca. She had not been notably successful at school, which was hardly surprising since she had often been working until late at night and had to sleep on top of a trunk in the dressing room. Her sisters were in more secure positions, but Franca presented an intractable problem until someone suggested that she enter nursing. The fact that she had a neurotic fear of blood was not viewed as an insuperable problem. The thinking was that she would be able to do home visits and if she were able to establish a round of thirty daily injections, her future was assured. Nursing College it would be.

Under prevailing arrangements, a student nurse was admitted to the training centre for a probationary period of two months. Franca's background as an actress was held against her and she had one especially vicious supervisor who used to rub her finger over Franca's cheeks each morning in an attempt to detect some trace of make-up, a sure sign of reprehensible activities. Franca recalls those months as a period of unending humiliation, and it may be significant that a hospital is adopted as a symbol of the police state in at least two of Dario's early plays. In the TV series, *Canzonissima*, she retold the story of the bullying supervisor, and received a letter of apology from the woman. In her 1990s one-woman piece, *Sex Yes! Don't Mind If I Do!*, she transferred into comedy the intense embarrassment she felt when a man, whose private parts she had been requested to hold while the doctor conducted an examination, had an ejaculation. On the expiry of the two months' probation, she was, to no one's surprise, told she was unsuited for the nursing profession. Her period of depression coincided with Dario's over his decision to abandon architecture.

She had set her face against any return to the stage. All her life, she claimed she had no love for acting or theatre. However, her stated aversion towards the stage was regarded in family circles as a girlish affectation, so she was sent to do auditions with a 'primary company', as her family referred to the big city companies. Her experience and her talents did her no harm, but the Milanese impresarios were mainly impressed by her looks. A young blonde, with perfect profile, seductive smile and soft eyes was a guaranteed draw. She was taken on with alacrity, and for one of her first parts was required to appear in an underdress. Her mother was in the stalls and was so shocked that she sent Franca an anonymous letter, in her own handwriting, saying that she was an admirer of this emerging actress, but that since she was so talented, she had no need to stoop to that kind of display. Franca was next hired for the show *Seven days in Milan*, by an impresario who was married to her sister. She had only one line to speak. Among the cast was Dario Fo.

He claims to have seen her photograph in the house of a friend, and to have been immediately attracted. During the run, he was too intimidated by this stunningly good-looking woman, who was always surrounded by hosts of admirers, to make an approach. He did portraits of her with which he covered the walls at home. When Bianca first met Franca, she recognised her immediately from the drawings and sketches she had seen. Franca claims to have grown increasingly irritated by this 'gauche, lanky, thin and somewhat ugly boy' who kept staring at her, but never made any move. Dario regarded himself as the ugly duckling who could never arouse her interest. As he wrote later for a woman's magazine, 'It wasn't that I hadn't noticed her. That would have been impossible. Franca was so pretty that all the men went wild over her. Anyway, she had a boyfriend, and was always pursued by hosts of men prepared to go to any lengths. I didn't want to enter the lists. I said to myself, with all those bees buzzing around her, she won't even see me. In addition, I didn't want to get caught up in the cyclone that was Franca, with all those pyrotechnics and confusion, or that jealousy and theatricality. I was working like a madman; I didn't want to think of her. I thought to myself – halt, danger, get out, flee, don't even look back or you'll turn into a pillar of salt'.[6]

And so it was that Franca made the first move, and with appropriate drama. They were performing in the Cinema Colosseo in Milan in 1952, and backstage she grabbed him by the lapels, pinned him against the wall, and gave him a long, passionate kiss until he was breathless. Bernard Shaw insisted that it is always women who decide who their partners will be, even if they normally allow the male the illusion of believing himself the hunter. Dario Fo could have had no such illusion. The two started seeing each other regularly, and, to the dismay of other members of cast, making arrangements onstage for what they would do later that evening. Franca's mother gave her subtle advice on what not to do, couched in the maternal language employed on such occasions. 'Be careful. Men are only after one thing.' Franca may well have overplayed her ignorance, but she fell pregnant. Money was collected from among their friends to pay for a back-street abortion, performed in a surgery but without anaesthetic. She was threatened with being chased out if she made any noise, so she remained silent. The doctor, whom she does not name, later became wealthy and famous, but after the legalization of abortion, he registered as a conscientious objector, but continued to perform abortions.[7]

The trauma did not undermine their relationship. 'When I was courting Franca, we were both poor. We used to cross Milan at night from the theatre where we were working to the house where she lived. I made her laugh all the way. I would jump and dance on the tramway, or stop and invent fantastic stories. We seemed younger than we were.' Their careers, however, required periods of separation and this created difficulties and break-ups. 'Before we finally got married, this gorgeous bitch had left me, a couple of times. Once it seemed it was for good. She had become famous. They called her the Italian Rita Hayworth. Visconti wanted her in one of his films. Someone else had written a script for her in one of those variety shows where she would be garlanded with feathers. And she left me. And I cried. I had to wait until we got back together in *A Poke in the Eye* to win her back.'[8] In June 1954 they were married. Franca insisted on a grand religious ceremony at the Basilica of Saint Ambrose in Milan, to please her devoutly Catholic mother.

Their partnership was often fraught, but personally and professionally the two came to rely on each other so deeply that it is simply meaningless to wonder what would have happened if, somehow, the two had operated separately. Together they came to create one of the great theatres of our time. Initially, Dario was slow to recognise the extent of her contribution to their joint work, and in a curious dedication to his early collection of his *Ballads and Songs*, he wrote: 'If you permit, comrades/ I this serenade/ wish to make to my partner:/ yes, to Franca, /to her who so many times/ has remained in the shadows/ to provide the accompaniment/ to suggest to us the words . . .' When the book was reprinted in 1976, this dedication was dropped, since by then Dario had come to acknowledge that Franca had given more than 'accompaniment' and that there was no cause for her to remain in the shadows.

CHAPTER 3

The Absurd at Work

Having appeared on radio, performed in theatre and exhibited his paintings, in 1953 Dario recorded his first song, a brittle, ironic number entitled *The Moon Is a Lightbulb*. The lyrics were his, the music was composed by Fiorenzo Carpi and the feelings expressed in a whimsical-absurdist style wholly in keeping with the *Poer nano* stories. The number happily parodied the sentimental motifs of the popular music of the time, touchingly recounting the torments of a spurned lover as he paces the street below the house where his unfaithful love, Lina, entertains Nino, a wealthy barber. His torments do not stem from a broken heart or unrequited passion but from the fact that the number 38 tram has already gone and the 28 taken off, leaving the tortured soul facing a long walk home. To make matters worse, his feet are hurting. Romantic clichés of the moon and stars as the comfort of unhappy lovers are also inverted.

> The Moon Is a Lightbulb
> And the stars like lemons traced in the water,
>
> And everybody knows you're with Nino, the barber
> Who's got stacks of cash
> And I'm walking up and down on the pavement
> And my feet are hurting, hurting, Lina.

The thirty-eight's away,
And the twenty-eight's been taken off
So I'll have to walk home . . .[1]

Dario's own recording had little success, but the song became a hit two years later when it was re-issued by Enzo Jannacci, a singer-songwriter with whom Dario would collaborate on many occasions. In the 1950s music, both Italian and imported, was already beginning to occupy a central place in popular culture. In the heady days following the Liberation, American music meant blues and jazz, but by the early fifties this was being replaced by mawkish, commercialized products. Italy spawned its own vocalists, including one Silvio Berlusconi who worked as a crooner on a cruise ship, who aped what was being done across the Atlantic. At the same time, there emerged underground in the cities a cult of music of a more subversive, unconventional kind, and Dario, who had already shown a flair for ironic ballads with a whimsical narrative, was ideally placed to meet this demand. His first number was followed by other numbers, such as *I saw a King*, featuring a monarch in tears on horseback, although the lyrics sought sympathy not for the king but for the horse, and the more famous *He Had a Black Taxi*, an updated version of the Cain and Abel story, with Abel a taxi driver and Cain a tyre thief. Dario was not the only writer attracted by the music industry. Italo Calvino wrote some wry pieces for a group called *Cantacronache*, while Umberto Eco and Franco Fortini also wrote lyrics. Their success was due in part to the encouragement offered by the Ricordi music company, a venerable, long-established family firm which had published the music of Verdi and Puccini. Nanni Ricordi, the unconventional scion of a highly respectable dynasty, set up a subsidiary intended to appeal to a generation in rebellion against their parents' ways. Ricordi became a friend of Dario and Franca, and was to be involved with them on various political and theatrical ventures over the coming decades. His studio in Milan became the meeting place for the new creative spirits of Milan, not only singers and lyricists.

As a singer, Dario may have had a limited range but his strong, idiosyncratic voice, which had character rather than melody, more than compensated. He had the presence, the intonation and character of a Charles Aznavour, and in this genre deficiencies can be glossed over as expressions of a distinctive style rather than as indications of limited vocal gifts. The number of songs authored by him over the years is extensive but most were conceived not as single numbers but as part of a show. It is something of a quirk that the plays which have travelled best have been without music, leaving many of his admirers outside Italy unaware that the majority of his theatrical works were built on a mixture of song and dialogue.

At this time, although he did many recordings of his own, his songs were brought to a mass public by other singers, particularly Jannacci, whose own compositions and humour were similar to Fo's. Jannacci had written a surreal song entitled *The Dog with the Hair*, which features a dog of unusual vanity who spends his time peering at himself in shop windows and endlessly adjusting his hair-styles. He goes into a shop to ask for three cigarettes, but is ignored by shop assistants unaccustomed to dealing with a dog with such hair. Nothing more happens. Jannacci sang this piece at an audition with RAI radio, but was dismissed with a wave of the hand. Some months later in the Ricordi studio, Dario burst in on him and said: 'You're the guy with the hair'. Initially Jannacci thought this stranger was making slighting comments about his hairstyle, but realised that the reference was to the dog in the song. 'Come home with me,' continued Dario. 'You must learn. He took me back to his place and made me listen to a song of his, which turned out to be *The Moon is a Lightbulb*.'[2]

There are parallels between Dario's songs and the French chanson, which was much in vogue in the early 1950s. Singers such as Georges Brassens or Juliette Greco found an audience which included both devotees of light music and adherents of existentialism, surrealism or the 'absurd'. Songs of Greco's featuring armed tanks filled with penguins and ducks would once have been consigned to the category of nonsense compositions, but were then viewed as expressing a philosophical outlook similar to Ionesco's or Adamov's. Some of Dario's early songs are redolent of that absurdist mood while others, notably those written in Milanese dialect for theatrical productions by Giorgio Strehler, are in folk song mode. Dario and Strehler collaborated on some of these songs while others were written by Dario alone, but the authorship was concealed since Strehler wished to pass the numbers off as the work of Anonymous. 'He wanted to let it be believed that we had collected popular songs from a city which had never in fact existed. There did exist tunes and pieces like *Porta Romana, El Barbisin, La Balilla* which had been sung in taverns and which we collected.'[3]

Song was integral to the revues produced by the theatre troupe Dario set up in 1953 with Franco Parenti and Giustino Durano. The new group, in a somewhat heavy parody of a popular comedy group called *The Hunchbacks*, took the name *The Uprights*, and performed in a genre similar to music hall or cabaret. There is not, as Umberto Eco once wrote somewhat wistfully, a tradition of cabaret in Italy to compare with Berlin in the twenties or Paris in the belle époque. The reasons he proposed for this absence were related to a lack of trust in democracy. 'Italian customs have remained Bourbon. Cabaret exists because it can speak badly of the authorities, and the authorities in Italy are not to be touched. The absence of cabaret in a country means that, in spite of appearances, liberty is allowed but not licence. And democracy thrives on licence'.[4]

Dario, having already displayed comic flair and irreverent talent in conventional revue, was ready to provide that licence. The new troupe negotiated the lease of the Piccolo for the summer months when it was normally closed. The writing for the first show, *A Poke in the Eye*, a title taken from a satirical column in the Communist daily, *L'Unità*, was done by Fo and Parenti, while Fiorenzo Carpi, who had been appointed the Piccolo's musical director, composed the music. Franca was a member of the cast and the work was eventually defined an anti-review. Somewhat oddly, Dario always denied that the show should be classified as cabaret, preferring to emphasise the satirical element and to place the work in the Variety tradition, as *avanspettacolo*, or curtain-raiser.

I've never done cabaret, but rather a form of theatre linked to popular traditions . . . When we did *A Poke in the Eye* with the Piccolo Teatro, the ambience was not that of cabaret – the space itself, 700 seats, a stage twelve to thirteen yards wide, a complete set, the number of people acting (there were twelve of us), and finally the concept of the piece which was not a string of sketches but had a logical continuity of its own . . . *A Poke in the Eye* was part of a history whose origins go back to the goliardic tradition, but was mixed with elements of *commedia dell'arte* and modified by my experience with the theatre of Strehler who, at that time, was truly revolutionary. It had little to do with the French or German tradition in cabaret. That is, it was something better than cabaret which forces one to adopt a certain unnatural format: a café performance requires a very private and intimate form of speaking. With us everything was expanded, the action, the amount of physical expression inherent in our way of acting, mime learned not from the traditions of the white mime, but from *commedia dell'arte* . . . Moreover, there was a popular element which consisted of the storyteller's visual narration, and this we used explicitly and directly.[5]

Dario had a tendency to impose retrospectively a seamless unity on his work. In spite of these later protestations, his first shows had much in common with the Parisian cabaret he had seen in the French capital. If he had not had the chance, as he put it, to experience the twin poles of Paris and Milan in the immediate post-war years, he would have been a different person.[6] If the approach *A Poke in the Eye* was satirical, it was not yet the blazing, violent flame of later years, but a flickering little light, still in need of tending. The impact was akin to Gilbert and Sullivan's gentle satire on the House of Lords in *Iolanthe*, not Karl Kraus's savage, frustrated rage in *The Last Days of Humanity*. Censorship made it difficult to deal with political matters, but at that juncture, with Fascism a recent memory, the work of re-evaluating national myths had an essential cathartic function. Fascist oratory and the Fascist education system had glorified all Italian achievements, real or imaginary, to produce a public version of history and a private cast of mind which were narrow, introverted and self-satisfied. Dario was out to puncture that conceit. The central drive was an attempt to dismantle the myths of history, to jeer at accepted wisdom, to laugh at the shibboleths of the tribe.

He was learning fast. He designed the costumes and scenery, and received all-round support from Strehler, who also designed the lighting scheme, and from Jacques Lecoq, who supervised the rehearsals and became de facto director. Lecoq, the leading exponent and teacher of mime for his generation, had arrived in Italy in 1948 to work with Gianfranco De Bosio's university troupe in Padua on their productions of Brecht and Ruzzante. In 1951, he moved to Milan at the invitation of Strehler and Grassi to set up a drama school at the Piccolo. In Lecoq's account, the Fo-Durano-Parenti company 'revived the radical spirit of Italian satire, both through the political commitment they showed and the physical language they used'.[7] The radical element might not be as strong as Lecoq suggests, but his own contribution in imparting a 'physical language' was decisive in shaping Dario's stagecraft. Lecoq in his turn was intrigued by the natural talent he detected inside Dario's awkward body. His grin was toothy, his nose jutted out like a small promontory, his arms dangled, his legs were seemingly out of proportion to his trunk and his gait was gangling and tumbling, as though he moved on short stilts. Lecoq helped him convert these oddities into assets, helping with 'the gags, the moon-faced expressions which are often the reverse of the content spoken in words and which remained one of Fo's favourite devices'.[8] He also worked on the voice, helping Dario acquire that range of laughs and onomatopoeic vocalisations which were indispensable to his monologues and enabled him to reproduce everything from storms at sea to tigers licking wounds. In later life, Dario, while retaining his regard for Lecoq, came to disagree with his general approach to mime, which he criticised as too abstract and too indifferent to the uses to which mime techniques could be put. He distanced himself from teachings which could be applied equally by the oppressed or oppressor, and were not integrated into some wider system of belief, political or otherwise.[9] In the rehearsals in the Piccolo, however, he was happy to be educated in technique alone.

The twenty-one sketches which make up *A Poke in the Eye* take a wry look at historical episodes and characters from classical to contemporary times, with the captains and the kings debunked and the conventional viewpoint overturned. Production photographs of the opening scene, *Egypt*, show the cast striking the customary rigid poses depicted on Egyptian tomb drawings and caricatured by generations of comedians, but the text, plainly inspired by Brecht's poem *To the Worker-Reader* asks who built the pyramids – the Pharaoh whose name it carries or the nameless slaves who transported the stones across the desert? In another sketch, Napoleon and Nelson squabble like two boys in a playground over their future glory as measured in the number of soldiers they will leave dead on the battlefield. Dario himself, in a sketch set on the plains of Troy, plays a nameless soldier who has the bright idea of ending the Trojan War by manufacturing a giant horse, but he gives all the credit for the invention to the decidedly dim but aristocratic Ulysses. The standpoint is that of the *Good Soldier Schweik*, the slightly baffled, unremarkable everyman who remains unawed and unimpressed by his betters. Dario was already experimenting with a dialectic between history and the present day. In future works, he would mount a sortie into history to find either metaphors for contemporary conditions, or to reconquer spaces in the past which he considered had been wrongly ceded to the victors.

The show was a success and went on tour to several Italian cities. Its black humour caught the mood of left-leaning audiences, and although it was well received by critics of right-wing papers as well, there were warning signs of a more hostile response from the political and religious authorities. The theatre in Trieste refused to host the company unless they agreed to cuts, the bishop in Vicenza requested the police to remove posters advertising the show and in various towns priests denounced the work from the pulpit. Undaunted, Parenti and Fo prepared a new script, *Madhouse for the Sane*, consisting again of satirical songs and sketches. It opened at the Piccolo in June 1954. Franca, who was pregnant, did not appear on this occasion. The show portrayed twenty-four hours in the life of an unidentified city with a close resemblance to Milan. The element of the absurd caused the Nobel Prize winning poet, Salvatore Quasimodo, who was then working as theatre reviewer and who followed Fo's work with sympathetic interest, to make the acute comment that the production contained not only 'an unnoticed return to *commedia dell'arte*' but also traces of 'decadent, surreal French poetry'.

The prevailing tone was ironic rather than surrealist, and the focus of the satire was this time on contemporary subjects and politicians in office. Individual sketches ridiculed the situation in Italy at a time when the Cold War was at its height and clerical domination on the increase at home. A magazine editor and publisher are shown in discussion with a journalist who is eager to explain his most recent articles. The editor is indignant at the suggestion that he should actually read the pieces before publication, since his job only requires him to count how often the terms 'nation', 'cradle of civilisation' or 'liberty' occur. The portrayal of Cabinet deliberations is hardly more flattering. The ministers discuss the state of Italy in grandiloquent terms, but cannot help noting that the roads, which under the Monarchy were the best in Europe, are now badly in need of repair. For this reason, one minister deplores the abdication of the King, since it had once been the patriotic practice of the inhabitants of villages to repair roads when a royal visit was imminent. Could we not learn from Russia, suggests another, an idea which causes dismay until he clarifies that the reference is to Czarist Russia. An official remembers that when Isadora Duncan or Sarah Bernhardt paid a visit to a town, people would throw coats or furs on the roads to conceal their real state, so could not the road problem be solved by dispatching attractive women on semi-official visits? A housing problem? Unpaid prison labour could be pressed into service, and instead of providing training for prisoners the solution might be to jail building workers. Agricultural unrest? In Britain, they send the Queen to trouble spots, and America had just appointed Clare Booth as ambassador to Italy. She attained notoriety by calling on the Italian government to take determined steps to root out Communism, so perhaps Mrs. Booth could be persuaded, for the good of Italy, to take on an out-and-out regal role?

The law in the 1950s required authors to submit their scripts in advance to an Undersecretary of State, who happened to be Giulio Andreotti, and who had been appalled by neo-realism in the cinema, particularly by the portrayal of Italy in De Sica's *Bicycle Thieves*. The application of censorship laws has always delighted connoisseurs of bureaucratic insanity, and Italy provided splendid examples. Sartre's theatre was outlawed but so too was Machiavelli's *The Mandragola*. Falstaff could appear in *Henry IV*, but only after certain lines were cut. The innocuous English comedy, *Kind Hearts and Coronets*, lay awaiting approval for many years because one of the female ancestors of the murderous aristocrat, played by Alec Guinness, had married an Italian. Distribution in Italy was permitted only when the offending character was made Spanish. There is no record of Generalisimo Franco's response. This bizarre response masked the heavy hand of the growing clerical-political domination of Italian cultural life, and national censorship was only half the story since the Church at local and national level imposed its own standards, with each parish issuing a list of approved and disapproved films and plays. There were various categories of refusal, and Fo and Rame became accustomed throughout their careers to having their work included among those which the Catholic faithful were most strongly advised to avoid.

Madhouse for the Sane was massacred by the censors. The script was sent back from Rome covered in red ink, so the staged version was only a pale copy of the original. Franca recalls that the stalls were filled with little men with little torches, peering at the script in the dark to make sure there were no deviations from the approved version, an impossible task with performers skilled in improvisation. It was to become a familiar experience. The work had a successful summer in Milan, but was less appreciated in the smaller centres to which it toured. After the run, the main figures in the company were unable to agree on the next move and the company split up. Durano returned to conventional revue work, while Parenti and Lecoq set up their own troupe. Dario had strong reservations about their favoured author, Eugène Ionesco, who remained a bête noire for him. Dario was and would remain distrustful of the avant-garde in all its manifestations, regarding it as opposed to the traditions of popular culture which he planned to cultivate. As regards Ionesco, he considered himself vindicated by the increasingly right-wing positions he adopted over the years, but ironically when Dario staged his own one-act farces a couple of years later, he would see himself described, by Quasimodo among others, as the Italian Ionesco.

If Dario associated Parenti's split with Ionesco, Parenti blamed the break on Dario's desire to move into a new medium, film. Italian cinema at the time was at its most buoyant and influential. The neo-realism of the immediate post-war years had given it an international lustre, and the willingness of directors like De Sica, Visconti and Rossellini to use film to focus on such topics as the Resistance, internal immigration, urban poverty and unemployment made cinema, not theatre, the main forum for discussion of political issues. In the early fifties a new wave which included directors like Pietro Germi and Ettore Scola, altered course and brought the lighter *commedia all'italiana* to the screen. In 1955, not long after the birth of their son Jacopo, Dario and Franca moved to Rome to work in cinema. By chance, their house was close to that of Roberto Rossellini and Ingrid Bergman, who were then being pursued by journalists and photographers anxious to report on their scandalous liaison. Dario hoped to find openings both as scriptwriter and actor, and brought with him a film-script in which he attempted, like Jacques Tati in *Monsieur Hulot*, to employ age-old clowning techniques to express human disorientation in a society which had become too complex, too mechanised, too incomprehensible, too fast. Dario had already devised such a character in the *Poer nano* monologues, although that figure inhabited a timeless zone, not a technological society. Similarly, in *Madhouse for the Sane* he had created a comic panorama of scenes and incidents in a cityscape no longer made in the image and likeness of man.

The script of *Lo svitato*, best translated as *Screwloose*, brought together all these elements. The central figure, Achille, showed Dario's preference for free-spirited characters rather than for ones with too tightly defined a role, but in cinema Dario was in the anomalous position of having a reputation sufficient to compel the film-makers to take his proposals seriously, but insufficient to justify him being given control. The expertise he had acquired in the theatre, he was continually reminded, was of no value in the cinema, which had its own rules and conventions. Dario found himself imprisoned in bumbledom and bureaucracy but he worked with producer Nello Santi and his Galatea Films company, and with director, Carlo Lizzani, a friend from student days. Lizzani had already directed a couple of successful films, including *Chronicles of Poor Lovers* (1948), and *Achtung! Banditi!* (1953), but he had no experience of comedy. The professionals agreed that Fo's script was interesting, fine, promising, showed his enormous ability and would, in due course, after reworking, make a good film. In all, five scriptwriters were brought in to do the retouching and rewriting. Fo, to his own later regret, felt obliged to give way to the greater experience and knowledge of his collaborators, although no one can now say how his original script would have worked. Nello Santi later described the result as representing 'six authors in search of a film'.

The film was shot in Milan and released in autumn 1956. The debt to Tati was obvious, although Achille was also the first of the many modern Harlequins Dario was to play. A somewhat dim but resourceful individual, with a level of naivety and gullibility which allows him to survive in circumstances which would have crushed a more intelligent man, he falls for a gangster's moll, and it takes him time to realise that there is another girl, played by Franca, who is in love with him. His home is a crumbling building long abandoned by all other tenants and surrounded by cranes and demolition machines, all waiting to raze it to the ground and replace it with some soulless structure. Achille is involved in a variety of bizarre mishaps, including a Keystone Cops chase pursued by a pack of grim and ferocious dogs through city streets jammed with cars and lorries. There are hints of protest against uncontrolled building work which was to dehumanise the city, and perhaps echoes of Dario's experiences as an apprentice architect, but the film was judged a failure both as a comedy and as a vehicle of protest. It was mauled by critics, and was no great success with the public.

The failure left a profound mark on the two. With just a touch of poetic licence, Franca described the film as 'the greatest failure in the history of the cinema', but continued to believe that Dario's original script had a vivacity and imaginative force which was destroyed in the rewrites. She was convinced that all could have been remedied had they had the resources to buy back the film and reshoot some of the sequences. Fo believed that his was a film without context and noted that Tati had not made an enormous impact when his films were first shown in Italy. He never reconciled himself to the flop, and laid the blame elsewhere, principally on the critics. 'When *Lo svitato* came out, the critics clambered all over it and stamped on it with both feet. I then understood how much joy there is in destruction in Italy. All right, there were some errors, but other works were re-issued and bought up by cinema museums.'[10] Years later he could repeat audience figures in various cinemas in Rome, recite box office takings in an experimental cinema in Milan and could even remember the acclaim which greeted the film in a festival in Florence and during the four brief days when it was given a screening in Rome. He was also appalled by the powerlessness of actors and writers in cinema, both in the creation and the eventual distribution of the film. In theatre he would always work with companies where, in principle, everyone had some say, and where he himself had some control over the final product.

In spite of this disappointment, Dario still nurtured an ambition to succeed in cinema. The couple remained in Rome until 1958, and Dario was taken on as gagman by Carlo Ponti and Dino De Laurentiis, the leading producers of the day. He submitted to the rigours and tedium of the endless rounds of meetings and discussions, and made a contribution as scriptwriter to various unremarkable films with titles like *Souvenir d'Italie*, and *Born in March*, both of which came out in 1957. Franca played some minor roles in such films as *Rascel Fifi*, and appeared in theatre in a Feydeau farce, *Don't Walk Around in the Nude*. One evening the Sicilian novelist Leonardo Sciascia was in the audience and was struck, as was the protagonist of his novel *The Knight and Death*, by the incongruity between the suggestive title and the thick house-coat which the censors required Franca to wear.

It was an unhappy, unfulfilling time. Franca found little satisfaction in the film parts which she accepted to help pay the bills, and encouraged Dario to start writing again for the theatre. In the free time he had from looking after Jacopo while Franca was working on the set, he produced a series of one-act farces. They vowed to have no more to do with a métier they decided was not theirs. Their life would be devoted to theatre. Dario made no further appearances on screen until the 1990s, and then in minor roles as a favour to friends. Dario and Franca remain the only actors of any established reputation in the post-war years who have made their name exclusively in theatre.

As with his study of architecture, Dario tried to draw some advantage from his exposure to film-making techniques, but the return from those years was scant. A benevolent critic might agree that in the comedies which he wrote during his so-called 'bourgeois period' in the early sixties there are traces of cinematic techniques in the slick switch of scene, in the sharp cuts from sequence to sequence, in the development of momentum and pace in his plots, but this is a meagre booty from three years of routine and unproductive labour. In *Tricks of the Trade*, he discussed how he had learned from cinema the fundamental value of montage and situation, but the directors to whom he referred were Eisenstein and Pabst, not the people he had worked with in Rome.

It was time to return to Milan. They contacted Paolo Grassi about the availability of the Piccolo, and were offered only the less prestigious summer season. They accepted and sold up in Rome. The Fo-Rame company made its debut on 6 June 1958 with four farces under the overall title *Thieves, Mannequins and Naked Women*. Spectators were continually tantalised by the promise of naked women in this phase of Fo's output, but nudity was limited to words on the hoardings. The Feydeau farce was originally part of the programme, but was replaced during the run by a new play of Dario's, *Bodies in the Post and Women in the Nude*. This play was the first of Fo's to be televised, but the censors insisted that the second part of the title be cut. Nudity, this time male, featured in another title, *The Naked Man and the Gentleman in Tails*, while the remaining titles were more chaste: *Decorators Have no Memory* and *The Virtuous Burglar*. The programme was such a success with audiences that its run was extended into the winter. It alternated with *Comica finale*, a second programme of four farces by Dario, which premiered in the Stabile in Turin, where the director was

Gianfranco de Bosio, who had invited Lecoq to Italy. Perhaps De Bosio had another plan. He was among the group who had rediscovered and rehabilitated the Renaissance actor-author, Ruzzante, who was already Dario's model and idol. De Bosio wanted Dario to perform Ruzzante, but the time was not right. Dario was intent on making his own name and establishing himself as writer and actor, and had no time for performing the works of other writers. He had debts to Ruzzante which he would pay, but not yet.

In the meantime, his debts were to the Rame family, since the farces in *Comica finale* were based on scripts from the Rame archive. As he would do repeatedly throughout his career, he selected material which he then rewrote, updated, modified and reinvented according to his own tastes and needs. Dario invariably moved in the past like Napoleon in Venice, looting what could be of value to him while still respecting Venice, in his own way. The two programmes represent twin aptitudes and contrasting attitudes to tradition. In the first, Dario operates as a writer portraying his own time and gives free rein to his own inventiveness, and in the second he displays a willingness to plunder and to operate inside a tradition. All the works can be classified as farces. If he had suffered from critical ill-timing with the release of *Lo svitato* before Tati became an icon, he enjoyed a piece of critical good fortune with the staging of his first one-act plays. In the fifties, when Beckett, Adamov and Ionesco in France had found farce the most appropriate means of expressing the senselessness and absurdity of life, this once despised genre basked in high critical esteem. Dario modified techniques of farce according to his needs at different phases of his life, but from the outset he was happy to crusade in favour of farce as such. 'I want to rehabilitate farce. Theatre critics have adopted the habit of saying that an unsuccessful comedy "declines into farce". Now, in my view, farce is a most noble – and modern – genre of theatre.'[11] He admired the clockwork precision of the classical French farceurs, their speed of movement and change of situation, the carefully phased chains of revelation, the nonchalant insouciance of the characters as they heedlessly pursued a logic which was clear to them but preposterous to anyone watching. Dario's farces had more in common with the slapstick boulevard variety of the nineteenth century than with dark existential farce of the twentieth. He read Feydeau, Labiche and Courteline, and used tools they provided to ridicule society. Far from standing in rage before the metaphysical emptiness of the cosmos, like Beckett or Ionesco, he encouraged in his audience an attitude of amusement at the arrangements of social life. This distinction between the metaphysical and the social was not fully realised in the 1950s when, paradoxically, Dario found himself viewed as the Italian exponent of the Absurd and as an importer of French philosophy and Parisian dramatic innovation.

He had no yen for that particular garland. There may be a point at which the surreal and the absurd can overlap with the merely burlesque, a point at which Labiche can be made to seem Kafkaesque, but in their origin and their objectives they are as distinct as Wasteland and Wonderland. Whereas for the writers of post-war farce, the absurd was a metaphor for the enduring absence of all metaphysical order, the absurd situations presented by the light-hearted farceurs of nineteenth-century Paris represented a state of merely temporary chaos. Feydeau made himself Lord of Misrule for a day but he was, as his third acts make clear, the most conformist of all writers. Dario had no comparable interest either in a mystical emptiness or in dénouements which reinforce the social status quo.

Satire is not the dominant force in the pieces that make up the first quartet of plays. *Decorators* is set in a brothel, and offers the titillation of scantily clad prostitutes prancing across the stage and gathering round the figure of the bordello owner's husband, frozen into a state of immobility by an injection which has the power to paralyse but not kill. It could be remarked that there are a number of stock characters and stock situations which will recur constantly in Fo's theatre. He had, in purely theatrical terms, a fondness for prostitutes, who will appear later as comic figures, as golden-hearted bearers of temperate values, as representatives of freedom from male oppression or from routine, or even as bearers of political wisdom. Similarly, the transforming injection would be a device he employed on many occasions. In this play, the injection has a purely comic function, administered by mistake to one of two house-painters, who is then immobilised. The husband, not having received his daily dose, comes round and denounces his wife for paralysing him since she was afraid he was too attractive to the other occupants of the house. All ends happily when the wife is injected and immobilised, leaving her husband and the painters to live in bliss with the frolicsome girls. This is as undemanding a romp as vaudeville could offer.

The most accomplished and successful piece remains *The Virtuous Burglar*, later given an off-Broadway production and gaining the honour of being the first Fo work performed in English. The play juxtaposes the moral code of the burglar and his wife, who are sexually faithful but indifferent to property rights, with the practice of the house-owners, who are rigid believers in property but faithless hypocrites in sexual matters. The burglar breaks into a well-to-do apartment but is disturbed by a phone call from his wife, asking him wheedlingly to bring her a little present. No sooner has he appeased her than the house-owner and his mistress arrive. The burglar takes refuge in a grandfather clock, where he overhears the husband attempt to entice the woman into the bedroom. The attempted seduction is disturbed by a further phone call from the burglar's wife, which causes the couple to fear that their liaison has been discovered, and the burglar's wife to believe that her husband is engaged on an affair of his own. There are further twists and no final resolution to this imbroglio, but there is no comfort for the comfortable bourgeoisie. Inversion of society's standards is the stock-in-trade of all comedy, and here the burglar is the positive hero. He emerges as the honest labouring man who expects a fair day's pay for a fair day's work. The burglar and his wife are faithful to each other, unlike the middle-class couple who indulge in casual but concealed infidelities. Hypocrisy has been one of theatre's favourite targets, but Fo gives the subject a mild class edge.

Fo's frame of reference is society, and he never strays onto the adjoining Beckettian wasteland where displaced individuals trade jokes while waiting for Godot or God. There are echoes of such conversations in *The Naked Man*, but they have the ring of pastiche or parody. The naked man in a dustbin cannot fail to recall Beckett's *Endgame*, while the two roadsweeps with a philosophical bent are reminiscent of the tramps in *Waiting for Godot*. The chatter between the two as they set to work covers such topics as the possibility of attaining truth and happiness, the nature of madness, the validity of yoga as a means of fulfilment, the Platonic view of the absolute, and the likelihood of the Pope's knowing where God resides, but their flow is interrupted by a distraught woman and a naked man. His confinement in a dustbin has an earthy explanation since it is revealed that he is an ambassador who had to exit quickly from his lover's bed. The tone is whimsical and jocular, and the plot develops according to a series of mistaken identities. The roadsweep spots a flower-seller still dressed in an evening suit which he had needed to sell bouquets in a night club. He purchases the suit for the ambassador but ends up wearing it himself, and being treated like a lord. So who then is the gentleman, the distressed Don Juan or the street cleaner decked out in elegant attire? Behind the temporarily upside down situation lies the tentative notion that possibly the world could be more fairly and equally ordered according to merit, but the laughter is genial and Fo is still less than a firebrand.

With the other four farce programme, *Comica finale*, tradition is vividly and exhilaratingly made flesh. Dario transformed the Rames' original pieces, sometimes retaining only single characters, but preserving the spirit of the source material. The recreated past is a fantasy age, with no connections or lessons for the present. *When You're Poor, You'll be a King* presents the kind of inversion which Mikhail Bakhtin, then unknown in Italy, identified as the core of the Carnival spirit. Four youths poke fun at a poor man who entertains the illusion that once he has squandered all he possesses he will ascend a throne. *Marcolfa*, a stock character from Italian comedy, follows the adventures of a serving girl of that name, famed for her ugliness, but discovered to have unsuspected charms when she is rumoured to have won the lottery, while *The Three Lads* unfolds in a fairy-tale atmosphere. The three are called to the castle to defend it but discover themselves the object of the attention of the daughters of the lord who had forbidden them from seeing other men.

Oscar Wilde once described *The Importance of Being Earnest* as a play 'about butterflies, for butterflies'. The same description could be applied to these largely escapist farces. Contemporary critics were impressed by Fo's natural clowning abilities, his impeccable timing and his improvisational skills. The two programmes commanded a great deal of critical attention, most of it positive, and the theatres were packed at a time of the year when, according to received wisdom, people were in holiday mood and had no interest in theatre. By the end of the run of the two programmes, Dario was a well established, even if slightly puzzling, figure in theatre. He had appeared in revues, in film, in farce, and had asserted himself as a writer in all these genres. It was now commonplace to say that he was a phenomenon. But of what sort?

CHAPTER 4

Being Bourgeois

Pinball machines caused much excitement in Italy in the late 1950s. Dario was addicted to these devices, and in moments of tension or vacuity found undemanding relaxation in mindlessly flicking balls up and down the table, around plastic obstacles and into little holes. However, in the Italy of the 'economic miracle', everything was scrutinised for its symbolic meaning and potential moral menace, so the pinball machine was, like the jukebox, the teenager, Hollywood films and Coca-Cola, deemed to be part of the new Americanised pop culture, and caused such alarm in pulpits and board rooms that the Ministry for the Interior proposed to ban it altogether. It was, in the words of an official communiqué, guilty of 'creating an atmosphere favourable to crime, taking up hours which could be devoted to work and study and causing the waste of money'.[1] In this context, Dario's decision to give the title *Archangels Don't Play Pinball* to his first full-length play had the double advantage of being both fashionable and polemical.

Dario and Franca had now become 'personalities', whose tastes, views and lifestyle were assumed to be of interest to the public at large. For readers of glossy magazines, Franca took on the role expected of fashionable actresses. She was happy to be photographed encased in furs, tight skirts, close-fitting jumpers or in staged *déshabille*, seducing the camera and the reader with a girlish pout. Dario let the world know that he was a supporter of Inter Milan, that his favourite food was *risotto*, that if he suffered from homesickness while abroad a plate of pasta helped, and that even rice would not necessarily serve this purpose because he would not trust anyone else to cook *risotto* as it should be done. The couple who were later to be the ideal revolutionary couple were at this time the envied model for a consumer society, he talented, witty, intelligent and politely radical, she talented, youthful, pretty, and both evidently destined for even greater success.

Dario developed, or had thrust on him, the image of a scoffing but jovial bohemian rather than of an enraged iconoclast. In the guise of the clown, he played and cavorted at the margins of society, exposing absurdities, jeering, sticking out his tongue, delivering derisive witticisms or satirical shafts, making himself a nuisance to the authorities, but knowing that he was breaking windows not pulling down temples or overturning altars. There was something very traditional and expected about his role at this time. The circus clown knows the rules as clearly as the court fool, and both know that to go too far is to risk the whip. Dario's overriding concerns were the urge to make his own way and have his own voice heard in theatre. He adopted the leftist positions held by many writers and artists, voting Communist, deploring the Christian Democrat rule, favouring divorce and advocating an increase in state ownership of industry. If his positions were dissident, they could be incorporated within the system. In a 1954 interview, he stated that the writers with whom he felt most affinity were Bernard Shaw and Chekhov. The choice of Chekhov, who was later to be dismissed as the very incarnation of bourgeois drama, was surprising, but the resemblances to Shaw at this period are clear. Both were inconvenient voices, determined to upset the status quo, but both accepted, at least for a time, the ease of a role as licensed entertainer-cum-oracle in society.

In January 1959, Dario made his first appearance on television in a comedy, *Five Lire Pieces*, and his celebrity was further increased by his starring role in a series of TV commercials. Television advertising and programming were both in their infancy and the directors of RAI, the public broadcasting authority, thought they could check the intrusiveness and power of the advertisers by clustering all the ads on a mini-programme called *Carosello*. The other programmes in those days of strict political and clerical control were so dull that *Carosello* was soon the most popular work on the screen. A mildly humorous approach wrapped in a narrative framework was the order of the day, and Dario was ideal for this purpose. That toothy smile, that India-rubber face, those eyes which seemed to widen to the dimensions of a screen, that range of odd gaits, that perfectly timed delivery boosted the sales of products from pasta and mineral water to petrol. The stories Dario acted out stretched the two-minute format to breaking point. In ads for Agip, the Italian oil company, he appeared in the guise of the detective Joe La Volpe, a parody of Philip Marlowe, who slouched about in bowler hat, badly fitting suit with revolver bulging under the jacket. The makers of commercials for Recoaro, the mineral water firm, chose a more absurdist approach. Dario and his partner, both zany carpet-fitters, would go into the house of some awkward housewife, only to grow exasperated with her demands and end up tossing her out of a window. 'Let's freshen up our ideas', went the refrain. 'Yes but what with? – Recoaro'. For the same brand, Dario created the figure of the garrulous signor Presenti, who talked and talked until his fictional listeners felt the need of refreshment with mineral water. He was also employed by Barilla, the pasta manufacturers, as a braggart who bored listeners at the bar with his accounts of fantastic exploits, only to be finally shown up as a windbag.

These were essentially side-shows, a means to put food on the table. The real opportunity came with an approach in early 1959 by an impresario, known familiarly as Papa, who managed the Odeon theatre in Milan. He had the shrewdness and acumen, as well as the philistinism, of the breed, and having seen the one-act pieces Dario had written, he recognised an emerging talent and realised there were commercial prospects to be exploited. He arranged a meeting at which he asked Dario if he felt able to write two or three-act plays. Dario hesitated but Franca took over to clarify that Papa was talking of a full-length play 'with music and song'. They quickly reached a deal specifying that the first play would open in September, at the Odeon, and that Dario would have full artistic control.[2] The style and content, be they satirical or conformist, comic or tragic, did not matter to the proprietor provided they put bottoms on seats. The Fo-Rame company was re-launched, with Dario as writer and lead actor, Franca as first actress, her sister Pia as wardrobe mistress, her brother Enrico as administrator and Carpi retained as musical director. Dario spent the summer writing, and from 1959, excepting only 1962 when they were involved with television, he turned out a play a year, always a comedy, always with music, generally for the Odeon, and always categorised, with hindsight, as 'bourgeois'.

Fo's 'bourgeois period' in theatre corresponded to the age of the 'economic miracle' in Italy. In Dario's case, this period, with nuances and qualifications, runs from *Archangels Don't Play Pinball* in 1959 to his break with commercial theatre in 1968, while in the case of the nation, the boom lasted from around 1958 to the slump whose effects began to be felt in 1963/4. Against all the prophecies made by the Left in the aftermath of the 1948 election, capitalism was working, the country was being transformed and wealth was trickling down. The new affluence was symbolised by the Vespa scooter, which carried Gregory Peck and Audrey Hepburn around the streets of the Eternal City in *Roman Holiday*, and by Fiat's economy car, the Seicento. It may have been a time of ideological disputes, but when the ferociously anti-Communist American ambassador, Clare Luce Booth, complained of the dominance of the Communist trade unionists on the Fiat workers councils, the workers obediently voted them off. Historians have seen a certain wry symbol of the times in a Communist trade unionist at Fiat who tried to whip up interest in elections to the factory councils, only to discover that his own members were more interested in brandishing the coupons giving them special terms for the purchase of the Seicento. Purchasing power was all. Dario himself performed in these years in the company restaurant of Rinascente, a department store with branches in most major cities.[3]

The tag 'bourgeois' was a polemical tag applied by critics and does scant justice to the actual content of Dario's works at this time. Certainly Dario was no revolutionary, nor could the works from this period be termed 'political' in the sense Brecht or Meyerhold used the term, but his comedies sat at an awkward angle to the expectations of a middle-class audience in search of a 'good night out'. They were bourgeois in the sense that they were played in commercial or 'bourgeois' venues, but in the 1950s there were no others.[4] The plays produced by the Fo-Rame company were not judged innocuous by the censors of the day, and on various occasions it was touch and go whether the show would be given authorisation. Approval for *Archangels* was officially withdrawn by the Ministry on account of the number of ad libs for which approval had not been sought. With the 1960 work, *He Had Two Pistols and White and Black Eyes,* the authorities ordered so many cuts that initially the company decided it was not worthwhile to proceed. Eventually, they chose to go ahead with the original script and risk the consequences: the censors backed down. For *Isabella, Three Caravels and a Con-Man,* Dario was subject of a report to the prosecution services because of a remark considered defamatory to the armed services, and actually received a challenge to a duel from an ex-cavalry officer. That situation was defused when Dario picked up the gauntlet but specified that the duel had to take place bare-footed, under the laws of Thailandese wrestling, of which he claimed to be national champion.[5] His opponent withdrew. One production had to be suspended because of a bomb threat, and at the end of another in Rome, the pair were attacked by a group of neo-Fascists. The zealous censors were such regular visitors that the view from the stage of torches shining on copies of the script resembled night-time in the countryside when the fireflies were abroad.

The new works were termed comedies rather than farces, but the distinction is at times imperceptible. There is assumed to be a greater sophistication to comedy than farce, but these comedies are a chain of farcical situations rather than one overarching plot. 'The choice of writing a comedy involves the choice of a more complex structure than that of farce. While the farce is based from beginning to end on a theatrical mechanism based on a single device, comedy has a structure articulated according to the storyline, and so the devices can be multiple', wrote Dario. The characters, especially the principal one invariably played by Dario, have a quality of impishness which makes them, at least in part, descendants of Harlequin, and leaves the impression that even the more stuffy of them could at any moment pull off the shirt and tie to reveal the lozenged costume. If they raise a glass to their mouth, they are as liable to squirt the wine over the face of their neighbour as to sip it politely. Dario's comedies do not provide a final-act unravelling of situations set up in the early sections of the play; the plot is normally a series of stops and starts and fresh beginnings, only some of which are resolved. His genius lies in his unrestrained inventiveness, but he often lacks the knack of channelling his creativity into structured plot, and endings were never his strong point. A Fo text is never complete. He will modify it in rehearsals, alter it during the run or rewrite it in response to audience reactions. At times, he succumbs to the temptation to concentrate on the detail or the individual scene and to incorporate, even at the expense of the coherence of the whole, all manner of visual jokes or gags, especially when they have some association with *commedia dell'arte*. At this stage, Franca was, by her own admission, too overawed by Dario's energy and inventiveness to make the critical contribution she would later make.

Dario, who always wrote at speed, produced *Archangels Don't Play at Pinball*, over the summer. The core of the work is a satire of bureaucracy, and the main players are a group of fairly innocuous hooligans or petty criminals, who live on the margins of society in some urban setting. Never before had Dario devised characters from a specified social grouping rather than from an abstract, almost metaphysical background.[6] This is not a work of social protest. The lads are jolly scoundrels who cheat bakers out of cakes and bread, but their actions do not invite judgement. Among them is one whose name is Weather, and whose first name could be Serene, Cloudy or Turbulent, but who is known as Lanky. This character, written by Dario for himself, was a cousin germane of Achille of *Lo Svitato*, and was the first of the many *faux-naïfs* characters who people Fo's theatre. His apparent simplicity is a mask behind which there lurks not an intelligence but a cunning and a pluck which will show up pretence and sham in society.

His friends gull Lanky into believing that a beautiful, wealthy Albanian woman has fallen in love with him and wants to marry him. The woman turns out to be a local prostitute, known ironically as Angela, but the 'wedding', with a phoney Coptic priest officiating, goes ahead. This wedding may be based on a similar event in Porto Valtravaglia, which ended in tragedy when the couple were drowned on the lake immediately after the ceremony.[7] When the two are left alone, the dialogue between them takes on an unexpectedly gentle and lyrical tone. Such moments of emotion are rare in Dario's theatre, and perhaps these passages can be seen as a reflection of the relations between Dario and Franca. He was the least autobiographical of writers, and intimacy or personal relationships were never in his area of interest. He was not a poet of the emotional side of the human psyche and was immune to any fascination with the manifold strategies which Jack uses in novels and plays to entice Jill into bed. There is no shortage of married couples in his works, but only with *Open Couple*, the other idiosyncratically autobiographical work in his canon, is the success or failure of the marriage the focus of attention.

The couple split up when Lanky informs her that he must be off to Rome to claim a pension due to him for a wound he received to his *osso sacro*, or sacrum, a bone which, with its odd name and embarrassing position, was always a favourite of Dario's. The pension claim takes Lanky into a Ministry, and allows Dario to satirise the workings of bureaucracy. There is something of expressionist absurdity in this scene of bureaucrats working like robots on a factory line, but it is another of those scenes which finds its worth only in performance. The words are secondary, and even the stage directions are as banal as cooking instructions on a packet. To his dismay Lanky finds that he has been registered as a bloodhound. The official registration is the only proof of existence, and since the form says 'bloodhound', Lanky must take on the characteristics and life-style fitting a bloodhound.

A plot with such an abundance of twists and changes of direction can leave the audience dizzy, and critics were still unsure of what to make of Dario's puzzling talent. His histrionic gifts were undisputed, but the theatre magazine *Sipario*, when publishing the script of *Archangels*, gave voice to the criticism which was to dog Fo all throughout his career. An enjoyable work of course, excellent on stage, brilliantly acted but did it have any value when set down on paper?

Farce rediscovers here – after references to reality which are anything but random – all its congenial slapstick and knockabout. It would be pointless, in an attempt to avoid losing the 'best', to look for the rest on the pages of the script; by the 'best', we mean the bare-knuckled struggle in which Dario Fo the actor and Dario Fo the author engage onstage to gain the upper hand in the show. Is it right to publish in *Sipario* a play which (precisely because of the genre to which it belongs) cannot boast sufficient literary autonomy? Let the reader judge, but let him judge by giving to the speeches of Lanky – it is an undemanding effort of the imagination – the intonations, the pauses, the accents, the absurd flurries, the stutters and the malicious cadences of the actor Dario Fo.[8]

The 1960/1 theatrical season saw Dario at the same venue with a more complex work, *He Had Two Pistols and White and Black Eyes,* a fable which reflects and distorts society with the devastatingly malicious wit of a Jonathan Swift or John Gay. Dario played both the leading roles, those of a priest who has lost his memory and of a bandit on the run. The opening scene unfolds in a psychiatric hospital 'which resembles the cloister of a monastery', run by doctors and nurses dressed in the conventional white coats but topped by white capes embellished with the red cross of the Knights of Malta.[9] The mental hospital managed by clerics provides an unsettlingly acerbic image of an Italy ruled by the Christian Democrat party, and allows Fo to introduce a favourite device of presenting the supposed madman as the representative of sanity. In a society which is corrupt and insane, the Lord of Misrule is the only legislator who can be trusted. Fo told his Danish translator Bent Holm that at this stage of his life he wrote largely according to instinct, but agreed that he was already drawn to that dramatic reversal of roles which Mikhail Bakhtin identified as the essence of carnival. Where the Italian constitution reads that 'Italy is a Republic founded on work', the crooks' trade union in the play wanted the statute altered to read 'a Republic founded on work and theft'. They put in a claim for a percentage of all theft, 'except for those committed inside Ministries'.

The public response to the play was gratifying. Official figures showed that the Fo-Rame company was attracting audiences far in excess of those attending the works of any other theatrical company in Italy. According to an unbreakable law of criticism, every plaudit induces an equal and opposite censure, so there were already reviewers suggesting that the attractions of the *beau monde* and of increasing prosperity had begun to blunt Fo's satirical purpose. Whatever the reason, the next season's play, *He Who Loses a Foot is Lucky in Love,* premiered on 8 September 1961, received some of the most hostile notices he was ever to draw. The Left-wing press, especially the Communist daily, *L'Unità,* was especially severe. In the play, Dario transfers the Apollo and Daphne myth to the Milan of his own time, and attempts to interweave a love story with criticism of construction companies involved in wholesale fraud. The criticism is not sustained, and in the attempt to build on the myth, the plot itself comes to resemble one of those ramshackle manor houses where each successive generation has added an extension. Barbs from the Left were not sufficient to enhance Dario and Franca's standing with the Establishment. The attack on corruption in business extended the circle of enemies.

Dario's theatre was beginning to win him an international reputation. Yugoslavia was the first country to stage a translation of one of his plays, but Scandinavia was also enthusiastic. By 1962 his work had been presented in three theatres in Stockholm, in two in Helsinki as well as in Denmark and Norway. Danish television presented *He Had Two Pistols and White and Black Eyes,* while other works were staged in Holland and Poland. As with a volcanic eruption, all the authorities in Italy could do was move as many people as possible away from the area likely to be affected. Apart from commercials, Dario and Franca were kept off the television screens, not difficult to achieve in a country where broadcasting was run by government placemen.

However, by 1962, the membership of the ruling Establishment was widening due to the change in government alliance known as the 'opening to the Left'. Pope John XXIII was on the papal throne, the modernising Vatican Council was in session, the liberalising trends which marked the 60s were already making their impact and the Christian Democrat party was suffering from public irritation with the scandals in which it was involved. Under Fernando Tambroni, they tried to bolster their declining position by establishing a coalition with the neo-Fascists, but this manoeuvre led to widespread rioting and the attempt was abandoned. Amintore Fanfani, then identified with the party's reforming wing, spearheaded a drive to the Left, aimed at prising the Socialists away from their alliance with the Communists. After an extended courtship, with the exchange of those half-hearted promises and mutual deceptions which characterise all mating procedures, a Centre-Left government, with Fanfani at the helm, was formed in February 1962.

Dario was among the opponents of a move which he saw as neutering the Socialists and giving new legitimacy to their Christian Democrat enemies, but for him the outcome was beneficial. In the first year of the new government, the law requiring pre-emptive censorship was rescinded, although in due course it became clear that this move was equivalent to the sixteenth-century legislation which legalised deer-hunting in the royal forests when there were no deer left to hunt. The importance of theatre had diminished value in an age when primacy in public entertainment, and in the expression of attitudes and beliefs, had passed to the newer media. In any case, Italian authorities, as Dario was to discover, retained sufficient control to deal with any troublesome thespian who looked likely to pose a threat. Local police chiefs retained the power to examine the content of the works in performance, and to take measures against anything which posed a threat to 'morals, good customs and public order'.

On assuming political power, Socialists were allowed to share not only government office but also what Italians cynically termed 'sub-government', that is, the right of appointment to the many quangos, boards, commissions, as well as banks and nationalised companies which were involved in the governance of the Republic. One of these was RAI, and in the early stages the Socialists' appointees let in gusts of fresh air. In the same year, 1962, RAI opened a second channel, RAI2, a minority channel in every sense. Since few existing licence holders had sets equipped to receive its programmes, RAI2 could be used as a ghetto for experimental programming or controversial works.

Dario and Franca were among the first to be invited to appear on the new channel, and five of the earlier one-act farces were transmitted. Dario directed the plays himself, receiving payment of three million lire, which was then a generous payment. The response was enthusiastic, and the couple were then invited by RAI2 to present a mini-series of the variety show, *Who's Seen It?* The show opened with a mock occupation of the studios by supposedly dissatisfied users, aiming to install comedians whose work was more in keeping with their own, iconoclastic tastes. The various sketches presented are said to have been unconventional, and the series is said to have stirred the waters of TV variety with its irreverent parodies of other TV shows. No one now can judge, since RAI later destroyed all copies of the programmes.

Emboldened, RAI then invited Dario and Franca to take charge of *Canzonissima* (The Big Song), the company's highly popular variety show, transmitted at prime time on the first channel. Conceived as an accompaniment to the national lottery, this programme had risen in popularity with the growth of the pop music industry. The programme included comic sketches, and the format had been altered after the first series to give the show a competitive edge. Each week one genre of song was featured, with the singer who received most votes from the audience at home going on to the final, where one overall winner was chosen. There were thirteen programmes in all.

Initially, Franca and Dario were sceptical and unenthusiastic. After the failure of their venture into film, they had devoted themselves to theatre and had been successful in building up their own audience. The first episode of *Canzonissima* was scheduled for October, which would mean missing a whole season and breaking faith with their public. In addition, *Canzonissima* was escapist entertainment, where relentless light-heartedness and light-headedness were prized. Television was not their métier, and they were unsure of what level of autonomy they would be afforded. On the other hand, it was not as though Italian theatre had been for them an arena of unrestricted liberty. The presence of prowling censors had been fatiguing, while their own experiences with *Who's Seen It?* had been positive. Provided they could reach a firm agreement that they were in control of content of the programmes, and were at liberty to reshape it, they decided to accept.

The Director-General of RAI2 was Sergio Pugliese, whom Franca described as open-minded and cultured. Schedules for all twelve programmes, excluding the final, were drawn up and submitted to him for discussion. Dario was prepared to defer to Pugliese's expertise in his own professional field, but he was determined that *Canzonissima* would rise above mindless giggles, chatter and sing-song. He insisted on the right to take a satirical look at contemporary Italy. This was accepted, and the format and outline scripts were agreed with the broadcasting authorities. Dario once again spent the summer writing, and the two sides met in a restaurant outside Verona and Franca remembers Pugliese laughing contentedly at the sketches Dario had prepared.[10] All seemed set fair.

The resultant programmes, a compromise between conflicting demands, do sound uncomfortable from today's standpoint, but accurate assessment is not possible, since RAI pulped these programmes too. The scripts are extant, as are the volumes of newspaper comment which followed the first and each successive programme. Choruses of high-kicking, scantily clad, sequinned dancing girls preceded mordant sketches on aspects of public life in Italy: a monologue by Dario was followed by close-ups of some idol of the moment singing his or her newest number on the pains of teenage passion. The theme tune composed by Dario, with its mockery not of the powerful and wealthy but of those who allow themselves to be gulled and tranquillised by the desire of goods and gadgets, set a satirical tone.

> Oh people of the miracle
> Economic miracle,
> Magnificent people,
> Champions of liberty (. . .)
> He who sings is a free man,
> Free of all thought
> He who sings is already content
> With what he does not have.
> Come now, let us sing,

Let us have done with thinking (. . .)
Let us hear the orphans sing,
And the weeping widows,
And striking workers
Let them all join in the song . . .[11]

Tired executives had not expected to while away their evenings listening to Dario pouring scorn on Italy's much vaunted 'economic miracle'. The well-heeled viewers were disconcerted by his focus on the losers in the economic process and by efforts to prick the vanity and vacuity of those who regarded themselves as winners. In one sketch, a deferential worker in awe of his employer thanks him for the scents he spreads in the air with his factory chimneys, for the light he puts into bulbs and for his kindness in increasing the size of the worker's pay packet – the actual packet, not the money inside it. 'Give to Caesar what is Caesar's' is taken as the motto of the employer, whose name is Caesar. In an attack on the paternalism of some employers, a demented employee is shown caressing a statue of the factory owner, and breaking into a lyrical number – 'Take this kiss. You give me work and life, take this kiss. You are my country, you are the air I breathe, take this kiss. Yours is the football and basketball team I support, take this kiss.' It was reported that this behaviour was then acted out in several workshops in northern Italy.

The greatest satisfaction for any satirist is to see from the bitterness and rancour of his opponents that his darts have found their target, so Dario must have been a contented man in the succeeding weeks. In Franca's words, 'war was declared on us by the Right.' The press inveighed against the freedom afforded to the Communist Fo to command the air waves. Methodical leaks informed newspaper readers of the concern felt in the upper echelons of RAI. The tempo was raised as the weeks went by. The Parliamentary Commission of Vigilance met in special session, and issued a communiqué saying that viewers expected relaxing entertainment, not politics. The Italian armed forces, a notoriously sensitive body of men, expressed outrage at a scene which poked fun at the uniforms they had worn during the war.

The Liberal party leader weighed in to opine that satire only served to exacerbate, not alleviate, problems. In the face of this pressure, the overall agreement covering all episodes was set aside and it was decreed that each one must be subject to rigorous internal scrutiny. A dispute between the managements in Milan, where the programmes were made, and Rome, where the RAI executive was based, added to the difficulties. The scripts were re-examined. Dario was asked to remove words like 'orphanage,' because it had inappropriate connotations in modern Italy, 'bed' since it had all kinds of promiscuous overtones and even 'liberty', since it might lead to revolution. His sketch on *Cain and Abel*, although performed on radio years previously, was red-pencilled, presumably on grounds of blasphemy. The director of the channel, Giuseppe Piccioni, later a senator, made a personal visit to the Fo flat in Milan where, according to Franca, he went down on his knees in front of the astonished couple to beg them to tone down their work. It is only fair to add that he denies this.

In spite of this sniffing over the scripts, there were points which still caused offence. In one programme, a woman played by Franca sent someone out to buy a water melon, with the advice to choose one which was good and red. A sharp-eyed reviewer spotted a subversive message in the preference for something red. That had to be a veiled message to the comrades, surely? In this climate, even rational people become capable of the most bizarre excesses, as happened to two valiant priests who denounced Fo in their parish magazine over a blasphemy they had detected in an anti-romantic love song, *The Boil*. The song, with tender pathos, outlines the plight of a young man who detects a boil under his earlobe, and knowing that his girlfriend cannot stand such things, fears that their relationship is at an end. The alleged blasphemy was not apparent to the naked eye, but Dario took the charge sufficiently seriously to raise a legal action. The penitent clerics admitted they had got it all wrong, and backed down.[12]

The quality of the programmes had suffered as a result of the interference of the censors, but there was no lessening of satirical attacks on sinister bodies no-one else had the courage to name. That year, one of the mafia's many internecine wars was underway in Sicily, but it was taboo even to admit in public that there was such a body as the mafia. On *Canzonissima*, Dario ridiculed the mob, and in reply, received a letter, stained with drops of human blood, containing the words, 'those who strike at the mafia, die by the mafia'. In an act of bravado, they stuck it up on the wall of their house, but reacted with more sobriety when their son, Jacopo, then aged six, was also subject to threats. For six months, Jacopo was escorted everywhere, to school and swing-parks, by police officers.

Unsurprisingly, audience ratings were climbing week by week. Some individual episodes were weak, but the series became the stuff of legends. It is still possible to meet taxi-drivers in Rome who will tell you that the programmes were a financial disaster for them. When they were being shown, they say, no one was on the streets. The crunch came in episode eleven with a sketch depicting a building contractor in a state of sham self-loathing over the apparent death of an employee who had fallen from badly erected scaffolding. To ward off criticism, the contractor feigns despair and promises improvement, but on learning that the worker's injuries were actually slight, he returns to his old cynical ways and threatens to punch any worker stupid enough to slip. The directors of RAI totally refused to sanction the broadcast of this sketch, particularly since there was a strike in the building industry at that time. Dario retorted with an ultimatum of his own – no sketch, no show. The week was taken up with an interminable round of consultations, but neither side would budge. Lawyers were consulted. The advice given to Dario and Franca was to abide by their contractual obligations, turn up as normal at the scheduled time and make the standard preparations for the show just in case the management backed down. On Saturday evening, they went to the studios, donned their costumes, hovered in the studio wings complete with make-up, still not knowing whether the programme would go ahead or not. Only when they heard the continuity announcer state that 'as of this evening, Dario Fo and Franca Rame have decided to leave *Canzonissima*', was the situation clarified. They put on their coats and went out into the night where, as the news spread, their progress along the street became a triumphal procession.

The fracas was headline news in Italy the following day. Leader columns debated the freedom of the air waves, the conduct of the RAI, the intrusiveness of politicians and the comic talents of Dario Fo. The couple were pictured seated on their sofa, with Franca wearing an expression of ferocious indignation. They came out of the whole fiasco well. Most commentators considered that they had been shabbily treated, and had behaved with dignity. Each side sued the other, and the case dragged on through the Italian courts for over a decade. Initially, Dario and Franca won and were awarded damages, but this was overturned on appeal, then further reversed, until finally the case went against the couple, who were compelled to pay high, but not ruinous, compensation.

The whole shambles secured their place in the public mind. There could not now be a person in Italy unaware of who they were. Previously, Dario had enjoyed a vogue as a writer and actor in theatre, but television bestowed on them fame in the full modern sense of the word – recognition in the streets, forfeiture of privacy, subjection to gossip, entry into public consciousness, attribution of glamour, conferment of an image and full public identifiability. The two were now 'personalities' or 'celebrities', with all the ambiguity that status confers, and their later careers are inseparable from that defining moment. They were barred from the television screens until 1976, when a further shift in Italian politics brought the Communist Party into a government alliance and permitted their return. In the meantime, having excluded themselves from cinema, they concentrated on theatre alone.

Canzonissima went on after the two walked out. The comic Walter Chiari took over as presenter, the competition to choose the best song was won by a number entitled *Quando, quando, quando*, and the regime did not totter. The affair dispelled such traces of innocence as remained in Dario and Franca. The cynicism of the powers that be and their tenacity in the defence of powerful interests took them both aback. The censors had backed down when Dario rejected demands for substantial cuts in *Archangels Don't Play Pinball*, but were intransigent when on the new, popular medium of TV he threatened to make full use of the power of direct address to a mass public. Dario and Franca returned to theatre, the medium they knew best, convinced that direct address to a mass public could be subversive, and determined to make theatre the vehicle for that appeal.

Echoes of the *Canzonissima* affair rumble through the next play, *Isabella, Three Caravels and a Con-Man*, premiered at the Odeon in September 1963. The Isabella in question is the Most Catholic Queen of Spain, and the con-man Christopher Columbus, making a return visit after his brief appearance in *Poer Nano*. Columbus, who requires royal patronage to realise his monomania for sailing to the Indias, has of necessity turned himself into a courtier who haunts the royal palace, where he is treated with condescension and impatience by his betters. There is a self-deprecating, satirical autobiographical undertow to this depiction of Columbus, whose dilemma reflects that of Dario in the corridors of RAI. In interviews prior to the production, he repeated that this was a serious farce, whose aim was to expose the compromises made by those leftist intellectuals who, after the 'opening to the left', were tempted to make their accommodations with the establishment. With his relish for irony, Dario revived the play on his return to TV in 1977.

To add to the multi-layered complexity and polyphonic diversity of this work, Dario also pitted himself against Brecht. Giorgio Strehler had that year chosen to put on *The Life of Galileo* at the Piccolo, and for a time the two productions were in performance in theatres within walking distance of each other. Both works turn to history to debate the present, both subject celebrated figures to critical scrutiny, and both employ to the full devices and approaches characteristic of the respective authors. As dramatist, Brecht presented himself as an iconoclast and non-conformist nuisance who used the stage as quasi-scientific, unemotional forum for debate. Dario too viewed himself as a breaker of conventions, but his theatre also includes elements of sheer mischief as well as of irony. Brecht's Galileo, perhaps in spite of his author's intentions, attains some aura of heroism, while Fo's Columbus is continually undermined by the sheer absurdity of all that surrounds him. The desire to arouse laughter is part of the tactic of subversion which is of the essence of Dario's drama, but he cannot resist a gag for its own sake. When the heavily pregnant Isabella stretches herself out on a sofa in the centre of a room where Columbus and the learned men are debating the shape of the planet earth, her grotesquely swollen belly is casually and nonchalantly employed by them as a globe to illustrate the routes that could be followed by ships moving around its circumference. The passage reveals nothing about Columbus, but it lightens the atmosphere and heightens the comedy.

The basic structure is the tried and tested play-within-a-play. The first sounds heard are of nails being hammered into a gallows where an actor is to be executed for the crime of performing a work which seems to be *La Celestina*, by Fernando de Rojas. It is carnival, a feast which permits the temporary dethroning of bishops, the replacement of reason by folly and the general overturning of established order. Fo was increasingly intrigued by this event.[13] As part of the carnival rites, word comes that sentence has been suspended, but not yet revoked, to allow the actor to perform on the scaffold the drama of Christopher Columbus. In the words of a guard, this freedom is granted 'so that it can be seen that in our country anyone can do what he likes on the scaffold; there is no censorship on this stage'. There are two audiences, the crowd on stage and the spectators in the stalls, and several time-frames, with the condemned actor referring back to the Catholic Spain of Ferdinand and Isabella and forward to the Catholic Spain of Franco, which is itself a metaphor for Christian Democrat controlled Italy. Dario was plainly still smarting from his treatment at the hands of the authorities, but was equally outraged at his own gullibility and at the complacency of others like him who had allowed themselves to be manipulated. Official annual statistics revealed that *Isabella* was the most popular production of the season.

Seventh Commandment: Thou Shalt Steal a Little Less, written for the 1964-5 season, sold out in the Odeon, causing him to hire the Puccini to extend its run in Milan. The subsequent tour inside Italy throughout winter '64 and spring '65 took in fifty-one venues, so that, according to official figures, over 200,000 spectators paid to see the show. There are elements of fantasy in the new work, but not a fantasy designed to create an elfland where problems can be smoothed away. This is

1984 or *Brave New World* rewritten for the Mad Hatter's tea-party, for underlying the new play, there is a real rage against an Italy mired in sleaze and corruption. Once again the image of an ecclesiastical mental institution is employed to depict the nation, but this time the citizens themselves are subjected to biting sarcasm for their passivity and inertia. The play marks a milestone in the evolution of Franca, who for the first time plays the principal part, the grave-digger, Enea. Instinctively deferential towards the forces of law and order, Enea initially applauds a police charge on strikers, but in the graveyard, she meets and forms a relationship with an accountant, who happens to have a mania for collecting and sleeping in coffins. Her consciousness of politics and laws deepens as she undergoes a process which sees her become another of Fo's big-hearted prostitutes, ('it is the only profession which emancipates, elevates, makes you feel someone'), before donning a nun's habit. The relationship with the coffin-maniac continues even when he has seemingly died. He revives and stumbles on the truth about the scale of corruption perpetrated by the hospital's governing body, but is silenced by surgeons who drill a curious rotating fan into his brain to reduce him to robotic acquiescence. Techniques of farce can scarcely conceal the savage violence of the vision behind it. The closing number, 'the song of the Italiot,' played with frenzied pace by a chorus of asylum inmates, arouses in the audience laughter which is as jarring and brittle as the sound of an open blade dragged along a stone wall.

> We are happy, we are content with the brain we have,
> We have the propeller which makes us follow the flow.
> If they tell us: he's thieving, he's stealing, he's on the fiddle
> We shrug our shoulders and smile like idiots.
> Because we are the ancient Indo-Phoenician race, the Italiots
> We are happy, we are content with the brain we have.[14]

Always Blame the Devil, premiered in September 1965 is set, like the later *Mistero buffo*, in the Middle Ages, an epoch which interested Fo. It provided a quarry for metaphors for the present day and was part of his reconstruction of an alternative history of the nameless, the poor, the dispossessed, the huddled masses who had been written out of the official chronicles. The Cathar heretics who find themselves facing Imperial forces in thirteenth-century Italy are comparable to the Vietnamese in their war with the Americans, and it requires no leap of imagination to see links between the Cathar 'communards', who preached the abolition of private property, and Italian Communists. Fo also believed that the Cathar heresy, or rebellion, represented both political protest and the authentic Gospel spirit. The heretics facing execution have had, as the executioner explains, the effrontery to suggest that 'Catholics should apply the Gospels to the letter,'[15] meaning that the Emperor and his court would have to follow a rule of poverty. The religious sentiments dramatised in Fo's works are primarily images for a political and social outlook, but that does not disguise the undercurrent of respect for authentic Christian belief which frequently surfaces in his work.

And all the time, Dario's reputation was growing. He had shows running in fourteen European cities from Reykjavik to Budapest. In 1966, the Fo-Rame company toured to sixteen countries from Scandinavia to Israel. The grandly titled *Annuario dell'Istituto del Dramma Italiano*, in its 1969 edition, announced that there were a total of 569 registered playwrights in Italy, although few of them were likely to be known to the general public. The same organ also revealed that of the works performed the previous year, 44 were written by Eduardo, Titina and Peppino De Filippo, members of the Neapolitan dynasty of actor-authors, while 20 were by Dario Fo.

The category 'registered playwright', which has no equivalent outside Italy, was a cypher for all that enraged Dario in the creeping institutionalisation and taming of theatre by the political establishment. The *teatri stabili* had now lost the vitality which had made them such a revolutionary force in Italian theatre in the post-war years and, more seriously, had de facto ceded their independence to the political bosses in local and national government. Appointments were made, as in every other sector of Italian life, on the basis not of competence but of party allegiance. Even the best of directors paid their dues to the system. Giorgio Strehler's work continued to be widely respected, although Fo was no longer among his admirers, but he would not have been able to continue had he not associated himself with the Socialist party who were uncontested rulers of Milan.

For years, Dario Fo and Eduardo De Filippo had stood, almost alone, outside this system, although now in the swinging, irreverent sixties, the mood of discontent was spreading. 'Registered playwrights' contained a sub-category of the 'non-performed playwright', a group which drew Dario's withering contempt. Many performed playwrights, who had had their work staged thanks to their deference to the structures of power, also drew his ire, since both groups were guilty of failing to produce plays which reflected contemporary society. Dario's preferred models were those who refused an easy accommodation with authority and who offered a challenge to society and grappled with history. 'I have heard the old lament on the crisis facing living authors, and on how only dead authors are performed, but I wonder if we are sure that these living authors are really alive? Rooting about in theatre history in all times, I find that where authors were genuinely tied to the history of their own age, they invariably found an audience to support and encourage them.' In contrast, he suggested a mind experiment in which researchers of the future attempted to reconstruct the history of our times from a selection of comedies and dramas which had been fired up into space. 'They would find nothing but a stream of grand concepts and of words playing blind man's buff without ever finding each other; there would be nothing but characters out of time and bereft of all sense of reality. Nobody could ever manage to guess when or by whom those works had been written. Days, nights, months, eras – all without context.'[16]

Dario was now worried that, although viewing himself as a trespasser on an alien habitat approximately defined 'bourgeois', he was being made too welcome. His humour, wit and taste for madcap jollity wrong-footed his audiences, but as a satirist his aim was to unsettle and irritate them. He was growing uneasy about the comfortable, prosperous audiences who filled the stalls, and who exited chuckling and laughing in evident delight. Had he missed its mark? He found a focus for his unease in one anonymous, fur-coated lady whom he espied in the foyer before and after a performance of *Isabella*. Her dress and demeanour singled her out as a member of the wealthy middle class, and if she of all people was not ill at ease, something was going wrong.

He felt the need for a new context for his own work. In the course of a trial for witchcraft in *Always Blame the Devil*, the judge discovers that the accusers are communards, and invites them to sing their hymn to him. The prisoners are bemused by the request, but the judge tells them: 'Make the people sing, said the poet, and you will see their soul. I am very interested in seeing this soul.'[17] This judicial view on traditional or folk music was one to which Fo become converted after his contacts with the *Nuovo Canzoniere Italiano*, NCI.

The NCI was established in 1962 to conduct research into popular history, folk culture, protest movements as these were expressed in song. They organised concerts, produced a learned periodical, cut several records and later established a research centre. Their first show carried the title – *The Other Italy: A Selection of Italian Popular and Protest Songs, Old and New,* so it was only a matter of time before they and Dario attracted each other's attention. The NCI attained national notoriety in 1964 with *Bella ciao!,* a programme of popular and Resistance songs performed at the Spoleto Festival. They had agreed to submit all their material to the festival managers, but at the last minute the lead singer lost her voice and her replacement sang an anti-war number from World War 1, *O Gorizia,* which had not received approval. It contained a line about 'treacherous gentlemen officers, who had always wanted war'. The delicate sensibilities of Italy's armed forces were offended and they sued.

Nanni Ricordi was now NCI manager and arranged a meeting at which Dario was invited to participate in the show which became *Ci ragiono e canto* (I Think It Over and Sing About it).[18] The group were conscious of their own lack of theatrical experience, but they were afflicted by an ideological rigidity typical of the sixties and determined not to be accused of the capital sin of 'selling out.' It is hard to imagine a less promising starting point, and indeed the production process was marred by both personal animosities and the group's protectiveness towards material they had gathered. The resultant tensions were expressed in ideological terms. Ideology, and its leering twin, jargon, now enter the Fo-Rame story. Certain of the arguments in the late sixties and seventies which caused co-operation to founder and friendships to splinter were conducted in a sub-Marxist jargon which is now as impenetrable as the disputations of medieval monks.

The agreement was that Fo would direct the NCI in the stage production of the material they had collected, but actually ceding control proved tricky. Factions were formed, with Fo and Ricordi finding themselves on the opposite side from Roberto Leydi, the show's author. Leydi left to join the Piccolo, a move regarded by others in the NCI as 'going over to enemy's side of the barricade.'[19] His departure did not resolve all disputes over production values and styles. Fo wanted to introduce movement and choreography in accordance with the visual requirements of the stage, but the NCI were chary of anything which smacked of trivialisation. He was accused of tending towards the 'grotesque' style, while the NCI wanted performance to be dictated by the rhythms and meanings of the songs. Fo countered that what was taken as grotesque was an attempt to establish some correlation between the rhythms of the songs and of the work which they accompanied. Some NCI members were outraged when Dario wrote some musical numbers of his own which he wanted to pass off as traditional pieces. An open letter, dotted with self-important italics, was circulated among the group. 'It is right not to present the songs according to a visual aesthetic; it is right to use a *historicising* presentation of them; but beware lest once they have been spruced up in that way, they lose that fire which comes from the fact that *they are also a presence in the contemporary popular-peasant world*: contemporaneity becomes the most important element of the process of theatrical historicisation, and this is the source of the provocative violence which the traditional popular heritage, together with the social song, brings with it.'[20] Dario was never moved by any undue reverence for the historical authenticity of material when he believed its immediate theatrical impact could be enhanced by rewriting. His productions were always defiantly impure. The author of the letter, Gianfranco Bosio, resigned from the production but took a menacing seat in the back stalls throughout the period of the rehearsals.

The work was staged in 1964, and televised much later in 1977 with many members of the original cast retained. The material is varied, including work songs, protest songs, nursery rhymes, cradle songs, love songs, political songs, anti-war songs as well as traditional folk songs from all regions of Italy. The production was moderately successful. 'The show perhaps was not what we would have wanted, and certainly was not what Fo would have wanted. It was in essence a difficult collaboration, but it did undoubtedly lead to a stimulating show.'[21] Probably that was the only judgement possible. The collaboration, however tense, forced Dario to deepen his notions of popular culture.[22] All sides were indebted to Gramsci, but the NCI group had engaged in more thorough, systematic, empirical research than Dario had ever considered until that point. They believed, as they wrote in the programme, that they were dealing 'not with a culture so much as with a civilisation' and one which was 'equipped with a great capacity for defence of its own values and for resistance in the face of the dominant culture'. Not all Leftist theorists were convinced by this notion, and in the ensuing debate, a dissenting voice was raised for the Communist party, the PCI, by Achille Occhetto, later party leader. The PCI, like its French counterpart, was never entirely happy with the notion of popular culture. Occhetto was concerned that this division of cultures would implicitly exclude the working class from the treasures of the mainstream Western culture, relegating them permanently to a lower spiritual division.

The immediate concern of the NCI itself was with the cost of lighting, scenery and costumes, which far exceeded estimates. When the extent of the deficit incurred by *Ci ragiono e canto* became clear, Nanni Ricordi handed in his resignation. He formed close links with the Fo-Rame company, and became administrator of the theatrical co-operatives they established some years later. His contacts both with the world of finance and with the upper echelons of the PCI were invaluable. One of the musicians, Paolo Ciarchi, also left to join the Fo-Rame troupe. Some members of the NCI, notably Michele L Straniero, later wrote about Dario with a ferocity of feeling which the passing of time had not served to abate.[23] The group itself was shaken to its foundations, and although there were two subsequent programmes of song, given the same title *Ci ragiono e canto* and produced by Fo in 1969 and 1973, the NCI as such was not involved. The third edition brought the Sicilian singer-songwriter Piero Sciotto into the group. Dario had been contemplating a show about prisons, and required a Southerner. A mutual friend contacted Sciotto, and although the original show was never made, Sciotto appeared in *Ci ragiono e canto 3*, and was an important presence in the life and work of Dario and Franca over many years.

CHAPTER 5

Viva La Rivoluzione!

Dario's travels in late 1966 took him both to Eastern Europe and Castro's Cuba, a Mecca for left-wing activists. He returned from Havana fired with enthusiasm not only for the vigour and enthusiasm Cuban companies displayed but also, temporarily, by the local version of 'poor theatre'. Their willingness to engage with issues of the day chimed with Dario's aims, but he differed over the question of production values. Stage design was one of the skills he brought to the theatre, and even when his company was later involved in touring from village to village, he refused to compromise on scenery and stage furniture. His vision of theatre, political or other, required the whole paraphernalia of costumes, artistically designed sets, elaborate lighting effects and props.

The 1960s in Europe were a period when a multitude of self-serving sins in theatre could be concealed under the labels of experimentation, happening or avant-garde. Dario, whose own interests were in the development of a line of theatre which had mass appeal, for the most part steered clear of such trends. However, he invariably offered generous support to fellow practitioners of whatever stamp, especially when they encountered problems with censorship. When the American radical, innovative director, Julian Beck, toured Italy with his troupe, Living Theatre, in 1966 they hired the Durini in Milan for their own style of happening, or *Free Theatre*, but it was too strong meat for the theatre's aristocratic owner, who summoned the police and had them turned out. Dario championed their cause and was responsible for having the company invited to the Parma festival to stage their *Antigone*. Whether this enhanced the standing of Living Theatre with the authorities is debatable, since when they returned to Italy in 1969 with *Paradise Now,* they were denounced for obscenity, refused an extension of the permits they had negotiated, escorted to the border by the police and expelled. Dario also became friendly with Eugenio Barba, the Italian avant-garde director who had established his Odin Teatret in Jutland. Barba's vision of non-narrative theatre, his desire to establish a semi-monastic community of actor-devotees was at the antipodes from Dario's notion of theatre, but the two shared a vision of actor-centred theatre, and Dario was impressed by Barba's attempts at achieving a primacy for the body in performance.

Dario's own position in commercial theatre was increasingly uneasy, but he performed twice more on the mainstream stage before breaking away. In January 1967, he produced, in the same Durini theatre from which the Living Theatre had been expelled, *A Sunday Stroll*, a version of a work by French playwright, Georges Michel. Only very rarely had Dario worked on the script of another author, and on such occasions his tendency was to dismantle the original and produce what would better be described as a parallel work rather than a translation. *A Sunday Stroll* was received coolly. The impression was that Dario was marking time.

Some of his best known songs were composed for a one-man show later that year starring Enzo Jannacci and entitled simply *22 Songs*. These numbers included *Veronica*, the song of the girl who liked music which was symphonic and harmonic but whose love was anything but platonic, and *The Priest Liprando*, the ballad of a medieval cleric who was forced to undergo trial by ordeal after denouncing his bishop for simony. Jannacci, like the NCI, wanted help with tempo, movement on stage and self-presentation, and he and Dario worked together in rehearsal for two highly intensive days.[1] The show went well, without the rancour which had marked the NCI experience.

His major work in 1967 was *Toss the Lady Out*, premiered at Milan's Teatro Manzoni in September. This free-wheeling play, which for once exploited the liberty of the sixties 'happening', is commonly given as the last in Dario's 'bourgeois period', although there is nothing bourgeois about the politics, an onslaught on consumerism and the American intervention in Vietnam. By 1967, Dario was plainly chafing at the bit. He needed to find a new form of theatre, but he by-passed the contemporary avant-garde in favour of the by-ways of theatre history. Clowns began to interest him, as they had Mayakovsky, whose influence on him was also on the increase. He made contact with the Colombaioni Brothers, two clowns who belonged to a well established circus dynasty, and devised his new play to incorporate their abilities. *Toss the Lady Out* was set in a circus Big Top, and all the parts were played by clowns or in the style of clowns. The actors in the company, including Dario, spent the months of rehearsals learning the new trade, walking on their hands, cartwheeling, employing falsetto tones of voice or plunging with the appearance of nonchalance into tanks of water. Franca mastered the techniques of the trapeze artist.

Within his discussion of clowns, Fo displayed again his tendency to stretch history. The clown was transformed into a cousin germane of the stock characters of *commedia dell'arte*.

> In our own days, the clown has become a figure whose job is to keep children happy. He is synonymous with puerile simple-mindedness, with picture-postcard ingenuousness and with pure sentimentality. Today's clown has lost both his ancient capacity to shock and his political-moral commitment. In other times, the clown used satire as a vehicle against violence, cruelty, hypocrisy and injustice. Centuries ago, he was an obscene, diabolic figure; in the cathedrals of the middle ages, on the capitals and the friezes above the entrances, there can still be seen representations of comic buffoons in provocative couplings with animals, mermaids or harpies, grinning broadly as they show off their organs.
>
> The clown's origins are very remote, and certainly clowns were already in existence before the advent of *commedia dell'arte*. It could be said that the characters of *commedia* were born of an obscene marriage between female jesters on the one hand and storytellers and clowns on the other, and that, after this act of incest, *commedia* spawned hosts of other clowns.[2]

The clown was given the status of forerunner of Harlequin, but in the show the fact that he was primarily an actor was to be kept in full view; the characters were known simply as Clown Dario, Clown Franca, Clown Valerio etc. While the performance constituted a declaration of affection for the scorned practitioners of a derided craft, the attacks on America over its conduct of the Vietnam war were boisterous. *Toss the Lady Out* can scarcely be regarded as a play, but the looseness of the circus format suited Fo perfectly. Some of his sketches were traditional, playful pieces of knockabout for its own sake, while others cocked a political snook at specific targets. The circus itself was one representation of America, as was the circus owner, the Old Lady, now dying, noisily and angrily, on the large bed which occupied part of the performing area. The passing of her inheritance to a younger woman, also played by Franca, signified the transition from an old to a new America that the accession of the Kennedy dynasty represented for many. Fo was not an admirer of Kennedy, but in the midst of deliberately grotesque imagery he devised an unexpectedly poignant depiction of the assassination at Dallas. The blonde circus-owner was seated astride a trapeze, wearing a straw hat decorated like a target board, and when she was shot, her body fell silently backwards, swinging lifelessly to and fro. It was only for a moment. Fo showed more enthusiasm for the various conspiracy theories, mocking the trajectory of the magic bullet which supposedly killed Kennedy and wounded Governor Connolly.

Toss the Lady Out was the last production of the Fo-Rame company, which then dissolved. Dario and Franca made the decision that they had to break completely with commercial, or 'bourgeois' theatre. Whatever success he may have had in integrating satire and politics into bourgeois comedy, Dario felt that the company was, both in its structure and stage policy, no longer the appropriate vehicle for changed times or for the political vision he wished to propose. In the sixties, writers were urged, when they needed urging, to conform to the idea of commitment enunciated by Jean-Paul Sartre, to mount the barricades, to identify with the proletarian cause or participate in pouring scorn on the bourgeoisie. Delicate members of the intelligentsia in New York, London, Paris and Rome found it necessary to consort with ferocious, and genuine, revolutionaries and could be heard opining that only an art based on the New Left or on Marxism as reinterpreted by Herbert Marcuse had any integrity or aesthetic justification. Marxism mingled with anarchism was the ideology preached, chanted and scribbled on walls by the students who took to the streets in Paris in May 1968, and by their Italian counterparts in the 'hot autumn' of strikes and demonstrations which shook Milan and Rome in 1969. No section of society was more affected by the new mood than the artists, writers and creative spirits of the time.

The movement of 1968 was in a very real sense a cultural revolution, but whereas in China Mao forced cultural operators into the factories and fields to experience proletarian life, in the West the ambition was to take cultural activities to the factories. No previous radical movement had ever been more self-consciously theatrical. It is tempting, in retrospect, to see some 'Punch and Judy' symbolism in the fact that the students who in Paris 1968 were proclaiming the end of the bourgeois order gathered in the Odeon theatre. In its August-September number that year, *Sipario*, the theatre periodical, issued a questionnaire to theatre workers to ascertain whether, in view of the student demonstrations and the strikes in factories, as well as the general sense of malaise in the world of culture, 1968 should be regarded as year zero for Italian theatre? Eduardo de Filippo gave a waspish reply, saying that it had always been the task of theatre to hold up a mirror to society, but people's success in deciphering the images they received varied with their own abilities. There were those who were ahead of the times, those who were in step with their times and those who would always be years, perhaps centuries behind, he said.

Dario was determined to be ahead, while official, commercial or bourgeois Italian theatre was, by the unanimous consent of the brightest and best, centuries behind. There were many straws in swirling winds. January saw an ill-focused strike by actors, although it was never clear who they were striking against, and the issue of imprecise promises by the government brought them back into line. The novelist Dacia Maraini set up her own, feminist theatre company in Centocelle, a housing estate on the outskirts of Rome to which she was guided by the

Communist Party, anxious to assist her search for a 'popular audience'. She later came to wonder if such a being existed, and said that most of her experience of 'decentralising' consisted of a search for this mythical creature. She worked her fingers to the bone in a converted garage which had been occupied by a karate school, and took on every theatrical role – writer, director, designer, actor and even cleaning lady.

The 'teatri stabili' which had been the hope of the post-war generation were now viewed as ossified structures, dominated by grey bureaucrats and ineffable politicians. Gianfranco De Bosio shook the dust off his feet as he resigned from the city theatre in Turin, as did Giuliano Scabia in Genoa. Giorgio Strehler was now in a more exposed position.

One morning, hearing voices outside the window, he looked out and saw a band of students shouting slogans and carrying banners and red flags. 'They're at it early, I thought. I wonder who they've got it in for?' He soon found out. 'They had it in for me; the banners and shouts left no doubt. Down with the tyrant of the Piccolo! Down with the baron of the stage! Get rid of the monster! Get off your throne!' Strehler . . . held a public meeting at the Piccolo with the demonstrators alongside the theatre staff and technicians. Then he took one of the marchers into his office, pointed to his armchair – the infamous throne, told him he could have it, and left.[3]

Strehler set up a new company, *Gruppo Teatro e Azione*, designed to explore political issues, but the company itself played only established theatres. This policy did not impress Fo, who was also determined to forge a new repertoire of popular, political theatre but who wanted to play to a new audience in 'alternative' venues. It was an aspiration shared with many playwrights and performers in many countries. In Holland the *Het Werkteater*, in Britain 7:84, in Italy the *Teatro Due* of Parma all declared an intention of taking theatre to the places where working class people would feel at home, and performing plays on issues which mattered to them. Fo expressed his own aspiration in a formula he was to repeat on many occasions: 'We were tired of being the *giullari* of the bourgeoisie, on whom our criticisms had now the effect of an alka-seltzer, so we decided to become the *giullari* of the proletariat.'

There was a certain rich irony, missed at the time, in the use of a term taken from medieval history as a self-description of Fo as he set out to create revolutionary theatre for today. The *giullare* was the strolling player of the Middle Ages, the all-round entertainer who moved from piazza to piazza to entertain an audience in its own idiom and in accordance with its own vision of the world. It is not easy to find a satisfactory translation in English. Etymologically, the word has the same roots as 'juggler', but its connotations are wider. The figure has much in common with the minstrel, or the Shakespearean fool. Perhaps the word 'busker' would pass muster if it were not so anachronistic, but the term 'jester,' provided it is not taken as the court jester, comes closest, and will be adopted here. The figure makes his first appearance in *Archangels Don't Play at Pinball*, when Lanky tells Blondie that his trade is to have people make a fool of him. 'Do you remember who the *giullare* was?' he asks. When she replies that he made kings laugh, Lanky agrees but adds that since there are no more kings, he is happy to make his friends in the bar laugh.[4]

Dario Fo set out in 1968 to be the jester for his own times, the spokesman for everyman. Historically, he believed, the jester was a representative of a popular culture, who shaped and gave voice to the discontents of ordinary people. His was the comedy not of escapism but of transmuted anger and dissatisfaction. This view of the jester is disputed by various academic authorities, who see him as a more neutral, less ideologically motivated figure, but that is to miss the point. Revolutionary rhetoric is not the currency of the stand-up comedian in musical hall, but his much-vaunted rapport with his audience conceals an instinctive identity of outlook, perhaps even of class. He plays to an audience in the stalls according to professional rather than political criteria, but expresses by his wit their scorn for toffs, idlers or social parasites, as well as for lords and masters. Fo viewed the jester as the articulate representative of an inarticulate culture, voicing deeply felt feelings of injustice. His own comedy is based, in another of his own formulae, on a combination of 'laughter with anger'. It can be merciless laughter. Fo recognised no boundaries of taste when he set out to flay the politicians or churchmen. Any idiosyncrasy of dress, defect of speech, oddity of behaviour or even sexual tendency which could serve to make a man of power ridiculous, and therefore less awesome, was grist to his mill. Satirical humour is pitiless, and as the jester, Dario was capable of verbal violence.

The attractions of the jester figure were varied and paradoxical. The jester was of his essence a one-man performer, and it must seem curious that Dario declared himself a reincarnation of the jester at precisely the moment when he was planning to establish a co-operative. At some level, perhaps still unconsciously, he must have known that a co-operative structure of performance would stifle his own talents, and would soon discover that the ideal of the co operative was incompatible with the reality of the unequal division of talent. His political desire to behave in accordance with egalitarian ideals was at odds with the personal urge to find an outlet and expression for his genius as an actor. Dario declared himself a Marxist, if an idiosyncratic and unsystematic one, and the jester represented a compromise between political ideology and theatrical aspiration. The performance style associated with the jester left Dario the unshackled freedom of the Victorian actor-manager, or the Italian *capocomico*. The jester belongs to established canon and illustrates one other paradox in Fo. While revolutionary in politics, he is traditionalist, indeed conservative and even reactionary, in theatre. Tradition is his theatrical habitat.

But in 1968, politics were all. Sections of public opinion in Italy, including many who viewed the prospect with horror, were convinced that the old order was about to be swept away in some onrush of popular rage. For Dario, the late sixties were, after the Liberation, the second moment of public enthusiasm he had known in his lifetime. He and Franca determined to forge a new kind of theatre in a new kind of troupe. Together with others, they set up *Nuova Scena* which, it declared, would be 'at the service of the revolutionary forces not so as to reform the bourgeois state, but to favour the growth of a real revolutionary process which could bring the working class to power'. The new company was established as a co-operative, to be run according to the principles of the socialist pioneers, with each member having one vote on all matters affecting the affairs of the association. Democratic assemblies would be held when needed, in the belief that after the full and frank expression of views, majority decisions would be respected. Each member was to draw the same salary, although that did not mean that they would all have the same income. A writer would retain his right to royalties as well as to the standard pay he would receive for his work as performer, or for whatever other function he carried out. The money to buy the props, vans and other needs was advanced by Dario and Franca, but as a loan. Most of it was repaid from takings over the two years the group remained together.

The new company was not a mark II version of the Fo-Rame outfit, but took in other actors and writers. Dario made contact with the *Theatre of October,* run by Nuccio Ambrosino, a gifted young director who had produced various shows in Milan. He in his turn sought out the actor-author, Vittorio Franceschi, who could have been Fo's theatrical twin. Franceschi was then 32, and like Fo had started out as writer-cum-performer in satirical cabaret. He had gone on to write his own plays, and in 1968 was in Trieste where the local theatre had performed two of his works. The previous year had seen him at the centre of a rumpus over an anti-war piece which had aroused the ire of ex-servicemen's associations. He too joined the new co-operative.

Theatre of October wanted to retain its own name and identity, so *Nuova Scena* became an umbrella organisation with, at least initially, two sub-groups, or souls. One was the *October* company, with Franceschi performing and touring with them, and the other consisted of Dario and Franca plus other actors, performing works by Dario. Legally *Nuova Scena* constituted itself as a club, since this status would afford them, it was believed, immunity from censorship laws and freedom from interference from police or magistrates. Its cultural politics were set out in one of its publicity brochures:

> Theatre, like all other means of expression, has always belonged to the ruling class, which makes use of it as an instrument of ideological and political pressure. The structures of theatre – architecture and site of the buildings, performance times, ticket prices – exclude popular audiences from participation, while that

theatre itself, in its choice of script and language, offers exclusively bourgeois-style products; it speaks to the society which supports it. *Nuova Scena* was born to replace this theatre with one which will establish an active and critical relationship with popular audiences and which, without concealment, operating on the basis of the political choice it has made, defines itself as an instrument of struggle for socialism'.

This explicit political purpose made for a complex relationship with the Italian Communist party, the PCI. The New Left everywhere in Europe believed that the established Communist parties were bureaucratic and reformist and guilty of abandoning their revolutionary aspirations. *Nuova Scena* may have agreed with much of this criticism, but members took a pragmatic view of the potential for change of the PCI. Franca had been a member of the Communist party for some time, and although her allegiance was faltering, she kept the party card until 1970. Dario, who had an innate distrust of all organisations, never joined, but both viewed the members of the party as their natural constituency. For this reason, *Nuova Scena* concluded that the 'alternative circuit' they sought should be provided by 'houses of the people' and community centres run by ARCI, the Italian Recreational and Cultural Association, a body close to the PCI.

The ubiquitous Nanni Ricordi was secretary of ARCI in Milan, and he and Dario met Achille Occhetto, the PCI spokesman for cultural affairs, who agreed that ARCI provided the ideal arenas. Ricordi moved to *Nuova Scena*, becoming its administrator. In ARCI, the recreational side of its activities had long since taken precedence over its cultural remit. Dario was fond of recalling that many of the centres had emblazoned above the portals a slogan which ran: 'If you want to give charity to a poor man, give him five pennies – three for bread and two for culture'.[5] In the same interview, Fo explained that culture did not mean simply knowing how to read and write, but also

> to produce, to express your own creativity, starting with your own conception of the world. The grave responsibility of the parties of

the traditional left lies in the fact of not having put themselves at the service of the creativity of the people, which is extraordinary, enormous. The principal fact of the Chinese cultural revolution is that it believed in the people, in its force of creativity and production, and above all in having goaded intellectuals to participate in a political life beyond their own artistic life, to enter into the class struggle.

With us, the influence of [Italian Communist leader] Togliatti destroyed this relationship between intellectuals and the popular masses. Togliatti showed himself to be an aristocrat. He was a professor and had maintained a bourgeois attitude toward culture. He considered intellectuals as people who should produce works, without ever involving themselves in politics. Politics was for politicians... In Italy, among 'men of culture' often given as examples, many were guilty of betrayal, had no dignity. Take Visconti, who today works for the Fascist industrialist Rusconi, or Pasolini and various other intellectuals who have sold out to the Right or to Social Democracy.

Apart from the inner core of actors and stage hands, membership of *Nuova Scena* was open. Subscription fees were set at a price between 1500 to 1700 lire, which entitled members to attend one show by Fo plus two others staged by the company. *Nuova Scena* was born as a touring company and where there was no established ARCI centre in a town, it was dependent on the enthusiasm of volunteers and supporters to adapt cinemas, halls, sports centres, disused theatres or to create totally extemporised performance spaces. Local members were also responsible for such pre-publicity as was issued. Whatever the space, Dario always insisted that there be some form of recognisable, properly equipped stage. He refused to countenance the suggestion that in political theatre, purely ideological values should have pre-eminence and the poetics of theatre could be viewed as secondary. 'When we arrived to put on a play at the 'houses of the people', we would turn up with a lorry packed with materials, and would spend the whole day creating a special stage. We would put up the lights, perhaps as many as forty or fifty reflectors, because we said that the people, with television, or in ordinary theatres, if they go there, are used to a particular sort of presentation . . . we must avoid at all costs giving them the impression that we are offering 'minor theatre', something tossed together, a theatre which is not up to using those means which, consciously or unconsciously, they are used to'.[6]

Frequently the cast had no changing rooms, and had to make shift with an overturned trunk. The entertainment followed an unchanging format – two acts of the scripted play followed by a 'third act', discussion with the audience. Mere agit-prop was taboo, although Fo ended up developing a new genre which could be termed didactic farce. In Britain, playwright John McGrath, whose militant comedy written for 7:84 had much in common with Fo's theatre, entitled the manifesto for his theatre *A Good Night Out*. Fo shared McGrath's objective of providing entertainment plus politics and of creating a carnival atmosphere. Laughter, Dario wrote, is the enemy of catharsis, which is to be avoided at all costs in a theatre which has a critical function but which should offer liberation from the humdrum and a venture into the dimension of imagination and fantasy. 'What do you mean by a show?' he asked himself. 'A show means enjoyment. Enjoyment is obtained by technical means, by stage devices which can be quite complex, as well as by the technical and ideological preparation of the actors.'[7]

If the decision to establish a co-operative was in keeping with the spirit of 1968, the choice of touring theatre was a return to the roots of Italian theatre, the theatre from which Franca had emerged. The success of *Nuova Scena* was due in part to the fact that *Canzonissima* had made Franca and Dario stars, but also to the fact that the company revived memories of a theatre common in Italy within living memory. Dario and his red guards were following in the footsteps of the touring players who had been the backbone of the Italian tradition, who had made theatre from *commedia dell'arte* onwards, and whose last representatives were companies like the Rame family. Prices were kept low, but production and travelling costs meant that every show would play at a loss, unless it attracted a mass audience. One of the few critics who took an interest in the new project reported with astonishment that he saw families who had never before been to theatre arriving an hour early, and remaining for debates which sometimes went on until three in the morning. 'Dario's first question at these debates was always – how many of you have been to the theatre before? There was invariably a large show of hands'.

During the 1968/69 season, *Theatre of October* presented a work entitled *Given That,* an attack on consumerism. Fo's own troupe performed a new large-scale, pageant piece, *Grand Pantomime with Puppets Large and Medium,* and, later in the season, *I Think It Over and Sing About It, No 2,* which was not a revival but a completely new show. In spite of the proletarian rhetoric which surrounded *Grand Pantomime,* its style and content linked it with the 'bourgeois' *Toss Out the Lady.* Grand pageantry with music and dance was intercut with episodes of slapstick and knockabout. The eleven actors and three actresses were dressed in neutral costumes, which allowed them to switch part rapidly, but wore masks which 'allude to *commedia dell'arte*'. Instead of using clowns as in his previous play, Dario hit on the idea, later borrowed by the French director Ariane Mnouchkine, of using puppets to enlarge the cast. The approach was that of the Medieval morality play, and the target was those revisionist writers and political leaders of the Left who had betrayed the heritage of both the Resistance and of Socialism. A monstrous, deliberately grotesque puppet, with outsize rubber lips, wrapped in mock medieval clothes towered over proceedings. Stage directions specify that it must be 'over three metres high', and that it must be seen as, 'a clear allegory of Fascism'. From its belly emerge equally allegorical figures representing Bourgeoisie, Capital, the General, the Bishop, the King and the Queen and their court. Opposing them is another puppet, a Dragon, with one actor supporting the head over his shoulders, and four other actors under the body of the beast, representing 'the Proletariat in struggle'. If the large puppet is an act of deference to the Italian carnival tradition, the dragon is drawn from Chinese sources. The dragon's arrival initially causes consternation among the establishment figures, but in modern society political rebellion can be stymied by sexual seduction. The Bourgeoisie figure is a voluptuous young girl with generous breasts, who is encouraged by Capital and Monarchy to strip for the good of the nation. The dragon roars and sighs, and eventually the leader of the proletariat is seduced and neutralised by the charms of Bourgeoisie. The pacifying of a rebellious proletariat is completed by the seductive pleasures of football, television and pop songs, leading a member of the proletariat to quote 'the old proverb – the television's on, the revolution's off'.

The first season went well. The company gave in all some 370 performances in a total of 125 centres, some of which were factories occupied by striking workers. In August 1968, they played in the occupied Steelworks in Brescia. The matter was reported to the local magistrate, who two years later charged Franca and Dario with trespass and infringing the rights of the owner, the first of many summonses they would receive. According to figures released by the Ministry, the total number of spectators attending performances amounted to 240,000, of whom 90% claimed never to have been previously to a theatre. These audience figures are all the more remarkable considering that the same source gave attendance figures for all theatres in Italy as three million. ARCI locally and nationally was impressed, and there seemed to be little in the plays to disturb friendly relations with the PCI.

Nevertheless, there was already friction inside the company. The idealists were coming face to face with the harsh theorem which lies at the basis of conservative politics, the belief, however formulated, that not all people are equal and not all are good. Bernard Shaw once wrote that any revolutionary movement will attract both those for whom the world is not good enough and those who are not good enough for the world. The first squabbles were over equality, an article of faith inside *Nuova Scena*, and it was on this point that Dario later wondered if he and Franca had not 'sinned of utopianism. In truth we were not on an equal footing. On the stage above all, we could only pretend to be equal.'[8] Actors in a given performance were listed in alphabetical order, a small thing in itself, but Dario and Franca had also ceded the leading roles to less charismatic, less talented and sometimes completely inexperienced members of the company. Gains for equality were outweighed by theatrical losses. Talent and training were needed to carry the burden of the performance, particularly in a theatre like Dario's, where the distance between script and performance is minimal and where acting skills are essential. There was also a clash between audience expectations and internal philosophy. Audiences, however enthusiastically they proclaimed their allegiance to the ideals outlined by the actors in the debates, were attracted by the fame and notoriety of Dario Fo and Franca Rame and were disappointed to find the two taking such a low profile.

The internal assemblies became interminable. The members of the company were invariably loquacious, articulate and self-opinionated, and had a command of a jargon which could, like all jargons, replace thought. Others looked on in despair at this turn of events. At an assembly in March 1969, Vittorio Franceschi recognised that they had all paid a high price in terms of 'physical exhaustion, psychological wear and tear and economic sacrifices' but he reminded the assembly that the audiences 'did not deserve our internal dissensions.'[9] Nuccio Ambrosino's group was the most alienated. They were dubious about the decision to stage *I think It Over and Sing About It*, which they judged insufficiently revolutionary and militant for the needs of the moment. A further source of strife at the end of the first season was over the future shape of the co-operative. Shows had been presented under the formula: *Nuova Scena* presents Dario Fo, or *Nuova Scena* presents *Theatre of October* in . . . The various sections of *Nuova Scena* performed on successive evenings in the same venues and, however much they doubted it at the time, the other groupings benefited from the drawing power of Fo and Rame on the first evening. Dario, with the agreement of Franceschi, believed the time had come for the co-operative to be wholly united and the subsidiary identities to be abolished. *Theatre of October* wanted to maintain its autonomy and title. 'For me Dario is fine as he is. I think it's right that he puts on his own shows with anyone he wants and in the way he wants. On the other hand, I do not want other methods, other work requirements to be snubbed or undervalued, much less castrated,' Ambrosino told the assembly.[10] The internal conflicts proved incapable of resolution, and in the first of many internal schisms Ambrosino and his troupe parted company with Fo and the others.

ARCI was still keen to maintain the collaboration, but wanted a fuller programme. The agreement was that in the following season,

Nuova Scena would present five works. In accordance with the co-operative principle, the task of preparing these scripts was shared out. Dario would write three, Vittorio Franceschi one, while the final work would be a collage of songs and sketches assembled and written by several younger members of the group. With this decided, the group broke up for the summer. However imminent the revolution, it would have to wait for *ferragosto* and the annual seaside holiday.

Tanned and refreshed, the company reassembled in late summer of 1969 to prepare for the autumn season. All sides in an increasingly divided company were agreed that they had to respond to the deepening political crisis in Italy in 1969, a year which marked the beginning of that state of turmoil which was to last for over a decade. That autumn passed into history as the 'hot autumn' of student unrest and trade union militancy. If the students made the headlines, the workers had the real clout, but for a time at least the two groups made common cause. Industrial contracts were due to be renegotiated, but the demands made by new grass-roots organisations were not merely for higher pay and renewed contracts of the same type, but also for improved conditions, for greater attention to safety at work and for salaries which were, as the new jargon had it, 'autonomous', that is, unrelated to business profitability or national economic conditions. Disputes, sit-ins, factory occupations, strikes, demonstrations involving private and public sector workers spilled from the workplace onto the streets in all the major cities of Italy. Clashes with the police became commonplace. In October in Turin, Fiat workers smashed the vehicles standing on the assembly lines. In the same month, a demonstrator was killed, apparently by a police bullet, in Pisa. The disputes widened in scope. In November a crowd estimated at 25,000 gathered outside the headquarters of RAI in Milan. On 19 November a police officer in Milan was killed in a brawl which followed a meeting during a strike for improved housing.

In this new climate, the established parties of the Left found themselves outflanked by new, extra-parliamentary formations. The PCI had initially been relaxed about these groupings, in spite of being denounced vociferously for their pains, but their position hardened during 1969. In accordance with Mao's writings, if not his practice, a thousand flowers bloomed on the Italian Left. The groups which were to dominate the extreme Left over the next decade, and would play no small part in the lives of Franca and Dario, made their appearance. The most significant were *Potere Operaio* (Worker Power), *Avanguardia Operaia* (Worker Avant-garde), and, the most important of all, *Lotta Continua* (Continuous Struggle). This latter produced a journal of the same name, whose first number appeared in Milan in November 1969. Not all Italian intellectuals were as enthralled by the new youthful movements. Pier Paolo Pasolini wrote a poem denouncing the students and siding with the police on the grounds that the students were the pampered children of affluent bourgeois parents, while the policemen were the sons of working class people, often from the poorer South. The poem aroused heated discussion, and the poet Roberto Sanesi wrote a counterblast accusing Pasolini of vulgar demagoguery. Leonardo Sciascia, with that deep disillusion which is the cultural heritage of the Sicilian, satirised in his novel *The Context* the new chic, patrician Left as nothing more than the bien-pensant conformism of the well heeled. Fo embraced the new ideology with the enthusiasm of the young Wordsworth hailing the French revolution, and in turn was hailed as the movement's spokesman.

The divisions of Italy were deeper and of a different kind from those becoming apparent in other western societies in those troubled years. If the rise of a revolutionary Left had parallels elsewhere in Europe and North America, the resurgence and mobilisation of violent neo-Fascist movements with historical roots in Mussolini's regime and with covert links to the ministries and police forces was unique to Italy. The 'reds' and the 'blacks', who even had distinctive uniforms of denims and donkey jackets for the Leftists and boots and gloves for the Rightists, clashed in the universities and on the streets. When the suggestion was first advanced that this right-wing terrorism was officially defended and even sponsored by sinister forces inside the ministries of Rome and the barracks of police and army officers, it was dismissed as left-wing paranoia, but the careful work of such investigative journalists as Camilla Cederna and Philip Willem has established the political complicity and guilt beyond all reasonable doubt.[11]

The first terrorist acts occurred in January 1969, and while they were milk and honey compared to what was to follow, they mark the point when terrorism became part of the fabric of Italian society. The aim of the neo-Fascist 'strategy of tension' was to create widespread panic which would lead to demands for a 'strong man' to restore the golden days of Fascism. The Greek Colonels had recently come to power, and many feared, with reason, that their *coup metadata* was a model for a future putsch in Italy. This fear dominated Left thinking, and obsessed Giangiacomo Feltrinelli, the millionaire publisher, who formed in the summer of 1969 the first of the underground Leftist groups, GAP, a name originally used by a partisan group in the Resistance. Feltrinelli, who had an enormous capacity for self-aggrandisement and self-deception, went into hiding, although no one was actually searching for him. Myriad left-wing terror groups, the Red Brigades and Front Line being the most important, began to emerge. Their immediate origins lay in the 1968 movement, although some saw their deeper origins in a culture termed 'Catho-communism', which linked the equal and opposing absolutisms of Catholicism and Marxism. Dario set his face unflinchingly against the use of the gun in politics, whether by the Left or the Right. Preaching revolution was one thing, but advocating bloodshed was another. His position was delicate and precarious. In the decade from 1969, he was on the crest of a wave; to change image, he was also astride a tiger. He had been denouncing reformism and revisionism, and was in every respect perfectly at ease with the political positions occupied by the revolutionary Left, but shied away from the advocacy of violence.

The 'revolution' he preached did not require definition. Utopianism is the poetic twin of naivety, and if Dario was never naive, he was certainly utopian. Marxism was one transient form of his enduring utopianism. His principal political motivation was horror of injustice, exploitation and every manifestation of man's inhumanity to man. Socialism is an elastic term, and Dario was not given to systematic formulations. He worked as tirelessly as Voltaire against individual miscarriages of justice, and carried the same passion into the public arena. He was one of nature's dissidents who would, as certainly as

André Chenier under the French revolution, or Mayakovsky or Essenin under Bolshevism, have been consumed by any successful revolution of whatever hue. If the man he most frequently quoted was Mao, his alter ego was Mayakovsky, who maintained his ironic distance from the Bolsheviks once they were in power. Dario was a man of the 'decency' George Orwell sought in writers who occupied themselves with politics – though he did completely suspend all use of his ironic faculties in regard to Mao.

For the vast, amorphous, disenchanted, dissident but unswervingly radical movement, often known simply as The Movement, Dario became an inspiration. 'Struggle' was a key component of the jargon for those years when the rhetoric of class warfare was routinely used by innocuous individuals who would never revolutionise a rabbit. Perhaps, in the post-play discussions, Dario became more of an oracle than any man should. Certainly both Vittorio Franceschi and Nanni Ricordi, neither of whom were middle-of-the-road liberals, came to think so, but audiences from Palermo to Trieste demanded his views on all manner of subject.

Before taking to the road for the 1969/70 season, the assembly had to approve the scripts. Fo and Franceschi had their promised scripts written. Franceschi's was entitled *A Dream of the Left*, an account of a young bourgeois who plays the part of the revolutionary militant for a season, only to scuttle back to his family and class when the stakes become too high. The other group had found the temptations of the beach too alluring, or the task too difficult, and were not able to deliver their text. With only ten days left if the agreement with ARCI was to be respected, the task was pressing. The assembly entrusted Franceschi with the task of cobbling together a performable text.

He decided to return to the kind of cabaret work with which he had begun his career. Writing various pieces himself and co-ordinating the work of others, he produced *MTM*, a series of songs and documentary pieces on the lives and experiences of working people in an industrial society. The finished work had to be submitted to the assembly, where one of his songs was subject to criticism which crystallised emerging problems. Franceschi had heard a news item about a young worker who had thrown himself under a high speed train. Enquiries into the suicide revealed that he had been suffering from nervous exhaustion after being threatened with redundancy. When travelling by train himself, Franceschi had been struck by the sight of butterflies which seemed to flock around the last carriages and appeared to follow the train over extended distances. He introduced this imagery into his song, but was reprimanded in assembly by one comrade who demanded to know what butterflies had to do with the tragedy of an exploited member of the working class. Was the poetic tone appropriate for a song designed to stir up feelings of anger? After anxious debate, the song was approved, and the show staged in the form Franceschi submitted it, but the temptation of overt agit-prop for members of the company remained strong. Fortunately Dario had unearthed a quote from Mao which said that actors should not use the stage as a political platform, otherwise they risked doing a disservice to both theatre and politics. There was no appeal against the authority of Mao.

Two of Dario's plays, *Chain Me Up and I'll Still Smash Everything*, and *The Worker Knows 300 Words, the Boss 1000, That's Why He's the Boss*, were approved without dissent. There was some perplexity over the relevance of the medieval setting of the third, the one-man *Mistero buffo*, but he got his way. To meet the demands placed on them, the company split into three. The first was headed by Franceschi and produced his two works; the second was headed by Franca Rame and staged the two works written for the cast, and the third consisted of Dario alone with *Mistero buffo*, probably his best known and finest work.

Mistero buffo was premiered at Sestre Levante on 1 October 1969, although there had been a try-out production in Milan University during a student sit-in. Dario subsequently performed the work, which exists in varying versions in all available media, in all five continents. Among his plays, only *Accidental Death of an Anarchist* has had comparable international success. With *Mistero buffo*, he fused his gifts as actor and author, revived historic popular theatre as a living force, found a subtlety of political expression he never again attained, while also giving himself a vehicle for his own unique stage talents. Initially, he planned to do the plays in the conventional style with several actors, but it simply did not work. The pieces required to be done by a single performer-jester, moving into and out of part, doubling as storyteller and as the characters who people the tale. The initial text has been expanded over the years with new sketches, scenes, monologues and extensive introductory material. One critic has calculated that if Fo were to perform all the material he has collected under the heading of *Mistero buffo*, the performance would last a full day and night.

The work consists of a series of scenes and sketches adapted, sometimes substantially re-written, from biblical and medieval tales as told by jesters. Dario had been combing ecclesiastical and theatre archives in Italy and in Czechoslovakia, Poland and Yugoslavia for jester material, and had uncovered a series of sketches but was uncertain how best to stage them for modern audiences. A philologically accurate version which could delight only the 'dry as dust' experts did not appeal, so he gave himself freedom to rewrite, and this in turn has led to debates on their historical authenticity. He has been accused of what could be termed reverse plagiarism, that is, of taking imperfect archival fragments as cues for the creation of new work which is then presented as a faithful translation of some lost comic jewel.[12] There is some truth in the accusation, although whether it matters is another question. On the first outing, Dario illustrated the performance with slides of medieval frescos and paintings, but discovered himself short of some images. No problem for a man of his talents. He spent the next day executing the images in the required style, photographed them and used the slides the following night as a reproduction of the work of an unknown master from the Dark Ages. There is no known medieval version of some of the better known pieces, such as *Boniface VIII*, or *The Birth of the Jester*. At most there are a couple of lines which have been elaborated and worked by Dario in the appropriate style. Behaviour of this kind has given experts a field day, but most people will view such polemics as the modern equivalent of the Swiftian dispute over the appropriate way to crack a boiled egg. Those who gingerly tap the rounded end and meticulously peel away the cracked shell to reveal the white and yolk view with disdain their more crass colleagues who blithely chop off the top and tuck in. Fo is to be ranked with both at different moments. He is as fastidious as a professor in the Sorbonne in his researches, but he has a sense of living stagecraft which is not part of that professor's armoury.

His erudition is formidable, even if the Middle Ages he presents on stage are as imaginary as Thomas Chatterton's. Ideologically, his imperative is to take sides and line up with one kind of history and one social class. His reading of the medieval texts led him to the conclusion that the jesters had inserted the protests of the poor and deprived inside these apparently religious texts. When the satirical protest was lacking, Dario added it. He repeatedly drew attention to the interweaving of social and theological themes in performance pieces produced by medieval Christianity and to the positioning of gargoyles alongside pious statues on the façades of medieval cathedrals. By temperament, Fo is at one with the sculptor of gargoyles. Unfortunately, not all his new comrades were of the same mind, and in the superdemocratic, ultra-leftist atmosphere of the *Nuova Scena* assemblies, he found it difficult to persuade them of the political relevance of his new enterprise. 'Speaking of religion, as did the jesters, I intended to speak about politics, while also making a play out of it. I came to religious theatre almost as a polemical reaction to the comrades I was working with, who, with considerable superficiality, branded the people's religious problem as a distortion with no cultural or political significance. The people's relationship with the divine, with the problem of God, with their own religion, with the religiosity of things is a problem which, regrettably, Marxists have never understood and have dodged.'[13]

It may be that there was a greater ambiguity in Dario's mind over Christian belief than his own pronouncements on the subject allow. His principal scorn was reserved for institutional religion but he also proclaimed himself a non believer, with no interest in religion itself. However, the subtext conflicts with his public statements. Christ is the final arbiter of what is decent and good, and Dario was drawn to Christian ethics and the person of Christ to an extent that appalled stern Marxists. This may be inevitable in someone of his background, but perhaps on this point his critics inside *Nuova Scena* saw more clearly than Dario himself. Two decades later, some Catholic writers would call attention to the pull of the transcendental in Fo, and even the

Vatican would thank him for keeping religious themes in the public eye. But that was in the future. In 1969, newspapers linked with the Church reacted with horror to this secularising of Christ and of Bible stories. Dario provided grist for their mills. Talking of *The Raising of Lazarus,* he described the underlying situation as 'the miracle seen as a conjuring trick and not as some victory of the spirit over death in the tragic and generous schemes of God. The approach is proclaimed from the very outset with the arrival of one of the characters in the graveyard. He asks the attendant if this is the place where the raising of Lazarus will take place. There and then the attendant fixes an admission fee for those who intend to spectate, and you can almost see him punching the tickets!'[14]

Christ is similarly humanised in the *Marriage Feast at Cana,* or even turned into a Bacchus-like, jolly god. A decidedly killjoy archangel, the sort of person who became dominant in the puritan traditions, and a merry drunkard vie with each other to recount the story of the changing of the water into wine. This Christ is no paladin of repression but an exponent of liberation and even gratification. 'Drink, good people, be happy, get drunk, don't save it till later, enjoy yourselves . . .!'

While *Mistero buffo* was offending the Vatican and the Christian Democrat party, the plays performed by Franca were upsetting the Communist party. *Chain Me Up and I'll Still Smash Everything,* a portmanteau title for two one-acters, was written, as was to happen frequently in subsequent years, in response to a request made in discussions after a show. The first, *The Boss's Funeral,* was based on an actual event when workers who had been occupying a factory found that their action had dropped from the headlines and was being forgotten. They decided to stage in the town a mock funeral to mourn their supposedly benevolent employer and thank him for all his generosity to them. The spoof worked, but the stage version changed and became a protest against injuries and deaths at work. A butcher comes on stage carrying a knife and a goat which he is about to slaughter, meaning to shake the audience from their inertia by inviting them to compare their distaste for the shedding of animal blood as against their indifference to industrial accidents. The work never satisfied audience or company and after a tepid reception in Florence, it was withdrawn.

The companion piece, *The Loom*, seriously irritated the PCI, and its anti-party bias was heightened when it was rewritten in 1972 as *Order! by GOOOOOOOOD*. On tour in Emilia-Romagna, the PCI heartland, audiences had raised the problem of the exploitation of domestic piece-workers, and Dario wrote this play on the basis of information provided. Husband and wife are both loyal Communists, but are trapped in a routine of drudgery and obliged to produce a certain number of items per week. The villain of the piece is a party official who is also employed as collector of the work they produce. In the later version, feminism became more of a force, so the couple's daughter is shown to be co-habiting with her boyfriend who belongs to an ultra-left faction. Their relationship upsets the father, but one of Dario's virtuous prostitutes helps all concerned to see their way through their political and personal dilemmas. In both versions, the mother is accidentally knocked unconscious by the father, who is driven to despair and smashes the looms, and in her delirium the mother has dreams of a more militant, less revisionist Communist party.

The real storm with the PCI broke over the accompanying play, *The Worker Knows 300 Words, The Boss 1000, That's Why He's The Boss*. The title was taken from a book of letters written by pupils, *Letters to a Teacher*, but it illustrated Fo's convictions on the role of culture. The action unfolds in an ARCI circle similar to the one used for performance. While the members are transforming the library into a billiards room, the books fall open allowing the characters to emerge and act out their drama. Gramsci appears to debate popular culture, while a Soviet official from the Stalinist era, dressed provocatively in the uniform of a Francoist official, conducts a show trial against the Czech Communist Resistance leader, Rudolf Slansky. Even more irritatingly for the PCI, Fo twinned American military activity in Vietnam with Soviet aggression in Czechoslovakia, denounced the 'historic compromise' between the PCI and the Christian Democrats by having the Communist mayor of Bologna waltz with the Cardinal of the city, and finally brought on Mayakovsky, here clearly Fo's spokesman, to defend his policy of performing to factory workers against an apparatchik who says such exhibitions are against party rules.

Giannino Galloni, the official theatre critic of *L'Unità*, the PCI daily, wrote a broadly favourable review, but he had misread the runes. The review was suppressed and he resigned in indignation. In the officially sanctioned substitute column, Fo was held guilty of 'errors of evaluation and perspective which are to be condemned'. The editor, Maurizio Ferrara, although he tried to cool the dispute by a column of his own, told an interviewer from *Panorama* that the work was an out-and-out attack on both the PCI and the Soviet Union. Giorgio Napolitano, an intellectual and theorist on the PCI executive who became Minister for the Interior in the late 1990s and later still President of the Republic, accused the work of 'crude, sentimental *qualunquismo*', where *qualunquismo* is a virtually untranslatable but gross offence which involves encouraging indifference and generalised hostility to all matters political. The debates in the Northern cities were lively affairs which made it clear that Dario had alienated large swathes of the organised Left.

Booking venues with ARCI became increasingly tricky, and there was no way of knowing if signed agreements would be honoured. Venues called at the last moment, sometimes even after the trucks with the sets had arrived, to cancel. The reasons given were varied and imaginative, including reports of flooding or infestation by rats, even when it transpired that these plagues had not prevented routine dance evenings or bingo sessions going ahead. To resolve the endless disputes, Franca was dispatched to Rome to meet PCI leader, Enrico Berlinguer, who was appalled at what she reported and issued a circular to the ARCI circles inviting them to be more open to self-criticism, and to avoid the mistakes made by the Soviet leaders in response to Mayakovsky. Improvement was only temporary. At every stop on the tour itself, they had to face hostile questions from PCI die-hards. Carlo Pagliarini, the PCI official who had negotiated the *Nuova Scena*-ARCI agreement, was now seriously worried by the feedback he was receiving from local bodies. He was present one evening in Sestre Levante when Franca burst into tears while responding to him. The overall strain, the sheer physical effort as well as her disappointment at the attitude of the PCI of which she was still a member were taking their toll. The following day she fainted during her performance of the Mayakovsky scene and had to be rushed to hospital. Initially it was feared she was suffering from a coronary, but eventually she was diagnosed as suffering from nervous exhaustion and had to be replaced for the remainder of the tour. At the same time, the police became more intrusive and insisted on their right to be present at performances, despite the fact that the company was registered as a members-only club. On some occasions, they were permitted to stay for the performance only to hear themselves bombarded with criticism in the post-performance discussions.[15]

To add to their troubles, Franca and Dario heard while in Sicily on tour that they had lost the latest round in the *Canzonissima* affair, which was still lumbering through the courts. The verdict in the lower court had gone in their favour, with RAI ordered to pay 7.2 million lire to Dario and half that to Franca for breach of contract. This was overturned by the High Court, which sent the case back for reconsideration. Internal relations inside the group were once again fractious. The composition of the company had changed following the decision of Nanni Ricordi to admit new recruits dubbed 'the politicals', people from the new ultra-left who, although unencumbered with theatrical skills or experience, were regarded as capable of ensuring that the comrades did not stray. Their presence was resented by those like Franceschi who feared a slide into overt propaganda or agit-prop. The group still included many idealists, like the future novelist Daniele Del Giudice, who cheerfully carried props and played minor roles. There were also assorted eccentrics. Several members recall a Trotskyite hairdresser who declared he had joined so as to be able to touch Dario. The dissensions were often bitter. Assemblies remained in session until seven in the morning, and there are accounts of tears and temper as well as of constructive debate. The survivors of those days all adopt now the same tone of nostalgic melancholy. They will insist that the good times, the companionship of shared ideals, the delight in the welcome they received in many places were strong forces in their lives, but they talk obsessively of the bad times, of the bickering, the cliques, the manoeuvrings.

As the Abbot of any monastic community will attest, it is not the major issues which wreak havoc. A monk who can live for years with a brother who differs on the nature of the Trinity will be reduced to a wreck inside a week by sitting at table opposite a brother who slurps his soup. Inside *Nuova Scena*, personal relations began to suffer and, as happens in any marital breakdown, the worst interpretations were put on all gestures. Dario was never capable of handling money, and indeed rarely carried any with him, so he would on occasions invite people for a drink only to discover that he had no cash to pay. He was branded 'mean', which is untrue. Franca, who had a keen business mind, was manager for the company and the family. She was capable of limitless generosity, but this liberality was construed in some quarters as an attempt to extend power and win votes for assembly decisions. Technicians in the company voiced discontents of a non ideological nature on discovering they were working longer hours than required by a commercial contract, for lower pay. Gossip had it that democracy was a sham and that an inner troika of Dario, Franca and Nanni Ricordi were in real control.

Dario was losing any respect for the PCI and its traditions, and was moving towards the newer extra-parliamentary groups. Although technically ARCI was independent of the PCI, a cooling of relations with the party inevitably had implications for collaboration with the sister cultural body. Dario was prepared to jettison the ARCI link, rather than soften his criticisms of the PCI. He also, while wishing to continue touring, came to feel that the company's objectives would be more easily met if they had a home base in Milan. Endless touring is tiring, especially when there was no fixed point where an administration could be housed, where rehearsals could be held and where productions could be premiered and finessed before the tour began. Others were worried about the cost of a theatre in the city, others again wanted to separate these two initiatives, to find a base but to continue touring the ARCI venues. Having laboured to establish a national alternative circuit, the prospect of rejecting it seemed to them madness. Meantime, ARCI itself continued wavering. Several circles wanted to withdraw all performance facilities, and when the central executive of ARCI convened a meeting, eight out of eleven threatened to resign if the facilities afforded Fo were renewed. The most frequent accusation was of breach of trust. By January 1970, *Nuova Scena* were told they would not be welcome unless changes were made.

Nanni Ricordi found the group a Milan base, a workshop, *Il Capannone*, in Via Colletta, a working class district of the city. An unpretentious, curved-roof, prefabricated building, concealed from the street in a backyard behind a row of high rise flats, it was no better or worse than the buildings Peter Brook was using in Paris. The acquisition of this property resolved one problem, but plans had still to be laid for next season. Dario had written a version of the play which would become *Accidental Death of an Anarchist*, while Franceschi had scripted a work on compulsory schooling entitled *Class Diary*. The plays were read to the assembly, which was open to outsiders. Accounts differ, but it appears that Dario's play did not require much discussion, non-approval being simply unthinkable. Franceschi's play was viewed favourably, but both Dario and Ricordi voiced doubts, principally on its failure to display adequate class consciousness. In a vote, it was decided that only Dario's play would be staged. For Franceschi, this was the last straw. When the company voted on continued collaboration with ARCI, a majority were in favour, with Dario, Franca and Ricordi in a minority. The minority decided to withdraw, and to set up a new company. *Nuova Scena* with Vittorio Franceschi continued to tour ARCI centres until the 1973/4 season, but its days as a revolutionary cadre were over.

CHAPTER 6

On The Road Again

The split in *Nuova Scena* was a schism rather than an apostasy, and Dario and Franca emerged with their beliefs in revolutionary socialism intact but their hopes in the co-operative ideal shaken. In October 1970, together with Nanni Ricordi and the musician Paolo Ciarchi, they set up a new group, *La Comune,* a name which recalled the 1870 Commune in Paris but had associations with Sixties-style communes and 'summers of love'. Regrettably, the new company was to be no more a prolonged love-in than its predecessor.

The establishment of *La Comune* represents the second disruption in Dario's career. After the 1968 break with commercial theatre, came the 1970 break with the PCI and the alternative circuit provided by ARCI. In search of an alternative to the alternative, Dario now threw in his lot with the 'Movement'. On legal advice, the private club status was retained, but membership of the new company, structured in a series of nation-wide self-governing circles, was once again open. Policy was to be determined by free votes in assemblies, although past experience had led Dario and Franca to diminish local autonomy over artistic policy and opt for a centralised secretariat charged with implementing decisions and overseeing administration. At its peak, the company had around 700,000 members divided into some 150 circles, which provided the basis of a fresh 'alternative circuit', separate both from bourgeois theatre and Communist spaces managed by ARCI.

From the outset, Dario and Franca were determined that *La Comune* would not become identified with any single one of the burgeoning extra-parliamentary Left groups. Freud wrote scathingly of the 'narcissism of tiny distinctions,' and it is often the case in politics that two alignments whose differences are imperceptible to outsiders are divided by a ferocity of mutual contempt greater than that which divides them from declared enemies. This was the case in those days with the bewildering array of groups of Maoists, Trotskyists, Leninists, anarchists, situationists and the like, all dedicated to achieving the red revolution. This sectarianism exasperated Dario, who hoped that *La Comune* could provide a rallying point for all leftist tendencies. As a document drawn up in 1970 had it, 'our aim is to put our work at the service of the class movement: being at the service of the movement does not mean placing ourselves in a pre-prepared dish, but contributing to the movement as such, having a presence, changing with it, its struggles and its real needs'.[1] Theatre-makers were viewed not independent artists but as spear-carriers in a proletarian army, while theatre itself operated not as a purveyor of rest and recreation but as a mechanism for challenging received ideas, offering an alternative vision of the world and resisting the encroachment into the people's imagination of alien concepts peddled by a hostile media. The Sixties generation was looking for a root-and-branch rethinking of human relations – political, economic, moral, social and sexual.

Granted this vision, the theatrical collective was only one branch of the new initiative, and when conversion work was completed on the Capannone, the company found they had spare capacity for offices for the many causes with which *La Comune* involved itself. Franca emerged as manager and focal point for both theatrical and wider political activities. The publication of little pamphlets was a thriving business in itself. The scripts of Dario's plays were often submerged by prefaces and postfaces made up of weighty analyses of social and political trends, of indications of the imminence of the revolution or of meticulously researched chronologies of recent events. Performances were still followed, and occasionally preceded, by debates.

Dario's writing in this period was more obviously didactic and more tied to the headlines of the day than previously. The first piece presented in the Capannone, *I Would Like To Die This Very Evening If I Thought It Were All Worthless*, premiered in October 1970, turned out to be an under-dramatised work which challenged the double standards which allowed the Italian Resistance to be regarded as a heroic liberation struggle and the Palestinian guerrilla war as a terrorist campaign. Dario had been researching deeply into the experiences of Italian partisans when King Hussein launched his offensive against Palestinians resident in Jordan. 'The play was a result of a discussion on the Amman massacre. Some comrades came to us because they thought that something had to be done. We collected writings and documents on the partisan struggles, and other comrades and political groups helped us out. The play developed from performance to performance. In fourteen performances, it changed completely because new material was added all the time.'[2] Readings were interspersed with songs, but in spite of the lack of rehearsal time, the play attracted more than 6,000 spectators in Milan alone, and gave the Capannone a place in the theatrical topography of the city.

If the times had been more peaceful, there is no knowing how the company, and Dario's theatre, might have evolved, but talk of revolution was in the air, and even if the word was devoid of concrete implications, such talk and the threat it carried provoked counter-moves. While there were comparable neo-Marxist movements elsewhere in Europe, Italy was unique in the fact that the extra-parliamentary Left was matched by the emergence of underground, neo-Fascist groups. There was much that was mysterious and obscure in the Italy of those days. One of the principal propaganda functions of Dario's theatre, as he conceived it, was to provide 'counter-information', to debunk misleading accounts whispered by government sources to compliant journalists. The strife between the 'opposing extremisms' of Right and Left was marked by a growing level of violence and, eventually, to a rising tally of deaths, but the suspicion on the Left, well founded as it transpired, was that the neo-Fascist underground was backed by prominent figures in ministries, in the armed forces and in the upper echelons of the police. The rightist 'strategy of tension' was wreaking havoc and slaughter, but no one was ever brought to book for these crimes. The first act in that strategy was played out at Piazza Fontana, in Milan.

Five bombs were planted in Milan and Rome on 12 December 1969, one of which failed to ignite. The three in Rome caused minor injury and damage, but the bomb in the Banca Nazionale dell'Agricoltura in Piazza Fontana left sixteen people dead and over ninety injured. It was recognized immediately as an atrocity of enormous dimensions, not only because of the number of deaths but because of the perception that it was the opening of a campaign, perhaps coming from the heart of political power. Franca was on her way to rehearsals when the news broke and it was she who brought the news to the company. She herself collapsed under the weight of what she had to reveal. The company around Dario was incapable of resuming ordinary activities. Over the following days, they reacted with anger as they watched news bulletins with new, and contradictory, information.

On the very day of the outrage, before police inquiries were properly underway, responsibility was laid at the door of anarchist groups. Pietro Valpreda in Rome and Pino Pinelli in Milan were immediately arrested and publicly identified as perpetrators of the outrage. There is something quaintly old-fashioned in the attribution of responsibility for this first bomb attack to anarchists rather than to new wave Marxists, as though the investigators had been digging out memories of childhood tales of the *fin de siècle* dynamiters. 'Monster' was the word used even by *L'Unità* for Valpreda and Pinelli. The police officer who led investigations and interrogated Pinelli was commissario Luigi Calabresi, a controversial officer loathed by the Left, but regarded as a brave servant of the state by the Right.

The whole affair was, and remains, as murky as any which stained Italian public life in those years, but the central fact was that the Italian public was invited to believe that they were exposed to danger from a clique of psychopathic madmen acting in the name of left-wing ideology. More careful inquiries over time made it clear that the perpetrators were in fact neo-Fascists whose responsibilities were to be the subject of tortured and protracted court hearings, but those revelations lay in the future. The day of the bombing Pinelli was in an anarchist club when the police arrived to invite him to come in for questioning. The word invitation does not require inverted commas. He was not arrested but requested to follow the officers to the police station, which he did on his own motor scooter. He never left the building alive. He was subjected to interrogation and perhaps to torture until around midnight of the night of 15/16 December, when his body crashed onto the courtyard below. It later transpired that an ambulance had been called before the fall was registered. Initially, the death was presented as the suicidal gesture of a man consumed with guilt, but there were signs of blows on the body. The Pinelli case became a *cause célèbre*, and various alternative hypotheses have been proposed by investigative journalists; that Pinelli had died under brutal treatment, that he had been pushed or even that he had accidentally fallen from an unstable position.[3]

The past career of Calabresi was investigated by the same sources. He had already acquired the nickname 'Inspector Parachute' for his alleged fondness for making suspects perch precariously on window ledges during interrogations. He had been deeply involved with the CIA, as well as with the Italian General De Lorenzo, who had attempted a *coup d'état* in 1964 so he quickly filled for the Left the position of monster which was foisted onto Pinelli and Valpreda by the press. He was believed responsible for the dubious convictions of trade unionists and left-wing activists. The far-left daily *Lotta Continua*, then edited by Adriano Sofri, who would play a prominent part in the later ramifications of this case, hounded him mercilessly and unremittingly. It appears that the witty but brittle cartoons the paper published undermined his increasingly fragile nervous equilibrium. One particularly vicious example showed a suspect presenting himself with a parachute strapped to his back at a door marked Luigi Calabresi. Another, with the caption, 'A good boy, good husband, father of one,' has Calabresi quietly playing at home with his daughter. The discordant element in this picture of domestic bliss is that the toy is a guillotine. Calabresi felt himself isolated, and under pressure from his superiors raised an action for libel against *Lotta Continua* and its editor, Pio Baldelli. The trial began on 9 October 1970, but the defence lawyers deftly transformed the hearing into an inquest into the death of Pinelli, with Calabresi in the dock.

The trial itself did not reach a conclusion, since on 17 May 1972 Calabresi was himself gunned down outside his house. *Lotta Continua* was openly exultant, while *La Comune* stated, somewhat callously, in a postface written for the Einaudi edition of *Accidental Death,* that the trial was suspended following the 'non accidental death of the actor'. At the time, no party or group claimed responsibility. In the febrile atmosphere of those times, it was believed in some quarters that Calabresi, who was showing signs of crumbling under the weight of isolation and public scorn, had been eliminated by elements of the Italian secret services. However, over the years, prompted by the campaigning of his wife, Gemma, and his son, Mario, who was only two at the time of his father's death but who became editor of two of Italy's leading newspapers, *La Stampa* and *La Repubblica,* Calabresi has been portrayed in a different light. Mario Calabresi wrote a book on the victims of the terrorist campaign, including his father, while Gemma gave many interviews and appeared on many platforms on the so-called 'years of lead' protesting her husband's innocence. In the eyes of his family and their supporters, Luigi Calabresi was a devoted family man, murdered only three years after his marriage, a dedicated servant of the state who did what he could to prevent young men from being drawn to political violence and above all a devout Catholic. The procedure has been opened which could lead to him being declared Blessed by the church.[4] Luigi Pirandello made Italians believe that personality is unknowable, or variable according to varying perspectives, so the personality of Calabresi is often described as Pirandellian, but this satisfies no one.

The Pinelli-Calabresi case pursued Dario all his life. It was reopened in 1988 when Adriano Sofri, Giorgio Pietrostefani and Ovidio Bompressi, all activists in *Lotta Continua* in the 1960s, were charged with Calabresi's murder on the basis of information given by Leonardo Marino, another member of the same organisation, as is discussed in a later chapter. In December 1970, *Accidental Death of an Anarchist* opened in the Capannone in Milan. In it, Dario unleashes a supposed madman with a talent for disguise on the successive accounts which the police offered to explain Pinelli's death in custody. The play has enjoyed enormous success world-wide and it may surprise those who have relished its wit, imaginativeness, humorous extravagance and comic rhythms that it is based on fact and is even a drama *à clef*, with most of the characters having a counterpart easily identified from news bulletins at the time. The 'second commissario' dresses in the polo-neck sweaters which Calabresi habitually wore, while the woman journalist was clearly the writer Camilla Cederna, who had done so much to demolish the official story. The only intruder in this identity parade of the usual suspects is the madman, played by Dario himself. This character, who has long antecedents in the Italian tradition, may be viewed as a modern-dress Harlequin. His madness, itself a common enough device in Fo's theatre, is madness with a method, an outlet for the earthiness, guile and low cunning showed by the classic Harlequin. He is gifted with a wit, perspicacity, divine insouciance and fearlessness denied those of conventionally sound mind. He enjoys fool's licence to blurt out truths which the authorities would prefer to suppress, but in an upside down world, where the worldly wise have made their peace with a society of unreason policed by violence, the madman is the only arbiter of decency and reason.

No play by Dario Fo ever reaches a definitive form even when in performance, but this work was designed to change daily to incorporate material which had emerged at that day's trial. The play is an acerbic counter-enquiry into official responsibility for the massacre in Piazza Fontana and the death of Pinelli in police custody, but the bitterness is clothed in Dario's unique style of farce. The refusal to arouse mere pity for an individual rather than a more all-embracing scorn and anger against all men governing, was intrinsic to his political poetics and to his choice of farce as a genre, but there is a boldness here which goes beyond theatrical convention. His farce unites seriousness of enquiry with guffawing, and on this occasion no-one could doubt his claim that his farce was an outgrowth of a tragic vision. The police station where the tragic events unfold is an updated version of the 'blasted heath', with the tale recounted by a Shakespearean fool. His jeering at painful events allows the underlying tragedy to remain in the mind, but the laughter is not the nihilistic variety which suggests that all life is senseless, but an uncomfortable laughter followed by anger, and hence, in Fo's view, by action and hope. As he said in one of the post-performance discussions:

> We do popular theatre. Not populist theatre. Popular theatre has always made use of the grotesque, of farce – farce is an invention of the people – to develop its most dramatic themes. We could produce hundreds of examples, but anyone who has seen *Mistero buffo* will realise that even to tell the story of Christ, the people do not use the dramatic methods favoured by the aristocracy, the one which aims to grab you by the throat or the guts, but tries to get there by a moment of violent laughter. Because laughter truly does remain at the bottom of the mind among the ferocious dregs which cannot be scraped away. Because laughter helps avoid one of the greatest of dangers, which is catharsis. That is to say, when people cry, they liberate themselves from pain.[5]

An outpouring of tragic grief was, he believed, a response which would not survive contact with fresh air on the streets when the play was over. Some deeper reflection was called for, some reflection which would be triggered by, but would not end in, laughter. The task was to reveal 'the reactionary nature of a state which was not "born of the Resistance," but was a continuation of the old Fascist state, with a few demagogic flourishes'. More immediately, the goal was 'to win the battle for the liberation of Valpreda and the other arrested comrades and to single out those who were really responsible for the killings, both at operational and tactical level. In this general framework, which placed a heavy responsibility on all revolutionary militants and on all sincere democrats, *Accidental Death of an Anarchist*, a grotesque farce on a tragic farce, had its part to play'.[6]

Judges, policemen, bureaucratic functionaries, bishops and army officers all emerge badly from this satire. Although he specifies that the action must unfold in 'an unremarkable office in the central police station', the device of having as his central character a madman-impersonator allows him to expand the range of his targets. The madman had passed himself off as a psychiatrist, but in the police station he plays judge, bishop and police officer as a device to point to the complicity of all sections of the Italian establishment in the crime and its cover-up. The mechanism of farce is unleashed when the arrested madman finds on a desk a folder referring to the case of the anarchist and carrying the name of the judge due to arrive from Rome to conduct an enquiry into police conduct. He transforms himself into that judge and initiates his own inquiry. The political denunciation is stepped up, but the dramatic impact lessened, with the introduction of the female investigative journalist. However effective this character may be from a political viewpoint, the unrelenting seriousness of her part makes it appear she has strayed in from another play. She is too obviously the didactic mouthpiece, the speaker of the unmediated truths the authorities wish to conceal. Many actresses have struggled with this part, and have been required to speak in squeaky voices or to wiggle about in tight skirts as uncomprehending directors did their best to extract comedy from the one wholly serious part in the play.

In addition to a myriad of incidental changes which he introduced during the run, Fo toyed with two different endings, neither totally satisfactory. In the first version, the madman secures a tape-recording of the conversations he had had with the officers, brandishes a bomb which had been concealed in a drawer, handcuffs the others to a clothes-hanger and flees. There is an explosion, the journalist frees herself and reports that a crowd is gathering around what appears to be a body in the courtyard below. A man played by the same actor as the madman makes his entrance, identifies himself as the real investigating magistrate from Rome and opens an investigation which takes the form of discussion with the audience. Later Fo amended this and had the work end with a declaration from the madman that the release of the tapes would unleash not revolution but scandal, 'the manure of social democracy', and that finally the Italians would become a social democracy, like the British or the Americans, and realise that 'we are in the shit up to our necks, which is why we walk with our heads high!'

Neither of these endings was used in the first British adaptation of the play by Gavin Richards for his Belt and Braces troupe. The play was initially produced on the London Fringe in the 1978/9 season, but was such a success that it was transferred to the West End in 1980. Dario attended the premiere in London, and however successful it was with the critics and audiences, he was appalled by it. He denounced it in the foyer at the interval and sat in gloomy silence at the post-performance dinner. It took all the efforts of Stuart Hood, who became general editor of the English translations, to persuade him that Richards had made a genuine move across cultures, substituting the British music hall tradition for the Italian tradition of *commedia dell'arte*. He was not mollified and remained outraged by the switch in spirit which, as he saw it, reduced the play to mere farce while ignoring the deeper tragedy inherent in the work. Richards' modifications were substantial, including cutting out the role of the bishop and even inserting a sneering reference, spoken by the journalist, to Dario's failure to give meatier roles to women. In place of Fo's ending, Richards devised two alternative endings, one which had the journalist rush out leaving the police and magistrate tied up while the bomb goes off, and a second in which she is duped into handing over the key to the Inspector, who promptly escapes leaving her to her fate. Whatever its deficiencies, the Richards version remains one of the few which preserved the vigour and comedy of the original without losing its political fervour.

Fo's judgements on most foreign productions of *Accidental Death* have been harsh. 'This exercise of the grotesque, of paradox, of madness could stand on its own even without the political discourse, so much so that certain directors (God break them on the wheel!), in their concern to achieve pure entertainment, have removed all indications of realistic conflict and have exaggerated the comedy to the point of making it pure clowning. They have ended up with a kind of surreal *pochade* where people are left rolling in the aisles, only to leave the theatre unburdened by any indignation or disturbing thought. This was the operation they conducted on Broadway, at the Belasco theatre, where the political element was literally murdered. The theatrical situation still worked, so the critic of the *New York Times* was able to write: In this play there are two murders; the first and most obvious is that of the play'.[7]

Accidental Death would not be the first work of mordant political satire to be relaunched, or neutered, as a jolly exercise of fantasy. Jonathan Swift, whose *Modest Proposal* Fo regarded as one of the supreme examples of biting satire, wrote *Gulliver's Travels* as a scornful denunciation of political shenanigans, but lived to see it treasured as a children's tale. Some directors have staged *Accidental Death* in the same spirit. More commonly, it has become the all-purpose protest play, used in different countries to satirise authorities and to mobilise opinion against some abuse of power in that society. British adapters incorporated references to Establishment spy scandals involving Anthony Blunt, and later to miscarriages of justice involving Irishmen wrongly imprisoned for crimes they did not commit. In Japan, it was used by environmentalists to attack the extension of Tokyo airport, while in Germany it became a vehicle to denounce abuses of prison regimes. Marco Ferreri wanted to adapt the play for the cinema, but when the matter was put to the vote in a *La Comune* assembly, the majority was opposed. Such permission would only be granted once there was a chain of 'alternative cinemas' to match the alternative circuit of theatres *La Comune* was striving to establish. Dario went along with the majority, but later regretted it.[8] Unsurprisingly, *Accidental Death* was the object of more than forty official actions and complaints, a higher total than any other single play by him.

While on tour, the company received bomb threats and had to endure petty problems created by the police and magistrates. In Bologna they were refused permission to perform in the grand Duse theatre, but attracted an audience of six thousand in the sports arena. The title was altered to include a reference to the death of the publisher, Giangiacomo Feltrinelli, whose dead body was found beneath an electricity pylon on 15 March 1972. Close by were various sticks of dynamite, and the official sources concluded that Feltrinelli killed himself accidentally while attempting to cut the electricity supply to Milan. This verdict was derided by Dario at the time, but later revelations about Feltrinelli made it appear likely that, on this occasion, the official version was nearer to the truth.

Dario returned to the developments surrounding the Pinelli and Feltrinelli case in *Bang! Bang! Who's There? The Police!*, premiered in December 1972. The armed forces, which had been absent from his life for some time, decided that this was the moment to reappear and raised their now familiar action for contempt. The published version with its lengthy, highly detailed chronology of events surrounding the Piazza Fontana bombing, thumbnail sketches of the protagonists and magistrates' reports on right-wing terrorism was a political pamphlet rather than a playscript. The work itself was written in a week and plainly found a resonance with audiences in those dark days. The actors wore no costumes, and read their lines from behind desks in an office inside the Ministry for the Interior. By opening night, Calabresi, who had also been appointed to investigate the Feltrinelli crime, had himself been assassinated, and in the play, his death is imputed to 'Machiavelli'. The work has an Orwellian atmosphere, with anonymous, Big Brother figures conversing about events relating to terrorism which are obscure to the man in the street but clear to those who have manipulated everything.

The attacks on established parties of both Left and Right made the organisation of touring schedules tricky. The company was routinely refused permission to perform in towns with a Communist town council, and *L'Unità* refused to carry publicity. Dario further alienated the established left-wing parties with *All Together! All United! Excuse Me, Isn't That the Boss?*, premiered in Varese in March 1971. Where had the Left in Italy gone wrong, where were the roots of the drift away from revolutionary socialism, he asked? The play carried the subtitle *Workers' Struggles 1911-22*, the period between the war in Libya and Mussolini's March on Rome. Unusually for Fo, there were no farcical or grotesque elements in the tale dramatised from the perspective of Antonia, a seamstress who had no interest in politics until her husband was killed by Fascist thugs. Her own political education begins there, and in due course she avenges his death by killing his assassin. Any interpretation of this act as support for 70s terrorism is nullified by Antonia's immediate regret for this impulsive gesture, since she realises she has 'killed the dog, not its owner.' Dario directed but did not appear on stage, leaving Franca, who gives the best of herself in dramatic roles, with the lead role in the play. All reviews agree on the quality of her performance both in bringing to life the flashbacks to the factory occupations in Turin in 1920 and in tracing the inner development of Antonia. The Socialist and Communist parties were united in expressions of outrage, the former because their historic leaders were derided, the latter because, probably rightly, they saw the attack on Socialist moderation yesterday as an assault on Communist compromise today. The film producer, Carlo Ponti was enthusiastic about the work, and negotiations were opened with a view to securing the rights for a film in which his wife, Sofia Loren, would have played the main role, but the discussions were inconclusive.

Being lead actress was only one of Franca's roles within the company. The burden of general administration fell largely on her shoulders, particularly after Nanni Ricordi resigned in 1971 to pursue his own interests in the family business. Dario and Franca's home became an extension of the *La Comune* office or a general debating chamber where friends and comrades met to discuss company policy and the questions of the day. Privacy, never a particularly strong concept in any part of Italy, was now denied them. Franca found the day-to-day stress of being wife and mother as well as being actress and general factotum of the company excessive. Dario, whatever views he later formed of male responsibilities in the abstract, never acquired an ability to assist in his own home. The exception was cooking, where he found as much pleasure in preparing risotto as he did in painting. When writing, he was capable of periods of the most intense, exclusive concentration, sitting at his desk for long hours at a stretch, not eating and scarcely sleeping, but he was indifferent to matters around him. When he was on his own, he would leave mail not only unanswered but unopened. Money was a special problem. On several occasions, taxi-drivers came to the door to ask for the refund of a fare for conveying a penniless Dario across the city. When Franca offered them the cash, she frequently found that she had also to refund the money they had lent him to buy himself dinner.

Franca had another role thrust upon her. *La Comune* decided to turn its attention once more on the plight of the Palestinian people, but opted for a documentary format. Somewhat to her dismay, Franca was elected to go to Lebanon to recruit some flesh and blood Palestinians. Late in 1971 she arrived in Beirut, to be greeted by a customs officer who assumed from her dress that she was a prostitute hired by some wealthy client. After some delay she was admitted to the country, where she toured the camps and invited a group of ten refugees back to Italy. The format of *Fedayeen*, presented in the Capannone in January 1972, was rudimentary. Franca appeared on stage with the Palestinians, who told their story in narrative and song. The company found themselves cold-shouldered by the Italian Left and even picketed by Palestinian students loyal to the main Palestinian organisation, Al Fatah, and later admitted they had behaved rashly. The ideology of *Fedayeen* was based on the critique made by the extremist Popular Front for the Liberation of Palestine, and *La Comune* had decided that Al Fatah was an establishment party, guilty of acts of deviation and compromise similar to those committed by the Italian Communists. They were embarrassed by pamphlets handed out at the door accusing them of aiding a Zionist game of divide and rule.

Official police and government files on both Dario and Franca were already bulging. In June 1971, Dario received a summons from a judge in Brescia for entering an occupied factory in 1968 to perform for striking workers. Franca ran into problems when she went to renew her passport to allow her to take up an invitation to perform in France. Initially the officer was relaxed, asking only if there was any outstanding legal business to be cleared up, and when she replied that there was only the *Canzonissima* case, he promised her a new passport within weeks. When she returned, she found the officer barely visible behind a mountain of paperwork referring to the various cases under investigation by magistrates the length and breadth of Italy. To have a passport issued, she would need to request permission from each and every one. Meanwhile, both were convinced that their phones were being tapped and they themselves followed by policemen. At times, the situation had overtones of black comedy. When they made two phone calls in quick succession, they could hear agents in some office discussing the first before they were connected for the second. At other times, the phone would ring and their entire conversation would be played back to them. Franca recalled once having a puncture on the way to the airport. She was on her own and waited until the officers who were tailing her drew up. Being not entirely bereft of gallantry, they got out, changed the tyre, bid her *buon viaggio* and got back into their own car to follow her. On another occasion, when attending a trial, she got into conversation with a 'charming young man'. When the verdict was announced, she was about to raise her clenched fist, when she felt him grip her tightly by the wrist and hold her arm down. 'That would cause you trouble,' he whispered, telling her he had been appointed to keep an eye on her.

There were definite limits to the comedy. Violence was now an almost daily occurrence. The Red Brigades had made their first appearance with an action at the Sit-Siemens factory in August 1970, while news filtered out of an attempted neo-Fascist coup d'état led by the 'black prince', Junio Valerio Borghese, in December. The Prefect of Milan, Libero Mazza, sent a much debated report to the Ministry for the Interior, in which he calculated that there were around 20,000 members of ultra-left groups in the city, to which had to be added an unspecified number of adherents of the ultra-right.[9] The police employed agents provocateurs, infiltrators and spies to maintain surveillance on left-wing groups, including *La Comune*. The magistrate Guido Viola, who was in charge of investigations into left-wing terrorism, regarded Dario and Franca as suspects. He ordered the prosecution of Dario for a poster, an ink drawing of a man, woman and child with blotches round their head, presumably taken to indicate blood, advertising *Bang! Bang! Who's There? The Police*. The poster itself was confiscated and removed from circulation.

The terrorist campaign plainly caused havoc in society, but in an unexpected way it polluted the atmosphere for the Left, even the revolutionary Left, where Dario and Franca positioned themselves. It drove the PCI into an even closer union with the Christian Democrats, but it also caused a certain tentativeness in left-wing circles as support ebbed away with each successive outrage. Such was the suspicion of Dario and Franca in official circles that, years later in 1998, when the crisis had passed, an official report revealed that some magistrates in the seventies had entertained the belief that Dario was the *eminence grise* behind the Red Brigades. Neither he nor Franca had any truck with terror or with violence, and spoke out determinedly and forthrightly against the cult of death which terrorism represented. On the other hand, the need for revolution was deeply felt, and more than once their plays ended with them spraying imaginary bullets from an imaginary gun over the audience. In that climate, innocent souls who would normally recoil at the sight of a bleeding nose could be seen happily chanting blood-curdling slogans and revelling in fantasy violence. One slogan which had great currency at gatherings, including those of *La Comune*, was the cry 'Never Again Without The Gun,' shouted in unison and accompanied by raised fists and yelling.

A sprawling network like *La Comune* certainly included among its members some who were at least sympathetic to terrorism, perhaps some responsible for terrorist acts and others who were drawn into terrorism through contacts they made there. This, by his own account, was the case with Mauro Borromeo, an ex-administrator in the Catholic University of Milan, arrested in 1981 for involvement with *Autonomia operaia*. As he explained, the turning point in his personal odyssey was the bombing at Piazza Fontana but his account of his gradual drift into terrorist circles was spiced with bitter criticism of Dario and Franca:

> I began to attend Dario Fo's plays, and I appreciated both his talents and political beliefs, but I ended up taking a critical view of certain attitudes of his and of Franca's. For instance, even if in the context of *La Comune* they preached the rights of Communist equality, in reality when on tour they always lodged in the best hotels, leaving the technicians and electricians to fend for themselves on their 5,000 lire per diem allowance. The Fo couple too, demagogically, took their 5,000 per day, but contrary to the anti-commercial ethic which had inspired the foundation of *La Comune*, they kept the entire income from the sale of scripts and recordings. It was at that time that I first heard of Red Aid. It was not merely a red charity which gave material help to prisoners and their families, but it had wider, deeper and unofficial functions. Specifically, it concerned itself with finding lodging for people who were being sought by the police . . .[10]

Borromeo was speaking after his arrest, and with an element of special pleading. He claimed that his group had operated inside the framework of Red Aid, and that 'practically unaware of what was happening, operating in conditions of clandestinity or semi-clandestinity', he had found himself engaged in finding safe houses for terrorists on the run. Red Aid itself had other, more peaceful, objectives.

It was Franca who, in 1972, set up Red Aid to work for prisoners' rights, to campaign for decent prison conditions and to provide for detainees and their families practical support, including legal advice, chains of comfort letters and food parcels. The organisation was established when, after a performance at the Capannone, Franca was approached by a woman who had been a baby-sitter for Jacopo years before. The son of a friend had been arrested in Florence following demonstrations at a meeting addressed by Giorgio Almirante, leader of the neo-Fascist MSI. She asked Franca if she could help in any way to alleviate the conditions the boy was facing in jail. Franca made an appeal from the stage, suggesting that some people might like to send a postcard or a postal order for 1000 lire. That evening seven people came forward. Within three months, Red Aid had some 10,000 adherents, and over the years of its existence they offered assistance to around 1000 prisoners. Franca was the organisation's administrator, spokesperson and public face but, as Gunther Grass found in Germany, it is impossible to advocate humane treatment or understanding of groups regarded by public opinion as satanic without attracting opprobrium. Franca's own public profile and image now changed radically. She was already widely viewed as La Pasionaria of the new Left, but her work with Red Aid made her both the most loved and the most loathed woman in Italy. In her own eyes, she was an Elizabeth Fry, and Red Aid a human rights campaign. For police, magistrates and sections of the press, she was a Rasputin or Mephistopheles, as well as apologist for terrorism. She became, even more than Dario, public enemy number one. She explained the objectives of Red Aid in a 1980 interview:

> Let's say it was a kind of welfare activity. A prisoner who needed it received a small monthly cheque, perhaps a parcel, books and letters, often hundreds of letters. Then there was the work

of counter-information, to demolish frame-ups, like the 'state massacre', or the Valpreda case. In the early stages, we only concerned ourselves with the 'politicals', but they themselves pointed out that this was unfair, and so we gave the same attention to the 'ordinary prisoners'.[11]

Franca found the work exhausting but also rewarding. Having repeatedly said that she was an actress by accident and that she would have preferred to some career of social service, she now found a sense of mission. This was, she said, the most 'grandiose' work she had been involved with. The Red Aid network was always somewhat ramshackle, but in the first place, since the police were indifferent to the plight of families of terrorist suspects, it arranged for families to be informed of the arrest and whereabouts of their son or daughter. The one-act play which Franca later performed, *A Mother*, was based on her contact with a woman who learned from television of the arrest of her son. The dispatch of prisoners to jails far from home became increasingly common when the anti-terrorist unit under General Carlo Alberto Dalla Chiesa established special prisons in remote spots. Franca revealed herself to be a highly efficient bureaucrat, keeping track of prisoners all over the peninsula and laboriously making cyclostyled copies of circulars to keep members in touch with each other. Later the word 'militant' was added to the title of the organisation, but the humanitarian aspect remained uppermost.

Initially Red Aid concerned itself with political prisoners arrested on demonstrations or sit-ins, but with the heightening of the terror campaign the nature of the crimes with which its clients were charged changed. They were not misunderstood lads from poor backgrounds, or the victims of miscarriages of justice. They had declared war on the state and were in some cases guilty of horrific acts of violence. The slightly twee phrase 'misguided comrades' gained circulation among those who wished to dissociate themselves from terrorism but not totally from the terrorists themselves, especially when they were exposed to maltreatment. Franca campaigned for the human rights of the prisoners, irrespective of their crime. 'I used to say to myself: I am not in agreement with what they do, but they are in jail, things are bad for them, because in jail things are indeed bad, and they will "pay" for what they have done. It is up to the court to judge, but meantime I must defend their right to be treated like men and not like beasts.'[12]

The Italian state replied to the terrorist threat by treatment which would, in an international context, have contravened the Geneva Convention. Stories of sensory deprivation, of psychological bullying, of petty vexations of the sort which saw short-sighted prisoners denied the use of their spectacles, were rife, but there were also tales of systematic beatings and torture, of prisoners left tied to benches for days, of starvation diets. Franca wrote a letter of protest to the President of the Republic:

> The letters, the stories, the dramas which have come to our attention all tell the same sort of tale – misery, despair, ignorance – and they cannot leave you indifferent. They are dreadful stories, of real torture, terrible stories not tolerated by the Constitution. There are some people who have preferred to die by swallowing fragments of blades, nails, spoon handles, or by garroting themselves rather than continue to live that life . . .
>
> There is one prisoner with his back broken by a prison guard following a revolt (we have the documents), another who had a testicle removed (it was no longer any use to him, since they had crushed it underfoot! We have the documents). Another had his arm broken with an iron bar, an arm which no one put in plaster. It calcified by itself. In time it ankylosed. (We have the documents).[13]

Alberto Franceschini, one of the founders of the Red Brigades, wrote in his autobiography[14] of his despair after being moved to Asinara, a special prison in Sardinia, locked up in a hut in the scorching heat without water, being finally given as food at 11.00 at night a few rolls which were too hard even to be bitten. Towards mid-day the following day, he heard some confusion outside, and the door opened to reveal Franca Rame whom he had known in the early days of the student movement. When Franceschini began to recount his experiences, the prison governor, Luigi Cardullo, hustled Franca away, on the grounds that she had no authorisation to speak with the prisoner. Only rarely was Franca permitted to make such visits, since, as Judge Viola revealed, there was a ministerial decree in force that all requests from her were to be routinely refused. Postal orders she dispatched to prisoners were, illegally, rejected and returned. Lawyers associated with Red Aid were victims of mysterious burglaries where nothing of value was stolen but correspondence was rifled; on other occasions, their doors were broken down and furniture smashed. *Agents provocateurs* were again active, and Franca sometimes received suspiciously generous donations, which she returned or handed over to the police, believing that they could be dirty money from drugs dealing or kidnapping. Once she received a parcel of false identity papers, with an accompanying note explaining that they would be of assistance to people on the run. Since the parcel looked like a crude trap, she took it immediately to the police. It was no doubt a coincidence that her home was visited by policemen that very afternoon.

La Comune now found itself subjected to harassment which affected its theatrical work. According to its own calculations, it played to some 700,000 people in a year, and had a membership of 27,000 in Milan alone. There were well over a hundred circles spread over all parts of Italy, and in 1972, sales of playscripts reached 60,000. Since the company eschewed the conventional theatre circuit, it often converted cinemas into temporary theatres, so the authorities hit on the ruse of refusing permission for such temporary conversions, or of threatening the cinema owner with the withdrawal of his projection licence. Since this meant bankruptcy, many owners, unsurprisingly, reneged on deals they had already struck. In addition, several police chiefs insisted on having officers present throughout performances or even rehearsals in case there were threats to public order. Dario refused to perform in the presence of the police, believing that the club status of *La Comune* gave it immunity from legal provisions regarding censorship.

The owner of the Capannone decided he too had had enough and in July 1972, served the company with notice to quit. He had no complaints over their tenantship, had received regular payments of rent and had seen his property improved, but he was under pressure and concluded the game was not worth any candle. The group went quietly. The premises are now in use as a car workshop, but the people in the bars in the neighbourhood still reminisce fondly on the bustle and excitement when they too went to theatre. The company signed a lease with the Pier Lombardo theatre (now called the Franco Parenti theatre, after Fo's early partner), but after it was signed, the management changed its mind.

The next problem concerned two senior magistrates, Guido Viola of Milan and Mario Sossi in Genoa, both of whom had taken an undue interest in everything involving Dario and Franca. The two men had distinguished themselves for their zeal in seeing red conspiracies everywhere, and for initiating prosecutions which were subsequently rejected by the Appeal Court. Sossi's attention was drawn to a doctoral thesis on prison conditions written by a student in Pavia, Irene Invernizzi, who was a member of *La Comune*. In Sossi's view, the work could be viewed as an invitation to revolt, or as incitement to escape. In his inquiries, he examined letters written by prisoners but intercepted by the prison authorities which made reference to Red Aid. An article appeared in the Genoese daily, *Il Secolo XIX,* written by Mario Massai, saying that Sossi had ordered an official inquiry, an essential preliminary to full legal proceedings, into Dario Fo and his relations with the Red Brigades. There were hints of some connection between a spate of riots in Italian jails and the activities of Dario and Franca, with the implication that the real aim of Red Aid was to establish a network of revolutionaries inside the prisons.

In October 1972, Dario was in Stockholm attending a session of the Russell Tribunal on the continued imprisonment of Pietro Valpreda, and on his return to Milan he was greeted by Franca and a journalist from *L'Unità,* who told him of these developments and of the likelihood that Sossi was about to transfer the case concerning him to Viola in Milan. Dario called a press conference the following day on the steps of the High Court in Milan, where he denounced the proceedings as 'fourth rate farce', and launched into what reporters present described as a devastatingly funny piece of mimicry of the two magistrates. The two had no need to be either 'actors or authors by profession', as they enjoyed those advantages which, according to Voltaire, made magistrates the most fortunate of performers. The show they put on under the guise of justice was essentially contrived to serve private interests, leaving them free of the need to win the favour of any audience, or even of public authorities. Several papers carried the story, with Ibio Paolucci writing in *L'Unità* of previous 'grotesque initiatives,' by Sossi.

Sossi raised a criminal, not civil, action for defamation against Fo and the *L'Unità*. The law's delays meant that it was January 1974 before the case came to court, but it then had to be further postponed for the most dramatic of reasons. On 18 April, Sossi was kidnapped by a Red Brigades detachment headed by Franceschini. Even in a country becoming hardened to killings, knee-cappings, bank raids and planned violence, the seizure of Sossi caused a sensation. In his autobiography, Franceschini admits that the group would have killed Sossi had it been necessary. During his captivity, Sossi's wife wrote to the Pope and the President asking for their intervention, and the Red Brigades replied with a communiqué saying that he would be executed unless members of the 22 October group, who had been put on trial in Genoa on Sossi's orders, were released. Franca had taken a special interest in this group, and was in attendance in court every day. The authorities held firm, but it appears that, once they were holed up with their hostage, some version of the Stockholm syndrome took over, and acts of violence against a somewhat pathetic figure became unthinkable. Sossi was released unharmed after 35 days.

The kidnap, as was made clear by the bulletins issued by the terrorists on his seizure, was related to his political stance and to his zeal in seeking lengthy sentences for terrorists. It was not related to Sossi's disputes with Dario or Franca, and Franceschini makes no mention of either in his account of the interrogations. However, on his release, Sossi returned to his attacks on Dario with two contradictory accounts. He simultaneously reported that the Red Brigades had referred to Fo with derision, and then made half-hearted suggestions that Fo was indeed the real leader of the entire underground movement. He said he had come under pressure to drop the Fo case, but that this pressure made it essential for him, in the interests of justice, to proceed with it, even though he would have preferred to abandon it. The kidnap made an enormous impression on Italian public opinion, and the possibility that Fo and Rame were indeed manipulators of terrorism was raised in various publications. Sossi was the hero of the hour. At the re-opening of the trial, he appeared surrounded by guards and plain clothes officers.

In the dock were Fo, Paolucci and Romolo Galimberti, editor of *L'Unità*. Dario's defence was that he was replying to an outrageous provocation by Sossi, as reported in *Il Secolo XIX*. Called to give evidence, the journalist, Mario Massai, first said that he had got the story that Dario was under suspicion directly from Sossi, then said that he had come to this conclusion after conversations with other magistrates. He then added that the offending article was not his, but was written by two other journalists, who stated in court that they had no memory of the events. There was also ambiguity over whether or not Sossi had issued a denial when he saw the story in print. At one point, he claimed he did not think it worthwhile, but later said he had issued a denial, but no one paid any heed. The final verdict was worthy of Solomon. Dario was acquitted since he had been put in a situation of 'putative provocation', which seemed to mean that he believed the newspaper story was true and responded as any decent man would. Massai came in for harsh words, but the unfortunate journalists from *L'Unità* were found guilty, although the fines imposed on them were light. How a journalist can be guilty of slander in reporting events or remarks which are themselves deemed free of all criminal taint will remain an enigma for those unencumbered with legal qualifications.

In the midst of all this, Dario and Franca were evicted from their home. The proprietor objected to their views on Palestine, and wanted them out. The press of the time carried various fetching photographs of Franca seated on suitcases, surrounded by armchairs and sideboards, in front of the house which had been theirs. Poverty was not the issue. They had a second house in Cernobbio on Lake Como, but finding a home in the city was now awkward. This troublesome duo were not welcome neighbours for the douce bourgeoisie of Milan.

CHAPTER 7

1973: *Annus Horribilis*

The year 1973 was on all fronts an *annus horribilis* for Dario and Franca. Problems were already developing inside the company as well as from the outside, so it is scarcely surprising if several of his associates recalled this as a period of embittered isolation. Dario was prone to extreme mood swings from exhilaration to depression and gnawing worry, and he gave expression to these feelings in an unusually forthright interview in February where he railed against people in the world of politics and theatre.[1] The duo of ex-friends who ran the Piccolo theatre were objects of special scorn. He slammed Giorgio Strehler for his expressions of jeering surprise over what he had termed Dario's decision to play for a bourgeois audience in non-bourgeois sites, and Paolo Grassi for his part in having him banned from the Chamber of Labour circuit. The lack of recognition in official circles was plainly beginning to irk him, so although normally free of all trace of braggadocio, he complained of being celebrated abroad but ignored at home and even suggested that in the prevailing political vacuum created by the rightward shift of the PCI, he *was* the opposition in Italy. The preferential treatment accorded Pier Paolo Pasolini in the Communist press rankled.

> He is supposed to be a left-wing director. I write about domestic labour, about riots in prison, but I do not exist for the PCI. They

are very good at praising Signor Pasolini, who chooses to do Boccaccio, in other words a reactionary writer in his own time who attacked the Ciompi rising, a workers' revolt. To make his *Decameron* acceptable, Pasolini inserts gratuitous pornography in keeping with the bourgeois pederastic tastes which he finds pleasing.

Dario would later change his mind on both Boccaccio and Pasolini. In 2011, he published a book, with lavish illustrations of his own, on Boccaccio, whose power he said he had discovered only after leaving the academy. In the blurb, he drew attention to the fact that 'a great man of culture, a free-thinker like Pier Paolo Pasolini, open to the value of this "narrators of tales," dedicated a film to his fables'.[2] However, in the 1970s, Pasolini was for Dario the very model of the bien-pensant, chic, salon radical. The two held sharply differing views on popular culture, on political theatre, on the use of dialect, but the savagery with which each expressed his animus towards the other cannot to be explained by mere politics. Later that year, at a time when Dario required public support, Pasolini was to reply in kind.

La Comune had been searching for a home since their eviction from *Il Capannone,* and found a seemingly willing partner in the owner of the Rossini cinema, but after agreeing a deal with them, he raised the rent. This was accepted but the police intervened to remind the proprietor of the terms of his cinema licence, so he withdrew altogether. In exasperation, *La Comune* occupied the building. To ward off any police action, the cast, then performing, ironically enough, *Bang! Bang! Who's There? The Police,* slept in the building.

Bombs were discovered under theatres where *La Comune* performed, and the couple's house in Cernobbio was set ablaze. Threatening letters arrived frequently, though the couple tried to treat them lightly. One particularly sinister missive, delivered by a group calling themselves *Boia d'Italia* (Executioners of Italy), was pinned to the living room wall. The caption, over a cartoon of a hanged man, read 'Red Pig, This Will Be Your End!' The level of surveillance on them had increased and Franca and Dario both remember a van which circled menacingly around their house. But this was nothing compared to the outrage perpetrated on Franca in March. It was not merely the inhuman savagery of the deed itself which was chilling but the fact, later proven beyond all conceivable doubt, that the attack was premeditated and planned with the connivance of officials in the Italian police forces.

On 9 March, Franca made by telephone an appointment with her hairdresser, and at 6.30 she left the Rossini for the salon. As she was walking on Via Nirone, near her own home and near a *carabinieri* station, she was seized from behind by several men, one of whom pointed a gun at her back. The human mind is prone to entertain the most incongruous thoughts at moments of great crisis and Franca later recalled that as she was being bundled into a van, her mind raced to the Costa Gravas film *Z*. 'Oh God', she thought, 'it's just like Greece here. Now they're kidnapping me and then they're going to kill me'. Lest there be any doubt about the political motivation of the attack, they jeered at her work in the theatre and at the activities of Red Aid. She was tossed onto the floor and held down by her captors who over the next couple of hours systematically tortured, punched, slashed and then raped her as they drove the vehicle around Milan. The men stubbed out cigarettes on her neck, cut her breasts with razor blades, stripped, slapped, punched and kicked her, and while one of the men held her down, at least three raped her. Franca thinks she may have fainted, causing the group to grow alarmed in case they had killed her. She remembers the man at her back complaining that he had not been allowed to rape her too, but they had been driving for some hours and the others were now desperate to dump her as soon as possible. They threw her ripped clothes around her and pushed her onto a street near the Sforza castle. She staggered around for some time before getting to a phone and calling Dario. He rushed to the spot and found her bleeding, bruised, dazed and weeping convulsively.

Back home, she said she had been assaulted but did not reveal the full horror of the ordeal. It would be years before she could tell even Dario that she had been raped. When word of the assault got out, people descended on the Rossini cinema to express their outrage and anger, and all over Italy in the following days, the fragmented Left came together for demonstrations of sympathy. Dario made a lengthy statement to *Paese Sera* outlining the full nature of the ordeal Franca had endured, but adding that it was part of the campaign of violence the working class was enduring in that phase of repression and reaction.

Ironically the magistrate put in charge of investigations was the same Guido Viola who was already leading the prosecution against them in other cases. He visited Franca, expressed sympathy, but his enquiries made no headway and some years later he notified her that due to lack of evidence he was shelving the case. Twenty-five years later, in 1998, when Italy's internal conflicts had been settled and the award of the Nobel Prize had consolidated Dario and Franca's position as international celebrities, the full background to the case was revealed, not by some excitable left-wing ideologue, but by a sober judge, Guido Salvini. Salvini had been asked to conduct a fresh enquiry into the responsibilities of neo-Fascist groups for the series of unsolved outrages from Piazza Fontana onwards, and was directed to focus especially on possible connivance between police forces and right-wing terrorists. His report ran to 60,000 pages divided into 92 volumes, based on over 400 interrogation sessions. Only two pages were dedicated to Franca Rame, but they established that the rape was, as the phrase had it, a 'state rape', and that the attack had not only been condoned but commissioned by high-ranking officials in the *carabinieri*. It was implied, but not proven, that authorisation might have come from higher up, from the Ministry for the Interior or for Defence.

The judge's conclusion vindicated what the couple had alleged at the time. The fact that the attackers had such precise information on her movements was puzzling, as was the fact that the *carabinieri* had not seen a thing even though the assault took place near their barracks. Shortly after the attack, a bug was found in their telephone at home. Franca suffered pains over the next twenty years and Jacopo believed she never fully recovered. She took morphine, but this caused hallucinations. Listening to the radio was impossible because the kidnappers played the radio as they drove around Milan, and the sound caused her to have flashbacks. Once at dinner the person sitting next to her accidentally burned her with his cigarette, causing her to go into hysterics. On another occasion, Jacopo put on a piece of pop music on a record player at home, but this simple act brought her hours of torture back to mind. Both the immediate physical and the long-term psychological damage were extreme.

> I could not sleep unless Dario was there, or unless Jacopo, who was not yet eighteen, cradled my head on his chest. I had no longer the same face; it was as if the blood, life itself had drained out of me. My hands were constantly shaking. I never went out, and when Dario persuaded me to go with him to a meeting in Pavia, people came up to him and asked how Franca was, when was he going to bring Franca, and I was there at his side, but no one recognised me. When I started to go out, I had to have someone with me. Once I threw myself into the arms of a traffic policeman, because I was sure I was being followed.[3]

Jacopo, now eighteen, took the attack on his mother particularly hard, and had to be dissuaded from joining one of the terrorist groups involved in the 'armed struggle'. 'I wanted revenge for my mother. My only aim was to kill the people responsible for her kidnap and rape,' he said.[4]

By May Franca, aided by Dario and Lanfranco Binni, a member of the company who collected and edited many of Dario's writings and speeches, felt able to resume work. *Enough of the Fascists!* a multi-media piece using video and recordings, recounted the experiences of partisan women. It was premiered in Lancenigo, with Franca performing various parts, but when she came to the episode of a female Resistance fighter beaten up by Fascist thugs, she broke down and had to interrupt the performance. The following month, she helped workers from the Fiat factory in Turin put together a play of their own based on the experiences of a family who had migrated from the South.

Franca dealt with her experience two years later by writing a one-woman play, entitled starkly, *The Rape*, but she did not immediately reveal that she was the woman who had undergone this brutality. In this case, there was no question of co-authorship: this work is indelibly and unmistakably Franca's. She wrote it in one sudden, unstoppable spasm of emotional power, showed it to Dario, who read it, fell silent, then embraced her. He was still ignorant, supposedly, of the sexual violence perpetrated on his wife. 'Probably he already knew, but I had finally managed, even if only on a piece of paper, to tell him.'[5] At a time when violence against women was more openly discussed, Franca felt an obligation to women to stage the piece and encourage debate about rape, but the courage to perform it herself always deserted her. It was left to other actresses until in Lucca in 1978 she finally found the strength to go through with it, but even then some concealment was needed. In post-performance discussions she maintained the subterfuge that the inspiration had come from an article in the woman's periodical *Quotidiano donna*. There was hardly a word of hers, she claimed. She held to this fiction until November 1988, when she told the truth after performing the monologue herself on a Sunday afternoon television show, *Fantastico*.

> There is no concealment in the writing, no ambiguity, no comedy, no grotesque, no retreat from the bitter, flint-hard truth.
>
> The blade they used to slit open my sweater is waved in front of my face a couple of times. I can't tell whether they've slashed me or not . . .
>
> 'Move your hips, whore . . . you're supposed to be giving me a good time!'
>
> Blood's trickling down my cheeks into my ears.
>
> Now it's the third one.
>
> It's disgusting to feel a man inside you like this . . . enjoying himself, grunting like a wild beast.[6]

Plainly a work like this, both as regards writing and performing, is drawn from inner sources beyond conventional considerations of the art of the stage, but it remains a remarkable transcription of a pain beyond most people's imagining. Dario too wrote, or improvised, a piece on rape, but in his own style, with anger contained and shaped inside the grotesque. The difference in approach is instructive. The sketch, *The English Lawyer*, featured a medieval law-officer who defends a nobleman charged with rape by throwing the blame onto the girl. Dario employed a mock-English *grammelot* to great comic and satiric effect but in his prologue he too let slip the comedy mask. He had read, he said, a report of four men attacking and raping one woman, and although a life-long opponent of capital punishment, he wondered whether it might not be justified in certain cases. (He decided it was not.)

The case had been officially closed but after Franca's 1988 TV performance it emerged that a neo-Fascist, Angelo Izzo, had told a court in Bologna of the collusion between right-wing terror groups and the Pastrengo division of the police. Izzo, already in jail for crimes of rape against two women, one of whom died, said the attack on Franca was aimed to intimidate her and warn her off the Red Aid work. He gave the name of one of the assailants, Angelo Angeli, and reported a startling conversation between two generals, Vito Miceli, then in charge of the secret services, and Giovanni Battista Palumbo, of the Pastrengo division of the carabinieri. Miceli suggested that Palumbo should sever his links with the National Front, an extremist right-wing organisation, while Palumbo retorted by reproaching Miceli for having coerced him into organising illegal acts against Fo and Rame. Izzo was not believed and the magistrate declined to re-open investigations, but in 1998, Judge Salvini confirmed Izzo's allegations in full. The enquiries revealed that the rape on Franca had been planned in the police stations of Milan, with the execution of the plan entrusted to thugs operating in the urban swamplands where common criminality and neo-Fascist terrorism met. Nicolò Bozzi, a carabiniere officer who later himself rose to the rank of General, gave an account of General Palumbo's actions which was in line with Izzo's. When Bozzi informed his superior of the rape on Franca, he remembered vividly Palumbo's reaction. 'High time,' he said. Bozzi added that the news was 'greeted in the police offices with euphoria, the commander was celebrating as though he had pulled off some splendid operation'.[7]

In the hubbub created in 1998 by the Salvini report, Franca spoke of what may have been another attempt at an apology. Years after the rape, 'the one who held me down started to phone me, telling me that he had become a decent man, that he wanted to meet me. I screamed in terror and slammed the phone down. Once, in the morning, a car blocked mine and a man came up to me to tell, "I'm the one", but I made off in desperation, without even seeing his face.'[8] Whoever he was, he had nothing more to fear. Twenty-five years had elapsed between the crime and the publication of the report, which meant that under the Statute of Limitations, no prosecution could be mounted.

Despite this private trauma, *La Comune* seemed to outsiders to be growing in self-confidence and prophetic dogmatism. According to the introduction to the third version of *I Think It Over and Sing About It*, which opened under Dario's direction in Genoa in February 1973, the task was no longer 'merely the recovery of the cultural values of the people ... but *also* – and it is here that there has been in our eyes a substantial step forward in the production values inside the theatre collective – the indication of the alternative, not only stated at the ideological level (Communism as strategic objective) but now present in the experience of the struggle'.[9]

Step forward it may have been, and outwardly confident it may have seemed, but this was to be the company's last production. The same combination of ideological, professional and personal conflicts which had led to the break-up of *Nuova Scena* was creating tensions inside *La Comune*. The deterioration in relations and the atmosphere of growing distrust manifested themselves in the drafting of lengthy documents, in arguments until dawn over obscure ideological points, in the summoning of interminable meetings and in the endless clustering of factions in bars and foyers. The failure of Socialism in one company was not an exhilarating spectacle. At stake were bruised feelings, basic emotions and primitive resentments that lay too deep for tracts. One unusually fanciful image gained great currency during the crisis. *La Comune* was likened to a penny-farthing bicycle, but was this inequality – inequality being the cardinal sin of a Marxist-Maoist co-operative – of wheel size to be corrected by reducing the size of the penny or by enlarging the farthing? The suggestion that the large wheel be reduced was advanced in all seriousness in assembly, although the means by which this could be achieved were not made clear. Franca countered with the proposition that surgeons and nurses could be regarded as equal, but that did not mean that a nurse should be left to perform operations.

Increasingly it appeared that the role of professionalism, or nature's unequal distribution of talent, created difficulties to which classical

Marxism could provide no answer. *La Comune* was rich in stage-struck enthusiasts who could not accept the attribution of secondary roles in the process of writing and acting. The fact that reviews spoke of Dario and Franca, and not of the sterling efforts of the others, rankled. Routine matters, like instructions given by Dario as director to one member to enter stage left, caused ructions, which had to be settled by an ad hoc assembly. 'It is important not to confuse democracy with democraticism,' said Dario, descending into ugly jargon. 'Perhaps that is one of the biggest mistakes Franca and I have made',[10] but once again the nature of the mistake is not clarified by the terminology. Franca added later, 'The dominant force in our collective had been a sort of damaging cult of democracy, which was the prime cause of so much dissent, so many conflicts and separations. Determined not to be star players, Dario and I committed the opposite error, in other words we had in fact left our collective without any real direction.'[11]

Many of the factions and groups operating inside the Movement had their own motives for fomenting trouble. Earlier Socialists had given priority to education, but the distinguishing feature of post-68 political activity was the tenacious belief in culture as the architecture of society. If culture could be revolutionised, the pillars of capitalism would crumble. Every groupuscule dedicated itself not only to pamphleteering, agitation and demonstrations but also to the establishment of a network for the diffusion of a new, radical culture. It seemed to strategic executives of various groups that *La Comune*, properly infiltrated and directed, provided a ready-made vehicle for this kind of work. Its leaflets already carried slogans declaring it to be *For A Revolutionary Culture, and Against the Bosses' Culture*. Dario was the main prize, and he shared the belief in the revolutionary potential of culture:

> And here it is worthwhile to recall – even at the cost of repeating ourselves and seeming tiresome – but only to certain advocates of the 'the only hope is with the gun' line – what Mao had to say: 'No culture, no revolution ... A man without culture will never be a real revolutionary. At the most he will be a rebel. A man without culture is like an empty sack. In the wind of the revolution, that

147

sack will be inflated and will seem full and powerful, but when it rains, and it often rains in the revolution, you will find that sack soaking at your feet, to trip you up.'[12]

He was disconcerted when *Lotta Continua* set up October circles as its own national circuit of political-cultural clubs. Several members left *La Comune* to join up with the new body, a move Dario denounced as 'sectarian' in a 1972 document circulated around the company with the title *Our Tasks on the Cultural Front.* He complained that the competition between *La Comune* and the new body takes place not on a political but on an economic level.

> The October circles give the impression of a commercial activity pure and simple. They are justified by the comrades of *Lotta Continua* themselves as a branch of the group, entrusted with the task of collecting funds for the newspaper or other activities of the group.
>
> Following this logic, you could 'hire' authors who 'have a following' and who bring in cash, like Pasolini and other members of the bourgeois cultural world . . . the comrades of *Lotta Continua* display an attitude of mean manipulativeness vis à vis cultural work. Showing films or organising recitals of songs takes on the prime function of making money . . . [13]

The broadly supportive Milan circle produced in March 1973 a paper of its own, snappily entitled *For a Revolutionary Culture at the Service of the Class Struggle Under the Guidance of the Workers' Vanguards.* [14] It traced in tedious detail the evolution of the group, identifying a first phase where it was no more than an extension of the theatre company, followed by a second phase where it developed its autonomous political life and faced the problem of 'mass intervention in communities, in factories, in schools'. If the theatrical collective was now only one branch of a broader organisation, Dario saw his critical autonomy threatened. This problem of liberty of action was aggravated when *Avanguardia Operaia*, another of the legion of Marxist movements of the extreme Left, started manoeuvring to reduce *La Comune* to the status of a branch of their movement. Harsh words flew. Dario and Franca refused to forfeit their right to act and write as they saw fit, and resisted all attempts to reduce the theatre collective to a platform for one group. For their pains, they found themselves accused of heinous and incomprehensible deviations such as 'bureaucratism' and 'adventurism'.

This fresh dispute needed fresh jargon. Dario and Franca declined to move from being 'militants at the service of the working class' to being 'artists of the left'. The distinction was an elusive one, but an artist of the Left was ultimately a servant of a party line, or a hired pen. To be viewed as 'artists of the left', wrote Franca, meant 'accepting compromises, being prone to opportunism, losing all rigour not only as regards the writing of scripts but also, and especially, as regards collective and individual behaviour, both externally and internally'.[15] Neither would countenance this demotion or loss of say over strictly political or artistic matters. In that topsy-turvy world, Dario found himself fighting the same battle for autonomy and against censorship he had waged with the executive at RAI during the *Canzonissima* fracas. As well as being involved in an ideological struggle, Dario was also engaged on a battle to win for himself the conditions in which his own talent could flourish. His model remained Mayakovsky who retained the jester's freedom to mock and to appeal to a sense of humanity which the Bolshevik commissars lost after 1917.

Dario was now facing the third split, cutting him adrift from elements of the Movement. At final assembly of the Milan circle in July 1973, Franca and Dario remained silent but came out deflated. Franca, who was still recovering from her own ordeal, resigned first, followed by Dario. The split was rancorous and poisonous, marked by petty acts of uncomradely dishonesty. It was discovered that one member, who had access to the bank accounts, had been giving herself and her husband a rise, even though the assembly had turned down the request. The company accounts were looted. Two signatures, that of Franca and another member, were needed on company cheques, and statutes laid down that no cheque could be for more than one million lire. On the day after the split, Franca had a phone call from the bank to say that the other signatory was coming to the bank every hour, to withdraw sums of one million lire. 'Let her,' said Franca. Since Dario and Franca took the decision to leave, they abandoned their rights to company property. All the props, stage equipment, costumes which had been accumulated in the course of a life in theatre were lost. During the debate, they formed the impression that *Avanguardia Operaia* sided with the faction which would command the reflectors and lights. Even the van remained with the rump of the company. It was found abandoned and rusting about a year later.

Officially, Paolo Ciarchi, the group's musician, took over as president and *La Comune* remained in being, although not for long, but on this occasion Dario and Franca decided that they too wished to maintain the company name, which they modified to *Theatrical Collective La Comune Directed by Dario Fo*. The other *La Comune* publicly expelled people like Lanfranco Binni for incomprehensible sins such as 'a vocation to scissionism.'[16] When Dario's company resumed performing, the rival faction rushed to inform the left-wing press of his dubious right to the company title. They did admit that Dario was indeed still formally a member of *La Comune* 'inasmuch as he is not expelled', but was 'not centralised to it.'[17] With the break-up of *La Comune*, unlike the splintering of *Nuova Scena*, a watershed had been reached. Dario and Franca had been forced to the rueful conclusion that the co-operative was not a viable structure in theatre, that plays could not be mounted if all decisions were devolved to assemblies. *La Comune* had hardly been a United Artists in the first place, and it may of course be that the disparity of talent was not something which could be incorporated within an egalitarian ideology. In London about the same time, Kenneth Halliwell was hacking Joe Orton to death because he could not breathe in his shadow, but could not flee it either. In Milan, no axes were wielded and no human flesh was torn, but the emotional havoc was immense.

That summer, there were other problems which pursued Dario. In June, the Ministry for Culture chose to issue a circular which, although not mentioning him by name, was dubbed by the media the 'Dario Fo Law'. Its small print stated that theatrical subsidies would be made only to companies 'who perform in public places or in places open to the public, and to which the public can have access by the acquisition of a regular ticket'. It was a classic sting. Dario was barred from public venues as defined by the law and was now being refused a subsidy to perform in the private spaces willing to host him. At the same time, the *Canzonissima* affair made a re-appearance. The Appeal Court decided Dario and Franca were after all responsible for the disruption of the programme, and ordered them to pay 26 million lire damages.

Dario retreated to his villa in Cernobbio on Lake Como. He was now forty-seven, at what should have been the peak of his creative career, but he found himself isolated. He never found occupying his time difficult. When not working, he could absorb himself in the most diverse activities, from watching B-movies on TV to painting, cooking risotto or indulging his interest in cycling races or Formula One car racing. More than one admirer has been disconcerted to be invited home after a performance only to have his expectations of stimulating conversation on life and theatre dashed by the spectacle of Dario slumped happily and vacantly in front of a TV screen, surfing mindlessly through channels. He conserved his energy for essential activities. That summer he spent some time working on a collection of puppets he had been casually assembling.

Both Dario and Franca felt they had been cheated and wronged, that they had made sacrifices of their own talents and resources only to be met with malicious misrepresentation and querulous disapprobation. Political quarrels with opponents were expected, but wounds left by squabbles with former friends or comrades were deep and hurtful. Since his debut, Dario had constructed and dismantled companies, had attracted and discarded successive audiences, be they bourgeois, Communist activists or new-left militants. Perhaps there was a fundamental clash between his politics, with the primacy of democracy and equality they entailed, and his theatrical talents, which required selfish self-assertion. He aroused in his colleagues either useless adulation or unfocused resentment so that, although personally endowed with bonhomie and generosity, he had been involved in various polemics and disputes all his working life. It is striking how often the less resentful explanations offered by others for the various breaks involve some inchoate expression of the sheer impossibility of living under a shadow as vast as his. During the death throes of *La Comune*, some gentle spirit with a touch of poetry in his soul complained that 'you cannot live always in the shadow of an oak tree; even the little trees must breathe.'[18] Others spoke in more curmudgeonly and embittered tones.

Now he was once again on his own and unsure of the next step. His new company might maintain the name *La Comune*, but the qualification 'Directed by Dario Fo' was important. The troupe was now a more conventional hire-and-fire company. For some years, he had been writing three major texts for the company per season. Summer was the season when he found most liberty to write, but that summer he wrote no major new work. Sections of the press were openly exultant, and there were sneering articles which suggested he was to be viewed as the flotsam and jetsam of a failed experiment.

There were other personal ramifications to the break-up. Dario and Franca had been planning to live in a kind of commune with friends from *La Comune*. Land was bought, division of property made and plans drawn up for seven detached houses in the same compound. With the growth of families and the endless bureaucratic delays, these plans were modified to one large block of flats with a communal area. Dario and Franca offered loans to the others, and when the local people objected to the lack of nursery facilities in the area, offered to incorporate a nursery into the building. This caused dissent, since some of the members worried about the consequent depreciation of value of property and, good Socialists as they were, even worried about having their children mix with the locals. When the work was almost completed, some of the others moved in, but the Fos, who were to have two flats in the complex, delayed. With the break-down of friendships occasioned by the split, and the rising fears occasioned by the neo-Fascist attacks on the two of them, they were told they were no longer welcome. Franca threatened legal proceedings and went into the property to recover some of her belongings. The architect in charge of the scheme accused her of having raided his office and taking keys. He raised an action, at which allegations against her were dismissed, but the couple were awarded only 170 million lire in recompense for 700 million lire they had invested in the project.

In spite of the break-up of the company Dario and Franca continued to receive appeals for help from trade unions and striking workers. To dramatise specific conflicts on the spot, Dario devised a new sort of improvised 'theatre of intervention', jokingly called a 'field-mass' after the open-air, religious ceremonies celebrated by military chaplains. They performed at a 'march for peace' in the Veneto, appeared in support of an anti-Fascist demonstration in Pavia and put on a sketch in the port town of Marghera near Venice, where some men were on trial charged with public order offences committed in the course of a 1969 industrial dispute. In Pescara, where some fifty prisoners were accused of offences committed during a prison riot, the group familiarised themselves with the facts of the case and, while the trial was in progress, made them the subject of an improvised, satirical, deliberately grotesque performance with the title, *God, Country and Jail.* 'The people knew nothing about it, they were uninformed. We gave a theatrical form to what was going on in the trial ... inventing situations, improvising ... certainly there was none of the fine rhythm, none of that marvellous balance when voices, lights, timing, cut-and-thrust merge ... there was very little that could give the satisfaction of "fine theatre" ... it was all chopped up with axes ... but, according to the comrades who were there, who saw the performance as an echo chamber for their political work, this was all right; they said – "more of these plays, even if they are indifferent" – (yes, indifferent, because we were not especially pleased with it ourselves).'[19] The collection of material on the Resistance continued, and both were enchanted by an encounter with a large, effervescent woman known as Mamma Togni. After her husband and son had been slaughtered by the Germans, she interrupted a speech by an official of the Republic of Salò and drove him away from the microphone with a club. A monologue based on her experiences became part of Franca's repertoire.

Prison conditions would have formed the subject of the next work had Dario not been galvanised by the violent overthrow on the night of 10-11 September 1973, of Salvador Allende, Marxist President of Chile. Parallels between Chile and Italy had been frequently invoked throughout the 70s. The Italian Christian Democrats had good relations with their Chilean counterparts, while the PCI was inspired by Allende's success at the polls. However, party officials were dismayed at how casually democracy could be overthrown when it produced results displeasing to local capital or to the Pentagon's ideal geo-political map. While many of his followers took to the streets in rage, PCI leader Enrico Berlinguer made a more detached analysis and developed a policy known as the 'historic compromise'. In his view, the *coup* demonstrated that the greatest threat facing a Communist party after electoral victory was 'isolation in power' and consequent exposure to American intervention. He announced that irrespective of the majority of seats it might eventually win, the PCI would make an 'historic compromise' by seeking a coalition with its traditional opponents, the Christian Democrats. Dario dissented from this line. The *coup* reinforced his belief that the support given by wealthy classes to democracy was a sham, and that any attempt by the PCI to win middle class approval by a rightward drift was both doomed to failure and a dereliction of revolutionary heritage.

Allende's overthrow provided Dario with a passion and a cause which shook him out of his lethargy. In slightly over a month, he produced *The People's War in Chile*, a denunciation of the military aggression in Santiago which also took Chile as a metaphor for Italy. Initially the play was conceived as an angry monologue to be delivered by Franca in the role of a painted whore, an allegory for the Chilean Christian Democrat party. This character was retained in the final version, with the whore expressing a gamut of changing convictions, denouncing Allende on his election, hailing the *coup*, then growing horrified when the military turned on the Christian Democrats and finally begging foreign support for a popular, anti-Fascist front. Dario altered and added as rehearsals proceeded. He expanded the work in length and scope to incorporate the piece on Mamma Togni as well as a collage of monologues and sketches reflecting the experiences of anti-Fascists in Chile and Italy. Among the Chilean and Italian songs in the show, the compositions of the folk-singer Victor Jara, who had his fingers cut off before being murdered in the Santiago football stadium, featured prominently.

The overall style was of the tried and tested variety, except for one new device, or 'provocation', which gave the play a startling, controversial force.[20] During the performance, Dario wore a collar microphone and in the midst of a denunciation of Pinochet, the audience heard a crackling noise, seemingly interference, come over the line, followed by what appeared to be a policeman's voice ordering patrol cars to take a detour to the north. Dario stopped in mid-phrase, eyes wide in mock consternation, joking with the audience that these policemen had been on his tail for days and now they were even interrupting the performance. The interference became more and more frequent, giving the impression that the patrol cars were bound for the theatre. Someone from the body of the theatre shouted that the telephone lines were down and that the radio had gone dead. Dario attempted to maintain calm, until another voice shouted, in supposed reassurance, that nothing could really be happening since 'this is Italy. It's not as if we are in Greece, or Chile. We have the Communist party, trade unions here . . . a *coup d'état* couldn't happen here'. The door burst open and a uniformed officer strode up onto the stage to announce that the performance was suspended and to read out the names of local activists who were to accompany him to the police station for questioning. The intention was that at this point a plant in the audience would start singing the *Internazionale,* which was to be taken up by the whole audience as an act of defiance, like the exiled French in *Casablanca* breaking into the *Marseillaise.* The individuals named were to believe that they were enjoying their last moments of freedom before an uncertain future, but in the course of the singing, the police officers were themselves to climb onto the stage, raise their clenched fists in the air and join in the chants. The stage directions recount that 'the audience will remain for a moment astonished, before realising that they have been duped. The reactions are various and always unpredictable. From here, an extremely lively debate *invariably* develops'.[21]

In fact, Dario's plausible inventiveness created mayhem on a par with Orson Welles' radio version of *War of the Worlds.* One unfortunate lad in Turin swallowed his address book for fear of incriminating comrades; another tried to throw himself out of a window, while yet another had to suffer the humiliation of watching his mother hurl herself, in spite of the efforts of Franca to restrain her, onto the 'police officer' screaming that her son had nothing to do with any extremist organisation. The same selfless thespian in uniform was several times threatened with knives. As a theatrical device, the false *coup* was a stunning success, but Dario was criticised by Right and Left for going over the top and devising a bluff of undue realism and violence. In some quarters, it was suggested that he had trivialised the seriousness of a real situation in Chile and of a potential threat in Italy. He rejected such accusations scornfully, and declared himself satisfied that he had both aroused the active reaction he had sought and had made clear the parallels between Italy and Chile.

In November, the schedule took the company to Sassari, in Sardinia, where they rented the Rex cinema for performances of the Chile play and *Mistero buffo*. The local police chief, Renato Voria, sent a request to see the script of the new play, but was rebuffed. On 8 November, he dispatched some fifty police officers to the performance. Dario refused them entrance but the performance was cancelled and the evening given over to public discussion of police activity. The following day, the police turned up during rehearsals. When Dario once again tried to prevent their entry into the hall, the officer in charge had him arrested. Some of Dario's colleagues seized hold of him and for a time he was hauled this way and that until the police succeeded in handcuffing him and leading him off to the station. He was charged with 'resistance and verbal violence to a public official' and kept in custody.

The Italian and international press corps descended on Sassari, and the story was the lead in every TV news bulletin and made the headlines in most papers. A photographer was somehow on hand to record the sight of Fo in handcuffs being led off, somewhat plaintively, to prison. Even those elements of the PCI which had been distrustful of him expressed their outrage at the conduct of the local police. In the town itself, a committee for the release of Dario Fo was instantly set up and groups marched on the prison to establish a permanent vigil outside the walls. Some marchers reported hearing the inmates reply with a chorus of *The Red Flag*. Franca and the other members of the company joined the picket, converting the demonstration into a 'happening'. Franca climbed onto the top of a car which had been requisitioned and performed various pieces, including Mamma Togni. In her account:

> Dario was arrested in the evening. That night there was a demonstration for Chile, and the representatives of the various groups, parties and trade unions agreed on the times and routes of the protest marches for the following day. The schools went on strike. There was an enormous procession. Some shepherds arrived even from Orgosolo. At the same time, for reasons of their own, the bakers too were on strike, and when they saw our demonstration they found out what was going on and they too joined in. The march stopped in front of the prison to welcome Dario, who was expected to be coming out after the interrogation by the judge. But he never seemed to be coming, and so while we were waiting we decided to put on a play. They put me on top of a *cinquecento*, between the police and the demonstrators; the police were lined up at my back, with the people at the front looking at me. On this unusual stage, I performed from ten o'clock until a quarter to two, with other colleagues taking a turn. We brought the bakers up on stage too, to explain their problems; everybody was enthusiastic.[22]

These words were written later, but at the time the outcome was not so certain. Dario was kept in captivity from 7.30 in the evening on 9 November until 2.30 the following afternoon, during which time he neither ate nor slept. He later said that when they put the handcuffs on him, the thought flashed into his mind that the *coup* really had taken place in Italy, but that most of the time he was aware of the preposterousness of the whole episode. The public outcry was such that he had to be released as quickly as the proprieties of the law would permit, but for all the harlequinade which attended it, the matter was serious enough. An actor in a democratic state had been taken from stage to prison cell for attempting to express views which were permitted on any reading of the constitution. Dario was aware that performers, minstrels, strolling players, acrobats and mountebanks had been subjected all throughout history to persecution and repression, and that only in this century had the actor been tamed by being converted into an object of cult in a religion of celebrity. The paradox was that Dario was a danger precisely because of his celebrity. One has to assume that some anonymous enthusiast from the acting profession would have performed unharassed. The further paradox was that the attentions of those same Sardinian police ensured that Dario Fo became again a force in public life.

Since the break-up of the *La Comune,* the smart judgement was that he was a busted flush, that the 'Movement' he had served was now tottering and that he would disappear under the growing force of the backlash. Sassari brought him back to public attention and he emerged with renewed vigour and self-belief. He was the object of various discussion forums and profiles in newspapers and magazines, most of which were unexpectedly eulogistic. The magazine *Panorama* produced a special supplement in which they asked various ex-collaborators, like Nuccio Ambrosino, or prominent theatre people, such as Giorgio Strehler or Paolo Grassi to express their view on the event. Whatever blows they had received from Fo in the past, they all weighed in with sincere support. The main exception was Pier Paolo Pasolini, perhaps still smarting from Fo's attack on him earlier in the year. 'My opinion on Dario Fo and his work is so negative that I refuse to speak of him', he opined, before going on to give the view he had refused to give. 'Fo is a kind of plague on Italian theatre.'[23] It was out of tune with the mood of the moment but a fitting epitaph for a miserable year.

CHAPTER 8

The French Connection

In January 1974, Dario received an invitation from the French Ministry of Culture to perform *Mistero buffo* in the Chaillot National Theatre in Paris. A French journalist dispatched to do an interview met him in Trento and concluded that 'In Italy Dario Fo is a kind of national phenomenon, a sort of Marxist Maurice Chevalier.'[1] There have been many varying descriptions of him over the years, but that was one of the most arresting.

He accepted the invitation with alacrity but in spite of the experience he had accumulated over the years, he was overawed at the prospect of performing in Paris and unsure how to proceed. He spoke French, but not to a standard which would allow him to do an act in the language. With Franca, who could not accompany him because of prior engagements, he devised a scheme for simultaneous translation, not word for word but via a colour-code intended to convey atmosphere, ideas and broad plot. The more important decision was to employ *grammelot*, the pseudo-language devised by Italian *commedia dell'arte* players when performing abroad, especially in Paris. To communicate with the audience, the players employed a vocabulary of plausible sounds in the accents of the language of the country where they were performing, but none of which corresponded to actual words or had any precise meaning.

As he was limbering up for the show, the stage manager suggested he peep through the curtain to see the audience. To his consternation, he made out 'the scientist who had played a leading part in the design of the French atom bomb', as well as 'famous artists, actors, musicians and celebrated prima donnas'. He also spotted Jean-Paul Sartre.[2] One of the first sketches he had chosen for performance portrayed Scapin giving lessons in etiquette. It involved grand pirouettes and gestures, but was also an invitation to the audience to seek out parallels with the cynicism of contemporary politicians. The applause was rapturous and Dario got into his stride. Never one for false modesty, he declared the evening a triumph.

The more enduring consequence of the visit to Paris was the encounter with Sartre. He went to hear him deliver a wide-ranging lecture on *Theatre of Situation and Popular Theatre*, beginning with the Greeks, proceeding through Atellan farce and medieval mystery plays and ending with a dissection of Elizabethan and modern theatre. Years later, he claimed to be able to reproduce that talk verbatim in *More Tricks of the Trade*, and if this was an exaggeration, there is no doubt that the notion of theatre of situation made a deep impact on him and recurs in subsequent lectures, workshops and articles of his own. Gramsci had earlier given him justification for viewing the style of drama he most admired, and which he believed he was producing, as popular theatre, but now Sartre provided him with grounds for asserting that 'popular theatre is first and foremost theatre of situation'.[3] So impressed was he by Sartre's book, *Theatre of Situation*, particularly the chapter on Beckett's *Waiting for Godot*, that he began to translate the work into Italian, but translation rights were refused by the French publisher. By the time he was persuaded to change his mind, Dario was involved with other projects.

It was Sartre who took the initiative in arranging a face to face meeting. Franca had by this time arrived in Paris, and the pair of them were overwhelmed by a request made by Sartre to Dario to participate in what must surely rank as one of the great opportunities *manqués* of recent decades. The philosopher had been invited by French television to prepare a series of programmes on the History of Europe in the twentieth century. He wanted the collaboration of writers from several

European countries, and wondered if Dario would be interested in preparing the programmes dealing with Italy. French television had raised no objection, and Dario, who never understood why Sartre had chosen him, was excited at the prospect. The two shared common left-wing, broadly Marxist beliefs, had both been galvanised by the revival of Marxist thought following the 'events of May' in Paris, 1968, and both were admirers of Mao and the Cultural revolution. Both too had taken up the cause of imprisoned terrorists, Sartre that of the Baader-Meinhof group in Mannheim prison in Germany, Dario the plight of many Italian terrorists in Italian jails.

They had meetings in Paris with intellectuals from other countries to discuss the project, and in July Sartre came to Rome. He wanted to begin work immediately, but Dario and Franca were committed to a trip to China in September, so the project was put back to autumn. Dario told the *Corriere della Sera* that the exact nature and extent of his involvement had not yet been finalised, but that he and Franca would make 'a contribution to the script, will do some pieces, as well as some sketches and some sung extracts. We will meet in Paris to put the final touches to the plans. However, what interests us is the encounter with Sartre, to whom my generation owes so much. All the great shake-ups, the things which have impacted on reality have come to us from him, so I consider this possible collaboration a great fortune. For me in particular, it could be an incentive to find new models, new formulae since, apart from anything else, the man is so stimulating.'[4]

If personal relations with Sartre were relaxed, those with Simone De Beauvoir were much less so. Franca was appalled at de Beauvoir's haughtiness and rudeness on their first encounter. 'In Sartre's house in Paris, the key turned in the lock, and there she was: shopping bag in hand, scarf on head. She threw a "don't smoke" at Sartre, and withdrew into the kitchen. Sartre, like a naughty child caught stealing the jam, stubbed out his cigarette or cigar. "Simone" he muttered. So that's who it was! I was more upset than Dario. Perhaps because I was a woman, I thought I had the right to at least a greeting.'[5] De Beauvoir appeared to believe the project was of little value, but in the event her opinions made no difference, since the scheme was aborted, seemingly on instructions from the Elysée Palace. General de Gaulle had taken a benevolent view of Sartre, regarding his activities with a tolerant good humour which his successor could not match. Dario and Franca were given to understand that President Pompidou had vetoed the proposal. This decision must have been a matter of regret. It is impossible to imagine what kind of wildly idiosyncratic, truculent and possibly ill-focused history might have emerged from this implausible coupling of unique talents, but the failure of the project must be regarded as a loss.

While in France, Dario met the distinguished actor and director, Jean Louis Barrault, who had also abandoned conventional theatre in 1968 but who had managed to establish his own permanent theatre, the Lilà, in a disused railway station on the outskirts of Paris. He also met Ariane Mnouchkine, of the *Théatre du Soleil*, who worked in premises rented from the City Council. These meetings heightened Dario's dissatisfaction with the nomadic life he had been required to live since his eviction from the Capannone, and on his return to Milan he made contact with the City Council to enquire about renting one of city's many empty buildings for use as a theatre. The councillor in charge of Council Properties was the Socialist Carlo Tognoli, an admirer of Dario's work.

The first response was promising. The two men visited various properties, and the choice fell on the disused Palazzina Liberty. The term 'Liberty' has nothing to do with freedom, but derives from the famous Liberty shops in London and is the standard Italian for *art nouveau*. Built around 1930, the Palazzina had originally been a central part of the fruit and vegetable market but had been left standing in solitary splendour in the middle of a park when the market was transferred to another site. It is a striking building, incorporating those elements of the pseudo-classical which could be reconciled with modernism. The royal crown and the coat of arms of the House of Savoy still stand atop the main entrance, while mosaics depicting a young woman languidly picking oranges in some mythical grove decorate the walls. Narrow columns surmounted by lions heads and little carved bunches of grapes leave space for grand oriel windows, and the whole is fronted by a long balcony which had never had any practical use until Dario pressed it into service as a stage for open air performances. By the 1970s, it was in a state of decay and only the intervention of Italy's leading conservation society, *Italia Nostra*, blocked proposals to have it demolished.

Tognoli and Fo reached an agreement on rent and the keys were handed over. In view of later developments and myths, it is worth emphasising that the first moves were made in strict accordance with the laws of contract. The understanding was that the company would be responsible for the restoration of the building and would oversee the provision of community facilities including a library, a crèche, rooms for meetings and assorted activities, all in addition to their own theatrical activities. In mid March, Dario and *La Comune* took possession. However, once Tognoli's initiative was presented to the City Council for approval, the Christian Democrats (DC) reacted with fury. In retrospect, granted Dario's notoriety, it seems curious that Tognoli had not done more to square his coalition partners, but the matter was clearly within his departmental competence and he had secured an excellent deal for the Council. Additional revenue was guaranteed, the Council would remain owners of the building, and the restoration work of an unused architectural jewel would be carried out by *La Comune*. Had it been anyone else, political agreement would have been a formality, but the DC regarded Fo as an enemy. Massimo De Carolis, the local party leader, declared his outright, indeed enraged, opposition to the move. De Carolis was already an important figure within the DC nationally, and would shortly enter Parliament.

The Council backtracked, and in a hastily convened meeting of 30 March Dario was ordered to surrender the keys and evacuate the building. He refused, and from that moment the occupation of Palazzina Liberty began. This was the time of occupations whether by tenants of apartment blocks or by workers of factories, but this case was different. Dario was entitled to believe he had been treated wretchedly. He had behaved with the propriety of a businessman-cum-philanthropist. He had undertaken to pay a fair rent, to restore life to a neglected building and to provide facilities to a run-down area of the city, only to have his good intentions flung rudely back in his face for the meanest and crudest of political motives. Certainly he had done nothing to ingratiate himself with the DC, but their conduct now confirmed all he had been saying about the nature of power and the standards of those who exercised it.

The company and their supporters swung into action. They organised a petition, and gathered perhaps as many as 20,000 signatures in support. Work was quickly started on a building whose only inhabitants were mice and rats. Processions of lorries carted away rubbish of all kinds and members of the group, aided by local people, started cleaning, scrubbing, brushing, painting and repairing. Meetings with residents in the neighbourhood were arranged, and after an early stand-off, local people formed the view that a revitalised Palazzina would be an asset. Several of them turned up with pots of paint they claimed to have found lying uselessly around their house, while others were craftsmen with valuable skills. Dario, with his architect's training, got to work on plans to transform the interior. Meetings were held each evening to discuss progress, and it was a matter of policy to schedule these meetings at a time convenient for everyone.

On 31 March, the day after the Council decision, a Committee for the Popular and Democratic Utilisation of the Palazzina was established. The Red Flag was unfurled. The first big rally in the surrounding parkland took place on 7 April, drawing a crowd estimated at anything between five and fifteen thousand people. Contemporary photographs show Fo, every inch the Roman tribune, standing on the raised balcony performing the *Lazarus* and the *Marriage Feast at Cana* from *Mistero buffo*, together with a short extract from Molière. Even for a man accustomed to playing to huge audiences in arenas, it was an astonishing tour de force. Those at the back could scarcely see him and certainly could not follow any facial expressions or gestures. The stage was the balcony which ran round the building and he performed without props, costumes or fellow actors, yet held the attention of a vast audience, many of whom were anything but theatre-goers. No doubt the general exhilaration of trespassing, of taking part in an act of impudence against the authorities contributed to the prevailing mood of shared excitement, but this was a day recalled later with delight by those who were there.

It was not all beer and skittles, for Dario demanded that attention be paid to local and national politics. Italy was about to face a referendum on divorce. The law legalising divorce had been passed by Parliament but the DC, led by Amintore Fanfani, had gathered the signatures needed to force a referendum to repeal the new Act. The Communist party entered the referendum campaign unwillingly, afraid not only of defeat but of a setback for their new strategy of alliance with the DC. Dario promised that the Palazzina could be used as headquarters and meeting place for the many groups involved in the pro-divorce side. He satirised the Milanese Christian Democratic party but in a typically oblique way, through an adaptation of the story of Fra Dolcino, the medieval Franciscan dissident who had featured in the earlier *Always Blame the Devil*. It is hard to imagine any other agitator advocating populist policies by reference to one of the leading heresiarchs of the Middle Ages.

The mass meeting was asked to approve a very bureaucratically worded motion backing the occupation and attacking the Council. 'Enough of the illusory, hypocritical promises of the Council which seeks only the demolition of the Palazzina, in the same way as the DC government allows the destruction of factories and countryside, in accordance with a logic that serves the profits of the boss class.' According to the motion, the Palazzina was to become:

1) A centre for *popular artistic production* open to all.
2) A centre for *cultural and political debate* at the service of the workers.

The Committee proposes the following initiatives:
- Opening of a *school of popular theatre* directed by Dario Fo, open to all young workers and students.
- Formation of *collectives of artistic production*.
- Organisation of *plays for children*.
- Works by the *La Comune Theatrical Collective* directed by Dario Fo, and other theatrical groups from Italy and abroad, who identify themselves with this struggle.

- Projection of *cycles of films and audiovisuals.*
- An *exhibition of popular art* open to workers, students, with the participation of progressive artists who support our programme.
- Cycle of *meetings, debates and conferences* (above all a series of initiatives connected with the *referendum*) and the opening of a *library* for further study of the subjects under discussion.
- Opening of a *nursery* where the children of those attending the plays and other initiatives of the centres can be left, and where the children can play together, be looked after and live collectively.
- A *weekly bulletin of information* on the Palazzina struggle.
- A *national propaganda campaign* on these issues.

Never before had italics been given such an overtly polemical purpose. In the following days, the professional sceptics and cynics of Right and Left joined in a chorus of syncopated derision. Where is the money to come from, do not people today prefer soap operas to the frantic pursuit of artistic excellence (popular or otherwise), is not Fo a dreamer when he is not a dangerous fanatic, should we not simply give him enough rope and leave him hang himself? No doubt Fo is a dreamer, a utopian dreamer with a boundless optimism in the capacities of the human animal, and in this project his utopian visions had the freest of reins. The Palazzina, according to these schemes, or dreams, was a combination of the Pompidou centre and the Abbey of Theleme. The utopian reformers and optimistic visionaries of Europe, that tribe of impatient improvers of man's estate, were leaning over his shoulder as he penned his manifesto for the building. His schemes had a breadth and nobility to rival those of the radical pioneers, of William Morris, Robert Owen, John Ruskin or indeed Antonio Gramsci. Like them he aimed to unleash in the individual a creativity which had been stifled, to encourage the growth of multi-sided talents, and to foster joy, happiness and a more glorious world. The individual was to be enhanced as an individual to permit him to attain the fullest richness of mind available to each. That is not the manifesto of dull politics, and indeed this project eschewed direct political activity, if one excepts the room left for debates and conferences, in favour of cultural activity. The programme rested on the conviction that education and the cultivated mind were the prerequisites of social change, and that Socialism was an attainment of the spirit before it could be a rule of society. The proposal voted on that day had the grandeur of an ideal, even if it provided easy meat for scoffers.

The City Council, indifferent to these high-minded utterances, was still intent on having Fo removed. On 10 April they offered to reimburse the company for the work they had done, but the offer was rejected. In off-the-record briefings, Council spokespeople made reference to the presence among the occupiers of revolutionary groups who advocated violence, and used Franca's plan to establish Red Aid headquarters in the Palazzina to justify vague and wholly unsubstantiated hints that the building was a den of terrorists or a hiding place for fugitives from justice. The suggestion was whispered that if only Dario and Franca were to separate themselves from the extremists around them, the Council would see them accommodated elsewhere in Milan. A deconsecrated church in some working class area was mentioned, but no one was hoodwinked over the seriousness of the offer. There followed an operation which descended into a harlequinade. The Council sent a team of workmen to construct a fence around the Palazzina. A crowd of local people gathered to demonstrate and the two sides faced each other with largely good-natured tolerance for a couple of hours until the Council employees concluded they were all members of the same working class, downed tools and went home. The Council cut off electricity supplies but this problem was overcome by the gift of a generator that provided energy for all the activities of restoration and creation.

Dario performed to another huge crowd on May Day. The park was flooded with people, while stalls selling food, trinkets and pamphlets were arranged inside and outside the building. Various bodies including the Radical Party, the Proletarian Bookshop, the Manifesto group, *Lotta Continua* and *Avanguardia operaia* not to mention several groupings of radical students came to demonstrate support. Two days later, the Council instituted court proceedings, but since the Mayor, Aldo Aniasi, failed to appear in person, the hearing was postponed until 17 May. The Court duly decided in favour of the Council, and the company was ordered by the magistrate to leave the building. Dario entered an immediate appeal which was, to general surprise, upheld. The Appeal Court agreed that entry into the Palazzina had been made in accordance with a legal agreement, and held that the Council had been unduly cavalier in overturning it. The Council counter-appealed. Court cases were to drag on for years, but meantime Dario and Franca had possession of their theatre. The police kept the Palazzina under continual surveillance. Fo's lawyer, the Sicilian Giovanni Piscopo, recalled meeting police agents whom he recognised prowling around the Palazzina in disguise. When challenged they replied that they were having their evening stroll. Others were prepared to employ more brutal means. On 13 June, sticks of dynamite were discovered in a telephone box in the street nearby.

Dario challenged De Carolis to a public debate. The offer was accepted provided it took place not in the Palazzina Liberty but before an invited audience in the local DC office. There was, as was to be expected, no meeting of minds. De Carolis was an astute politician, confident of his own positions and not likely to be cowed by Dario's wit or irony. His case was that Dario Fo had every right in a democracy to full freedom of opinion, but no right to preferential treatment. What was his entitlement to the use of public property when his purpose was to establish a platform from which to express subversive views? Dario retorted that the core of the problem was the role of culture in society. He attacked the Christian Democrats for having overseen the decline and degradation of cinema and TV, and for resorting to censorship when they risked losing the argument. Had the DC sunk to the level of replying to ideas by recourse to (metaphorical) violence? De Carolis rejected the accusation, saying that revolutionaries like Dario had always been spoiled by the system, and concluded that if the Palazzina Liberty were to be given to anyone, it should not be to him, who would use it from morning to evening to spit on the Christian Democrats. He was undoubtedly right. Dario had never had any hesitation in biting the few hands which fed him.

Meantime, the transformation of the Palazzina was in full swing. The company scoured Milan for seating, but discovered on several occasions that would-be benefactors were put off by phone calls advising them against association with an illegal occupation. Undaunted, Dario announced that 'the occupation of the Palazzina Liberty is one of the most important shows we have ever produced'. The Chilean artist, Sebastian Matta, painted a series of grand murals in his own idiosyncratic style, combining elements of magic realism, allegory, pure fantasy and political spleen. The subject of the cycle was *The Death of the General,* showing the assassination of a warlord. This work adorned the main hall of the Palazzina, and later hung above Franca's desk in her office.

Dario intended to open the premises with *God, Fatherland and Prison,* a play he had on the stocks but he decided the moment was not right and it was again postponed. Instead, the Ferrari company of puppeteers, with a workshop on the history of puppets in the morning and a show in the afternoon, became the first company to perform in the Palazzina. In the first three months of occupation, twenty-five theatre troupes as well as twenty groups of singers, from Italy and abroad took the stage. Dario's own first production was one of his few complete flops. Still anxious to establish continuity with popular culture from other periods, he had been reading two dialect poets, the Milanese Carlo Porta and the Roman G C Belli. In May he put on a script which was barely more than a dramatised reading, *Porta and Belli Against Power,* but it pleased no one and was withdrawn after a week.

The promised playgroups and workshops for children were instituted. The Xerox copier, an indispensable instrument of left-wing activity in the era before the photo-copier, was installed and bulletins were produced in profusion. The inhabitants of the neighbourhood were bombarded with earnest little leaflets, some written in the jargon of the time but others couched in the spirited irony which was Dario's own trademark. One much appreciated leaflet read: 'After years of being left to enjoy themselves in the Palazzina Liberty, *The Mice Wish to Thank the Christian Democrats for the efforts they have put into preventing the Palazzina being taken away from them and saved from collapse.'* The City Fathers looked on aghast as demonstrations followed one after the other in the park around the Palazzina. On 9 June, demonstrators gathered to protest against 'imperialism, Zionism and internal repression in the Middle East'.

In mid-June, the Palazzina hosted a grand, three-day Conference on Culture. According to leaflets distributed around the neighbourhood, discussion was to focus on lessons learned from the take-over of the Palazzina, move onto the role of the intellectual as producer of culture and lead to the identification of common ground on this topic between rival strands of left-wing thinking. It was optimistically promised that the use of abstract or ideological jargon would be outlawed in favour of the examination of practical experience, but since the event drew an impressive number of scholars, researchers, journalists, theatre practitioners, political activists and members of far-left formations, the possibility of prohibiting polysyllabic speech was remote. The event offered Dario, who was more a polemicist than a systematic thinker, an occasion for clarifying to himself his own thinking on popular culture. With a microphone in his hand his thoughts were as clear as when holding a pen, and was quick to respond to the provocations and prompts of debate. His forte was the lively phrase or the unexpected insight enlightened by a combination of wit and imagination, but always based on genuine knowledge. He was widely read which provided him with a private library of quotes, many of which have unfortunately never been uttered by the writers to whom they were attributed, but which served to illustrate the tenor of his own thinking.

Since the break-up of the first version of *La Comune*, Dario had spent many anxious hours reconsidering the relationship between art and politics, and specifically trying to determine which should have primacy. Socialism and the revolution – he still failed to define exactly what 'revolution' entailed – constituted the only creed he professed, but all around him he heard voices suggesting that art was *de trop* in the political struggle, or that, in his own phrase, the artists were 'like confetti, or the filling of a cake or the trimmings alongside the main course.'[6] The artist, he feared, was expected to view himself as the clown in motley whose task was to drum up interest and entice along the crowd but had then to move aside when it came to the serious work of propaganda and agitation. Slightly less fearsome was the possibility, which at different times Mayakovsky and Elio Vittorini had rebelled against, that the writer would be required to create according to preordained paradigms, and forfeit autonomy of action. Dario was anxious to establish his right to an autonomous space and to demonstrate, at least to himself, the political value of his work as writer and performer. The dangers and benefits of amalgamating political discussion with entertainment had always intrigued him, but the encroachment of self-appointed commissars instinctively appalled him. Fortunately Lenin and Mao were on hand to lend him support.

> The concern is, and we are reminded of it in downright peremptory terms, to recall Lenin's phrase, a phrase which is too frequently distorted: 'What is art? Art is a small cog in the mechanism of the class struggle.' Well then, this cog has become smaller and smaller in the minds of many comrades of the various groups, to the point where it has become superfluous. In other words, they mean that if you remove this cog, the class struggle will go forward under its own steam. No, when Lenin spoke of the cog, he did not mean it was superfluous. He said that this cog was as important as other larger cogs. Without the cog of culture, without the cog of art, of class art obviously, the machine would not go forward. It may be small, but it is important to understand that it is essential, that it is part of the whole problem of revolution.

Mao was even more helpful.

> Mao says: a man without culture will never be a revolutionary. At most he will be a rebel . . . So, it is clear, without culture there will be no revolution. And what does Mao mean by culture? He means another vision of the world, he means changed relationships between men. He means a particular concept of love between people, one quite different from that which the bourgeoisie expresses, for theirs expresses all the forces of capitalism. Mao insists that *before* the revolution cultural work must begin, that *during* the revolution there must be cultural work and that *after* the revolution cultural work must continue.[7]

There was no appeal against such masters. In a perspective shared with many post-1968 activists, Dario advocated the rethinking of relations between man and man, and man and woman. Art was not a flimsy wrapping designed to make palatable the stern maxims of *Das Kapital*, but an indispensable element of a life devoted to the 'struggle', that other voguish word trotted out at conventions. However, Dario was still in search of some overall poetic of popular culture and of the kernel of difference between it and the hegemonic culture. Lenin and Mao were of limited use here, but Dario's new friend, Jean-Paul Sartre, was invaluable, particularly when he wrote that bourgeois culture was polluted by a vein of pessimism and of distrust, or even contempt, for humanity itself. Bourgeois writers inhabited a *cul de sac* of their own making, and could construct no exit. The cardinal sin of those who gave voice to the angst of the age was an inability to believe in the prospect of change and improvement. As a corrective, Dario appealed to a long tradition of people's culture dating from the middle ages, critical in nature and casting a satirical eye on the doings of the holders of power and authority. While it was true that strands of popular culture were vacuous or mindless, he found in authentic popular culture a vitality which outshone the shallow nihilism of the avant-garde. He was delighted to find that Brecht had spoken of 'the sheer happiness of theatre,' and even commended Strehler for finding the theatrical means for expressing that happiness. 'What does a play mean?' Dario asked. 'A play means enjoyment,' he explained. Theatre was not didacticism, nor a lecture on ends and means but a release of pressure and an occasion for the expression of communal joy. This placed on the makers of popular theatre the obligation to work to the highest standards. The bourgeoisie were not to have the best tunes. The slapdash was not acceptable in popular, political or ideological theatre. The enjoyment which theatre offered could be attained only by the 'technical and ideological training of the actors' and by using the best available scenery and the finest lighting and sound equipment. A cultivation of popular values did not excuse a sacrifice of professional standards.

With the ideological framework clear, Dario was able to face anew certain problems, notably the problem of the 'fourth wall' and of the 'aside', which may not have concerned ideologists but which had been debated in theatre for generations. The link between the 'fourth wall' and the 'aside' was that both assumed a lost immediacy of relationship between stage and stalls. Any aesthetic which constructed barriers between performer and spectator, or which reduced the spectator to a condition of passivity was anathema to him. 'Is the fourth wall only that magic, rectangular space fixed by the framework of the stage, which divides the audience from the performers? No, it is also the footlights which create a particular kind of atmosphere ... the corpse-like make-up on the actors' faces, their gestures and their habit of emitting sounds in special cadences ... which put the spectator in the condition of a peeping Tom spying on a story which has nothing to do with him and which is on the other side to the fourth wall.' The construction of a 'fourth wall' was responsible in its turn for the suppression of the 'aside.' The actor who inhabited the closed space of the stage, supposedly ignoring the presence of an audience observing him, was deprived of the possibility of turning away from fellow actors and addressing remarks directly to the audience. The premise for Fo's wish to rehabilitate the 'aside' was a wish to do away with all division between the two sides of the footlights. Rather than access to the character's hidden fears, the 'aside' was an invitation to the audience to participate and hence to form a community. It also had implications for the style of acting permitted. 'The aside means that at the moment the actor says something to another actor, he can give an immediate denial, he can do a commentary for the audience. He can *criticise* the character from outside, he can detach himself from the part. In other words, he can act in an epic style.' The use of Brecht's terminology was not accidental. Dario too believed that an actor should seek not to identify himself with the character he was playing so much as *present* that character. 'Presenting means making continual use of the "aside", in other words speaking to the audience, and to be able to speak to the audience the actor must be able to exit from the part, mediate it, present it, indicate it ... this is the basis a completely different idealogical vision of creating theatre or cinema.'

Fo now found himself at odds with the two leading twentieth-century theorists of theatre, Stanislavsky and Brecht. He was never totally at ease with either. He respected the German playwright as the great precursor and teacher in political theatre, and generally ascribed any disagreements between them to deformations introduced by unintelligent directors or slavish acolytes. Nevertheless, the differences are real, particularly over the value to be ascribed to the popular tradition. Towards Stanislavsky, on the other hand, Fo displayed the consistency of unremitting biliousness. Dario disliked the entire Stanislavskian approach, which he dismissed polemically, and comprehensively, as 'the worst, reactionary, conservative, bourgeois position in history'. Stanislavsky's fault, in Dario's interpretation, was to envisage the creation of an intimate, closed theatre, where private traumas or individual affairs of the mind or heart could be scrutinised. His ideal was big, rumbustious, public theatre, where clashes which affected an entire community and its way of life could be aired and dramatised. He disliked a theatre where audiences had the role of eavesdroppers or voyeurs, ogling a spectacle which they had encountered by chance. Inherent in this concept was the further notion, which he rejected even more strongly, that the actor should delve in his own ego or subconscious or into his own store of emotional memories so as to act out dramas which were his alone. If the spectator identified with these traumatic memories of the actor's, that was for Stanislavsky a bonus but not of the essence.

> When we arrived at the need to knock down the fourth wall, or when we got to the point of talking of collective problems, we found ourselves in completely opposing positions over the question of identifying the actor and the character. I the actor will try to find inside myself all the odds and ends, all the guts, all my defects, all my qualities so as to dress myself in the character . . . this is Stanislavsky . . . But for my part I try to create the vision of a community, of a chorus, of a communion. Obviously I try not to talk too much of myself, but of problems which are collective. If I look out problems which are collective, my speech, my language will be different, will be of necessity epic. That is why all popular theatre is always epic. Because at the bottom there is a clear ideological factor. There is the ideology of the community, of interests, which are social interests, interests of living together, of producing together, of dividing what is obtained.[8]

This outlook is far removed from the commercial imperatives of modern theatre, and perhaps from modern theatre *tout court*. Once again there is a historical depth to Fo's thought. His ideas of epic acting derived less from Brecht than from the nameless medieval jester-actors who preceded *commedia dell'arte*. 'We also understood', he told his audience in the Palazzina, 'why in medieval theatre the actor tended to present himself alone on stage and construct several characters . . . Because only in that way could he produce with his own repetitive presence the epic moment of the performance, of chorality.' The jester was never meant to erase himself and become his character. When required to address his audience directly, he had scarcely even to exit from his part, no more than Dario had had to do in *Mistero buffo*. There was always a touch of aesthetic egoism in Fo. When talking about the stage, popular theatre or even acting techniques, he inevitably provided a *raison d'être* for the display of his own skills. By the end of his discourse on popular theatre, he had established that Dario Fo the jester was entitled to be always and everywhere Dario Fo, and never, unlike an Olivier, a Barrault or a Gassman, sink his own being behind that of a Lear, an Othello, an Orestes or a Faust.

Discussions of theory were all very well, but work had to go on. In June 1974, within a week of the conference, Dario and Franca and the company were in Brescia where, in late May, Italy's most recent terrorist outrage had occurred. A bomb had been left in a portico, timed to go off when a demonstration by the United Anti-Fascist Committee was passing. Eight people were left dead and over a hundred were injured. The President and the Prime Minister were jeered when they visited the town to attend the funeral of the victims. A few days later, members of Dario's *La Comune* organised in Milan a 'people's trial' against the perpetrators of the outrage, calling on eye witnesses, journalists, lawyers, ex-Resistance fighters and local members of *La Comune* who had taken photographs of the event. On 21 June, the company moved to the premises of their Brescia branch, and invited those who had participated at the demonstration or who had been sheltering in the portico to recount what they had seen. The company then put together a show which they performed that evening in the main square. Some pieces were reprised from the recent play on Chile, Franca again did her monologue on Mamma Togni and various Chilean and Italian Resistance songs were worked in. The central part of the work consisted of the direct testimony of those who had seen the massacre and who wished to denounce the neo-Fascist groups responsible.

Over the summer of 1974, Dario was engaged in writing the work to which he gave various titles, before settling on *Can't pay? Won't Pay!* As was common practice in these years, Dario drafted the script but then discussed it with colleagues and with the first audiences in factories in Milan. 'Following the debates, we realised there were gaps in the script, scenes which should be played differently. The genuinely constructive criticisms made by our comrades convinced us to change and rewrite the finale. This is, in our view, the correct means of creating "collective" theatre.'[9] The seemingly innocuous last sentence carries a polemical sting. Taking soundings from real people who draw on their own experience is the best way to construct political theatre, whereas heeding an ideological commissar is not.

The play, a more fully rounded and well-made piece than Fo had written previously, was born of the observation that the principal problem facing working people in the 70s was not unemployment but inflation. Hourly wage costs rose by 24% in 1970, as employers and government strove to control the dissent unleashed by the 'hot autumn'. Economists blamed this rise in on-costs for a drop in investment and for inflationary pressures in the following two years. A modest increase in productivity was registered in 1973-74, but this came to an abrupt end with the oil crisis. Monthly inflation statistics spiralled out of control, as interest rates rose to levels not seen in Europe since the depression of the 1930s. The continual rise in prices played greater havoc with the lives of employees and their families than had a decade of terrorism. Even at the height of the violence and mayhem, it was possible for ordinary people to continue with their day-to-day lives, but unbridled inflation represented a different threat.

Anger at inflation produced a genuinely spontaneous rebellion. Men and, more especially, women took matters into their own hands by embarking on a course of action to which political activists, who had not initiated it and could not control it, gave the dignified name of 'proletarian expropriation', or 'auto-reduction.' Baldly stated, people refused to pay increased fares for public transport, higher bills for gas or electricity, higher tariffs in factory canteens and, above all, rising prices for goods in supermarkets. Some customers continued to pay the old price, others offered only what they themselves deemed a fair price, while in other cases groups of women simply took what they wanted from supermarket shelves and refused to pay at all. It was, in its own way, a challenge to the system and to the economic status quo, but it was a campaign which dismayed parties on both sides of the political spectrum.

Later it was said, by friendly critics, that Dario had intuitively or magically foreseen this development before it got underway, and by hostile critics that *Can't Pay? Won't Pay!* was the inspiration for shoplifting. In fact, the first recorded acts of 'proletarian expropriation' pre-dated anything Fo had written. Instances of non-payment, or 'auto-reduction,' occurred at a rock concert as early as 1971 when an event in Milan featuring Led Zeppelin led to prolonged and violent clashes between the police and fans demanding free entrance. The fans claimed they had a 'need for music' which no economic system had a right to deny them, and that in demanding entrance without buying a ticket they were taking control of the 'musical product'. The riots led to the banning of all rock concerts in Milan for a period. Newspaper articles at the time reported that in some neighbourhoods people took 'collective action' to loot cheese and fruit from supermarkets. In March 1973, Joan Baez went in Rome to do a concert and was asked to play free for the 'proletarians' in the Magliana district. Initially she agreed, but then backed down. *Stampa Alternativa* (Alternative Press) organised a protest and handed out leaflets which read, 'Joan Baez says yes to the masters, no to the proletarians. Tonight the police are going to massacre the proletarians who want to get in without paying. WE say no to Joan Baez . . . servant of the Yankees.'[10] This situation, with its mixture of popular resentment and street burlesque, was bound to appeal to Fo.

In addition to focusing on a new situation, *Can't Pay? Won't Pay!* dramatised those basic human urges he always identified as in *commedia dell'arte* or in the theatre of Ruzzante. He had long been fascinated by how certain street performers and writers of the late Renaissance had devised mechanisms and gags which wrapped the basic appetites for food, shelter and sex inside comic situations and now invited people to see parallels between his own play and 'the old Venetian and Neapolitan popular farces (in which) the basic key is hunger. To resolve the atavistic problem of appetite, the initial, instinctive solution is for everyone to look after number one, but this can be switched into a need to act collectively, to organise and to struggle together, not simply to survive but to live in the fullest sense of the term . . .'[11]

However, *Can't Pay? Won't Pay!* has more in common with French farce than with *commedia*, and it is no coincidence that Fo termed the new work a *pochade*, a description he had used for *The Virtuous Burglar* in the fifties. The plot has a slickness and deftness which had been absent from his assembly-line products, giving it the quickfire, hurry-scurry of Feydeau, as well as the relentless momentum, breathless busyness and non-stop rhythm farce requires. The action unravels through endless twists and turns, as Dario closes in on the various characters in turn, allowing each to make their contribution to the situation. There was also a greater balance in the writing and characterisation than had been evident for some time. Dario played Giovanni, and Franca his wife, Antonia, but these two do not dominate the stage to the exclusion of the others. It would be possible – just – to read the play and wonder which part Dario had written for himself. It is interesting to speculate if this too was a consequence of the break-up of the old-style *La Comune*. Now that he was directing a standard theatrical troupe he could count on the experience and skill of his fellow actors.

As a bonus, in this work Fo restrained his tendency towards pulpiteering. The politics arose from the fantasy of the plot, although that did not make the politics any less dangerous, as the police presence at various points on the tour testified. The play is rooted in the conditions experienced by two working class couples living in unremarkable city flats. Antonia and Margherita enter burdened with foodstuffs 'liberated' from the local supermarket in the fracas which followed the discovery that prices had been raised overnight. A voice was heard to declaim

'You're fully entitled to pay what is right! This is like a strike, except that in a strike the workers have to give up their pay . . . but this time it's the bosses who'll have to cough up something.'[12] Antonia's exhilaration is tempered by her fear of explaining what she has done to her husband, Giovanni who, as a stalwart member of the Communist party, is never willing to deviate from the party line. The PCI in the mid-seventies was more papist than any Pope, to employ the Italian expression, and had adopted the puritan ethics of the secular Humanists and the law-abiding politics of caution and moderation. Politics aside, Giovanni is the incarnation of the good-hearted, gormless, credulous idiot who has provided entertainment on European stages from the days of Aristophanes or Plautus. 'You can tell him any load of cobblers you like and he'll swallow it,' says Antonia of her husband.

Giovanni and Luigi make up a Laurel and Hardy double act. Giovanni arrives home to find a police raid underway, and is astonished to find himself in conversation with a Maoist constable who recites from the Little Red Book, and whispers that at heart he is in sympathy with the militant direct action of the housewives. The revolution is still far off, and meantime a man, especially one from the poor south of Italy, has to eat. The various situations interlock. The women conceal their booty by wrapping it around their stomachs making them look pregnant. Giovanni hears of the raid on the store, and tells Antonia that, unthinkable though it is, if she had been involved in those scenes he would be driven into a homicidal rage. Thereafter the play proceeds at the pace of a fast-forwarded movie, swinging between two centres of focus. Giovanni is hungry and unwittingly devours cat food; he sees Margherita no longer pregnant and believes a tale that a new device is available for the transplant of unborn babies but fears that his wife, in her innocence, may have offered her womb to help out her friend. There is, within the logic of farce, a totally satisfactory stitching together of all these bizarre dangling threads, and even a happy ending when Giovanni sees the error of his blind support for the party.

There was more to the play than was realised at the time. Contemporary critics concentrated, not surprisingly, on the advocacy of 'auto-reduction' and the championing of the actions of the housewives in Milan. Only a few mentioned the continued anti-Communist party satire, and none drew attention to the wholly new element, which was the first tentative blossoming of feminism. Franca Rame's thinking about woman's estate had been evolving with the emergence of feminism in Italy and the parts Fo wrote for her reflected this evolution. *Can't Pay? Won't Pay!* is Fo's first feminist play. Antonia takes the initiatives; it is she who denounces the inadequacy of the party line, and she who develops fantastic tales needed to gull the police. Certainly, the dilemmas she faces are not those feminist writers were then addressing, nor those which would appear in Franca's own work shortly afterwards, but Antonia shows herself a plucky individualist who has emerged from the shadow of her husband to adopt her own independent positions. This independence was not what was becoming known as 'separatism;' the independence was a claim for women's rights and autonomy inside the family. Antonia is not Ibsen's Nora, and no such figure would appear in her theatre. Franca's independent woman will always remain wife, mother and family woman. Similarly, the discussion of the position of women in society made in this play assumes an orthodox Marxist perspective. Oppression is a function of class, not gender.

The prospect of tragedy striking Dario and Franca was never completely absent. On the night of 21-22 December, a bomb exploded outside the Palazzina Liberty. According to the police, it was an amateurish device, but it caused considerable commotion and shattered windows in the vicinity. Several people sleeping in the park had to be treated for shock. Dario's views still aroused violent responses.

Can't Pay? Won't Pay! was revived at the Palazzina in 1980, and excerpts of it were broadcast on Italian television as part of *Trasmissione forzata*, a series of variety programmes Dario and Franca co-presented in 1988. It was also the first of Fo's plays to reach the British stage, and thus the first to be subjected to a very British process of transposition, adaptation, cutting and reworking to make it conform to the director's notion of what a British audience can cope with. A translator was asked to prepare what British theatre calls 'a literal translation', and the stage version was prepared by Bill Colvill and Rob Walker. Walker was resident director at the Half Moon theatre, and directed the play when it was staged in 1978 under the title *We Can't Pay? We Won't Pay!* The English version retained, and perhaps even heightened, the comedy but it never achieved anything deeper than belly laughs. Most of the directors who stage Fo are drawn to him by a meeting of minds over political viewpoints as much as by an admiration of his stagecraft, but rarely attain the balance between, in Fo's own terminology, laughter and anger, or between tragedy and farce.

In 1981, after *Accidental Death of an Anarchist* proved a hit in the West End, the other play too was given a West End run, under the snappier, and now accepted, English title of *Can't Pay? Won't Pay!* which later became the slogan of the anti-poll tax campaigners. The play was revived in Milan in a substantially revised form in the aftermath of the 2008 financial crisis, and produced in Britain with the new title *Low Pay? Won't Pay!*[13] For a moment, to the delight of Giovanni, it seemed that capitalism was on the point of collapse and a new world was in the making. Dario directed this production in Milan, and turned his fire on financiers, bankers and on Silvio Berlusconi, who was by then the new force in Italian politics.

CHAPTER 9

Home and Abroad

There was consternation, accompanied by jeering hilarity in the more effete of Italy's literary salons, when the news broke in February 1975 that, on the initiative of the Swedish Pen Club, Dario Fo had been nominated for the Nobel Prize for Literature. He himself regarded the nomination as a venture into Never-never Land, and dismissed the proposal:

> You'll never see me in tails; it doesn't suit me. As to bows, I have become famous for my aversion to reverences and genuflections of any kind. This business of the Nobel Prize is really funny. I can just imagine the faces of certain prefects, magistrates and politicians of my acquaintance. There they are, beavering away to shut me up and clap handcuffs on my wrists, and the Swedes pull off a gag like that! Can you imagine how embarrassed they would be if they had to arrest a Nobel Prize winner?

When he was asked if he would accept the prize if it were offered, he fended off the question:

> It would be really amusing, almost like one of my own comedies. Can you see me in Stockholm? The king summons me, I present myself: "Good morning, sir, no I mean King, no I mean Majesty . . . (What the hell am I supposed to say?) There's a prize

for me? Thanks, what an honour for my country! By the way, are you aware that in Italy they chase me out of all the places I go to perform, and that I'm involved in a lawsuit with Milan City Council because they don't want to let me have an abandoned building that's due for demolition? But who cares? I have won the prize and I am cheered up . . . Give us a kiss, your Majesty." Can you imagine a more grotesque scene?[1]

The more sober reasons he gave why he would never win the Nobel Prize were, firstly that the award of the Nobel had, like every other such honour, political overtones, and that therefore 'it's highly unlikely that they are going to give it to a pain-in-the-arse like me,' and secondly, that while other playwrights like Shaw, Pirandello, O'Neill and Beckett had received the award, his theatre was not written 'to pass into history. I write and perform satire linked to the events of the day, to everyday news. They are scripts which immediately burn up their contents.'[2] Dario's opinions varied on whether or not he believed he merited status as author of works of enduring value. At other times, he stated firmly, and with justification, that his texts were more than rough sketches, that they had merit in a popular tradition, which was distinct from, but not inferior to, that of the standard repertoire of classics.

In 1975 the award went to Saul Bellow, but history has its own ironies. In due course, the Swedish Royal Academy would come round to his point of view on the popular tradition, and in due course Dario would be happy to don tails and bow before the King of Sweden. Equally, in 1997 his comments and ridicule would be trotted out and used against him when a renewed nomination was accepted by the Swedish Royal Academy.

Now that the Palazzina Liberty was established as company base, the project of re-establishing a national 'alternative circuit' was de facto abandoned. By the year's end there were 85,000 members of the new *La Comune* in Milan alone. Any other professional or city theatre in Italy would have regarded half that number as a sign of success and popularity. Other companies and campaigners made use of the venue, and in the run-up to the municipal elections of June 1975, left wing parties used it for meetings and conferences. The venue was still controversial. At an event in May, Romano Canosa and Antonio Bevere, two magistrates who were members of the left-leaning Democratic Magistracy, announced their doubts about proposed measures on public order. Their speeches were reported and the two were reprimanded by their superiors.

Turbulence continued on the streets of the city. On 15 May, a group of Red Brigades terrorists burst into the office of Massimo De Carolis, Dario's opponent on the City Council. He was subjected to summary trial for misdeeds against the people, found guilty and shot in the leg. In the prevailing savagery of the terrorist campaign, De Carolis was lucky. A month later, Margherita Cagol, known as 'Mara', one of the founders of the Red Brigades, was killed after a shoot-out with policemen who had stumbled on her hide-out while searching in the Monferrato hills for a kidnap victim.

Franca was still the object of newspaper speculation about supposed links with terrorism. According to one story mysteriously leaked to sympathetic journalists, witnesses had reported a certain resemblance between Franca Rame and the woman who drove the getaway car on the evening of the kidnap of Mario Sossi back in 1974. The woman had blonde hair, and that obviously clinched the matter. A Milanese daily, *La Notte*, ran a story in May saying that the police were closing in on her, and even implying that she was the real financier of the Red Brigades. Franca issued a statement denying it and pointing out that on the night in question she had been 500 miles away performing in public. Although exhausted by endless dealings with the law and lawyers, she raised an action against the journalist and the editor of the paper, which issued an apology.

The general election campaign of 1975 brought Dario back to the television screens for the first time since he had walked out on *Canzonissima* in 1962. The Democratic Party for Proletarian Unity invited him to appear in a party political broadcast. Being broadly sympathetic, he accepted, but made it known that he maintained his independence and was not a member of the party. Although appearing with sober politicians, he clowned in his own satirical, grotesque style, mocking opponents but also raising the issues of the moment including arbitrary arrest and questions of law and order. In a reassuring tone, he promised that if the Left won, they would be gentle with the Christian Democrats. 'If we win, we will allow them back onto the TV screens in thirteen years.' The Establishment was piqued. 'Politicians of other parties were outraged,' wrote Dario. 'What's going on? An actor, a song and dance man coming here to steal our job, speaking to people in a language they can understand . . .' Parliament rushed through emergency legislation, forbidding singing or acting on party political broadcasts.[3]

Dario also included in the broadcast excerpts from the play he was preparing, *The Kidnapping of Fanfani*. Amintore Fanfani was one of the founding fathers of the DC and held the office of Prime Minister on six occasions. In 1963, he led the 'opening to the Left' which brought the Socialist party into the government coalition with the Christian Democrats, but thereafter, he shifted to the Right. More than Andreotti or Moro or any of the other chieftains of the DC, he was identified as the principal enemy of the new Left and strongest spokesman for reactionary forces. The Bertani publishing house of Verona produced at that period many militant works on left-wing political philosophy and on conditions in Italian factories, and had become the quasi-official publisher of *La Comune*. Its version of *The Kidnapping of Fanfani* was accompanied by an apparatus of articles and analytic pieces explaining why Fanfani was an especially dangerous opponent and denouncing policies associated with him. The prologue described him as 'incarnating Fascist corporativism and Catholic neo-corporativism', and identified him as the leader of a tendency inside the DC which was using the struggle against terrorism as a cover for a sinister campaign of 'pre-emptive militarisation of the country . . . and of the imposition of a 'Chilean solution' on the workers' movement.'

A curiosity of some interest is an article which appeared in *Il Manifesto* on 29 November 1973, entitled 'Supposing They kidnapped Fanfani?' Whether Dario got the idea from the newspaper or not, the fantasy kidnap of Fanfani was the theme of his play. The writing was completed in eight days and the play, which opened on 5 June 1975, was intended as a contribution to the election campaign. Lacking the finish of *Can't Pay? Won't Pay!*, the new work is a throwback to the off-the-cuff, rough-and-ready lampoons Dario had staged in previous years. Fanfani is kidnapped at the opening of a charity event to raise money for Vietnamese children, but it transpires that the kidnapping was the work not of the Red Brigades but of the Christian Democrats. The plight of the party is so desperate that their only way of warding off defeat in the forthcoming elections is to appeal for a sympathy vote.

Once unleashed, Dario's inventiveness careers off under its own steam, sparking against rocks and knocking bark off trees. He once said that every good playwright is a good thief, and where he cannot create, he borrows. On this occasion, he borrowed from an incident during the kidnapping of J Paul Getty, when captors clipped off a piece of his ear and sent it to the family. Fanfani's kidnappers report that the press is sceptical about the seizure, leading party colleagues to suggest that one of his ears would be enough to convince them. Mixing whimsy and malice, Dario has the gang find refuge in a convent, where the nuns specialise in abortion. Fanfani is disguised as a woman, and, in an echo of similar situations in earlier plays, has his stomach pumped up until he gives birth to a black-shirted puppet. The exertions are such that Fanfani dies and ascends to heaven, where the Madonna, played by Franca, berates him and his party for their crimes. She also prophesies that their days are numbered and that the international working class will shortly spew them and their like out of office. Fanfani awakes to discover that it was all a dream, and here the initial version ended. In rehearsal, however, Fo rethought the finale, and introduced a double bluff. Fanfani wakes up alive and on earth but facing two armed gangsters dispatched by his party colleague, Giulio Andreotti, who is convinced that Fanfani's kidnap will indeed guarantee victory for the DC. As he is dragged off, Fanfani cries out that it is all useless since 'they will have their revolution anyway . . . it will all come true, all come true'. Whatever disappointments he may have endured from his comrades, Dario still had no doubt that the red revolution was at hand. 'It is on this point that I cannot agree with the parties of the traditional left or with the Communist party,' he wrote. 'I believe in the creativity of the struggles, in the fact that silently, perhaps underground, even in Italy, everything is in readiness for the great clash.'[4]

What captured attention was the brio of the production and the wit of the devices employed to excoriate Fanfani, who was diminished in the most literal sense. The real point of the play was its merciless evisceration of the DC as a whole, but Fanfani was more than a symbol of the party. Like the great satirists of history, Juvenal or Jonathan Swift, Dario was motivated by *saeva indignatio*, and did not shrink from violent, derisive, ad hominem malice. He took every opportunity to demean his target, and Fanfani lent himself to such treatment. Short of stature, slightly stout and famously choleric, he had an off-balance physique which delighted cartoonists. To find a means of exaggerating and reproducing in comic form Fanfani's physical oddity, he delved into *commedia dell'arte* where, in what one critic described as an 'extraordinary case of reincarnation,' he discovered that there had existed the stock-character of a dwarf called Fanfanicchio. Dario played Fanfani, and created the dwarf effect by having a plank placed a few feet above the stage, while he put shoes on his hands and a tiny pair of baggy trousers over his arms. His head and that part of his upper body which remained on view made a diminutive human being, whose arms were provided by another actor. It was a *tour de force*, recognised as such even by those, on this occasion a majority, who did not admire the play. 'It is difficult,' writes the critic Franco Quadri, 'to convey by other than a direct statement the monstrous acting skills of Fo as dwarf, weaving his way through dances, scratching his nose with his shoes, launching himself into flight or strolling along the walls, never forgetting (the character's) fixation with law and order or his Napoleonic poses.'[5]

The Left made substantial progress at the polls, although the revolution remained on the far side of the horizon. De Carolis, happily recovered from the terrorist assault, was upset by the outcome of the vote, and was quoted as saying that 'it is clear that a society in which girls can go around without bras is not likely to produce nuns'.[6] This delphic comment was the subject of much puzzled and whimsical debate, even if its literal truth was scarcely in dispute. The socialist Aldo Aniasi became mayor of Milan, and at the time things seemed likely to be easier for Fo in his dealings with the Council in the still unresolved dispute over the Palazzina.

The Kidnapping of Fanfani was linked closely to the political classes in Italy, and as such had little appeal abroad. It went on tour in northern Italy, and played to eight thousand people in Turin. Fo used his visit to the city to involve himself in other causes. In July, he paid a visit to the members of an organisation calling itself the *Gruppo Abele*, who were then on hunger strike, to express support for their work in rehabilitating addicts. The visit was the first public demonstration of interest in drugs, an issue which was increasingly to occupy the mental and emotional energy of Dario and Franca in coming years. The group provided meeting places for users and drug-workers but also dissented from the voguish cult of drug use in western society, arraigning not only pushers but poets, singers and intellectuals. They set their sights on the likes of Timothy Leary, Bob Dylan, the Beatles, the Rolling Stones, as well as the whole beat or hippie culture, not to mention surrealism, Rimbaud, William Burroughs or the brand of Indian mysticism which George Harrison had made popular among western youth. The use of drugs, they reckoned, was the consequence not only of poverty, hopelessness and unemployment, but also of aspects of the prevailing youth culture.

Also in Turin, Dario and Franca joined in protests in support of the lawyer, Giambattista Lazagna, imprisoned in the town of Fossano. The story of Lazagna was a curious one, even for those baffling times. Under the pseudonym, 'Saetta' (arrow), he had attained legendary status as a partisan leader in the later phases of the Resistance. After the war, he set up a legal practice in Genoa, but in March 1972, to general disbelief, he was arrested for supposed association with terrorists. In May, police investigating the activities of Giangiacomo Feltrinelli let it be known that there had been connections between Feltrinelli and Lazagna, although it was never shown that this acquaintanceship was linked to terrorist acts. In September 1974, Lazagna was again arrested as a result of information passed to the police by Silvano Girotto, known as 'Brother machine-gun'. Of all the exotic fauna which flourished in the undergrowth where terrorists, self-serving criminals, double-dealing informers, mythomaniacs and assorted conspiracy theorists fed each other's diseased fantasies, none was more bizarre than 'Brother machine-gun'. This man had genuinely been a Franciscan friar but left the order to move to South America, where he joined, or claimed to have joined, some guerrilla grouping. He returned to Italy wearing as a war medal his past as a combatant and was able to make the acquaintance of leading figures among terrorists. He turned informer, and gave information which led to the arrest of two of the founders of the Red Brigades, Renato Curcio and Alberto Franceschini. Leaflets found in Bergamo allegedly demonstrated links between Girotto, Lazagna and the Red Brigades. This link was expanded in the press to the point where Lazagna was indicated as the evil genius behind the whole left-wing terror movement.

His case was taken up by Franca's Red Aid, but by the time Dario and Franca were in Turin, Lazagna had been in jail for nine months. They joined in a march from Turin to Fossano, where pictures show them standing outside the prison with their fists raised, shouting slogans of solidarity with the detainees they regarded as political prisoners. Those inside replied with shouts of gratitude. Dario gave a statement to the press, saying that 'Lazagna is a fundamental step in the repression. He is in prison on the basis of a political frame-up which originated with the false accusations made by Girotto. But we are not marching only to demand the immediate release of Lazagna. He is only the tip of the iceberg, because the repression has also struck representatives of Democratic Magistracy, as well as lawyers and workers. Italian democracy cannot allow this game to go on.'

Dario remained in the news all throughout that summer. In *Il Giorno*, the columnist Giancarlo Vigorelli published an attack on *The Kidnapping of Fanfani*, but thirty-eight journalists published an open letter protesting against the 'neo-Fascist tone' of the article in question. It was an odd incident in itself, showing how little the freedom of speech is respected when it is expressed as freedom for awkward views, but also showing the level of support Dario commanded. Things were easing for him in other respects too. The democratic Left had made substantial advances in the 70s, and the Communist party held, or at least shared, power in Milan, Turin, Genoa, Rome and Naples. Opinion polls gave the party a commanding lead for the general elections due in 1976. The Socialist party had representatives on various state holding companies, and one of these Beniamino Finocchiaro, who was on the board of RAI, the Italian Broadcasting authority, chose this moment to wonder whether Dario should be allowed back onto the television screens. 'Thirteen years ago, Dario Fo interrupted his participation with *Canzonissima* because the scripts of which he was author had been censured. In the new course of the company would this be possible? Censorship, I mean. The Chairman says not.' The suggestion was not immediately followed up.

On 20 August, a group comprising Dario, Franca, Jacopo and about twenty members of *La Comune* set off to visit Maoist China. Other members of the party included Mario Capanna, a leader of the 1968 student movement who had recently been elected to the Lombard Regional Council, and Hrayr Terzian, a psychiatrist and director of a mental hospital in Verona. 'To know, to understand how the Chinese live and work, you would probably need three lives, while we have only three weeks at our disposal', said Dario on their departure. 'We can only promise not to waste even one minute of our time.' The pre-arranged itinerary took them to Shanghai, Beijing, Canton, Nanjing, Tianjin and Jinan.

From his many references to Mao and Maoism in debates on theatre and politics, it is clear that at this time China was another pleasance where Dario's benevolent utopianism flourished, and that the Cultural Revolution was an essential moral, political and aesthetic point of reference. He was not alone in thinking that way in the seventies. Men who are desperate for a solution are easily persuaded because they wish desperately to be persuaded, wrote J K Galbraith in *The Age of Uncertainty*. Bolshevism having self-evidently failed, large swathes of opinion in the west were in thrall to a fantasy of the Great Helmsman and attributed to China the legendary status occupied in antiquity by Atlantis. Devotees saw Mao as the anchorite or the benevolent ascetic who, in the Cultural Revolution, had stepped down from his throne to lead a campaign against deviation, corruption, bureaucracy and even against his own regime. Maoism, and the cult of the Little Red Book, provided the underpinnings to the politico-philosophical convictions of the European, especially French and Italian, New Left. Romantic Maoism became the jargon of a generation.

Dario's case was more complex, but party and people in China were recipients of transferred loyalty. Dario and Franca went to China in the frame of mind of pilgrims on the milky way to Santiago de Compostela. 'China is today the highest moment of socialist experience in the world . . . in Europe the cultural revolution has determined the nature of contestation,' he wrote. When Dario and Franca got there, they saw what they expected to see. They accepted what they were told, found confirmation of all they already believed, and came home with their faith nourished.

At the time of their visit, China was still shaken by the aftershocks of the Cultural Revolution, while the upper echelons of the party, aware that Mao could not survive much longer, were engaged in jockeying for power. The most recent campaigns launched by the cadres of the party had identified as enemies, however improbable they appeared as bedfellows, the philosopher Confucius and Lin Piao, a party functionary once close to Mao but who, after losing out in a palace putsch, had fled and had died in a plane crash near the Soviet border. Much more is now known about the career of Mao than could have been known by Franca and Dario at the time of their visit. The portrait which emerges from recent biographies[7] gives Mao rank among the great politician-criminals of the twentieth century, alongside Hitler, Stalin or Pol Pot. In the seventies, however, little was known of the hundreds of thousands who were slaughtered, tortured, maimed, exiled, imprisoned or driven to suicide as a result of his activities, nor of the up to twenty million who died of famine as a result of the campaigns masterminded by Mao and his inner coterie.

This was not the China Dario and Franca saw. 'Over there they are constructing a new humanity. I know, it has been said many times, now it is almost a cliché, but it is really true. I have been to Russia, to Eastern Europe, to Cuba but what I saw in China cannot be compared with the reality of any other country.'[8] Dario had watched China from afar, in the spirit in which William Wordsworth, Beethoven or Ugo Foscolo watched the unfolding of the French Revolution. He believed himself in the enviable position of witnessing a major, irreversible shift not merely in society but in the very nature of humanity. Society was being transformed from predatory capitalism to a gentler form of co-operation, bringing closer that state of justice and happiness to which human beings had always aspired. He recounted uncritically the history of the Cultural Revolution as it had been recounted to him.

> A university lecturer, who lived through the entire revolution, one evening talked us through the various 'passages' of the revolution. There was nothing random about it; the revolutionary movement was carried forward in a precise way by the Communist party and by Mao. It all began with some violent criticisms of a film, which featured a character who lived centuries ago, and who was portrayed as a saviour of the fatherland. In reality, he was a leading bourgeois. Mao wrote some important letters, of considerable weight, about the film. Shortly afterwards, a series of articles came out, all signed by a group calling itself "the three families", in which they advanced some considerations on girls' tresses, on fashion, and they hoped for the return to certain forms of hair style and to all that, in journalistic language, goes under the name of 'colour'. Life, they say, is not only class struggle, but also taste, nostalgia for green days gone. Finally there was the famous comedy, *The Mandarin*, I say famous because it marked the beginning of the Cultural Revolution.[9]

There ensued, in Dario's account, a mass mobilisation of between 90 and 150 thousand people from all over China who converged on Beijing in support of the Cultural Revolution. So numerous were they that Mao found himself compelled to use a car to inspect them all. Groups from the far left, particularly around the universities, took advantage of the situation created by the mass assemblies, and there were clashes leading to deaths among the workers, who 'did not react'. The Communist party took a low profile in these encounters, 'unlike other Communist parties, thereby showing its trust in the working class.' In the rail yards in Shanghai, Dario was told by a fireman, 'who spoke as though he was a story-teller,' of the resistance the workers put up to the bureaucrats and directors. The central role was played by 'cultural propaganda, that is, by cinema, newspapers, great debates in assemblies, theatre, story-

192

tellers. All these means were adopted to make people understand the importance of the fight against revisionism. There were stand-offs between railway workers and some directors, there were clashes, some directors went so far as to block trains and ships. The workers reacted in the only way possible, making propaganda in the packed station at Shanghai, among the thousands of passengers waiting to depart, sometimes even climbing onto the roofs of carriages. Finally they managed to bring to their knees the directors who had been attempting in every way possible to create disorder, difficulties, chaos, anything to impede the advance of the revolutionary movement.'[10]

The lack of critical independence Fo displayed in the many interviews he gave on his return is startling. His glowing account of the devotion of the Chinese people for Mao and the Communist party reads like the life of a saint in a devotional manual, but all throughout his life, the coruscating satirist dismayed by injustice or abuse of power is the twin of an idealist in search of some lost purity. If it is the former who is better known through his major works from *Accidental Death of an Anarchist* to *Free Marino!*, the latter is always present in the folds of the pages. It is a pity that the utopian Fo was given fullest voice in a meeting not with some imaginary Shangri-La or El Dorado of his own devising, but with a historical land in which real people lived and suffered. In the China of the Cultural Revolution, he found a society which satisfied his aspirations. Whether it corresponded with the historical China of 1975 is a different matter, but if Fo was a fool, he was a holy fool. Unlike the fellow-travellers in Stalinist Russia, he did not justify executions, the imprisonment of dissidents, the state persecution of minorities. He coined no smart slogans about necessary crimes or about cracking eggs to make omelettes. He simply did not see the darker, more cruel side.

His disenchanted, satirical stance vis à vis power wholly deserted him when the holder of power was Mao. Years later, when much more was known about Mao's years in power than in 1975, he still replied when asked by a journalist for an example of a politician with a sense of humour: 'Mao Tse-tung, crude but with a sense of self-irony.'[11] On his return to Italy, he gave many interviews, and it was clear that Maoist China was all that the west could and should be:

The first thing that struck me was the matter of merchandise. Here, man is an object, a piece of merchandise in fact, who tends to sell himself at the highest possible price at every moment of his life: when he offers his labour, when he is looking for a wife, even when he is getting dressed. With us, there is a sharp division between concepts of good, morality and relationships of production. In China, on the other hand, eating, drinking, getting dressed, principles of morality are all part and parcel of the same thing. There is a profound conception of life which determines everything. There is the new man because there is a new philosophy.[12]

When he was asked if there was much opportunity in China for the expression of dissent, Fo replied in enthusiastic terms about the spread of liberty of speech:

It seemed to me that there is ample space (for dissent). You will understand this immediately from the debates, if you are a bit alert. Everyone says exactly what they think. So the bureaucrat and the real revolutionary emerge, the one who would like to apply the principles of Maoism as though they were pieces on an assembly line and the one who tries to get to grips with the reality. In any case, there is a real confrontation, no blah-blah.

In a meeting with the Jinan Artistic Company, the spokesperson told Fo and the *La Comune* actors that they had been once misled by 'the revisionist line of Liu Shao-chi, and for a time had gone down the wrong path; we did not succeed in satisfying the needs of a socialist society. Through the struggles of the Cultural Revolution and the campaign of criticism against Confucius and Lin Piao, the artists of our company have acquired new vigour and have transformed themselves. Under the direction of the party, they take as a weapon Marxism-Leninism and the thought of Mao Tse-tung, and undertake to follow the orientation indicated by Chairman Mao and to put "art and literature at the service of the workers, of the peasants and of the soldiers".'[13] This was delicate ground for Dario, who had struggled against state censorship and against the imposition of party line. He replied only that *La Comune*

194

aimed to be a company run by 'workers, peasants and progressives, by those who moved forward the struggles in Italy. The Chinese Cultural Revolution was the principal reason for our decision.' He also told them that 'the repression under way by the judicial system, by the authorities is extremely violent, and many comrades are being arrested.'[14]

Having been invited principally as a man of theatre, he had meetings with fellow actors and theatre directors in China. Strangely in none of his first interviews does he mention hearing the tale which would later become *Story of a Tiger*, one of his best known monologues. He and his colleagues acted and sang in many factory canteens, in streets, in private houses. In the Bejing Opera, he performed the *grammelot*, in cod English, of the American technocrat and his failure to build a rocket which could take off from the ground, together with extracts from *The Kidnapping of Fanfani*. By his own account, the piece met with great success, and everywhere they went, they were met by people who demanded 'Do us your Fanfani!' The performance was greeted by laughter and questions – 'But is it really true? It can't be! Did he really say those things on the defence of the race? Is he really so sure of himself? Couldn't we invite him to China? That would be funny!' The joke was on Dario when, later that year, the vicissitudes of global politics caused the Chinese authorities to issue an invitation to Senator Fanfani together with Franz Josef Strauss and other representatives of the European Right. Fo wrote a humorous piece, telling Fanfani not to be troubled if during visits to schools children came running up to him to see if he was kept moving by some trick device.

Fo had his own beliefs on popular theatre and performance techniques confirmed by the practices he found current in China. 'In Nankin, I saw a worker perform by himself in a square, without mask or make-up, in front of a small crowd. In other words, he was performing a Chinese *Mistero buffo*.'[15] 'The area around Shanghai is filled with story-tellers who recount new and ancient stories, or tell tales from the newspapers. For instance, there is a jester, alone on the stage, who reproduces, playing all the parts himself, a trip in a tram round the city ring road: (he recounts) what the people say, comments which have nothing to do with politics, the pushing and shoving, discussions

195

about work, salaries, the struggle against Lin Piao. There is one man who believes that Confucius is a party functionary, another who has not understood a word of the recent instructions. All of this is done in a grotesque, exhilarating style, accompanied by rolls of drums which convey the rhythm of the situation, and with the underlying indication that that is the correct line. It is something which reminded me to an extraordinary extent of my work on popular theatre, *Mistero buffo*, for example.'[16] It appeared that on all important points there was a complete identification between the theatre performances and beliefs of Dario Fo in Italy and the practice of his Maoist counterparts in China as sanctioned by the Cultural Revolution.

On his return, Fo became embroiled in controversy with the film director Michelangelo Antonioni, who in 1972 had released the film, *Chung Kuo*, for which he had received the assistance of the Chinese authorities. The work was seen by critics as a return to an earlier documentary style which he had abandoned for films such as *Blow-up* or *Zabriskie Point*, although Antonioni himself preferred to describe his work as 'travel notes'. The voice-over is largely descriptive of what the camera records, with little attempt at analysis or contextualisation of a society or culture which Antonioni, as he readily admitted, lacked the knowledge to penetrate in any depth. The film had aroused the indignation of the Chinese, and on his return Dario made himself spokesman for their discontent. The core of the dispute concerned the possibility of understanding Chinese culture granted its profound divergences from western ideas and assumptions, and the interpretation of the political conduct and turn of mind of Chinese people.

'Rather than phoney, Antonioni's China was escapist, he limited himself to providing local colour on things without explaining them. And in China, this is easy, granted that everything is uncovered, exposed to daylight',[17] wrote Dario, who had made use of film material to prepare himself for the trip. He claimed that Antonioni had given a naive picture of the 'candour and dignity' of the Chinese, while he had found a people 'filled with irony, subtle and profound, proud and, when they set their mind to it, malicious.' Antonioni issued a bad tempered retort, accusing Fo of oversimplification and arrogance in claiming to have grasped the nature of China after a visit of twenty-three days. 'The actor was there a few days, and on his return to the west, all the enigmas on Mao's regime have vanished,' wrote Antonioni. Fo countered by berating Antonioni for producing a set of commonplace banalities which had caused gratuitous offence. He pulled from his knowledge of folk wisdom an Italian proverb which ran: 'Someone who goes looking for frogs, will perhaps find frogs; he is not likely to find mushrooms, which do not grow in ponds. Which means that when you want to find something, you should not let chance take you there . . .'[18] This is probably good, if gnomic, advice, but it is advice Dario himself could have taken to heart in rethinking his own experiences in China. He had found the frogs he was searching for, but missed the poisonous mushrooms surrounding the pond.

CHAPTER 10

Dealing With Drugs

The mid-seventies brought no abatement of the turbulence in Milan. 'Between the years 1974 and 1977, the city experienced difficult hours,' wrote the journalist Giorgio Bocca.

> There were clashes with the Fascists: mile-long marches which paralyse the centre and give foreign tourists the impression of a revolutionary Milan, while it is nothing more than neurotic. Everywhere proletarian circles and free radio stations spring up . . . in Milan more than in other cities the risky interdependence between new left culture and the Movement appears. In the city and its hinterland the most important extra-parliamentary periodicals are concentrated . . . it is not possible to know how far the professors behind these reviews, in particular those with explicitly revolutionary programmes, realise how much their opinions, their ideas impact on the Movement.'[1]

Demonstrations which always threatened to erupt into violence, continued apace. In January 1976, during a demonstration against the Shah of Iran, lorries were burnt in the centre of Milan. In February the Central Station was immobilised for hours until the police made a baton charge into ranks of the strikers. More serious, but small scale, events involving the beating-up of individuals or the throwing of home

198

made Molotov cocktails were so frequent as scarcely to merit detailed reporting in the press.

New groups began to show their hand and different forms of protest were used. On 17 January 1976, a group of thirty feminists stormed the cathedral, while in February, violent scuffles lasting several hours followed a 'happening' jointly organised by various alternative factions to coincide with a religious ceremony. Julian Beck's company, Living Theatre, added to the disruption of day-to-day living during a return visit to Milan in March. Their anti-nuclear show performed in the Galleria near Piazza Duomo involved bodies being laid out end to end. The company also appeared, together with Dario and Franca and a left-wing pop group calling themselves Stormy Six, at a factory on the outskirts of Milan occupied by striking workers. Dario and Franca were still subject to threats and harassment, and if they coped well enough, others surrounding them found it a greater strain. The warehouse of Giorgio Bertani, publisher of Dario's plays, was set on fire on more than one occasion, and he and his family received several anonymous, threatening telephone calls. The accumulated problems proved too much for Bertani, who in March attempted to take his own life, although the bullet missed his heart and he survived.

Militant action was not limited to Milan. Rome's homeless occupied some of the many empty buildings scattered around the city. The squatters were acting in the spirit of *Can't Pay? Won't Pay!* and expected, and received, full-hearted support from Dario and Franca, who in January 1976, performed in the open area in the centre of the occupied flats. In the same month, the couple took part in a midnight demonstration outside San Vittore prison in Milan after word got about that the Red Brigades leader, Renato Curcio, was about to be moved. Curcio had briefly escaped, but was back in captivity after an armed raid on his flat. His stay in San Vittore was brief, since he was moved by the authorities after a mysterious incident inside the prison in which three alleged terrorists were stabbed in the course of disturbances. Six prisoners and a prison guard were charged in connection with the assault. A lawyer, Sergio Spazzali, who had worked for Red Aid, was also among the intended victims, and only escaped injury because he was in the shower when his cell door was broken down by the attackers. The demonstration was concerned with prison conditions as much as with the transfer of Curcio.[2]

The occupation of Palazzina Liberty was still a matter of political debate in Milan's council chambers, particularly after the return of Massimo De Carolis to active politics when he recovered from his assault by the Red Brigades. Some socialist councillors had been seen at shows, but officially the Council was still intent on repossessing the building. De Carolis raised the question of modifications to the Palazzina interior for which no official permission had been requested, and went on to accuse the new municipal office bearers of not pursuing the action against *La Comune* with due diligence. 'In the meanwhile, Dario Fo continues to produce his shows (his is the only company in Milan which has its own venue provided gratis, at the expense of the City Council), not to mention the conferences where it is explained that the Council drugs children in the nurseries (conference held at Palazzina Liberty on 8 February), or the meeting of Red Aid or the League for abortion.'

The complication for the city authorities was that Dario's residency was now viewed as a fixture by the neighbourhood committee as well as by the various groups who used the building as headquarters. *La Comune* drew its support from the constituency to which the Socialist party wished to appeal, making it difficult politically for the new Council to simply evict the company. Negotiations were opened in February between Dario and the Council, and two months later it seemed that the question had been amicably resolved. The company would end their occupation and take up residence in a new, purpose-built venue near Piazzale Cuoco. Ownership of the Palazzina would revert to the Council which would not seek retrospective rental but would offer no compensation for the restructuring work undertaken. The proposed new building would take the form of a vast, spherical geodetic structure of glass and steel, of the kind originally devised by Buckminster Fuller and made famous by its use in the Montreal Expo in 1967. When complete, it would hold 1200 spectators.

Dario's comments were moderately sanguine. 'I have only one regret. When people thought of the Palazzina Liberty, they were by now used to thinking of it as a theatre. Reaching an agreement is positive but having restored the Palazzina, the idea of starting from scratch does not fill me with enthusiasm.' Even De Carolis offered a form of support. 'I am not sorry that Fo will be moving to another Council area. I have no problems with Dario Fo as an actor; he is one of the possible components of a pluralistic society. What I did not like was that he had transformed the Palazzina into a kind of Mompracem where he did what he pleased.'[3] Unfortunately, the residents of Piazzale Cuoco did not share the prevailing optimism. The prospect of seeing a quiet, empty space converted into a bustling social centre did not appeal to everyone, particularly since the promised hurly-burly would bring with it heightened police vigilance and the threat of violence. In addition, the earmarked area had previously housed an ad hoc theatre put up by the local community. They declared themselves devastated by the 'decision which fell from on high from the Council'.[4] Dario could hardly oppose such expressions of popular culture or popular democracy, so the agreement was never ratified. *La Comune* remained in Palazzina Liberty.

There were many other legal cases pending, but the judgements were now frequently in his favour. The first break occurred on 1 April 1973, when a judge, Antonio Soda, had referred a case to the Constitutional Court to determine if Dario was justified in his argument that the police had no right to interfere with the operations of a private club. Prosecutions were being brought under a 1931 Fascist law, and the judge asked the Upper Court to decide on the rights of a citizen in a democracy whose political philosophy differed from its statutory law. The wheels of Italian justice grind exceedingly slowly, and in March 1976 the Constitutional Court had still not reported, but Dario was acquitted by a court in Pordenone after being charged in May 1970 with having prevented a public official from entering the building where *La Comune* was performing. The celebrations in the Fo camp were short lived. The prosecution entered an immediate appeal.

While not as yet in a state of disenchantment over the prospect of grand political reform, or revolution, from this period in the mid-seventies the energies of Dario and Franca were largely channelled into social projects. They both lent full support to the pro-abortion campaign, even if their high profile presence created difficulties. At one demonstration, several young women appeared on a platform to announce they had undergone abortions, but the following day they were charged by magistrates. The Palazzina housed press conferences and discussion groups on the issue, while Dario cast his public support in the form of the semi-theatrical, grotesque satire. The early versions of the bill before the Chamber of Deputies required the doctor authorising abortion to satisfy himself that the woman really wanted one. The problem, Dario suggested in a spoof dialogue he devised between a doctor and a woman, was that gynaecologists and private clinics had been living for years off the profits of semi-clandestine, illegal abortion and had no interest in seeing a public system established. In addition, he said, the proposed law required the gynaecologist to convert himself into a magistrate or police officer. He wrote a sketch where the doctor accuses the girl of two-timing her boyfriend. Since the authorities had to be pro-active and had to know who the real father was, they had filmed her every sexual or intimate act over recent months. The doctor explains.

> There was no other solution. This law which lays on the doctor, and on the doctor alone, the responsibility of deciding on abortion is either a nonsense, in which case let's forget it, or else it's serious, and then the doctor who really believes in it and wants to apply it is obliged to turn to methods which are not exactly democratic. They are an outrage to the privacy of the woman as well as requiring a kind of body-search on her. In other words – more babies and less freedom!

In a fine excess, the doctor climbs onto the window ledge and exclaims – 'Make love all you women. Who cares if you're young, mature or mere girls, because I'm filming you and have ways of checking up on you! Don't think you can escape by turning out the lights. We have infra-red film. We see everything! Every embrace is checked. Women married or unmarried. Every foetus is on file!'[5]

Dario and Franca began to take greater interest in Italy's drug problems. They had visited a group in Turin who helped addicts and on the China trip had made the acquaintance of Hrayr Terzian, a Marxist doctor who was a specialist, if an unorthodox one, in the field. They were concerned that their son Jacopo was mixing in circles in which drugs circulated freely. Years later, Dario recalled the atmosphere of those years.

> Twenty-five years ago we were at the time of the "free needle", of the first arrests for possession of "small quantities" of hashish, even for personal use. Above all these were the days of the petty moralists, of the rigid scientists who pointed their finger at young people and screamed, "Watch out! Taking grass is the quickest way to end up shooting up with heroin." Franca and I, together with the whole *La Comune* company, were still performing at the Palazzina Liberty and were constantly engaged both with agnostic spectators and with friends and comrades who were passionate about the problem of the slaughter of youth from overdoses. The most bitter debates exploded among the young, including our son, Jacopo.[6]

On 3 March, a bar near their home was attacked by a unit which left leaflets claiming that it had been selected because it was a 'centre of the heroin trade'. The document carried the slogan – All Power to the Armed Proletariat.[7] The proletariat, armed or otherwise, may have been waking up to the problem of the use and diffusion of drugs, but their self-appointed, intellectual avant-garde was not quite sure how to react.

Debates concerned threats to health or life but also exposed fissures and stresses in the whole mish-mash of ideas which made up the culture of the amorphous Movement. The disputes reflected the contrasting components of the mindset of many on the new, post-1968 Left, including members of *La Comune* – unbending political anti-capitalism on the one hand and the libertarian social and sexual attitudes of the swinging Sixties on the other. Was drug-taking a protest against exploitation or a new form of exploitation? The politicals and the hippies could make common cause on many issues; the same people turned up on demonstrations, had the same dress sense, made the same statements of non-conformism, listened to the same music and viewed the same politicians as hate-figures, but the gulf was wide. 'Drop out' urged the siren voice of Timothy Leary from California, but the injunction was rejected by those who wanted social commitment and political involvement. Drugs offered bliss and the artificial paradise Rimbaud had preached, while Marxist doctrine aimed at the creation of a real paradise for all. At this time, a more mournful voice began to make itself heard, the lament of those ordinary working people who simply saw drugs as a scourge which poisoned their neighbourhoods, made their streets unsafe, inflicted disabilities and sometimes death on their children. Dario chose to pay heed to this voice.

'I had two scripts prepared,' he recalled.[8] 'One on China, and the other a family of shack-dwellers near Piazza Duomo in Milan. I did a reading for workers and people from the neighbourhood. They told me – yes they are fine but there are more urgent problems to discuss, for instance, drugs. So I set to work and have produced this play.' The work, premiered in the Palazzina on 2 March, was eventually given the title *Mum's Marijuana is the Best*.[9] The first published version of the play was furnished with enough material to make a treatise. Like Hrayr Terzian in his essay for the volume, Dario appealed to the Chinese experience as providing the model approach. 'Look at the Chinese', he told a representative of the Campaign against the Spread of Drugs. 'They don't put addicts in prison. They've never said that after the revolution, hey presto! no more addicts.' He deplored the fact that there were no structures in Italy to help addicts who wanted to give up, but concluded that 'for me, the problem is cultural, not abstract, and must be put in those terms'.[10] Dario conducted many conversations, visited various centres and undertook a programme of research, but it was Dr. Terzian who provided him with the perspective in which, at this stage, he viewed the whole problem. He also gave him the slogan which turned the problem into one of class. 'A sentence by Terzian, a real luminary in this field, is significant: in the sub-proletariat, it is the drug which uses the individual, while among the rich it is the individual who uses the drug.' The rehearsals in the Palazzina were open to the inhabitants of the area, who felt free to drop in and make suggestions.

Mum's Marijuana is a didactic farce, a genre which Fo had forged. The plot is based on the overturning of expectations. Franca played the mother and Dario the grandfather, but it is that generation, not the rebellious young, who are using drugs of various sorts, one a recognisable herb and the other an absurdist 'scorpion's bite'. When the youthful Luigi comes home from work at mid-day, he discovers his mother and grandfather guiltily concealing traces of the drug and admitting not only to smoking it but also to growing and dealing in it. The mother, Rosetta, spokesperson for the author's opinions, has the most dynamic part. This role is another indication of the increasingly high profile accorded female characters, although it is striking that Dario can only accord such roles to the mother figure.

There are other notions swirling about. A bent policeman advances the notion that abuse of drugs is all the fault of the CIA, which 'is inside to control the whole Movement', while blaming the Chinese for the circulation of drugs. The grandfather proposes that the real problem is unemployment, hopelessness, under-education, but there is a deeper undercurrent to this play since Dario knew he was dealing with forces which surpass politics and which go to the very heart of human experience. As he told the campaigners, 'We have to pose again, in correct terms, the question – what is life? What is man? What is woman? This leads to the question – what is love, love for your own body, not hatred for your body, not suicide and especially not suicide while staying in a sitting position. If you stay sitting down, as the system wants, what are you doing? You can toss yourself off, but then you get fed up with that. You can drink, but with the rubbishy wine that's going around, you get an ulcer. At that point, drugs are only a tiny step on a path that is already marked out.'

With *Mum's Marijuana*, Dario found himself at odds with many of his youthful audience, still wedded to the view that 'pot is the symbol of a generation in revolt'. Although unswervingly instructive in purpose, it is nonetheless a confused play, and Dario later admitted that his ideas were not altogether clear in his mind at the time of writing. A lightly dramatised debate intercut with a sequence of jokes and gags, the work is dependent for its impact on a feeling of outrage which has as yet no precise focus. There are three underlying notions being advanced, but none very convincingly: that drugs are a class problem, that the powers-that-be manipulate public attitudes so as to justify wider repressive measures and that everyone is prone to taking an inappropriately moralistic stance on the question.

The play concludes on an unexpectedly Chekhovian note with two long speeches from Rosetta, which transcend all talk of Machiavellian CIA plots to ponder deeper dilemmas pertaining to human beings in a technological society. To some extent, Dario was expressing the alienation from a soulless society which Marx saw as the basis of religious sentiment and which Herbert Marcuse, the ideological brahmin of the sixties, saw as the ultimate condemnation of capitalism. He was venturing onto territory on which he had rarely trespassed previously. The emotional life is not the stuff of his theatre. The speeches were given to Franca who talks first of loneliness, and then tells an allegorical tale of three prisoners in a cell, fed by their captors only on fish and meat so hard that it cannot be chewed or digested. The first prisoner devises a way of beating the food into a mash which can be swallowed, the second files his spoon into a sharp knife with which he cuts the food into tiny segments, while the third sinks into despair and hopelessness, refuses to take any measures and grows so weak that he is on the point of death. At this point the first prisoner intervenes and prepares a mash for the dying man. After a couple of days, the second prisoner gives a hand and explains why he is scraping away all day at the prison wall with his sharpened spoon. He is cutting a hole in the cement between the bricks of the cell, so as to let in the light and afford hope of escape.

> Through the hole, and only that way, we can make our escape. But watch out! A little window with bars won't do, no matter what some people say. "Let's make do with it . . . then we'll see." No, a hole or nothing, a breach in this bastard wall . . . maybe we should knock the whole wall down . . . air, air! Keep on burrowing away . . . doing what we can until they all come flocking to give a hand . . . to knock down the wall . . . until we see the whole sky . . . all of it, great and deep as it is![11]

It is a fine, rousing flourish to bring down the curtain, implying a revolt as much against heaven as against a society which is askew. The tone must have jarred with the author himself, since this speech was cut in the greatly modified version published in 1998.

In May 1976, Dario was elected president of the Italian playwrights' federation. The post, though largely honorary, was an indication of regard from fellow writers. Franca meanwhile continued with her Red Aid work, and took up the case of Umberto Farioli. Farioli was one of those hauntingly Dostoevskian characters who emerge in the histories of terrorism, in Italy or elsewhere. Pathetically, doggedly bent as much on self-destruction as on the overthrow of the state, he had been arrested, not for the first time, the previous November for allegedly planning the kidnapping of Gianni Agnelli, a situation Dario was to use in a later play. Farioli was a semi-invalid, with a heavy limp, and the day after his arrest the Red Brigades had issued a statement saying that he was ill 'and in constant need of medication'.[12] He was refused this care in prison until Franca took up his case. She issued her own statement making it clear that she had no sympathy with the violence used and advocated by the Red Brigades, and that her involvement was purely humanitarian. Her intervention brought Farioli some relief.

The company spent June in Rome, performing in a specially constructed marquee. Aware of the criticism of some of his recent work, Dario decided against producing anything new, preferring a retrospective of productions not previously seen by the Roman public. The programme included *Mistero buffo*, *The Kidnapping*, *Mum's Marijuana*, and *Can't Pay? Won't Pay!* He was stung by the response to *Mum's Marijuana*, especially the criticism from normally well-disposed sources who feared that he was over-reaching with the unremitting demands he made of himself.

Meanwhile political opinion in Italy continued its swing to the moderate Left. The Movement and its terrorist flankers captured the headlines, but the constitutional left-wing parties were growing steadily. The Communist party increased its membership from 1,496,000 in 1969 to 1,798,000 in 1976,[13] and was generally expected to overtake its opponents in the general election scheduled for June 1976. The DC had been involved in various large-scale scandals in the mid-seventies, the most notable of which was the Lockheed Affair, which led to the resignation of President Giovanni Leone. On the other hand, there was still a widespread fear of any party carrying the label 'Communist', and during the campaign the right-wing journalist Indro Montanelli coined the memorable phrase which helped save the DC bacon – Hold your nose and vote Christian Democrat! Many did, so although the Communists succeeded in winning 34.4%, the Christian Democrats recovered to register 38.7% of the vote. The DC knew that they could not govern without PCI support, so they called on the wiliest of their politicians, Giulio Andreotti, to form a government of 'national unity'. Under the agreement, the PCI, while not formal coalition partners, had the right to be consulted before legislation was introduced, and in return offered support, or at least non-opposition, from the opposition benches. Both Dario and Franca regarded these moves with undisguised dismay

After the Roman season, the couple retired to Cesenatico for their annual summer break. Cesenatico on the Adriatic had always been a favoured resort of many Milanese, and Dario and Franca had been going regularly since they were first married. In the 1960s, they had purchased an old farm building well away from the hubbub of the beach and the sea-front promenades, and some years later were able to buy the adjoining property so as to make one spacious, luxury holiday home. In spite of the substantial amounts they had distributed to assist striking workers, to help out with the legal costs of militants facing trial or to support the various causes they espoused, they were now a wealthy couple. In addition to income from their own work as actors, they were also in receipt of royalties for performances in Italy and overseas. They built a large, private swimming pool in the land surrounding the house, although privacy was never guaranteed. Children in the immediate locality had free use of the pool and the home was always liable to be invaded by friends from the city, as well as by directors or actors from other countries who wanted an exclusive workshop on how to produce Dario's plays. In spite of that, Cesenatico was a haven where they could work and relax, and where they were accepted without fuss by the local people. It was there that Dario did much of his writing.

They could be a demanding couple. Neither of the two suffered incompetence with any gladness. When he felt he had been let down or cheated, Dario was liable to react splenetically. His polemical armoury included a sarcastic wit which he did not reserve for national politicians or internationally famed writers. Occasional correspondents in newspapers who criticised him or the causes he championed were liable to find themselves subjected to sardonic disdain. That August, he was pursued by journalists anxious to find his response to a dispute with Domenico Modugno, the poet and singer best known for his song, *Volare*. Modugno was recording for television a series of protest songs, and hoped to include both in the programme and on a disk some pieces written by Dario. Modugno's version of the disagreement was that he had proposed a programme on the riots in Bronte, the Sicilian town where, shortly after Garibaldi's landing in 1860, the inhabitants had risen against the landowners and aristocracy. Dario asked him to set to music some of his verses, and while Modugno was enthusiastic, pressure of time meant that the project was not carried to completion. Dario, on the other hand, claimed that a year earlier he and Modugno had explored the possibility of putting on a performance at Palazzina Liberty. 'The production was one of a series of artistic initiatives of ours, with the takings going to help workers who had been laid off by their employers. At the beginning, Modugno seemed enthusiastic, but when the time came for production and performance, he couldn't be traced. Now I hear that that he has made a record, but I am no longer in agreement, and I will do everything in my power to block him. What he has done is very serious and uncivil. It amounts to a form of artistic expropriation. I am sorry but I will not put up with certain kinds of behaviour. He has decided, on his own behalf, to bring to fruition a project which we had tossed about together, and which had quite different origins. I have not the slightest interest in having Modugno sing my songs.'[14]

A more acrimonious dispute followed Dario's acceptance of an invitation issued by the Communist party to take part in a debate on theatre at its national *Festa dell'Unità* at Prato. Dario was promised that the contributions to the debate would be published in the party's theoretical journal, *Rinascita*. What appeared was a highly partisan mixture of reporting and derogatory comments written by the party's official theatre critic, Alberto Abruzzese.[15] He dismissed Dario's theatre with lofty disdain, as though looking down from a plateau, offering luke-warm praise but conveying an overall impression of amused, patrician tedium. In Dario's words, he adopted 'the tone of a verdict from the *Upper Tribunal of the Cultural Court*, making his sentence beyond all appeal'. The crux of his complaint was that Dario lacked 'any genuine dramaturgy', that he had never developed any adequate theory of theatre to explain and justify his activities as writer and performer. His poor awareness of the relationship between theatre and class consciousness had caused him to use implements which were too blunt and unsubtle, meaning that the politics were entrusted to direct delivery by the chief actor. Normally people who wrote of him in these terms conditioned their criticism of the writer by praise of the actor, but Abruzzese sneeringly described these skills as those of the 'craftsman'. There was more than a touch of snobbery in Abruzzese, shared by many Communist intellectuals, apparent in Pasolini's disdain for Fo, and expressed as a preference for the *avant-garde* over popular theatre. Abruzzese regarded Fo's theatre as simplistic and plainly had no instinctive sympathy with popular culture. This left him in a dilemma over the theatre of Brecht and the writings of Antonio Gramsci on this topic. Brecht he left aside, but since Gramsci occupied for a Communist intellectual in Italy the place occupied by Aquinas in the Catholic Church, he could not ditch Gramsci. He neatly side-stepped the problem by claiming that Dario had misrepresented and misunderstood him. For good measure, he accused Fo of being 'moralistic.'

Dario's lengthy, outraged reply was polemical in the extreme. His first appeal was to the authority of Mao. Was Abruzzese familiar with a passage where Mao attacked 'the stereotyped and sententious language of certain party bureaucrats? Re-read it, it might be useful to you.' Dario was defensive towards his own audiences, people 'who understand what we are saying . . . who enjoy with their brains even when we say things that do not meet with their full agreement, because they love the fantasy and imagination we offer them'. As for the lack of 'dramaturgy', Dario insisted that even reactionary authors had a theory of drama, clinching the case with a reference to Ionesco, the man who had been his favourite reactionary dramatist since the break-up of the Parenti-Durano-Fo group in the 1950s. 'It cannot be denied that even (Ionesco) possesses a clear theory of theatre; it might nauseate you, but he had it, as do the authors of a *pochade* and of Grand Guignol. Science and theory are not the exclusive heritage of Marxists . . . At least on this, Albert, you will agree with me. So, how can this be? You concede dramaturgy to many people but not to me. Why not?'

There was a hurt tone to his defence of his record in maintaining independence from state interference, and to his attack on the 'cultural decentralisation' practised by the Piccolo Teatro and supported by the PCI. This he viewed as 'cultural colonialism, a joke and swindle which were at times downright vulgar – a tramp's dinner offered by Ladies of Charity with spumante and cake once a year, at Christmas . . . and for the rest of the time, shit'. However, he astonished many of his followers by his assertion that his model and aspiration was Milan's famous opera house, La Scala, where an audience like his could sit in well-heated comfort and watch a show where everything worked to perfection and where nothing had to be roughed out. Until that pinnacle of perfection could be attained, Dario told radical theatre practitioners to forge their own path, create their own theatre, find their own public and not sit about waiting for subsidies or state aid. Italy is full of plangent playwrights or frustrated actors who complain about the existing structures and lack the will to take their own initiatives. In Dario's view, it was time for them to display 'the dignity and the courage' which come from enjoying autonomy from control imposed by interested bureaucrats in charge of funds or cultural programmes.

> In the meantime, while struggling to take over the structures which the authorities do not wish to cede, I do not think we are entitled to stand idly by, much less to come to some deal by submitting (with the noble alibi that we "must get along somehow") to shameful blackmail and coming to a compromise with the powerful in return for grants and circuits with a guaranteed minimum or maximum. They will make you pay dearly by imposing on you its policies and ideas.

The point was clinched by recounting an Arab-African fable which had been told to him, he claimed, by a member of the Fedayeen. A lion chased a zebra from dawn to dusk, but could not catch it. Dragging himself home defeated, he struck up a conversation with a lynx which had watched the hunt with amusement. The lynx was derisive but when the lion invited him to do better, the lynx demurred saying that the zebra was too fast and too resourceful for one like him. 'But Your Majesty cannot allow himself to be humiliated in this way. You must punish this animal, otherwise what remains of your dignity?' The lynx summoned all the animals of the forest to a congress, at which he would make a speech in the lion's name.

At the conference, there was also a 'neo-critic, who kept himself to one side'. The lynx proposed that the zebra be severely censured for its contemptible behaviour and banned from the forest. 'Why, asks the crocodile, because you felines cannot manage to catch it?' Not at all, replies the lynx, who insists that his species had always upheld the sacred right of each animal to defend itself in any way it saw fit, but there were ways and ways. The horse or the giraffe knew how to maintain their dignity while fleeing, unlike the zebra, who was prone to exercise its undoubted right to flee in 'an unacceptable, ungainly way, bereft of all style'. The expulsion motion was passed, and the edict scratched into the bark of the trees. The zebra, who was illiterate, had to have the edict read to him by 'a monkey with a hairy bottom, of the species bureaucrat', but he reacted with disdain and anger. 'I'll show them a thing or two about style,' he determined. He took lessons in dance, learned how to walk gracefully on his hind legs and even attempted a complex *pas de deux.* The watching monkeys went into ecstasies, and even the lion admitted he would have to rethink his objections. 'It would be a real pleasure to chase an animal of such delicacy, so delightfully rhythmical in its steps.' Having uttered these words, he leapt on the zebra and sunk his teeth into his ribs. The zebra tried to run off while maintaining the grace it had acquired, but the lion jumped onto the animal's back and killed it. 'Such a pity, groaned the monkeys. A very noble animal has perished there. He cared more for his style than for his skin. A real artist. Amen.'

In the *Rinascita* piece, Fo said that the moral was evident, but he spelled it out in another journal.

I am not the zebra who is going to fall for someone else's model. I have a model and have no need of a science and an elegance which are not mine. The concept which they, *Rinascita* or the Communist party, have of dramaturgy is up to them. Let me say, I have my own dramaturgy, you don't notice it, just as the zebra had. My dramaturgy lies in the relationship with people; my way of making theatre consists of breaking up the play with interventions, with reality. As for being a craftsman, this is an attitude which is a consequence of a dramaturgy. What *Rinascita* is making is an aristocratic, not a progressive, statement. The men of the Renaissance attended a studio before they could be artists. They boasted about their art, and their art was their craft.[16]

There were other, more predictable matters to be attended to. In November, he faced trial in Reggio on the familiar grounds of having, on 11 April 1970, resisted a police officer in the pursuit of his duties. The disputed duties involved attendance at a performance from which Dario felt entitled to bar the officer because of the company's status as a private club. Dario won his case since the judge decided that the acts in question did not constitute a crime. That same month, works of his were being performed in Malmo, Copenhagen and Stockholm while Ingmar Bergman's Dramaten theatre in the Swedish capital had taken an option on *Order, by Gooooood!* In response to an invitation from the Stadsteater in Copenhagen, he was contemplating doing *Hamlet,* not Shakespeare's tragedy but a version of a Danish popular play from the late fifteenth century. 'There were the first revolts by the Scandinavian peasants and weavers, and the voice of the ghost is the voice of the people emanating from the mouth of a hanged man. It is a project I am very keen on,' he told the *Corriere della Sera,* but it was a project he never managed to bring to the stage.

There were other offers which he did not feel free to reject. The election results led to a loosening of Christian Democrat control of the institutions, especially of the broadcasting media. RAI had been a DC fiefdom, but the new management now made overtures to Dario to see if, after fourteen years exile, he would be interested in returning to the television screens.

CHAPTER 11

Televised Anathemas

Since the *Canzonissima* fracas, Dario and Franca had been ambiguous about television. As would be expected from any strong minded individuals, they replied to the ban with expressions of robust insouciance, implying, if not quite stating, that television was irrelevant to the task they had set themselves of updating the popular theatre tradition, of finding their own audience and talking directly to them in the medium of their own choosing. Dario in particular missed no opportunity of expressing his dismay at the brainless light entertainment broadcast on RAI, and of denouncing the cynical political management of a supposed public service by the Christian Democrats for the Christian Democrats. However, Hans Enzenberger once wrote that in a *coup d'état*, the insurgents occupy first the broadcasting station, then the chancelleries, and the two were clearly frustrated at their denial of access to the principal medium of communication and entertainment in modern society. They recognised that television was a centre of power from which they were excluded by an act of political will.

After the 1976 elections, the Socialist party was given de facto control of the RAI2, a newly established channel. Dario responded positively when Massimo Fichera, the channel's director, wondered if he would be willing to let bygones be bygones and return to the television screens. 'It may not be the ideal,' he said, 'but even television has been forced to reflect the collective consciousness of these years. I have seen some programmes where it was possible to call a spade a spade. On the other hand, we must take advantage of the contradictions which emerge. These plays of mine have been seen by some 350,000 spectators, *Mistero buffo* by perhaps a million or more, but the chance of reaching 6-10 million viewers is impressive.'[1]

The first proposal was to turn back the clock and begin with the episodes of *Canzonissima* which had caused so much controversy fourteen years previously, but a search of the archives revealed that the programmes had been destroyed. The next proposal was for a wide-ranging retrospective of Dario's theatre during the years of his absence from the TV screen, but Dario was nervous about introducing his work too abruptly to an unprepared TV audience, who might be unaware of the controversies these works had aroused. 'I decided to go for my theatre of the sixties, so as to permit a gradual approach by the television audience to our stage language and to our style of putting on shows. If we had offered our more recent work, the impact might have been too violent. Plays like *Accidental Death of an Anarchist, The Kidnapping of Fanfani, Bang! Bang! Who's There? The Police!* might well have been too strong a shock for people brought up on yesterday's school of mind-numbing television.' The series was given the humdrum title *Theatre of Dario Fo,* and would feature *Mistero buffo* for a total of five and half hours television time; *I Think It Over and Sing About It,* which was also to be broadcast in two parts; and the plays, *Seventh Commandment: Thou Shalt Steal a Little Less; Isabella, Three Caravels and a Con-man; Toss Out the Lady* and finally a new piece on the condition of women.

RAI demonstrated the importance they attached to the series by announcing it would be filmed in colour, still in its infancy in Italy, but the management was aware of the worldwide sales potential of any initiative involving Dario Fo. He set his face against special adaptation for the screen and made it a condition that the filming be done in the Palazzina Liberty, not in a television studio, 'first of all, (because) the Palazzina has become a symbol for us. And then what I have in mind is not a TV show in the strict sense, but something which conveys the significance of the Palazzina in relation to our theatre, to the debates which take place there, to the participation and intervention of an audience which is not only popular but also, to a large extent, bourgeois. The bourgeois audience pays by experiencing scandalised emotion, for example when the police arrive to kick us out.'[2]

The prospect of RAI, a public corporation, filming inside the Palazzina Liberty caused ructions inside the Milan City Council. Carlo Bianchi, a DC stalwart, raised the question in the Council chambers, referring with some indignation to newspaper reports that RAI and Dario had already signed a contract. How could this be, he wondered, since Fo was supposedly on the point of vacating premises he had no right to be occupying? He was assured that the company would be leaving in a couple of months, and in any case no municipal expenditure would be involved. RAI would put its own generators in place.

Initially the contract envisaged a total of eight or nine hours of broadcast material, but there would appear to have been greater flexibility in broadcasting circles than would be tolerated nowadays. In any case, all those involved were carried away by their own enthusiasm and ended up with a total of eighteen hours of programming. The material was broadcast in two cycles, one in spring and the other in autumn 1977. Curious journalists and people from the neighbourhood turned up to watch the filming, although public access had to be restricted because of the general confusion of wires, reflectors, moving cameras, technicians and engineers which are all part and parcel of filming. Dario was an early casualty; he fell over an extended wire, rolled down the stairs of an emergency exit and ended up with his leg in plaster. The sacred rule that the show must go on was observed. The schedules were altered, and filming began with *I Think it Over and Sing About It*, which he was only directing, rather than with *Mistero buffo*.

For the series as a whole, Dario was involved on all fronts as writer, actor and director. He modified aspects of the plays, reducing the length of *Toss Out the Lady* but introducing into it the dwarf routine he had perfected for the Fanfani play. The *I Think it Over* piece was a distillation of the three successive productions and allowed Dario the freedom denied him at the first staging to use choreographed movement alongside the songs. There were very few modifications in *Seventh*

Commandment: Thou Shalt Steal a Little Less, neither in the rhythms and development of the plot nor in the central attack on corruption. 'Scandals are always with us,' he said. He also pointed out that what had seemed outrageous flights of fancy, such as the use of lobotomy in dealing with criminals, had been practised on members of the Baader-Meinhof gang in Stammheim prison in Germany. The final programme of broadly feminist sketches and one-act plays, eventually given the title *Let Us Talk About Women,* was new work specially written for TV.

In the frantic lead-up to the first programme, scheduled for Friday 22 April, Franca found time to accept an invitation to go to Portugal to join in the celebrations for the revolution which had toppled the dictatorial regime, but both were otherwise fully engaged on a round of interviews and personal appearances in the unnecessary attempt to drum up interest. The press responded with gusto, though in those days of civic unrest, tension and terrorism, there was no shortage of alternative topics. Giorgio Gaber, singer-songwriter and friend of Dario's, announced in Rome that he would be abandoning the stage to return to his earlier career as an accountant. (He later changed his mind.) This dramatic announcement followed attempts by left-wing groups, with whom he was in broad sympathy, to behave in accordance with the principles of *Can't Pay? Won't Pay!* They forced their way into a concert, paying only the ticket price they themselves thought fair. Some, offended at the bourgeois distinction between performer and audience, went further. A group claiming to be admirers of Gaber's tried to storm the stage in Rome, and demanded the opportunity to sing their own songs. 'The stuff about some people being tuneless is a bourgeois invention,' they stated. In the early months of 1977, the University of Rome was occupied by disgruntled students. When the respected trade union leader and Communist activist, Luciano Lama, went to calm the student body, he was greeted by jeers and mockery. The police moved to evict the students in April, but in the ensuing turmoil two police officers were killed by gun fire. Meanwhile, accusations of corruption had reached the highest level of government. Two ministers, Luigi Gui and Mario Tanassi, were impeached in February for their part in the Lockheed affair.

In spite of this flurry of newsworthy activity, it was the return of Dario and Franca to the TV screens which commanded most column inches. 'The Great Return' was a favourite headline, followed by variations on the theme of the 'prodigal son' or the 'heretic readmitted to the fold'. The original scheduling would have seen the series open on 22 April with *Mistero buffo,* but the serendipity of TV progamming meant that Franco Zeffirelli's film *Jesus of Nazareth,* with Robert Powell in the title role, was serialised on television the same month, with the final episode due for transmission on the evening following Fo. Although personal relations between the two were cordial, Zeffirelli, an ardent Catholic and an enthusiastic supporter of the DC, represented everything in Italian artistic life which Fo abominated.

Dario used several of the interviews he was now routinely giving to denounce Zeffirelli's interpretation of the figure of Christ. He excoriated Zeffirelli with scornful violence, accusing him of having ignored the Bacchic joyfulness, the sybaritic eroticism, the delight in sensual appetites, the disdain for the rich and powerful which are integral to the popular reading of the story of Christ.

> In *Mistero buffo,* I accepted the popular approach in its totality. I turned back to the popular tradition which is not made up of boorish inventions, as some have always believed. What do I regret in Zeffirelli? That all the moments of grand, generous sexuality, of festivity, of joy, of song, that is, of the Dionysiac rite, have been eliminated. It is not a casual mistake, because each time the body should be on stage, when the body has its part, he intervenes to cut it out. The first example is Mary Magdalen ... In the popular tradition, Mary Magdalen is a sensual woman, always depicted with long hair. In Simone Martini's *Crucifixion,* Mary Magdalen embraces the cross, embraces Christ by the legs and once again wraps his feet in her hair. Not in Zeffirelli. He cuts, castrates, emasculates. He is ascetic, Platonic, Aristotelian. It is an Aristotelian concept of Christianity. It is blasphemous. [3]

The accusation of blasphemy was to be heard more frequently and stridently in Italy that April than at any time since the heyday of the

Holy Inquisition, but it was Dario who was indicated as the blasphemer. If his views on the earthiness of gospel conduct would startle biblical exegetes or moral theologians, his principal charge against Zeffirelli was in itself clear and coherent. Dario was invariably an egocentric critic. The strength of his criticism lies not in the acuteness of his observations on other writers or actors, but in how his criticism clarifies his own artistic and political credo. For him the gospels were not a source of religious revelation nor a privileged access to moral absolutes, as they were for Zeffirelli, but an integral part of the only tradition he recognised, the people's tradition. He was never more Gramscian than when he discussed religious practices. The value of the Bible for him was not in the canonical interpretation handed down *ex cathedra* by bishops or scribes, but in the folk vision of it which had been incorporated into the worship, the festivals, the carnival rites and the workaday lives of the poor and dispossessed.[4]

He was equally at odds with Zeffirelli over his depiction of certain incidents, such as the expulsion of the merchants from the Temple ('because he makes Christ hysterical. He uses the Christ of Fra Angelico ... The yelling and screaming of Masaccio will never be part of Zeffirelli's vision; it was not by chance that Pasolini turned to Masaccio'). Equally, he found fault with Zeffirelli's portrayal of Judas. For Dario, Judas was a member of a different class, 'the only intellectual among the sons of carpenters and fishermen. Judas knows how to read and write, he knows Greek, Judas is from a wealthy family.' In the popular tradition, Judas was never accorded any respect or forgiveness. 'In *Mistero buffo*, I inserted a sophisticated monologue where Judas ... tries to save himself with dialectic, overturning the truth. I leave Judas hanging from a tree.'

Presumably that expression of views should have been warning enough of the nature of the vision which underlay Dario's work. Ignorance was in this case inexcusable. *Mistero buffo* had toured the length and breadth of Italy in performance before coming to the TV screen, but seemingly nothing of its contents had permeated the consciousness of Italy's parliamentary or ecclesiastical authorities, or of their representatives in the press. The day after the broadcast the plain people of Italy were treated to a display of outrage and indignation which would have been excessive even if Dario had advocated dethroning the Pope, demolishing Saint Peter's basilica and defacing Michelangelo's *Pietà*. The Italian Senate and Chamber of Deputies, the Vatican, the Conference of Italian Bishops, RAI, every newspaper of whatever political slant, every weekly including those which normally concerned themselves with sport or sex set aside their normal activities to debate what was immediately dubbed 'the Fo question.'

Normally sane men and women, charged with responsibility for governing the affairs of church and state, lost all sense of equilibrium. 'On Television the Fo Bomb Has Gone Off,' thundered Genoa's *Secolo XIX*, and that was one of the more moderate responses. 'Indignation Among Catholics After Fo's Programme', was the expression used in *Il Tempo*. 'The Jesus of Dario Fo,' ran the *Corriere d'Informazione* in bold capitals, before adding below, 'Polemics Explode on the *Mistero buffo* Broadcast Last Night on Channel 2.' In the article itself, the paper reported that 'this poor Jesus never does finish dying'. Explosions of the type the headline referred to went off all over Italy that week, but fortunately only in the editorial offices of the national dailies. Father Romeo Panciroli, official Vatican press officer, excelled for the sheer intemperance of his comments. 'A disgusting, crass and degrading broadcast,' he opined, 'which offended the Catholic faith and the religious sentiment of the Italian people, and one which,' he added, warming to his task, 'has considerably lowered the level of television programming. I believe that this is the first occasion when a national television network has, in the time that television has existed in the world, broadcast a programme of such blasphemy.' Fo had secured himself a place in history, or at least in that section of history controlled by Fr. Panciroli, as the most blasphemous of writers. Fo himself retorted that this was the 'finest compliment the Vatican could pay me, apart from the fact that I do not consider the Vatican sacred'.[5]

The upper echelons of the Vatican hierarchy entered the fray. Cardinal Ugo Poletti, cardinal vicar of Rome, sent a telegram to Italy's Prime Minister, Giulio Andreotti, expressing his anxiety over the damage this programme had done to Italy's image abroad and voicing deep concern over wounded religious sensibilities. 'Speaking for innumerable citizens and organisations of Rome, I express sadness and protest over the blasphemous and anti-cultural television programme, *Mistero buffo* by Dario Fo, to which should be added profound humiliation for the inconceivable vulgarity of a public broadcast which demeans the Italian nation before the whole world.' The Conference of Italian Bishops also telegrammed the Prime Minister demanding respect for 'the religious sentiments and conscience of a considerable part of the Italian people in these difficult moments which require not division and anathemas, but the concord and collaboration of all'. There was no shortage of anathemas. The Vatican daily, *Osservatore Romano*, reminded parish priests of their duty to denounce such irreligious talk from the pulpit, and went on to demand a purge at RAI. 'How is it possible,' it asked in Latinate prose, 'for the authorities responsible for radio-telecommunications in Italy to permit an operation so clearly destined to wound the consciences of Catholics?'[6] Although consciences among the faithful appeared intact, the Vatican itself was in a state of shock. *Panorama* reported that on the Sunday following the broadcast, the highest authorities in the government of Vatican City, including Cardinal Jean Villot, the Secretary of State, Cardinal Benelli, Archbishop of Florence, and Monsignor Agostino Casaroli, Minister for Foreign Affairs, met to consider an official diplomatic protest to the Italian Republic. They decided instead to encourage the Italian faithful to make their own protests.[7]

This they did in varied ways. Italian law still contained a provision outlawing 'contempt of religion', and the Roman magistrate, Rosario de Mauro announced that he had received dozens of official complaints from private citizens and from such bodies as 'Catholic Parents' or 'Ex-Salesian pupils' inviting him to open proceedings against Dario. De Mauro, clearly a man of some independence of mind, declined to take any action, since he could find no trace of any attack 'on moral values or on the divinity. The figure of Christ, for example appears clearly contrasted with that of Boniface VIII. The sensation drawn from the work is of respect for the spiritual heritage of the Catholic Church, in contrast to the representation of human behaviour which deviates from the values of that heritage.' His was a whisper into a storm which continued to rage.

The board of RAI was in more or less permanent session, and had to decide whether to screen the second episode. It was hopelessly divided, with one half threatening to resign if the series went ahead, and the other half threatening to resign if it did not. RAI was still not a fully independent body, and the puppet masters were the party bosses. On the floor of the Chamber of Deputies and in the parliamentary Committee of Vigilance on Radio and Television, protests grew in intensity and shrillness. The Committee chairman was the veteran Christian Democrat, Paolo Emilio Taviani, formerly Minister for the Interior and later the subject of a venomous, derisive letter written by Aldo Moro while held in captivity by the Red Brigades. The committee itself contained thirty-seven members, of whom fifteen were from the DC, eleven from the Communist party, three from the Socialists, with one each from the Social Democrats, the Republicans, the Liberals, the Independent Left, the Radicals, the neo-Fascist MSI and the Democratic party of Proletarian Unity (PdUP). Two days after the broadcast, Taviani received a telegram from the Italian Women's Committee, one of the leading Catholic organisations, demanding that the programmes be immediately suspended. He wished to reply immediately to the Vatican and the Women's Committee but was stymied by procedural wrangles dreamed up by the PdUP, whom Dario had supported in a party political broadcast.

Taviani emerged as the most vehement of Dario's denouncers. 'The initiative of the DC group in raising the matter means that the DC is echoing in Parliament and elsewhere the bitterness and contempt felt by Catholics and by the millions of citizens whose religious feelings have been outraged,' he intoned. If that was not denunciation enough, he went on to say that 'this programme reminds me of Nazis who burned books and attacked both the *Osservatore Romano* and the boys from Catholic Action.'[8] He explained that he was speaking from the standpoint of a man 'who had always liked culture', who had been involved in the restoration of the Teatro Argentina and in reforming RAI, therefore as one 'who is entitled to raise (his) voice'. His objection was firstly to the fact that Dario had been granted the privilege of having his entire repertoire shown on TV, a privilege not extended even to Eduardo De Filippo, and secondly to 'the contents, a unilateral act of violence against fundamental religious values held by many citizens.' Lest he had been misunderstood, he accused Dario of 'ideological hooliganism . . . the anti-clericalism of seventy-years ago.' In another interview, he denounced Fo as 'an ideological fraud, a liar, the mongol brother of Jacques Tati.'[9]

Judging by press reports, it would seem that no topic other than *Mistero buffo* was being discussed from the Swiss border to the southernmost tip of Sicily. From the unmanageable mass which *Mistero buffo* had become, Dario had selected four sketches – *The Grammelot of the Zanni, Saint Benedict, the Raising of Lazarus* and *Boniface VIII*. The first two sketches were plainly considered innocuous, leaving two main sources of conflict – Fo versus the DC over Pope Boniface VIII and by implication over political and ecclesiastical power in Italy, and Fo versus Zeffirelli over Lazarus and therefore over religious belief. In the whole incredible business, it was Zeffirelli who conducted himself with most tact and restraint. He was used in the columns of the *Osservatore Romano* as the seraphic counterpoint to the Mephistophelean Fo, but while disagreeing with Dario's use of religious iconography, he continued to express his admiration for him as man of theatre. Two newspapers, *Milano Sera* and *La Repubblica,* brought them together for face-to-face confrontations, covering largely familiar ground. Zeffirelli defended his own film, saying that he had wanted to emphasise 'pacification and love. My *Jesus* is created so as to enter into people's lives without disturbance . . .', which was the opposite of the effect Fo wished to create. Dario, he said, was out to overthrow the altars. Zeffirelli repeated that Dario 'was one of the great Italian theatrical phenomena',[10] and he had the subtlety to recognise that he (Dario) operated in the frolicking goliardic tradition which was offensive and debunking by definition, but he was unhappy at the terrain he had chosen. Zeffirelli was upset at the unseemly squabbles which attended the miracle of the raising of Lazarus from the dead and by the introduction into a sacred scene of costermongers, pedlars, hucksters and assorted tricksters plying their trade while waiting for Jesus to work the miracle. While claiming to be sophisticated and tolerant himself, he adopted the standpoint of the plain, uneducated Catholic. 'That type of scurrility cannot be proposed to a television mass audience without careful preparation. This is not a question of censorship. Fo can say what he pleases, but he himself performs in one way when he plays for workers and peasants, and in another when he performs for a radical bourgeois audience.' For a moment, Zeffirelli sounded uncannily like the defence advocates in the *Lady Chatterley* obscenity trial in London, worrying about the impact of such literature falling into the hands of 'wives and servants.'

Dario was entitled to his perplexity when he wondered if his work would have been acceptable if it had remained in basements and chamber theatres where only a select audience had had access to it,[11] but the fact was that *Mistero buffo* had not been written or performed for an élite. Behind this whole discussion of the public reception of the televised version of the play, lay the wider question of the power of television. *Mistero buffo* was not a new work premiered in 1977. In the years since the first performance in 1969, the work had been seen by vast numbers of people. Dario put the figure as high as 1.5 million, and even if that is excessive, the numbers of spectators were very high. But television in modern society has a power and a reach which theatre today can never have. The debate over *Mistero buffo*, involving as it did the hierarchies of church and state, was ipso facto a debate about power, power over minds, power over the circulation of ideas and thus the power to determine what Gramsci called cultural hegemony. The fracas demonstrated the truth of the charge that censorship of theatre had been lifted but retained on television when television replaced theatre as the prime medium for entertainment. Having been spurned by TV all these years, Dario was given a dramatic lesson in exactly why he had been ostracised. The year 1977 on Italian television terms was one of those rare open moments when contentious, rebellious ideas could be aired. It was a brief interval.

The debate over power in church and state focused on the sketch satirising Pope Boniface VIII. The sketch showed Boniface revelling in the pomp of office, vesting himself with magnificent robes which proclaimed wealth and influence, all the while bullying the altar boy in attendance on him. While processing in imperial splendour through the streets of Rome, Boniface meets Christ carrying his cross. Christ refuses to recognise his successor in the opulent figure of Boniface, a refusal symbolised by the kick with which he sweeps the Pope aside. The anger and scorn in Dario's portrayal are palpable. The medieval pope was not a straightforward allegory of the contemporary pontiff, but when critics said that his depiction of Boniface represented a challenge to contemporary ways, there could be no denying the charge. Without identifying the two, Fo did, in his preface to this sketch, make fun of Pope John Paul II. But Boniface VIII was also a historical character and here Fo's critics faced a situation of some delicacy. The historical Boniface was a contemporary of Dante, whose position as Italy's supreme poet, and indeed as Europe's Catholic poet *par excellence,* could not be placed in doubt. Dante despised and hated – no milder words will suffice – Pope Boniface with a ferocity Dario Fo could never equal. Dante made it clear that there was a place in hell reserved for Boniface, who was still alive in the year 1300, the year in which *The Divine Comedy* was set. When Dante reaches *Paradiso,* Saint Peter himself berates his successor for desecrating the papal throne with such virulence that the celestial rose of heaven, where the souls of the saved are clustered, turns red with shame. To condemn Dario over his treatment of Boniface is to condemn Dante Alighieri. It would be easier to have people believe that the Sacred College of Cardinals had embraced Calvinism.

There is much innocent fun to be had with the newspaper columns of those days, and even with the reports of parliamentary debates. Daily papers found space, among reports of terrorist attacks or of events in Vietnam, for learned articles on medieval history and in literature. Those who had forgotten what they had learned at school found that Boniface had also been a target for the venom of the thirteenth-century Franciscan poet, Jacopone da Todi, who had been left chained to a wall for years on Boniface's orders. 'Boniface VIII in Parliament' ran a headline in the *Corriere della Sera* on 26 April. An absolutist Pontiff, some six centuries dead, found himself the centre of a debate about liberty and libertarianism in twentieth-century Italy. 'Jesus Is a Star' ran another headline, which did not refer to Andrew Lloyd Webber. The French medieval historian, Jean Chesneaux, commissioned by the *Corriere* to assess Fo's depiction of the Middle Ages, concluded that he had deeper and more accurate knowledge of that epoch than most professional historians.

Dario was now the centre of a national disputation which recalled the controversy aroused a decade earlier when Hochhuth's *The Deputy*, with its accusation that Pius XII had declined to intervene to defend the Jews from Hitler, was staged in Rome. As it developed, the polemics went well beyond the issues raised by *Mistero buffo* itself and quickly degenerated into a debate of the deaf. Dario's more prosaic, political defenders railed against censorship, defended democracy and free speech, while the more aesthetically inclined spoke of the freedom of creativity and the extension of cultural boundaries and of challenges to sycophancy of mind. His opponents, huddled on the opposing citadel, raised banners proclaiming the rights of religion, denouncing desecration, upholding respect for the sacred and questioning claims for absolute tolerance and free speech. The brilliant cartoonist, Forattini, produced a wicked *vignette* showing Fo crucified, but on a carefully worked rearrangement on the letters TV. His head was positioned at the crook of the V, while his arms were stretched out under the upwards-sloping sides of the same letter, allowing his hands to emerge, nailed to the extremities of the T.

There were other ironic points which emerged in the course of the controversy. In April, Amintore Fanfani and other DC notables travelled to Florence to speak at a conference in defence of the freedom, absolute freedom, of painters. The decision to focus on artists rather than writers was dictated by the logic of the Cold War. Some painters in the USSR wished to exhibit their work but the exhibition had been disrupted by the KGB. Their canvases were not politically motivated but did not conform to prevailing tastes in the upper echelons of the Soviet Communist party. By supporting the rights of artists in the Soviet Union, the Right in Italy believed they were embarrassing the Kremlin, while also putting their own Communist party on the defensive. An alert journalist remembered that the Venice Biennale in 1976 had been dedicated to the theme of 'dissent'. The question was obvious. When and where was dissent permitted and indeed encouraged? Did pictorial artists have greater rights than those enjoyed by writers? Was Fo entitled to be regarded as a dissident? Was Italy on a par with the USSR?

Dario had blown apart the silence of servility or of habit which underlay acceptance of the status quo, as the ecclesiastical and political Right in Italy fully recognised. He was plainly perceived as a threat by Christian Democratic Italy. The threat to religious belief itself was not intentional, but the threat to the established order and hierarchy of Church and State was. Transcendental theology held no interest for him, and he steadfastly rebuffed any effort to enlist him among the ranks of the twentieth century's mystics without a creed. 'I am not even distantly a follower of any religion,' he told *Panorama*. 'I am a convinced atheist, a Marxist, a materialist. These are for me points which cannot be touched.'[12] At the same time, he was no proselytiser for secularism, nor did he jeer at doctrines or dogmas. Nowhere in his theatre did he pit the religious against the materialist vision of the cosmos. His scorn was reserved for the growth of the institutional church into a centre of power and wealth, and its uncritical cohabitation with oppressive forces in the state. His researches into the history and development of popular theatre, especially of medieval theatre, had convinced him of the centrality of the religious experience in the worldview of ordinary people, and led him to conclude that there is a subversive element in the popular interpretation of gospel teaching.

> Boniface VIII, what is he? He is the violence of the power of the church. What happens? Boniface VIII bedecks himself in finery, sacred finery if you like, but today people want a different church, not the mired down church they see ... I offend power, not religious feeling.[13]

The Fo case was rapidly caught up in the thickets of party politics at a time when Italy was governed by a series of daily deals between the DC Cabinet and the PCI opposition. As such it rapidly became a nuisance for the respective leaderships, each of whom had reasons to fear the ramifications of the 'Fo affair'. One journalist wrote the Fo affair presented the most serious risk not only to the continuance of the government in office, but also to the whole process of integration of the Communists into democratic life and of the normalisation of relations between the PCI and the other political parties. The plan was three-pronged: 'to force the Christian Democrats and the Communists to vote against each other in the parliamentary commission, to offer space to those inside the DC who were still prepared to ride the tiger of anti-communist intransigence, and to turn the remaining fifteen episodes of the *Theatre of Dario Fo* into so many bombs against PCI-DC dialogue.'[14] Other countries looked on bemused. Fo was invited to France in May to explain on French television exactly what was going on in Italy. He told them he was aghast to discover that Boniface VIII had his defenders in modern Italy. The rest of the series went ahead undisturbed, watched by more viewers than any other programme in Italian television history. Dario expected *Seventh Commandment: Thou Shalt Steal a Little Less*, with its mockery of political-commercial corruption, to be controversial, and perhaps it should have been, but in the event it passed off more quietly.

When the first approaches were made to him, Dario was asked why he wanted to return to RAI which had treated him so appallingly in the past. He replied that he had not changed but that RAI had. This was true enough, but was only a part of a wider truth, as the ecclesiastical-political establishment came to realise in the course of the fracas. Italy was no longer the clerical or confessional state it had been when Alcide De Gasperi and the founding fathers succeeded in making Christian Democracy the natural governing party in the Republic. In the 1970s, there was no longer any meaningful sense in which Italy could be described either as a Christian Democratic state or even as a Catholic country. The watershed date in this transformation of Italian society was undoubtedly the 1974 referendum on divorce, when electors rejected the advice of church and of the party which was its political arm. There was a wild exaggeration to the entire Fo affair, but the hysteria of the response was also a belated recognition in certain quarters of fading powers. Vatican anxiety and Vatican policies had the advantage of logic, even if it was the logic of *realpolitik*. The working arrangements between the DC and the PCI meant that the PCI was no longer the pariah party, but also that Italy was no longer a monolithic society. Dario Fo, as was shown by the bugging of his phone, the bombing of theatres where he played, the threats issued to collaborators and the persecution he had endured from police and prosecution services was very much a *persona non grata* both to the official ministries and to the unofficial masonries which held sway in the governance of the Republic. He was principally the singer of this process, but he had also played his part as composer and orchestrator. And he was proud of both roles.

CHAPTER 12

Liberating Franca

The final TV programme in the series, given the downbeat title *Let's Talk About Women*, was recognition that the feminist movement in Italy was becoming increasingly vociferous. Franca was never comfortable about identifying herself as a feminist *tout court*, but she was a vigorous and vociferous supporter of the demands being made by women. Although not fully recognised then, the work marked the opening of a new phase in the career of Dario and Franca, with Franca assuming a higher profile.

There were other shifts, perhaps imperceptible, in their overall stance. In 1977, the two published an interesting booklet whose prosaic title *The Political Theatre of Dario Fo* conceals a certain depressed bafflement.[1] The work contained two play scripts – *Mistero buffo* and *Isabella, Three Caravels and a Con-man*, a preface by Dario, an article by Franca and a cartoon version by Jacopo Fo of the TV theme song *Who Makes Us Do It?*, but the focus and the critical gaze throughout were retrospective. Dario reflected on the theatre he had already produced, defining it in newly discovered Sartrean terms as 'theatre of situation' unlike the 'bourgeois theatre of Chekhov or Pirandello . . . (whose was) a theatre of characters who recount to each other their own stories and their own moods which are then the key to mechanical conflicts. We were always concerned to take a different approach, the situation approach'. Even the term 'political theatre' now seemed to him of dubious validity.

'As far as the works staged by *La Comune* are concerned, I would have preferred to call them "popular theatre", on account of the discourse they contain, meaning that they succeed in reclaiming a certain type of class theatre.'

The term "political theatre" was coined by Piscator, as a polemical provocation to distinguish it from "digestive" theatre, which is a theatre removed from all contingent, dramatic, lyrical problems. Piscator's was a political theatre in the decisive fact of being managed directly by the working class.

With the employment today of the term "political", I would not like to make people's hair stand on end. Perhaps they are right, because "political theatre" has become a kind of subtitle for tedious theatre, know-all theatre, schematic theatre, non-enjoyable theatre.

Now, as is well known, all theatre is political, all art is political. It is when someone wants to hide the political value, as with Feydeau, that we have the most stridently political theatre, in this case bourgeois-political.

These statements were unremarkable, but what followed, even if couched in terms of historical analysis, was a more important recognition of a new strand of thought, the politics of the personal.

Greek theatre is political theatre, indeed commissioned theatre. The *Oresteian Trilogy* was commissioned by the then hegemonic authorities in the *polis*. By adopting the absolutist, or the mythical and religious, approach, they hoped to make grand-style, great-power propaganda, that is, they hoped to ensure the election of a man to office. This theatre set itself against the archaic, peasant, rural tradition which saw the female as sacred, as the mother not only in the sense of progenitor but also as the source of culture and repository of the values of tradition.

For the first time, Dario chose to highlight the female aspect, but the emphasis on the mother figure is a more idiosyncratic foretaste of one of the main strands of the new feminist theatre Dario and Franca would produce. In the same booklet, Franca contributed a piece which united elements of Maoist self-criticism and feminist consciousness-raising. She looked back over the type of role she had played in the fifties as a jobbing actress and in the work she and Dario had produced in the sixties. These parts were, as she readily admitted, essentially decorative. In the 1950s, the empty head under a blonde hairpiece, atop characterless eyes and an inviting smile, the whole perched above a generous bosom, were the indispensable characteristics for the rising female star. Federico Fellini succeeded in seemingly satirising this iconic figure, while in reality indulging the frisson it provides, with the scene in *La Dolce Vita* where Anita Ekberg, her body inflated beyond the dreams of any fetishist, wades provocatively in the Trevi Fountain.

Franca now conceded that in this sphere she had not been a life-long rebel. When she appeared in the revue *I Fanatici* with the *Billi e Riva* troupe in the fifties, she was photographed in sultry poses, leaning provocatively against pillars, or bedecked in low-cut dresses and wearing ribbons which resembled the rabbit ears worn by Playboy Bunnies. Franca's head then was no more empty than Jayne Mansfield's, but she shared the American star's physical attributes and allowed herself, she now believed, to be reduced to sex-symbol status. By the seventies, she had discarded this image. As was noted by a writer in the women's magazine, *Noi Donne:*

> In the years when together with Dario Fo she created revue theatre, she entertained people principally by her provocative attractions combined with a "vamp" style of performance: today, in the years of a theatre strongly committed at the level of social, political and ideological militancy, Franca Rame, still attractive though she may be, is more and more prone to refuse to make a display of her still appreciable features. She disguises herself, she makes herself ugly, conceals her profile and acts in such a way as to permit her to set out ideas and facts. She has chosen that style of acting which overrides differences between man and woman, between actor and actress, which eliminates sexual attributes as focus for attention . . .[2]

There is more than a touch of exaggeration in this estimate. The sexual charge in Franca's performances remained strong, but she regretted opportunities lost due to the sexist climate of earlier times. In the same interview, she went on:

> In Italy, in the theatre and cinema circuit, a disconcerting super-ficiality and banality were current. Since, as I have already said, I have certain physical characteristics, in other words those of the dumb blond, I cannot do anything other than the vamp. This is true today, never mind then. In each and every film, I "logically" played the vamp (but one who was amiable and a bit unlucky), and was never offered the role of an ordinary woman, who just might have been able to speak and think for herself.
>
> I carried this kind of sexist burden for many years. Even in Dario's plays, I was never, ever asked to display any kind of skill, craft, stage sense . . . well, if it was there, so much the better . . . this, obviously, from critics and not from Dario, who has always tried to create precise and concrete, as well as human, characters. Obviously he could hardly make me hunchbacked, but he gave me at least a minimum of brain.

This situation evolved over the years. It was Enea, the seeming simpleton of *Seventh Commandment: Thou Shalt Steal a Little Less,* who revealed the scheming and corruption all around, while Franca had the leading roles in both parts *Isabella,* both as the domineering queen, and as the mad Joan. With *Can't Pay? Won't Pay!* the female character took charge and became not the comic 'feed' but the principal comic actor.

By the late seventies, both Dario and Franca felt it necessary to make the position of women in society more central to their work. She wrote, 'for a theatre like ours, which both keeps up with what is going on and is fashioned by it, to have avoided associating ourselves with questions raised by women would have been a serious matter. The woman question is too important nowadays.'[3] The remaining problem was to find the appropriate style. In the discussions following the first production of *Let's Talk About Women,* she stated that 'speaking about women is easy. Everybody does it, perhaps too much. The difficulty is to do it in the theatre, and to say something serious on the condition of women while laughing and entertaining.[4] Theatrical means had parity of importance with content, but there were problems over content too. Franca was uneasy over aspects of contemporary feminism. In her brief contribution to the booklet, she made a sharp, polemical distinction between her own position and that of 'feminists'. Occasionally, very charily, she would use the term 'feminist' to describe herself, but more commonly 'feminist' was a word applied to other women whose idealism and fervour she admired but whose ways were not entirely hers. However much she may have been branded an extremist in social and economic politics, Franca was a moderate in sexual politics:

> These girls, these women have done extraordinary things even if, as in every movement, there have been negative, mistaken phases. But this happens with all real movements. Were there not mistakes in 1968? We can well admit it, since we are paying for them now.
>
> I have a great deal of respect for the feminists, especially for those who do not take up positions of out and out antagonism to men, and for those who are working courageously to change reality, beavering away in their own localities, carrying out abortions etc. I am not a militant feminist, in the sense that the greater part of my time is already absorbed, apart from the theatre, in other activities such as Red Aid and the thousand and one things needed to 'look after the shop'. But I do follow some initiatives and activities of the feminist movement. I was present, for instance, at the work of a group of young women who carry out abortions, and I must confess I was dumbfounded. I watched them (both those who performed the abortion and those who underwent it), and they were truly . . . heroic.

Feminism which was anti-male in tone was not for her. The manifesto of the American group called SCUM, (the Society for Cutting Up Men) filled her with uncomprehending dismay. It is facile to put this down to her age and background, as was done by some women who belonged to the category of 'militant feminists', but her rejection of this stance was determined primarily by her Marxism. Her political thinking was

234

essentially class-based, where the classes were the exploited and the exploiters, or the proletariat and the bourgeoisie. She was never able to afford women the status of an independently exploited class. The priority to be accorded to socialism or feminism was a theme which recurred endlessly in the conferences and gatherings of those years, and Franca' stance was unyielding. The only revolution to which she gave assent was one which would liberate all proletarians, male and female. In the socialist perspective, men too, she repeated, were oppressed, and her 'feminism' was aimed at the raising of all consciousness, male and female. She never swerved from this view. Two years later, in an interview with a Sicilian paper, while on tour with *All Bed, Board and Church*, the final form of the work premiered on television, we find her saying:

> I am not a feminist in the sense of militant. In fact I have never been a member of any group. I am a feminist by personal and political choice. I am not a separatist. For women to liberate themselves, it is not sufficient for us to change our heads, or that of men, we must change society. In my play, there is also a pitiless exposure of a society by means of laughter. I have always wanted to make people laugh while thinking, and to make them think while laughing.[5]

Encouraging rethinking by laughter had been the aim of the theatre which Dario and she had produced, and she had no wish to change tack. Leftist intellectuals in Italy, like Alberto Abruzzesi, had had problems with Fo's humour in the years of political militancy, and now the same attitude of *a priori* refusal emerged in response to the broadly feminist theatre the couple created in the late seventies. Humour which was subdued, subtle, dry or satirical was acceptable, but tomfoolery, knockabout or laughter which was festive, raucous and boisterous seemed somehow inappropriate or demeaning for serious subjects. In an article which appeared shortly before the broadcast of *Let's Talk About Women*, the novelist Natalia Ginzburg, who had always been prickly towards Dario, wrote that he was not a real comic because real comics were 'tragic and ingenuous', and displayed an ability to be 'forgetful, dismayed and alone'.[6] Franca heard the same objections, and grew exasperated with critics who told her that her comic approach was an unacceptable compromise.

Many women's theatrical collectives were set up in those days, although Franca never considered joining. She received plays from women writers, but these rarely met her professional standards. Any depiction of women as victims, or any self-pitying portrayal of women was instantly thrown in the bin. 'I launched a kind of desperate appeal to some feminist comrades: "Help and Solidarity! Sisters, help!" Some scripts were dispatched to me: tales, autobiographical stories, collections of letters, but all things which it would have been very difficult to transfer to the stage. Anyway, I tried, but what a disaster. Scripts that would never stand up, not even with the support of a crane.' Her discussions with feminist writers were a re-run of the debates inside *Nuova Scena* and *La Comune*.

Franca now grew more noticeably assertive about her own part in the creative partnership. She and Dario had always worked together but her role had been overshadowed or downright neglected. Until the late seventies, the plays were published under Dario's name alone, and Franca received credit neither for her contribution to the reworking of the texts during rehearsal, nor for the rewriting and editing, which she did alone, in preparation for publication. Dario by himself is unlikely to have left any published trace of his work, and could always blithely quote Shakespeare to justify indifference to the printing press, but the truth was that the tedium, the routine, the concentration on unrewarding detail challenged his attention span. The show has always gone on, the plays have always been written, the rehearsals keenly supervised and the post-performance discussions attended to with unswerving attention, but Dario's horizons are marked by the play's run. Once that is over, his interest wanes. Stage directions, for instance, were never his *forte*; in the published versions of the early plays, they are entirely lacking. It was only when Franca decided they were indispensable that they began to appear. The final script will be an amalgam of all the various modifications, rewrites, changes and alterations which have been introduced in the course of rehearsal and performance, so that any aspiring editor would find himself, or herself, faced with piles of scribbled pages from which to extract a publishable version. Perhaps only Franca could have done the job of editing and publishing. Shakespeare's folios were produced by two fellow actors after his death, and they deserve grateful credit, as does Franca. There would be no Fo folio without her.

Franca began to speak of 'our' theatre, and from this period the playbills, programmes and the spines of the books began to accord her due credit. It is worth noting that while Fo is invariably quoted as being the world's most performed living playwright, it is the jointly signed works which have been most frequently staged. There is no reason to believe that any change in the creative process actually took place at the time of *Let's Talk About Women*; it is rather that Franca finally received belated credit for what she had always done. Dario invariably deferred to her sense of theatricality, of timing, of what works on stage. Her demands on other actors could be severe. She taped every performance and summoned the actor if his or her timing was faulty and a laugh was missed.

Most probably there was no real change during this "feminist" period, when the plays began to be jointly credited. Often disagreements between them over first drafts were intense. Franca made the point that whereas friends and colleagues could duck the awkwardness of dissent by expressions of *bello, bello* and admiration, she knew she would have to give life on stage to the words written. Writers who have struggled with their work are not always amenable to criticism, no matter how incisive or constructive. Franca recalled that once when she had been highly critical, Dario had her pinned against a wall, demanding that she explain herself. Jacopo, who was still young and had never seen his parents fight, was reduced to whimpering – What are you doing, what are you doing? In the case of *Almost by Chance a Woman, Elizabeth*, Franca told Dario he had produced a stimulating essay on Shakespeare but not a drama. He responded huffily and threw the manuscript into a drawer, but when he drew it out later, he agreed with her judgment and re-wrote.

Dario told Franca to try her own hand at writing, and she did make an effort but by her own account, without success. She would later be acclaimed for her own monologues, but at this point she still required Dario's support. As she wrote, 'At a certain point, Dario came down from his Aventine hill, and gave me a hand, in all truth, fortunately, two hands. He took up the pile of sheets of paper and scribbles and set off to make something of them. Well, I must say that one or two pieces came out more or less as I had always imagined them. They seemed (finally) to have been written by a woman. And there was more of mine left than I expected could be used.' Dario's version was more or less the same. He told an American magazine that *Accidental Death* was a work of his, but when asked about the monologues played by Franca, he replied: 'they were based on some ideas by Franca, but the definitive writing, the treatment I did. And then in due course Franca adapted them for performance.'[7]

Her collaboration allowed her to ward off criticism at the premiere. While prepared to accept that there were deficiencies in the scripts, she would not accept the criticism that the monologues were inferior or unacceptable because they were written by a male.

> It is a criticism I do not accept. I have always helped Dario in the composition of his theatrical works with suggestions, criticisms, proposals, but this time – I really want this to be understood – everything was completely different. In fact – and I want this to be clear – I even put my name on the title page, because if I did not write it in my own hand, I built it up verbally in long discussions with Dario. Some parts, indeed, I wanted to have redone, because they did not convince me.[8]

Dario had begun work on *Let's Talk About Women* some two years prior to the first performance in 1977, but then put it aside to take up the *Fanfani* and the *Marijuana* plays. Before the TV version, the work went on stage at the Palazzina in March in the presence of a tolerant but frustrated audience. Dario painted special backcloths, one featuring a parody of the traditional *Flight into Egypt* motif. St Joseph was shown seated comfortably on horseback, while the Virgin Mary, in a state of evident exhaustion, staggered on ahead, holding the lead of the horse in one hand and the infant Jesus in the other. Another drape depicted a parody of the *Creation*, with the woman seeing the light as she emerges from the rib of the lordly male and immediately kneeling at his feet.

This first version was a cabaret-style miscellany of assorted pieces, consisting of one-liners, songs, monologues and sketches, some of which were plundered from earlier works. The protagonist was Franca, with Dario supposedly her straight man, although this was a part he had some difficulty in maintaining. The pieces showed Dario's penchant for history, especially sacred history. One sketch featured a discussion arising from a dilemma enunciated by Erasmus of Rotterdam over whether women have a soul and whether Eve should be regarded as the daughter of darkness, another paraded Elizabethan female figures, including Juliet and Ophelia, all played by bearded men as a satire on the contemporary ban on allowing women on stage. Franca performed the monologues of the Resistance heroine, Mamma Togni, and of the mother of Michele Lu Lanzone, the Sicilian trade unionist killed by the mafia, and who was herself confined in an asylum for threatening to denounce his killers. One of the musical interludes had Franca attempting to sing a folk song entitled, *I Am My Own Person,* but being symbolically drowned out by Dario blaring a blues number into a microphone. Another sketch featured a man whose anti-abortion convictions are put to the test when he himself falls pregnant. The most successful piece was the monologue, *Wakening Up,* which subsequently became one of the most frequently performed pieces in the Fo-Rame repertoire.

These last two pieces reflected current debates, but it is not hard to see why seventies feminists were mystified by the other sketches. The theological disputations of Erasmus, the debates on women on the Elizabethan stage may have intrigued Dario and were doubtless part of the traditional underpinning to women's subaltern position in history, but they bewildered younger women who had honed their activism on divorce and abortion campaigns, and their critical thinking on the writings of Julia Kristeva and Luce Irigaray. Franca accepted some of the points made in discussions after the performance, while remaining baffled by the aggression of some of her critics. 'It is an old project, some years old,' she told one critic. 'Let me make one point clear. We did not plan, nor have we provided, a feminist work, or a work on the condition of women. We aimed at the construction of some female figures without in any way wanting to exemplify the problems of women as such. We picked up on some topics – to deal with them all would take a thousand hours.'

Post-1968 feminism had set itself a different agenda, and the most frequent criticism was that Dario and Franca were out of touch with the times. There is no Italian word which exactly renders the English term 'generation gap', but the reality existed. Dario and Franca were among those who lived through the turbulence of 1968, but the times they were a-changing, as Bob Dylan sang, and the daughters, if not the sons, were out of the parents' command. In the same number, Dylan also advised people not of the younger generation to start swimming, lest 'they sink like a stone'. Dario and Franca were swimming, but to their surprise they found themselves, if not sinking, certainly buffeted by cross-currents. One critic present at the premiere recorded reactions. 'The gist of the various contributions is that they do not see their themes in the play, because those featured are old, and not of their generation. There is no mention of sexual exploitation, of the black economy, of the authentic liberation of women or of any criticism of the system. Nor did the feminists there recognise themselves in the mother of the murdered trade unionist. In other words, the whole thing did not go down with them in the slightest.'

'Authentic liberation' in Franca's eyes, was to be found embedded in the experiences of the women featured, not trumpeted in an abstract discourse on patriarchy. Her theatre was an arena of voices, all speaking of their distress but expressing, however awkwardly, a brave optimism that conditions could be changed. Her characters live lives of emotional and spiritual aridity, represented in tones of mockery and self-mockery. The comedy of the plays is not a rejection of their woeful experiences but a cry that happiness is possible, that human relations can be improved, that life for women, and for men, can be made richer.

Franca was unsettled at this period, and the experience of appearing in plays written for her crystallised her discontent. She had on many occasions expressed her dissatisfaction with life as an actress. 'If I could go back, I would without any question choose another kind of work. The job does not give me any kind of fulfilment.'[9] Having been brought up in a family of travelling actors and entertainers, she was immune to the romance of the stage. The tedium, the chore, the routine of displaying herself in parts which presented no challenge, in a medium which familiarity had led her to despise had always depressed her. Hovering in the wings before a first entry on a first night may have set the adrenaline coursing through the veins of actors who joined the profession in adulthood, but having been on stage since her tenderest years, she regarded walking on in front of footlights as humdrum. Only duffers, she implied, puff out their chests at plaudits for reciting lines and leading someone else's life, or grow fearful at the prospect of making a fool of themselves in public. She gave the impression that she had sleepwalked into the profession. 'If there were no limitations to one's choice, I think I would have dedicated myself to trade unionism or social work.'[10]

She was already engaged on works of charity or philanthropy with Red Aid, but it was proving too much for her. When asked why she had begun to go her own way in 1977, she replied that it was necessary to look back to the years from 1968, when she and Dario left the established theatre circuit. 'I continued acting, but there was also all the rest. I looked after the administration, sold the tickets, kept things in order and out of "revolutionary morality" I had no domestic help. Then as an afterthought, there were those ten thousand prisoners that I was involved with. That was how it was then: politics first. If it so happened that there was a good part for an actress in the script, so much the better. If not, "the political discourse has to work, so you, what the hell do you want?" And in fact I asked for nothing. But I was absolutely ground down.'[11]

The voguish slogan said that 'the personal is political' so Franca introduced politics into her own life. She went on strike. The event has become part of family and company legend and, as with all legends, there are various versions of how she went about it. In some, she put a notice up in her home alerting her husband and her son that if, from that point on, they wanted clothes washed or ironed, meals prepared, rooms tidied, phone calls recorded, they would have to do it themselves. In another, she informed the company and the groups who used the Palazzina that she would no longer be available for the various services and tasks she had previously performed. In further versions, she announced that she was retiring from the stage. Whatever form it took, her announcement galvanised those around her. Dario declared his agreement. Previous requests for domestic help had been refused on the grounds that it introduced the class system into the home, but now the guardians of revolutionary morality decided that flexibility was in order, that domestic work had no greater or lesser dignity than any other proletarian sale of personal labour, that it was not *ipso facto* exploitative, and that provided a domestic servant was well treated and generously paid, there was no reason why one should not be employed. A woman, later replaced by a Filipino couple, was taken on as cleaner and cook. The number of employees grew, and a decade later Dario and Franca were surrounded by secretaries, agents and personal assistants. They were in general well treated and well paid, but the demands put on them, especially by Franca, could be high. She worked on high octane energy, and when stressed or fatigued, was prone to fits of temperamental intolerance or displays of excitable emotionalism. In later years, the house in Milan became a workshop, and there was a high turnover. Some assistants left in high dudgeon, and others were summarily dismissed.

Dario was disconcerted at the prospect of Franca abandoning acting. He wrote a further set of monologues, *All Home, Bed and Church,* in eight days, and presented them to her. 'We put it on, with me acting. On my own. After the premiere, which was a success, I could have given up. I had shown myself that I could do it. And my insecurities vanished.' The idea that Franca Rame, who had grown up in the acting profession and had been performing since girlhood, required reassurance about her on-stage abilities, is bizarre, but she had little experience as solo performer and had watched Dario perform in that style since *Mistero buffo* in 1969. To that extent, *All Home Bed and Church*[12] was a new departure, and marked the opening of a new phase in her career, as solo performer. She would travel all over world performing these pieces, and indeed in many countries her fame was associated exclusively with the one-woman *feminist* (italics are de rigueur) monologues she performed, and had authored or at least co-authored.

The new programme was first staged in Milan in December 1977. Initially there were five monologues, one of which, *Wakening Up,* had survived in modified form from the television series. In the first version, an alarm clock wakes up a woman who runs around the house preparing her child for nursery and herself for work, only to realise that all her rushing is unnecessary since it is Sunday. In the amended form, the woman abandons herself to a utopian dream of peace and harmony, where she can stroll at leisure in a world where work has been humanised, where relations are relaxed and idyllic and where 'there is no egoism, only communism'.

Same Old Story exploits the grotesque to strong effect. Rather than making love to her husband, the narrator is shown as compelled by him to copulate. Her fear of pregnancy is swept aside with rough words, and in the course of the monologue the woman changes into a gynaecologist and a woman giving birth, before becoming the new baby and then, with devastating suddenness, a doll which is the uninhibited doppelganger of the conventional, repressed woman. To the woman's initial disgust, the doll unleashes a flood of obscenities and of scatological, foul language. The woman tells her baby a fairy tale which turns into a grotesque parody of itself. The story twists and turns in an obscene Wonderland peopled by a dwarf who falls in love with the foul-mouthed doll, but sees his plan to marry her thwarted by the arrival of a ferocious wolf, who turns out to be an electronic engineer, transformed into a wolf by a wicked witch. The man explodes, leaving the woman free and in control of her body. She walks off into the sunset until she reaches a tree whose branches shelter a group of young women, who agree that they all have the same old story to tell.

The swelling ebullience of the piece is intoxicating, but the most intriguing aspect is the use of the doll as double. The woman is twee, stiff and demure but the doll can kick over the traces and unshackle herself from the demands put on women in society. If woman's liberation was an aim Franca accepted, release from convention presented a difficulty for her. She always adhered to standards of propriety and decorum. Until she liberated herself in 1994 when performing *Sex?Don't Mind if I Do,* an adaptation of a manual written by her son, she always responded with a shudder to words which could be regarded as vulgar. However incongruous it may be in one of her rebellious views, there was always something of the mannerly bourgeois about her. She was more at ease in dresses than in blue jeans and blouses. Several actresses elsewhere in Europe were objects of her disapproval when their productions of her shows were damned as lacking in taste, or as 'vulgar'. One woman in Finland had the misfortune to trick out with outsize phalluses the set she was using for her own version of Franca's monologues. When Franca got wind of it, she immediately withdrew performing rights. In a translation I did of a later play, *An Ordinary Day*, I grappled with the problem of finding a word to express the part of the male body which an enraged prostitute had a habit of biting off. In the original, the word was the polite *coso*, which is more properly rendered as 'thingummy.' My translation, 'prick', was certainly more direct than the original, and when the English was re-translated into Italian for Franca's approval, the translator used the word *cazzo*, which is even more crude than the English. Franca was incensed, and bawled down the phone from Milan that Dario would never use such improprieties.

A Woman Alone caused Franca to be picketed by English feminists when she performed it at the Riverside theatre in 1982. The work was a protest against harassment, but in London the problem was the see-through negligée which Franca chose to wear. To English eyes, any form of nudity or semi-nudity was equivalent to the presentation of the woman as sex-object. Franca reacted with disbelief and regarded the protest as a manifestation of traditional British puritanism. The woman was kept locked at home by her jealous husband, making contact only with a crippled but sex-crazed brother-in-law and an unseen female neighbour living opposite. She is also beset by peeping Toms, whom she wards off with her rifle, but during her uninhibited monologue she persuades herself that the gun would be better used on her uncaring husband, and the finale shows her seated quietly, gun across her knee, awaiting his return.

Over the years the number of monologues grew, so the volume published in 1989 carried the title *Twenty-five Monologues for a Woman*. Their success all over the world eventually rivalled that of *Mistero buffo*. Like Dario, Franca went on stage to address the audience in improvised prologue about issues of the day in whichever country she happened to be, before performing the written script. These pieces represent Franca in her own right, if not quite in her own write. The underlying demand is not so much for a rethinking of female identity as for a new deal for women in their everyday life. If it is true that Italian feminism has contained in itself the competing themes of equality with men and of the intrinsic diversity of women,[13] Franca only really engaged with the first. The language and the structure have a touch of surreal clowning, but the agenda could not be more concrete.

These plays dramatise the day-to-day plight of ordinary women enslaved by household chores, of housewives dealing with inflation at the micro level, of wives dealing with emotional neglect and physical overwork, of women hoping for change. 'Franca's theatre is not meta-feminist, in the sense that it doesn't question the sex of God and the existence of the individual,' wrote one critic, somewhat heavily, before adding that 'the "painful proximity" that characterises her voice results in a fusion of writer, performer, subject and audience that bypasses the necessity of intellectual argumentation'.[14] It is true that these monologues are never adventures in ideas, which is why they disappointed those who expected more intellectual fare. The fundamental conviction is that human beings, male and female, huddled together for a brief period of consciousness on earth must behave towards each other with respect, fairness and decency. This statement has the crystalline banality that, as G. K. Chesterton put it, is the mark of a truism. There is always a need for some alchemy in literature: the alchemy in Fo and Rame is a humour which is zany, surreal, adventurous, grotesque but never merely whimsical. Humour is the artifice which mediates and transforms, and yet, like some of Chekhov's short stories, these sketches impress and disconcert by their seeming lack of art, by their ability to cling close to lived life. 'Gentlemen, you live badly,' Dario had been saying for years, and now Franca's riposte was 'Ladies, do not put up with it.' Both continued to chorus that the fault was in the system, in the structures of power which left both male and female oppressed and alienated.

Franca's feminism was not especially revolutionary. A relationship marked by mutual fidelity, love and commitment, underpinned by a previously unknown equality in every domain was the ideal. Her

Marxism did not persuade her to follow Engels in questioning the family itself, nor did her feminism ever lead her to take an interest in 'separatism'. The witnesses she lined up in her theatre may have experienced misery and dissatisfaction in their married life but, even in *A Woman Alone,* they craved fulfilment in shared heterosexual life. The passion they expressed was for parity of consideration. There is no ideology of anti-male feeling at any level other than the purely jocose. She was appalled when, while she was performing in the Palazzina, a group of young women outside started jeering and dancing around Jacopo because he had the misfortune to be male. On another occasion in Rome, a group of twenty female students arrived to find the theatre full. They declared themselves to be feminists and demanded entrance. Franca apologised, pointing out that all tickets were sold, but offered to arrange seats for them on the stage. The leader of the group demurred, saying that there were several men in the audience who could be ejected. Franca refused, saying that her plays were intended for a male audience as well. 'Yes I am a feminist, if it has a political edge, not when it involves a sterile struggle against men. Yes, if it means walking hand in hand. Women need to be helped to liberate themselves.'[15]

These same students might have expressed surprise, even shocked dismay, at the recognition that the central figure in Franca's drama was the mother. The stock character of much feminist theatre, the normally youthful woman who asserts her independence and makes her brave journey on her own in a hostile world, is simply not present. Franca's maternal heroine is a figure with deep roots in Mediterranean culture and mythology. She makes her first appearance as the Virgin Mary, standing desolately at the foot of the cross in the sketches from the Passion which were added to *Mistero buffo* in the 1976 summer season. In one, Franca is shown rejecting the Archangel Gabriel's attempts to comfort her while her son hangs on the cross, telling the archangel that only a mother who has suckled her baby, who sat beside him when he cried as he was teething can understand her plight; in another, she is shown lamenting that her thirty-three year old son will never have a family, and arousing the compassion of a Roman soldier and of the other women at Calvary, not because she is a queen or her son divine, but because he is human and she is experiencing a mother's pain. This medieval Madonna returns in the closing vision in *The Kidnapping of Fanfani* as the eternal mother who mourns for all her children, everywhere. 'I am on earth, at every moment I am on earth . . . I am inside all mothers devastated by suffering and by your violence. I am inside the withered flesh of Vietnamese women, holding in their arms their slaughtered sons . . . I am in the anguished cry of black mothers, embracing the feet of their children lynched by racists . . . it is my tears which fall on the head of a poor Chilean boy, gunned down in the stadium in Santiago . . .' The same figure dominates these new sketches, most obviously *The Mother*, a play based on the experiences of a woman who had contacted Franca through Red Aid. This mother, who had lost touch with her son until she saw television footage of him being arrested for involvement in terrorist activity, is a direct descendant of the *mater dolorosa*. The women in *Same Old Story*, *Wakening Up* or *The Freak Mamma* may be facing all the dilemmas of modern women juggling work and home, but they are first and foremost dedicated, sacrificing mothers, whose first thought is for their children. Feminism represents liberation inside the family, not from it.

These plays also revealed Franca's real range as actress. Not being devoid of vanity, she relished the appreciation she received abroad where she was known for her own achievements and not simply as Dario Fo's wife. She happily reported that she had been listed in France as 'one of the three great, world-class epic actresses'.[16] In Italy, she had only appeared in plays written in Dario's style, so had made her reputation as a comic actress. The television part in 1981 of Mrs Warren in George Bernard Shaw's play was one of the few exceptions, but for the most part she had denied herself the opportunity normally given to celebrated actresses such as Eleonora Duse, Sarah Bernhardt, or indeed Vanessa Redgrave and Madeleine Renaud, to test themselves in melodrama, modern comedy and classical tragedy. It is always intriguing to speculate on what Franca and Dario might have been had they not known each other or if, having met, they had formed an antipathy towards each other. How different, wondered Pascal, would history have been if Cleopatra's nose had been longer, and if Anthony had not been attracted to her?

And if Franca Rame's nose had been misshapen, and Dario not drawn to her? There is no sign that Franca wished any such dispensation, but, holding wider speculations at bay, it is reasonable to assume that Franca's acting career would have taken a different turn. She would have done more film and TV, and might have had the chance to perform in styles other than the comic. The life she chose gave her no such possibility, but some of these stronger monologues, notably *Medea* and *The Mother*, gave a glimpse of what might have been. They revealed in her an inner force, an integrity, a spiritual quality, a stillness, a capacity to induce in spectators that reflective and deeply felt silence which is in theatre a more profound sign of appreciation than noisy applause.

CHAPTER 13

Tiger, Tiger

A new mood, one of those unaccountable, unplanned alterations in the public humour which can unexpectedly seize nations took hold of Italy in the late 1970s. Given the name 'ebb-tide', it implied a weariness with political activity and campaigning, and a withdrawal into the private, emotional, perhaps even domestic sphere of life. The Movement, and terrorism, had by no means totally collapsed, but there was a growing if grudging recognition that the Bastille could not be stormed, that perhaps in modern society there was no Bastille to be stormed. Retiring into the private dimension was still put forward as a gesture of contempt towards the 'system' and an assertion of individual purity, but the view commonly heard was that the days of grand public strategies had passed and that people were entitled to turn their minds to private matters, to culture, ecology, agriculture, self-fulfilment, hedonism, cuisine (which enjoyed a boom), or to marrying and raising families. The more opportunistic, those who would in future decades occupy parliamentary seats, editorial offices or judicial authority began to distance themselves from what it was convenient to term the excesses of youth.

The new mood did not mean that interest in politics had died, far from it, and it certainly did not indicate the end of terrorism, but it presented a problem for the far Left, especially since it was accompanied by a growing disquiet with the ideology of terror and violence. Instead of bringing the state to its knees, terrorism was producing a disabling malaise and even nausea among the adherents of the 'Movement'. For many leftists, the response to terrorism was as much an issue as the struggle against the capitalist order. The state itself had closed ranks, with the Communist party backing the hard line taken by the Christian Democrats and railing against the infantilism of intellectuals or youthful militants who advocated violence or 'revolution'. The Authorities, with a range of special laws and newly instituted police units, were now making headway against student and industrial dissent. Carlo Alberto Dalla Chiesa headed a newly instituted police division, and many of the first generation terrorists were in jail.

Like the novelists Leonardo Sciascia and Alberto Moravia, Dario found himself subjected to constant sniping for his supposed ambiguity towards terrorism. The televising of the second episode of *Mistero buffo* coincided with the killing of two policemen during the occupation of Rome University, and Antonello Trombadori, Communist member of parliament, veteran of the Resistance and author of some volumes of verse, suggested that Dario should insert a condemnation of these killings in his programmes. Dario replied that he had no objection to this in principle, but would prefer it to be part of a wider condemnation of all violence, certainly including 'those who shoot and kill policemen', but also including the poisons spewed out in July 1976 by the chemical plant in Seveso, and 'the provocations which have been causing blood to be shed in this country for the past nine years'. He added, 'Of course I am opposed to violence, ferociously opposed, firstly because people are killed, a most serious sin. Secondly because in this way, we fall into the traps laid by the Establishment.'[1]

Franca was similarly criticised in December 1977 by a correspondent from the *Corriere della Sera* who took exception to the closing scene of *A Woman Alone*, where the woman settles down with a rifle on her lap to await the return of her abusive husband. Dario penned an acid reply, wondering at the selectivity of the correspondent's distaste, pointing out that the heroine could plead self-defence since she was preparing to ward off attacks on her. He emphasised that no violence occurred on stage and wondered why there was no objection to the violence of

Medea, 'but you can't accuse Euripides of being an instigator of violence or of terrorism. By God, he's a classic!'[2] The implacable Trombadori went back on the attack after seeing a petition in the magazine *Cinema Nuovo*, which protested against the treatment in a German jail of Irmgard Moeller, a member of the Baader-Meinhof group who had been found in her cell with stab wounds in the stomach. The signatories, he suggested, were not humanitarians but covert sympathisers with terrorist violence. Dario replied, 'Trombadori is a terrorist in the sense that he creates terror. A natural terrorist. No, he does not point a gun, but his index finger . . . I insist in saying that Trombadori is a terrorist because his aim is to terrorise all those who do not accept the logic of the defence of violence offered by any regime, at any cost, against any person guilty of any crime, for the simple reason that that person is a human being.' Dario also took exception to Trombadori's habit of casting aspersions on Franca. 'In each of your writings, you never fail to refer to "the well known actress, Franca Rame", portraying her as a kind of suffragette who - these are your words - "has certainly never experienced real Fascist violence." And I am not here to remind you how out of place and in bad taste this expression is. But where were you, Honourable Vigilante, at the time of the Fascist aggression Franca did endure?'[3]

If criticism from the despised Communist party could be brushed aside, it was harder to silence doubts from inside the Movement. It was felt on all sides that there was a manifest need for rethinking and regrouping. A grand meeting, to embrace all shades of left-wing opinion, was called to take place in Bologna in September 1977. The official topic was Repression, in itself an acknowledgement, however grudging, that the government's measures against militancy and terrorism were proving effective, but the real agenda was a vague unease and a sense that a decade of unrest had produced scant results and that it was time for maps to be redrawn. Dario stated that the Bologna meeting had two urgent tasks: 'to take soundings inside the Movement and to evaluate the weight which an 'armed party' ideology has, both quantitatively and qualitatively, in the Movement.'[4]

The choice of Bologna, the traditional stronghold of the Communist party, as venue was deliberately provocative. The new Left had made a habit of attacking the 'Social Democrats,' that is, the Communists, for their abandonment of revolutionary ideals, while in reply PCI leader Enrico Berlinguer dismissed those planning to attend the conference as *untorelli*, a word used in Alessandro Manzoni's classic novel, *I promessi sposi* to describe spreaders of the plague. Conferences, especially those involving such disputatious groups as the Italian Left in those years, were always tricky events to manage. The previous year, *Lotta Continua* had simply disintegrated during its congress in Rimini when such constituent parts as those representing workers and women failed to find sufficient common ground to allow them even to meet in the same room.

In Bologna, the Communist administration of the city smothered its opponents with kindness. It announced that those attending were welcome to roll out their sleeping bags in the city parks, and mobilised the city's social kitchens to provide meals at give-away prices. The management of the conference itself was a more delicate matter. There were many events billed, and each room or building was occupied by a different faction of the disunited Left desperate to proselytise their own cause. Since the various groups kept largely to themselves, when they did not actually come to blows, there was little meeting of minds. The distinguished visitors had a hard time. Felix Guattari and Gilles Deleuze, two of the leading French leftist opponents of the better known *nouveaux philosophes*, were in attendance but they were confronted by the Italian press at its most chauvinistic over the insolence of the French in daring to criticise human rights in Italy when the guillotine was still in use in France.[5]

Dario's principal contribution to the proceedings was the premiere of *Story of a Tiger* on 22 September in the Palasport. The setting is in China in the days of the revolutionary war and the tale opens with a soldier who injures his leg on Mao's Long March, holding up the progress of the army. When Brecht at his most Stalinist devised a similar situation in *The Measures Taken*, also set in China, his activist accepted death rather than impede revolutionary progress. Dario's soldier, on the other hand, refuses the 'offer' made by one of his comrades to shoot him, but he is abandoned and takes refuge in a cave, which turns out to be the lair of a tiger and her cub. The tiger heals him by licking his wounds, and the three then form a surrogate family. However, the soldier finds himself relegated to a position of servant and flees to a nearby village. The animals follow him, causing the villagers initially to disperse in panic, but they come to appreciate the advantages of having a tiger on their side when they are attacked first by the Japanese and then by the forces of Chiang Kai-shek. As reinforcements, they fabricate false tigers using carnival masks and costumes, and live peacefully until a functionary of the now victorious Communist party arrives to inform them that tigers must be returned to the forest forthwith since it has been decreed that they are 'anarchistic, lacking a command of dialectics and so cannot be assigned a role in the party'. Instead, the peasants enclose the tiger in a henhouse, allowing them to tell future apparatchiks that instructions have been complied with and that the occupant of the henhouse should be registered as a 'tigered hen'. Later, higher commissars arrive to compliment them on their initiative in disobeying petty officialdom, now regarded as revisionists and counter-revolutionaries, but issue new directives that, in the absence of enemies, tigers are to be confined to a zoo. The only reply is the roar of the tiger, in itself sufficient to keep all placemen in subjection.

This multi-layered tale transcends its allegorical elements. Dario lists the allegories in his prologue, starting with an existential revolt against passivity and death contained in the soldier's refusal of euthanasia, and the Camusian revolt and re-statement of humanist values in the call for 'resistance even in the face of death'. This statement of the value of life in itself was of a sort Brecht was not called to make in the course of his own political activity, unlike in the abstraction of fictional political theatre, but Dario found himself compelled every day to express his own disagreement with those 'mistaken comrades' who had chosen the 'armed struggle' and arrogated to themselves the power of life and death. The fable also contains other allegories, and chimed in with the anti-party, anti-authority mood of the Bologna conference. In China, the tiger is, according to Fo, associated with all the qualities which distinguish honest candour from fawning servility, so 'to possess a tiger means never to delegate anything to anyone, never to invite others to resolve problems, not even those people who have previously been given a mandate, not even the most highly esteemed of officials, not even those who have demonstrated their know-how on countless occasions, the most trusted and honest party secretary . . . no, never!'[6]

If this call to take autonomous political responsibility against authority and bureaucracy is powerful and rousing, there is more to this enigmatic tale than politics. In a unique way the man, female tiger and cub form in the forest caverns a kind of holy family, whose relations are tight, exclusive and satisfy all needs and cravings of creatures, human or animal, for shelter, warmth, nutrition, care, comfort and affection. The cave is the home, where the tiger is moved to help the sick and dying male. Once he has overcome more obvious feelings of fear towards a beast known in legend for its ferocity, the soldier develops feelings of delicate affections towards the tiger. The tiger acts as nurse for her injured mate and there are even fairly explicit sexual overtones to the description of the tiger licking the soldier's wounds, and of the man sucking milk from the tiger's teats. On his recovery, the male becomes hunter and provider, showing the wild animals the benefits of cooked meats, so when he flees to the village and to human habitation, he leaves behind a feeling of betrayal and disloyalty.

When the tiger comes looking for the soldier, the villagers may be terrorised, but the focus is not on their fear of the beast of the jungle but on the mutual recriminations between the partners as the tiger reproaches the man for ingratitude after her efforts to nurse him back to health. The man in his turn tells the tiger-mother how he had helped her by feeding from her breasts when they were expanded and causing discomfort, so gradually domestic peace is restored. The narrative parodies but reproduces in gentle terms the style of the romantic, happy-ever-after novel. The man is driven to explain how the family had been formed: 'you know, when there is love in a family . . . we made peace. I stroked her under the chin . . . the tiger gave me a lick on the . . . the cub gave me a little kick . . .' The distance between civilisation and the jungle evaporates, but so does the gap between this piece and the monologues which had proceeded it. Both express a demand for continued love and loyalty. *Story of a Tiger* bestrides political commitment and the 'ebb-tide' culture of Italy in the late 1970s.

Not even in *Mistero buffo* did Dario create for himself such a platform for his acting talents. Here he gave a demonstration of his own, non-Brechtian style of epic acting, switching effortlessly from one character to another, turning lightly to address the audience as though the fourth wall were an alien imposition to be ignored rather than destroyed, transforming himself from man to beast and filling the stage with armies which only the crassly unimaginative could fail to see. He summoned the audience into person to person confidence, wheedled, coaxed and coerced them to see the world through his eyes. His hands and flaying arms painted pictures of men holding weapons, of wounded soldiers, of menacing tigers, of houses spaced around a village, of hen-houses and cages, and even of precisely positioned walls. In a Fo performance, the body is king. In *Story of a Tiger*, he crawled like a man in pain, pranced like a child, paced like a feline, ran like a crowd in terror, all the while producing a flow of sounds which reproduced the roar of animals, the creaking of rusty doors, the cawing of birds, the crowing of cockerels, the clanging of bars and the scuttling of soldiers in fear of death. He impersonated a deer captured in a hunt and even a bullet as it emerges from the barrel of a gun. Nothing was more astonishing than the lightness and grace of movement this now heftily built, no longer young man, could achieve. He combined mime, mimicry and ventriloquism in a bravura style which was a reminder that once he had learned a trade with Jacques Lecoq, but that he had applied his learning in a way Lecoq never intended to become in succession orator, teacher, performer and tribune of the plebians. The ideology to which he had dedicated his life was still detectable in the words that flowed in torrents, but his solitariness as he strutted back and forth spoke of an actor who as actor could not give assent to notions of equality. Some talents cannot be acquired but having been inherited demand display; art leaves no space for democracy. Dario is an instinctive *generalisimo* of the stage, and while he had in other days attempted to rein in his tendency to elbow others aside or to leave them in the shadows, now he strutted as lord and master. Even Italian audiences required the guidance of the mime and gestures, since Dario performed in a synthetic dialect with elements taken from Venetian, Lombard or Paduan speech but spoken by no one in the form he employed it. Communication depended on non-linguistic devices, above all on *grammelot*.

There is some mystery over the origins of the work. The canonical explanation is that the tale is an elaboration of a story Dario heard recited by a Chinese story-teller during his visit to China. However, Dario is not a reliable guide to his own sources or inventiveness, and in none of the many interviews he gave on his return from China does he make any mention of the tiger story. He does refer to the history, not of a tiger or a soldier, but of an old woman who liaised with the partisans in the war against the Kuomintang. A boy tries to reach her hide-out, is wounded by pursuing soldiers and is hidden by the woman in a washing basket. When the soldiers rummage about looking for him, the boy coughs, but the woman coughs in unison and confuses the men so deeply that they end up throwing their leader down a well.[7] There is no tiger. Bent Holm, the Danish dramaturg and Fo translator, drew up an alternative, admittedly speculative, genesis of the tale.[8] He points out that it is inconceivable that in the conditions prevailing in Maoist China any story-teller could have made the criticisms of the party which are implicit in the closing sections. His own suggestion is that elements taken from a book by the scholar Enrica Colotti-Pischel, overlaid with the tale told by the Shanghai story-teller, could have provided Dario with inspiration for the parts of the story dealing with the march, escape from death and refuge in the village, but that the introduction of the tiger instead of the old woman is an original invention. The closing attack on grey bureaucracy and party apparatus is pure Fo, and the real targets are Italy and Italian Communism. In any case, the tale has, like Shakespeare's comedies, an authenticity and charm independent of any putative sources.

Franca had to face problems of a purely private nature when in January 1978, while on tour in Genoa, she was knocked down by a car. In addition to injuries to the spine, arm and hand, she suffered damage to the central nervous system. She was kept in hospital several weeks, and was subject to strange, troubling bouts of hallucination when she believed her arms and hands were on fire. The pain was intense and her recovery was never complete. She only regained partial use of her hand and arm, and for long afterwards she required pain-killers to continue work. Even slight changes of condition or temperature could cause a relapse. During the time of convalescence, Dario and Jacopo, she said, looked after her like a baby, washing her, dressing her even at times feeding her. 'It is thanks to them that I did not give way to despair, that I was able to return to acting in autumn, that I did not die. Believe me, I am not exaggerating. That's why I say that perhaps it is right that I have suffered so much if this suffering has given me the certainty of such great love from my husband and my son. It is love we are talking about, not pity. If they had only felt pity, they could have hired a nurse or put me in a clinic. I have had proof of love which few women have in their lives, from Dario and Jacopo above all, but also from the comrades who perform with us, who organise our company.'9

Franca was still convalescing when, on 16 March 1978, the whole of Italy was thrown into turmoil by the kidnapping of Aldo Moro by the Red Brigades. Andreotti's government had resigned in January, and Moro had been working behind the scenes to stitch together a stronger Christian Democrat - Communist alliance which would give the PCI greater influence while still denying them cabinet posts. His efforts were successful, and he was on his way to Parliament to vote on the confidence motion when his car was ambushed. The five men in his escort were slaughtered, and Moro himself dragged away. He was to remain a hostage in the 'people's prison' for fifty-five days while the police searched the length and breadth of Italy for some trace of him. The terrorists threatened to kill him unless their conditions, which included the release of 'political prisoners', were met. The government, supported by the PCI but not by the Socialist party, replied with assertions of the need for 'firmness' in the face of blackmail. From captivity, Moro wrote a series of anguished letters to his wife, to party colleagues, to political opponents, to civic leaders and to the Pope begging for their intervention. The Italian authorities were unyielding. Moro was assassinated on 9 May, and his body left in the boot of a Renault in Via Caetani in Rome, half way between the headquarters of the DC and the PCI.

Italy was split over the desirability of negotiating with terrorists. The main argument against doing a deal was that enunciated memorably by Rudyard Kipling - 'If once you have paid him the Dane-geld/ You never get rid of the Dane.' Paradoxically, the most forceful advocates of a negotiated settlement to save a human life were those who most abominated all that Moro represented politically. *Lotta Continua*, the extreme left newspaper which had survived the disappearance of the party, was highly critical of the Red Brigades. Leonardo Sciascia, who had revealed himself in his novels a virulent opponent of all the DC stood for, came out in favour of negotiations, and was attacked by Giorgio Amendola, a leading Communist, for his trouble. Dario and Franca, in total consistency with their rejection of all violence, criticised the Red Brigades and interceded for Moro's life. They took their stance on fundamentalist notions of human rights and the sanctity of life which had been the basis of their objections to the use of terror and to the torture or ill-treatment of terrorists. Dario, together with Marco Pannella, leader of the Radical party, and several dissident Communists and independent bishops, was a signatory to a petition prepared by an ad hoc 'party of negotiation', which only *Lotta Continua* would publish.

Franca was invited by the very authorities who had attacked her fiercely for her work with Red Aid to use her influence and act as intermediary. She travelled to Turin to meet the imprisoned Red Brigades leaders who were on trial in the city. One of their number, Alberto Franceschini, gave an account of the meeting:

> The last request for intervention was made by Franca Rame. She came to the prison in the name of the Christian Democrat undersecretary for Justice, Renato Dell'Andro, asking for the unconditional release of Moro . . . the conversation with Franca, almost a year after her visit to the Asinara (an island prison off the coast of Sardinia), was brief and dramatic. On that occasion I had been struck by her human expression, the expression of a woman sincerely upset by the conditions in which we were forced to live. But now she seemed to have aged, as though more than a year had passed; there were signs of suffering on her face, her arm was in plaster as a result of a road accident. She had difficulty in

finding the words she needed, perhaps she was not happy with the role she was called on to play. She weighed attentively every word and began by talking about the accident. She was authorised to talk only to Renato (Curcio), Roberto (Ognibene) and me. We take a hard line. We concede her nothing, not even a smile or a greeting. We tell her we are enraged with her for having agreed to come to make such a proposal to us: Moro's life when they make us live in such inhuman conditions? The Ministry has suspended meetings with our families, while we can freely meet with her without guards or glass partitions. Does not she, who had always been so involved with the problems of the families of inmates, realise what all this means? Instead of making proposals of this sort, she should be trying to modify our living conditions, then we could talk. She replies that there is nothing to be done. All we can do is rise to our feet in the court and say that Moro must be freed. If he is assassinated, things will get worse for us. I read the anxiety on Franca's face as she transmits what they have told her. We do not know what to reply to her, we remain in silence for some seconds, perhaps some minutes, exchanging glances between the three of us, knowing glances. We cannot make a declaration of that sort, not even we who had released Sossi without obtaining practically anything in return. The Moro kidnapping is not the Sossi kidnapping. It was Renato who spoke for all of us. We did not await Franca's reaction. We filed back to our cells.[10]

The Moro kidnapping presented Italy not merely with a dilemma of *realpolitik* but also with a crisis of spiritual vision for which a largely secularised society was unprepared and ill-equipped. Dario was deeply moved by the systematic defamation of Aldo Moro by those who had been friends and acolytes but who now denigrated him for cowardice, or who suggested that the 'real' Moro was already dead and the man writing those letters was an empty shell. He was overwhelmed by the spectacle of a man of power at bay and by the glimpse of his humanity suddenly and unexpectedly, in extremis, revealed. In the final letters Moro had cast off all false trappings or pretensions, Dario wrote, and spoke as someone who had seen the imposture which had been his life as holder of power.[11]

Moro's murder, preceded by the stripping away of prestige and dignity seemed to Dario to constitute the basic matter of tragedy. In the people's prison, Moro found himself facing the primal fear of extinction, the anxiety of that human impotence and terror in the face of the irrational which tragic writers had dramatised in *Oedipus* or *King Lear*. Dario set aside his other work, and announced that he wished to dramatise the plight of Moro. For the first and only time in his life he decided that tragedy in the prime, Aristotelian sense of the word offered the appropriate key to understanding the catastrophe which had overtaken Moro himself and Italy as a whole. Tragedy had always been an obsessive interest of his but, like Samuel Beckett, Eugene Ionesco or Eduardo De Filippo, he was convinced that for twentieth-century society, tragedy could be made acceptable only when presented in the garb of farce. When contemplating Ruzzante, Molière or the figure of Harlequin, Dario was intrigued not by the comic devices they employed, or not only by them, but by the layers of tragedy which underpinned their comic vision. He admired Ruzzante's ability to create laughter which eschewed escapism, and to fashion a granite-hard farce which did not soften the realities of hunger, fear, poverty or sexual cravings. In Dario's view, tragedy was an intrinsic part of grotesque humour and satire, and their ultimate justification. 'Satire is nothing other than the comic treatment of tragedy; without tragedy, there is no satire. It provokes the laughter of the conscience, of the intelligence,' he once said.[12]

However, a satirical farce of the *Accidental Death* type would be an inadequate response to the spiritual and human traumas of the Moro case. The clashes and contrasts between 'the safeguarding of man, his liberty, his dignity, his life', and 'the reasons which we today call *raisons d'état* and which were once called the great law of the gods with, as its base, sacrifice, renewal through the sacrifice of the scapegoat, through bloodshed', lay too deep.[13] Instead, Dario composed an austere, classical tragedy, *The Moro Case*, but he had no experience in the genre, was never satisfied with the final work and never allowed it to be performed.

However, extracts have been published and the whole work is preserved in the Fo-Rame archive.[14] The leading figures in the Christian Democratic party, including Giulio Andreotti and the then Minister for the Interior (and future President of the Republic), Francesco Cossiga speak the words they uttered at the time, as does Pope Paul VI and Moro himself. The cast is completed by satyrs and Bacchantes, a Shakespearean Fool, a Tiresias-like Elder and a chorus borrowed from the Greeks. Behind this tragedy there lay a quasi-theological anxiety, worthy of Dostoevsky, over the mentality and motivations both of the terrorists and of the holders of public office, over the willingness of both sides to weigh human life like a commodity. The distinction between the differing concepts of destiny in Sophocles and Euripides aided his quest for understanding:

On the one hand the imponderability of the destiny of men overwhelmed by fate, which determines everything and against which reason has no sway, and on the other the conceptions of Euripides who sets his face against the absolutism of fate, who focuses on the reason of men. There are two key tragedies in this respect, *Philoctetes* and *Iphigenia*. You will recall in particular the terrifying encounter at the moment when Iphigenia was to be sacrificed to the possibility that the Achaeans, the Attics and the Illyrians might find unity, a unity of action which strongly resembles the situation of the coalition between the PCI and the DC. You could also consider the crucifixion of those who preferred to sacrifice the assumptions of the agreement, of the conquest etc., who considered it preferable to save the life of this woman who was the scapegoat. Finally all the falseness, the hypocrisy, the madness of this group of men in power, to convince themselves that this sacrifice had to be made. The same could be said of *Philoctetes*: he is wounded, he could be saved but the word is that his gangrene is incurable. It is easy to make out the meaning of this gangrene, this isolation, this expulsion, this decision to leave him for dead before he really is, but there is the other fact of his bow. What is his bow? It is the allegory of his strength, of his credibility, of his history and could be the pivot of his victory. Therefore it is necessary to sacrifice *Philoctetes* to take away his bow . . .

Dario's work has the heavy rhythms of oratorio or a *Dies Irae,* and perhaps could be performed if set to music, although it might need the talents of a Palestrina.

Dario performed an updated and rewritten version of *Story of a Tiger* at the Palazzina Liberty in February 1978. It was to be his last appearance there. Milan City Council's action for his eviction came before Court of Cassation the following year, and this time the Council's petition was upheld. The order did not have instant effect, but the Council had the option of serving it when they chose. Perhaps in deference to their own sense of changed times, perhaps ground down by the dogged perseverance of the Council, Dario and Franca decided to abandon the struggle. The Council promised not to use force, and announced that the next step was to calculate how much had been spent on restorations as against what was owed in rent. Dario undertook a disillusioned, half-hearted search among ex-cinemas and assorted halls for another venue, giving as his minimum requirement a building with at least a thousand seats. 'I am not interested in subsidies,' he said. 'All I want is compensation for what I have spent.' According to his own estimates, he was owed 100 million lire, plus legal expenses.[15] The company remained in the Palazzina until 1981, when they bowed to the unceasing pressure and left. They did not find another venue, so the Palazzina Liberty was the last theatre Dario and Franca had as their own. The building was subsequently used, officially, as a venue for chamber orchestras, puppet shows and touring companies and, unofficially, as a refuge for drug-takers and the urban destitute.

The days of the 'alternative circuit' were closing. Declining energy and enthusiasm undermine dedication to all causes, and both Dario and Franca began to speak with some nostalgia of the great theatres where they had performed at the beginning of their career. While rehearsing *Mum's Marijuana,* Dario had spoken enviously of the Piccolo theatre or La Scala opera house, with their superior facilities, properly equipped stage, comfortable green rooms and plush seats for the audience. Maybe, suggested Franca, we have neglected the middle class? Do not they have rights, should their dilemmas not be dramatised, or at least should they not be given the opportunity to face the problems confronting working class people? Is it really an act of apostasy, the couple asked themselves, to return to the official circuit if we retain faith with our own style of theatre and our own politics?

Dario was put to the test when he received a call inviting him to direct Stravinsky's *Histoire du Soldat* for La Scala as part of their bicentenary celebrations in 1978. The idea originated with Claudio Abbado, principal conductor and joint artistic director of the company, but although the production was to be part of the official programme, it would be staged not in the main auditorium but in the Piccola Scala. There was talk of a series of collaborative ventures, and a new opera by Luigi Nono was mentioned, but in the event the Stravinsky was the only work which reached the stage.

The decision to work with La Scala, normally viewed as the venue of choice of the wealthy and privileged, was made easier when Dario was able to recall that it had never been the chosen home of the 'conformist bourgeoisie', but had hosted satirical works which undermined the social status quo, such as *William Tell*.[16] A meeting with Abbado clinched the deal. The maestro explained that for the first production in 1914 Stravinsky had planned to put on 'a narrative opera with satirical scenes referring to the political and social situation of the time', but the conditions in the year of the outbreak of World War I had compelled him to scale down his ambitions.[17] To ensure that his work was staged, Stravinsky cut back the number of characters, leaving him with the devil, the soldier and his girl not to mention the rifle and the violin. Abbado wondered if Dario might like to return to Stravinsky's original vision and undertake a reconstruction of the never-performed original script, but warned that there remained only scattered excerpts and newspaper reports. Dario said that only his scant acquaintance with Abbado stopped him from embracing him on the spot. He decided immediately that the production would require to be done on an epic scale.

Later, he complained that some sections of the company were anything but enraptured with his work or his presence, and that he was being undermined from within. He was irked that the secretary general of La Scala had failed to alert Stravinsky's heirs of the plan and to seek due authorisation, and that only his intervention with the agent had prevented the production being aborted. When he required balancing weights to hold the high panels in place, the props department refused to provide them, but he resolved this problem with the unlikely expedient of procuring plastic bags from a supermarket, and filling them with sand 'which we asked workers on a building site to give us'.[18]

Until this point, Dario had limited himself almost exclusively to staging his own work. In 1967, he had directed *Sunday Parade*, loosely based on original work by Georges Michel, but after *Histoire* he accepted invitations to direct the work of other writers. 'Directing' is hardly an adequate term for the kind of transformation and rethinking involved in a Fo production. With Georges Michel, with Stravinsky, and later with Rossini, Molière, Brecht and Ruzzante, puzzled or outraged critics would point out that the script or score had been so comprehensively manhandled as to make it a full part of the Dario Fo canon with little of the spirit of the original. Whatever he stated, or even believed, Dario had not the selflessness to limit himself to releasing an energy in the text as he found it. He imbued and perhaps enriched it with his own fantasy, imagination, creativity, vision and personality, so Stravinsky's *Histoire du Soldat* became *Storia di un Soldato* and, as one reviewer pointed out in a trenchant but generally favourable notice, Dario's name was mentioned twice in the programme as against the one mention of Stravinsky. Fo was credited with the 'scenic action' as well as with responsibility for 'directing, scenes and costumes'.[19] The original script writer, Charles-Ferdinand Ramuz, was de facto written out. Explaining his thinking, Dario said:

> I love the *Histoire*. I consider Stravinsky to be one of the greats, much greater than is suggested by this stage and musical action, which had of necessity to be entrusted to a few actors. Ramuz's script seems embarrassing, highly dated, full of lines of phoney philosophy with no meaning, like, "nothingness is all, all is nothingness . . ." It restricts the action in the tale, nothing happens on stage, everything has already taken place. That's why I tried to have everything recounted, with few words and many gestures . . .

Ours is, rather than a means of re-reading a great, exciting author, an act of love towards Stravinsky.[20]

The original Stravinsky-Ramuz work was completely overturned. 'I had two and half months to get the show ready, with all the work done on stage, and not a word written at home.'[21] In fact the rehearsals lasted four months, and the script, if that is the appropriate word, emerged as ideas occurred to Dario in the theatre. By accident, he was using the improvisational techniques of *commedia dell'arte*. Where La Scala had expected a 'chamber piece', Dario chose to give them a 'piazza' piece. He introduced other compositions by Stravinsky, including the *Octet*, composed in 1923, five years after the *Histoire*. He considered inserting some Ragtime numbers, but concluded it was not feasible. The orchestra was not concealed in a pit but in full view on a raised platform in the centre of the stage, with the action unfolding around them. Instead of the one dancer which Stravinsky and Ramuz had intended, Dario created an instant collective with thirty unknown young actors from the Piccolo Teatro's drama school. Dressed in informal but brightly coloured costumes, they performed with riotous, festive joie de vivre, waving coloured banners and streamers and creating a sea of arresting images. Each took it in turn to play the part of the soldier.

The plot ended up resembling Ruzzante more than Ramuz. 'The action was completely reversed, in both dramatic and ideological terms,' wrote Dario in his introduction.[22] A poor peasant makes his way to the city, where he arouses the attention of a devil-flatterer, who tries to rob him of his violin, that is, his soul. The peasant is persuaded to enlist for what he believes to be a crusade, but finds it to be a war of profit. On his return, no one recognises him. In disillusionment, he sets sail in a 'ship of fools', only to be shipwrecked. He escapes to an island, ruled by an enormous skeleton made of reeds. The skeleton, who is king and head of state, is beset by a detachment of hooligans brandishing the P.38 (the favoured weapon of Italian terrorists) and surrounded by argumentative, unscrupulous courtiers, each desperate to grab positions of power. The king has a sickly daughter, represented on stage by a huge puppet, whom the soldier tries to coax back to life by playing his violin. The marriage of the two saves the state, but only to a dubious future of social democracy. The final scene has all the mimes, acrobats and actors, wearing *commedia* masks, seated in a semi-circle which resembles the Italian Parliament, speaking in *grammelot*, but moving restlessly from right to left, from one political formation to another, as self-interest dictated.

Critical responses were mixed, but the most ferocious came from the novelist Marta Morazzoni. She was no doubt right to conclude that 'almost nothing remains of Stravinsky, his music and his story, except for a musical theme kept as a distant background sound,' but her real objection was to 'the evident and flavourless political satire, which recalls television political parodies'.[23] In addition to criticisms from theatre and music critics, Fo found himself yet again engulfed in controversy with the political authorities of the city. His old adversary, Massimo De Carolis, came to see the premiere in Cremona, but left without a word. Dario paid tribute to his 'intelligence, ability and political wile' but suspected him of employing that wile to foment trouble for him behind the scenes.[24] Objections were raised to Dario's employment by a publicly financed company while he was still engaged in unfinished legal business with the Milan City Council, and further complaints that he had overspent his budget.

Dario succeeded in his central aim of attracting a mass audience to a work which had previously been regarded as only suitable for an élite. He calculated that in a season, La Scala would expect to play to around 20,000 spectators, whereas *Storia di un Soldato* had attracted 60-70,000 in Lombardy alone. La Scala, like many other theatres and opera houses in Italy, had accumulated a huge debt, but when Dario was blamed for adding to the deficit, he retorted that his production was one of the cheapest and most successful that La Scala had mounted for some years. He delightedly gave out detailed financial accounts to anyone who would listen, boasting that his production had cost only 25000 lire per spectator, as against the 40,000 lire which was the company average. He also received invitations to bring the production to London, the Edinburgh Festival, Belgium, Sweden, Holland and Germany. If these invitations had been taken up, it is reasonable to expect that all the costs could have been recovered, but opposition in the Council and inside the company was so intense that none of the invitations were accepted and the run ended in Milan in 1979. It was a storm in a teacup compared to past quarrels, but Dario's problems with official Italy were not over.

CHAPTER 14

On The Defensive

Dario's heightened profile after his return to television in 1977 brought unwelcome press articles, some questioning his account of his activities during the period of German occupation in the last days of the war. The fact that several of the journalists responsible for this renewed interest were motivated by political spite did not lessen the gravity of their charges. The basic facts were not in dispute. The Fo family lived in the territory where Mussolini, after being rescued by German paratroopers from captivity, had established his *Repubblica Sociale d'Italia* (RSI), whose capital was Salò on Lake Garda. Dario received call-up papers to join the Fascist army and eventually did so, initially explaining that his aim was to protect his father who was engaged in escorting escaped prisoners of war across the border into Switzerland.[1] He went first to the camp at Varese, believing that the detachments there had no military equipment and that he would be sent home. When he discovered this information was false and he was likely to be sent to Germany, he volunteered as a delaying tactic to join the parachute division in Tradate. Members of the RSI army were later called '*repubblichini*', a word which defies exact translation. The meaning is not 'republican' but something more contemptuous, like 'soldiers of the little republic of Salò,' but since it serves to indicate adherents of Mussolini's last regime, the unadulterated or polemical sense is 'Fascist'. The other damning term from that time is *rastrellatore,* that is, a member of the anti-partisan, round-up or death squads.

Dario was frequently challenged on this subject, particularly in the 1990s when Silvio Berlusconi, with the backing of the neo-Fascist National Alliance, came to power. The question of the status to be accorded the 'boys of Salò', once regarded as traitors or cowards, became a subject for renewed debate, but in Dario's case the issue was first raised in February 1977 when the extreme right-wing periodical, *Il Nord,* which circulated in Piedmont, published an article written by one Angelo Fornara, headlined 'The Red Fo Called Dario Once A Fascist.' The language was deliberately offensive, containing accusations that Dario was a 'turncoat, a histrionic, a social-climber, a clown who spins in every wind, a Fascist, a radical, a Communist, a fool with his snout in every trough'. This was bad enough, but Fornara went on to claim that Dario had been a *repubblichino* and a *rastrellatore* and that he had been enrolled in 'the Mazzarino battalion of the National Guard of the Republic of Salò'. This detachment had been responsible for a massacre in the region of Romagnano Sesia, and a fear of being recognised explained why, the article continued, Dario had never been able to tour in that area with his theatre company. Although *Il Nord* had a limited circulation, the allegations were reported in other media and questions were raised in Parliament. The daily, *Il Giorno,* carried the story while the magazine *Gente* dispatched journalists to dig more deeply.[2] These two publications later apologised and agreed there was no substance to the allegations, but *Il Nord* refused to publish a retraction. Fo raised a case for criminal libel against the writer of the article and the editor of the periodical, Gianni Cerruti. He hired as his lawyer, Giovanni Cappelli, who had acted for Franca's Red Aid and had defended some Red Brigades terrorists.

The hearing opened in February 1978 in Varese, where the magazine was published, and dragged on for over a year. Even by the standard of libel actions, it was a singularly nasty and contorted case, and turned on complicated political, ethical and historical questions concerning the period of Nazi occupation and the Resistance. Historians now agree that there were three wars underway in 1944: an anti-occupation uprising, a partisan movement, and a civil war between two sides with conflicting visions of post-war Italy. Cappelli focused on narrower issues – was Fo a *repubblichino*, was he guilty of being a *rastrellatore* and specifically had he been involved in the 'massacre of Romagnano Sesia', where many partisans were killed.

The crux of the case was not to establish whether Fo had been in the uniform of the RSI forces, since this was beyond discussion, but the level of commitment he had brought to the cause. This was a difficult case to argue in law. Failures of memory and bad faith meant that reliable witnesses were hard to find, but it was possible to produce documents to validate Dario's alibi at the period of the massacre. It was shown that he enlisted on 3 April 1944, the last time call-up papers were issued, and did choose to go to Varese, in accordance with his statements. His movements were complicated, in part because he escaped from one camp, in part because, surprisingly, he received an official pass to allow him to continue his studies at the Brera. He was able to prove that he could not have been involved in the death squads, but only by producing papers which reminded people that he had been in other military bases with *repubblichini*, not on the mountains with the freedom fighters.

Cappelli questioned the motives of those who had raised the action. His case was that when Dario returned to the TV screens after being banned for years, his *Mistero buffo* had aroused hostile reactions in certain quarters. The calumnies against him over his days with the militias of Salò were an attempt to 'bring out the most tragic, bitter moment of his life to discredit him before the masses who love him. The Fo who was a boy of seventeen is an attempt to kill off the Fo known today as an actor and artist'.[3] This may have been true but it did not serve to prove or disprove the charges. Dario himself went into the witness box, and admitted candidly that he had served in the RSI army and so had been a *repubblichino*, but an involuntary one. His decision to join the army when he received the call-up had been made with the agreement of the partisan forces operating in Alto Verbano, and was necessary to defend his family, especially his father who was helping smuggle prisoners of war and Jews across the border to Switzerland. 'I did enrol as a volunteer with the parachutists of the RSI, but my intention was to cover the partisan oganisation based in my house in Porto Valtravaglia . . . after the 8 September, my father, Felice, a station master near the Swiss border, took charge of the Resistence organisation in the Alto Verbano. I was only seventeen years old, and with others who were even younger I was employed on tasks appropriate for someone of my age.' His submission was that while he had worn the RSI uniform, he had always been anti-Fascist, and that the decision to join was a ruse to avoid suspicion falling on him and his family.

This account caused several columnists to enter the debate. The distinguished journalist, Indro Montanelli, who did not know Fo personally and had no sympathy with his politics, wrote that he was astounded that he had raised the legal action in the first place. 'Red or Black, the Fanatic Never Changes,' read the headline to his article. For Montanelli, the central point was not whether Fo had been a Fascist, since 'the right to make mistakes must be granted to everyone, especially the young', but he added that Fo's explanation 'does not persuade us particularly'. He went on: 'above all, we find it very strange that to escape military service under the banners of Mussolini, Fo found no better means than to enlist of his own accord. Enlistment for enlistment, Fo could even have chosen to enlist in the partisan bands, as did many of his contemporaries'.[4]

The lawyers representing *Il Nord* produced a grainy photograph, which had previously been produced in *Gente,* of Dario with a group of young recruits, all wearing the uniform and beret of the *repubblichini.* This added little to their legal case, particularly since Cappelli was able to show that Dario had not belonged to the Mazzarino detachment at the time of the engagement with the partisans. Military records, however incomplete, of Dario's movements disproved another allegation, that he had been a participant in massacres perpetrated during the suppression of the 'Free Republic' which the partisans had established in the town of Ossola. It was also established that, in spite of Fornara's allegations, Dario had toured with his company in the province of Novara on at least six occasions.

The most serious of the allegations was that Dario had been a *rastrellatore* and had actively participated in massacres of partisans and Resistance fighters, especially in the Val d'Ossola. A certain Sergeant Milani, who had served with the notorious *Folgore* unit, came forward to say that Fo had been at his side in one of the bloodiest and most barbaric of these round-ups. He declared that in October 1944, Fo had been there when the *Folgore* disembarked at Cannobio during an ambush at a cemetery near Falmenta in the operation against the 'Free Republic', when several partisans were killed. Milani said the event occurred in October, Fo insisted it was September but in any case was able to produce documents showing that he had only enrolled with *Folgore* in November, that is, after the massacre. In accordance with Italian court practice, the two men were brought face to face before the judge. Dario held to his assertion that he had joined up only to ward off suspicion from his father, but agreed that he had known Milani in that period. Milani continued to insist that Dario could not have known him in early November 1944, since at that time he was on service in Piedmont. The court found unconditionally in Dario's favour on this point.

If there was no proof of the major allegation of being a *rastrellatore*, Dario was compelled to admit to embarrassing exaggerations in previous accounts of his activities. In an interview with Chiara Valentini published in *Panorama*, he had said, 'I was always among the partisans', but in the witness box, he modified this statement to the more modest, 'we once went to bring food to some friends'.[5] Cappelli conceded that Dario may have been guilty of some hyperbole over his role in the Resistance, but invited the court to view his statements as a boastful 'grandfather's account to grandchildren'. Some friends in the Resistance became 'in that kind of dream' partisan leaders, while the fact of having given some assistance would be sufficient 'to transform the Fo home in a refuge for partisans, and indeed into their headquarters'.

However, the story of the Fo family's involvement with the Resistance was placed in doubt. The most damaging statement came from General Giacinto Lazzarini, a Resistance leader and hero whose credentials were beyond all question. He headed the bands active in the area where the Fos lived, and in one of his more extravagant moments Dario had claimed that Lazzarini was a myth for him. He even claimed to have searched in the hills and valleys for the Lazzarini group, but to have been unable to locate them. In the witness box, Lazzarini denied having ever heard of the Fo family's involvement in the struggle, a denial which referred not only to Dario but also his father. He asked the question which puzzled many people. If Dario 'had joined the parachute division on the advice of a partisan leader, why had he not said so immediately at the Liberation? It would have been a title of honour for him. Why keep hidden for so many years an episode of such merit?' On the other side, Dario produced letters from partisans who had operated alongside Felice Fo, while Leo Wachter, a Jew and partisan, contradicted Lazzarini by stating firmly that he had been given refuge in the Fo home.

In his summing up, the Public Prosecutor, Franco Mancini, who had a role because the charge was of criminal, not civil, libel, focused initially on the nature of the struggle in1944 in Italy which had been portrayed more as 'hagiography than history', meaning that the losers were afraid of the consequences of being on the wrong side. 'There has been an enormous multiplication of people who attempted to acquire the merit of having fought alongside the victors, and of reclaiming political virginity.'[6] He went so far as to ask for Fornara's acquittal. *Il Nord's* lawyer, Leandro De Maio resorted to grand rhetoric, asking the judges to see Dario not as an unbiased citizen but as a politically committed artist who advocates 'to his audience the destruction of the values in which, rightly or wrongly, the majority of people place their belief'. What right has a man who holds nothing sacred, who has criticised 'God, the saints, the Popes, but also the Madonna and politicians', to deny the right of criticism to a citizen like Fornara?[7] This argument ignored the fact that some specific allegations made by Fornara, not his overall civic rights, were at stake.

The verdict was recorded in Fo's favour, but many saw it as a Pyrrhic victory. Fornara was condemned to pay damages of 200,000 lire, a penalty judged mild by the press, and kept so low because the judges found unequivocally in Fo's favour only on one point. They rejected totally the accusation of participation in the raid on Romagnano Sesia. There had been death squads operating in that area, they stated, but there was no proof that Dario had any involvement. On the other points, the judgement was more indecipherable and the published verdicts reek of prejudice. 'It is certain', the judgement ran, 'that Fo wore the uniform of parachutist in the *repubblichino* ranks of the "Blue Battalion" of Tradate.' He himself recognised this point, – indeed could do no other, since there was circumstantial evidence supported by numerous additional documentary and testified grounds – even if he attempted to mitigate his voluntary enlistment, maintaining that he had played the part of an 'infiltrator', engaged on a double bluff. 'But his mental reservations', the judgment continued, 'leave things unchanged.' It is a puzzling assertion. 'Mental reservation' is a Jesuitical category which the court had introduced of its own accord. It was not part of Dario's case. He claimed his enlistment was a gesture to aid the Resistance and to ward off suspicion from his father.

The allegation that Dario had been involved in the operation against the Free Republic of Ossola was dismissed, but the finding over whether he could be called a *repubblichino* or even a *rastrellatore* was damaging to him. The reasoning was tortuous, but the verdict was that it was legitimate to use these descriptions. 'While it is certain that the Tradate parachutists were employed in some death squad activities ... it is not certain, indeed it is debatable, whether Dario Fo was so employed.' To a non-lawyer the absence of proof would seem conclusive, but the judgement continued: 'this circumstance is, in the view of the court, of negligible value ... the meaning is that Fo's militancy in a *repubblichino* battalion which certainly carried out some round-ups makes him, in a certain sense, morally responsible for all the activities and choices operated by that school which he had, by his own free choice, decided to enter.' This final judgement flies in the face of all jurisprudential logic and was bereft of any legal or moral sense of individual responsibility. The reasoning was that since Dario had been a member of an RSI body, he could be held 'morally co-responsible for all the activities and all the operational choices of that school which, by his own free choice, he had decided to enter.' Dario had been a member of a particular company, *ergo* he could be held responsible for every outrage committed by that body, whether he consented or was even present.

Even if there were some columnists who expressed bafflement at the court's judgment, the terms *repubblichino* and even *rastrellatore* were carried in the headlines the following day. If criminal law is based on the principle that a person is responsible only for his own actions and that guilt by association has no legal force, it is hard to see how it could be right and lawful to legitimise the use of a description based on actions which Dario had not committed. The term *repubblichino* would be flung in his face thereafter, even when he won the Nobel prize. 'The first *repubblichino* to win a Nobel prize,' sneered various newspapers when the award was announced in Stockholm. Pier Paolo Pasolini, no friend of Dario's, delighted in the use of the term.

Dario hailed the verdict as a victory but in truth the verdict pleased no one. *Il Nord* announced, inevitably, that it would appeal, while Dario raised an action against Milani, who was eventually acquitted. Dario was free of the slur that he had been a Fascist by conviction, and certainly free of any allegation that he had ambushed partisans or taken part in murderous attacks, but the fact that he had been in the RSI army was now in the public domain. It was also clear that some of his early accounts of his activities in the days of the Resistance were embellished and exaggerated. In all his theatre, no myth, no legend, no call to arms had more strength than the call to revive and abide by the values of the Resistance, but Dario had not been involved in that struggle. As one friendly but puzzled critic put it, '(Fo's) hero General Lazzarini was operating in the zone where Fo was living, and at the moment the conscription papers arrived. Why not join him?'

No one living in comfort has the right to judge those who lived in darker days, and Dario was not shown to have committed any enormity. The face in the photograph was that of a very callow youth. There was no shameful, concealed history to be compared to that of Martin Heidegger, Paul de Man or Kurt Waldheim, but there was a less than glorious story of subsequent exaggeration and occasional evasion. He was dogged by the story. In 1990, on the publication of an autobiographical work by Roberto Vivarelli, who had volunteered for the RSI army, Dario was interviewed and declared that, unlike Vivarelli, he had joined up not for ideological reasons, but 'to attempt to dodge the draft, to get home with my skin intact'.[8] He returned to the subject in subsequent autobiographical writings, where he spoke of the partisans who found refuge at the Fo house, of the activities of his father and uncle and of the risks he himself ran in assisting British prisoners of war to flee to Switzerland. He added new information that after the forty days training as a parachutist in Tradate, he and a friend absconded from the camp. Dario made his way home, but his father immediately took him to the village of Caldé where he had a friend who owned a house in the woods. He spent the last month of the war in an attic, being fed when friends judged it safe to visit him. He was finally able to get out when he heard bells ringing out and went onto the roof from where he saw people coming up from Caldé, shouting that the war was over.[9] In an interview marking his ninetieth birthday, he spoke candidly but not defensively. 'When I went back, the people in my village did not call me Fascist. I only tried to save myself. I was a boy.'[10]

At the trial's close, Dario and Franca were off to Sweden to play *Mistero buffo* and *All Home, Bed and Church* in theatres which had been sold out weeks in advance. Dario proceeded to Jutland to meet up with avant-garde director, Eugenio Barba, and his Odin Teatret, while Franca went on to Cologne. Part of that summer they spent in Umbria with Jacopo, who was now making a career for himself as writer and cartoonist with a satirical weekly, *Il Male*. With the assistance of his parents, he had bought a large wooded estate between Perugia and Gubbio, with abandoned farm houses and medieval watch towers scattered over the area. This he transformed into a hippy-cum-cultural compound which he named the Free University of Alcatraz, and embellished it with arresting, occasionally weird, sculptures or paintings done by his father and with gnomic graffiti of his own. It has hosted many relaxed seminars on a variety of topics from arts and crafts to psychotherapy and the techniques of cartoon-drawing. Dario and Franca, not to mention many others writers and performers, used the centre to give classes for aspiring actors from all over Europe.

Legal matters which had been pending for many years were resolved. In February 1979, the trial against Dario for threatening a police officer in 1973 when on tour with *The People's War in Chile* opened in Sassari, but he was acquitted of all charges. In July, he and nine others were acquitted of a similar charge relating to an event in Pordenone in 1970 when public officials had been barred from entering a venue where *Mistero buffo* was being performed. The Fos being still deeply controversial and divisive both in politics and in theatre, their lives were of interest to the media, and this interest was heightened when Franca was invited by RAI to present a series of twenty programmes to be broadcast from January 1980 under the title *Buonasera con Franca Rame.*

Once again, Dario wrote most of the material, but on-screen roles between the couple were reversed, with Franca taking the lead role and Dario guesting as 'feed'. Franca was now fifty-one and had been a public figure at least since the *Canzonissima* episode. Her position as one of Italy's leading actresses was well established, yet she felt that only with the rise of feminism and with her own solo performances had she won a position of parity with Dario. The couple insisted that the programmes be scheduled for a time when housewives, including both their mothers, would be watching. The new series gave another opportunity for a further settling of accounts. The treatment meted out to them at the time of *Canzonissima*, and the subsequent destruction of the film reels, still rankled, so they decided to re-record and broadcast sketches censored in 1962. They also found space for some pieces from the *Let's Talk About Women* staged three years previously, topped and tailed with fresh material. Some of the new sketches, like one featuring the ideal husband who turned out to be a robot of such terrifying efficiency that he was substituted by a flesh-and-blood man, or the piece on a mythical Batman-male, were a continuation of one-act plays Franca had been working on. Another such piece on a nurse tending an ex-minister, who had much in common with the Social Democrat ex-minister, Mario Tanassi, jailed for his part in the Lockheed scandal, struck the familiar note of political satire. The programmes were among the few occasions when Franca sang solo.

Apparently *Buonasera con Franca Rame* represented some kind of test or challenge she set herself. When asked by an interviewer if she of all had women had been successful in attaining equality in her marriage, she expressed herself in seemingly assertive but still troubled terms:

> Yes, now I have, because with *All Home, Bed and Church* I have shown other people that I can walk by myself, but it has taken me a lifetime to get here, and I have had to overcome so many conflicts, so many mortifications. This show has had for me the value of a wager. I said to myself: 'If it does not go well, I will close it down after three days and open an orphanage.' (An orphanage has always been an obsession of mine). It has gone well, so now I can tell you that my relationship with Dario is on an equal footing.[11]

Franca now found herself placed on a pedestal she had no wish to occupy but which she found impossible to vacate. She was the subject of profiles and endless requests for interviews, often beginning with the words – we know all we need to know about Franca Rame the actress, but who is Franca the woman? She was always accommodating, if somewhat impatient. Lalla Mori, asked her what age she was when she had her first sexual experience, (21, have I wasted too much time?), if she was passive in her relationship (Why should I be? There's me as well as him), if she had ever been attracted to another woman (No, never), although she agreed that many women had fallen in love with her, (I was embarrassed), but she initially declined to answer when she was asked how she made love. (Did your mother never explain to you that there is such a thing as privacy?). However she reminded herself that she was a public person, and so had an obligation to give an answer, but changed the question to how a woman should make love. There are six stages: Don't make too much fuss first; take a lingering bath, perhaps with your partner; clean and perfume yourself; kisses, sweet kisses, and caresses; careful not to overexcite your partner in the preliminaries; don't fake by uttering moans and little cries . . . but don't worry about being stroked and kissed in the right place . . . and have a good time![12] Franca might have made an excellent agony aunt.

Nevertheless, for the first time, in some of these interviews, Franca allowed readers a glimpse of dissatisfaction with her private life and relations with Dario. It was by no means the only, nor even the dominant, note. When asked if she was still proud to have Dario as husband, she replied in breathless tones, 'More than proud! We have been married more than twenty-five years, and there is a beautiful relationship between us, a relationship of absolute regard of one for the other, of respect, of love, love in the deepest sense of the word. We cannot do without each other, this is undeniable. You have no idea of how marvellous it is to have a man like Dario at your side.'[13] She spoiled the effect by adding that they no longer had sexual relations with each other. 'After twenty-eight years of marriage, there is no longer an exchange of sexual emotion between us, and I have tried to understand why not. I have thought it over and have arrived at the conclusion that we love each other too deeply to be lovers. It might seem incestuous to us.' That was not to say they were each living lives of monastic chastity and renunciation, and gossip on this score too was reported in the press. Franca gave voice, perhaps unconsciously, to a different kind of resentment when she referred to public reaction and judgment of their lives. She and Dario were equal, she said, before drawing back to add the qualification:

> Or nearly, because there is always a substantial difference: the judgement of your fellows. For instance, if Dario were to come to Spoleto and happened to meet up with a fascinating young girl, and were to spend the night with her, no one would think twice about it. [14]

But if she did so? It was an ancient complaint, made by women in Shakespeare or Ariosto, dramatised by Madame Bovary and Anna Karenina. Feminism, Franca implied, could not change men's conduct or society's judgement. An older man involved in an affair with a younger woman will be congratulated, while society will 'condemn, invariably and inexorably the relationship between a woman who is, let's say, more than 40 years old, and a man who is younger than her, even by very little'. She gave vent to feelings which were obviously more than socio-political:

> A woman over 40 is seen as an old lady, and she herself will be filled with complexes. She no longer has the right to fall in love

279

at all, let alone with a man younger than herself. This is the proof that we still live in a society made for the benefit of men, but it seems to me that there is nothing squalid about the relationship between an adult woman and a boy if it is conducted with dignity, conscience and appropriateness. On the contrary, if the woman is profoundly woman, it cannot but be positive. An adult woman knows how to love completely: and when she loves completely, she gives everything, she is more patient, more understanding than younger women, more maternal, more loving. In addition to this, the act of love with a womanly woman is extremely important for a young man. It helps him discover what sex is.

However, the quest to help youthful males to discover sex can turn sour. With a touch of deeply felt exasperation, Franca went on: 'The only problem is that then you can't get rid of him. Even if they are relationships with no future, even if they are tortured relationships, they are still lovely and rich and when they end they leave a good memory, do they not? I do not allow myself to make moralistic judgements. At the end of the day, with money you can buy anything, so why not buy yourself a little bit of an illusion?'[15] Dario was well aware that Franca too had her affairs, the most public being with Nanni Ricordi. When in the already mentioned interview with Silvia Truzzi, he was asked if Franca had ever betrayed him, he replied:

> I think she did so out of spite. I suffered because of it, but I felt very guilty. She was in the right, but these were incidents, stumbles. They were never the key to our relationship. For Franca, I felt absolute, overwhelming, boundless love. I remember that when she had a car accident and had to sleep on a firm surface, she lay on the floor because she could not stay in bed. I lay down beside her on the ground.[16]

In none of her feminist plays, with the exception of the deeply ironical *The Open Couple*, does Franca depict, much less idealise, a woman in an adulterous affair, whether the pair in question are of the same or different ages. Such conduct by men or women never won her outright approval.

If Franca puts herself forward as everywoman, she also, in lightly disguised form, advances personal views of what liberation for women should mean. The perspective is frequently that of a woman whose salad days have passed and whose life is neither totally satisfying nor totally frustrating. There is a vein of deeper sadness to her self-portrayal, explicitly so in the interviews and implicitly, on a careful reading, in the stage monologues. 'The problem with escape,' as Theodore Zeldin put it, 'is knowing where to escape to.'[17] Franca had no clearer answer than Zeldin. She was an accomplished, successful, beautiful woman, whose career was enviable, whose talents were celebrated and yet who was nagged by a persistent sense of dissatisfaction, based on a feeling of inadequacy as much as of inequality. Professionally she had known only success, but personally she wanted more. She isolated herself from new wave feminists by seeing some form of resolution of existential, female dilemmas in a non-revolutionary language of love and loyalty. It was something she feared was now missing in her marriage.

She said that for the first eighteen years, Dario had been unswervingly faithful to her. With the availability of the pill, women, especially young women, enjoyed a sexual liberation women of Franca's generation had never known and to which she could not entirely adjust. Franca blamed, no doubt rightly, inner complexes and outer social judgements for her own predicament. 'In making love, I saw "Sin". And each time I "sinned", there was my mamma standing severely between us, at the foot of the bed.'[18]

Dario, on the other hand, found himself surrounded by liberated and admiring younger women who had cast off the shackles of restraint and inhibition. He emerged blinking into a new landscape changed utterly by the new permissiveness and sexual politics of early feminism, and he cheerfully adjusted. The Italian press does not pry into private lives in the way the British or American press does, but photographs of young women alongside Dario began to appear in various publications. Franca began to pick up the phone and hear calls not meant for her, and even to take receipt of presents sent for Dario. She later said she set aside a trunk marked 'Gifts, Girls, Dario' to contain the 'belts, scarves, socks, gloves, books, perfumes' he received from female admirers.[19]

Something of her resentments, and perhaps even of his guilt, are apparent in the sub-text to *The Open Couple*, a work which is an anomalous part of their output. The play was premiered in Stockholm in 1983, the only one of their works to receive its first staging outside Italy. It was also the only time, leaving aside the politically determined decisions made by the co-operatives of the later 1960s and early 1970s, that Dario declined to take the leading role in his own work. The reason, paradoxical as it may seem, was that this play did have autobiographical overtones, albeit veiled behind the surface irony, and he had no wish to be publicly identified with the character.[20] The play, in his account to me, was written by Dario as a private gesture to pacify Franca after a quarrel over his affairs with other women. It was meant to be read to a few close friends and not intended for the stage, but was picked up in their house by Carlo Barsotti, who was impressed by its potential and who, together with his wife, Anna, translated and produced it in Stockholm's Pistol Theater. Dario recalled meeting an Italian journalist in an airport who requested an impromptu interview about his recent success. He assumed she was referring to *Story of a Tiger*, but she was on her way back from Stockholm where the *The Open Couple* was playing to packed houses. On the back of this success, Dario directed Franca in an Italian production.

The play dramatises the contradictions, complications and, from a woman's perspective, the injustice of the 'open couple' relationship. It tackles the unequal power balance that such relationships involve while also probing, with a seriousness belied by laughter, the delicate emotional complexity of all relationships. The militants of previous decades had now settled down with families but, at least the males, retained the libertarian philosophy of their salad or hashish days. The recommendation in the play, even if it clashed with Dario or Franca's personal conduct, was to live in fidelity and mutual respect. The supposedly adult agreement allowing the married couple to respect each other's right to indulge in casual affairs begins to grate strongly with the wife who realises she is passing an increasing number of evenings alone, but then, in a comic overturning of expectations, the husband is disconcerted when his wife casually announces over a game of cards that she has initiated a relationship with a fascinating man, a nuclear physicist who is also a rock star. The husband becomes increasingly frantic at this turning of the tables, initially scoffing, then pleading and finally threatening to kill himself. He is left to choose his own catastrophic end as the wife strolls off with her fabulous prince charming.

This comedy of modern manners was probably Dario's most unexpected success, and a work far removed from his normal terrain. Its power derives from the combination of surface farce and a dark, or tragic, undercurrent of sadness and poignancy. The play was taken in some quarters as an affirmation of the 'open relation' provided that male chauvinism was rejected and the woman was granted equal freedom and the right to sexual fulfilment, but in the intention of the authors, and in Franca's own convictions, the underlying moral was one which would satisfy the most rigid of traditional monogamists. It gave a contemporary twist to old beliefs on the need for mutual trust, on the value of fidelity, on the inevitability of jealousy when trust was betrayed, and it constituted an attack on the capacity for manipulation by the powerful, i.e. male, partner in any couple. The 'open couple' ideology was, Franca believed, a fraudulent front for egocentric male behaviour, advocated by men of all sides of the political spectrum because it satisfied their purposes. She said: 'the "open couple", if it means the belief that a couple can have affairs without the relationship being damaged is simply impossible, because there are feelings involved, feelings of love, and one of the two always suffers. Normally it is the woman who comes off worse, but that is not the main point of the play . . . For couples of my age, it is much worse, because men do not look for mother figures, or run off with women of 80. They go off with young girls, and for the wives it can be traumatic.'[21]

Dario and Franca were now receiving invitations from all around the world, both individually and jointly. In 1980, they were invited to the USA to perform at a Festival of Italian Theatre in New York. The American consul in Milan, whose name, Anthony Perkins, delighted them, expressed his admiration for their work with addicts, which was similar to work he had done in America, and said there would be no problem over the visa. Piero Sciotto was now company manager and he was dispatched a month in advance to make preparations, but the State Department refused the request for a visa on the grounds that they were founders of Red Aid. The ban applied to Dario and Jacopo, causing Franca to be further outraged because Red Aid was not recognised as entirely her initiative. The deeper grounds for their outrage were that the two had invariably set their faces against terrorist violence. Their sponsors in America appealed, but the authorities in Washington refused to budge, leaving Mr Perkins embarrassed.

Their American hosts had the wit to organise in New York on 25 May, *An Evening Without Dario Fo and Franca Rame*. Sciotto remembers that before the refusal of the visa, the visit was awaited in theatre circles with a measure of polite interest, but was hardly a burning issue for society at large. 'Afterwards, they all reacted as though they were old school friends of Dario, devastated at being deprived of his company.' The *Evening* attracted the support of the foremost names of American literature and theatre. Martin Scorsese, Arthur Miller, Joe Chaikin, Sol Yurick, Bernard Malamud were all in attendance. Norman Mailer promised to be there but crashed his car en route. Students put on a production of *Can't Pay? Won't Pay!*, a letter from Dario and Franca was read out, and the two received more publicity than if they had been there in person.

That summer Fo finally found the appropriate means to dramatise the thoughts that had been circling in his mind since the Moro assassination. He had written various scripts which did not, in his own view, stand up, and had not produced any full length play since *Mum's Marijuana* in 1976. 'The tragic paradoxes which (I) kept on inventing were outdone by even more tragic and paradoxical events.'[22] In the summer of 1980, the ideal approach occurred to him. *Trumpets and Raspberries* was completed in ten days and premiered at the Cinema Cristallo in January the following year. Although inspired by an event which had occurred only two years previously, the play was stylistically and ideologically something of a throwback to the kind of work performed in the seventies, and even brought back the good old days of questions in parliament, objections from the PCI and complaints to the police about the reading on stage of letters written by prisoners in Trani jail, where there had been riots. This reading was taken as further proof of support for violence and terrorism.

Dario would write many more plays, and have many more successes, but this was the last of the noisy, rumbustious, didactic political farces for which he is best known. The Moro case was treated obliquely by presenting the kidnap as that not of a politician but of Italy's leading industrialist, Gianni Agnelli, owner of Fiat and of Juventus Football Club. The basic elements of the plot were borrowed from the misadventures of the twins in Plautus' *Menaechmi*. A worker in Fiat, Antonio, happens to be in the vicinity when the car carrying Agnelli is attacked by a gang of kidnappers. Antonio covers the disfigured body of Agnelli with his jacket and takes him to hospital. The doctors find in the jacket a photograph of Antonio, and use it to reconstruct Agnelli's appearance. Dario played both of the now identical characters with a variety of quick-change routines and unrestrained comic horseplay. The Agnelli-Antonio character is suspected of involvement in the original kidnapping, causing secret police to swarm around the home of Antonio's divorced wife, played by Franca. The new man is taken hostage, a scene which led to press attacks on Dario for tastelessness, since shortly before the opening night, a judge, Giovanni D'Urso, was kidnapped by the Red Brigades. In the play Dario has his Antonio-Agnelli recite words from the letters written by Moro in captivity. In the fiction, the hostage is released. Moro was only a politician, but Agnelli represents Capital, so the state bows to the kidnappers' demands. The play was received coolly in Italy, but was a great success abroad.

It is worthwhile wondering why there was such a divergence of reception. In the changed political climate of Italy, audiences may have had a surfeit of Fo and his political theatre. It was not so beyond the Italian frontier, but with many translations and adaptations of his work being staged internationally, the problem of how to present Fo was now acute for directors and translators. His theatre at its best, for instance with *Accidental Death*, has a carefully arranged rhythm and pace, which means there are certain phases where there are no laughs, but his reputation as writer of hard-hitting political work *and* slapstick farce has caused some directors and actors, even those motivated by similar

285

political views to Dario's, to panic and assume that their production is failing if it does not produce a laugh a minute. To compensate, they exaggerate, but are often unsure which side of the duality to emphasise. The balance is more difficult to attain on stages outside Italy where translators and directors face the added difficulty of staging events which were well known to Italian audiences. Dario's brand of what can be termed didactic farce is unique, so the temptation of nervous directors is either to overdo the clowning or to step up the political thrust. Dario himself winced at many of the versions of his work. 'I have seen few good works,' he wrote. 'Some were respectable, others appalling, either on account of the actors, the director or the text itself which had been supposedly corrected but often cheapened.'[23]

He was present at the 1981 London premier of *Accidental Death of an Anarchist,* adapted, very freely, by Gavin Richards from a literal translation by Gillian Hannah. The English version was translated back for him by Tony Mitchell, and he was upset by what he heard. Anxious to have the play performed in Britain, he reluctantly gave consent, but he was enraged at what he saw on stage. Stuart Hood, who translated and edited other works, had to go to great lengths during the interval to calm him. Other people who were present remember the post-production dinner as a grim affair, with Dario sitting grumpily at the end of the table, staring into his plate. The sins of the production in Dario's eyes were that it cut itself too far adrift from the original, and in its desperation to raise laughter had degenerated into a clown show bereft of the undercurrent of tragedy in the original. One of the problems with his response to foreign productions is that Dario is author not only of the script but of the entire complex of factors which constitute stage-craft, and is touchy about alterations. Gavin Richards took on the Fo role not only as actor but as complete play-maker, re-arranging and re-writing, to Dario's distress. However, for all the liberties it took with the original, the Richards adaptation remains the English-language version which has most successfully married the comic brio and passionate commitment of Fo's theatre. With its switch from something akin to Italian *commedia dell'arte* to something akin to British music hall, it also represented a successful transition between cultures.

Dario had an opportunity to appreciate the dilemmas of translation from the other side later that year when the *Teatro stabile* in Turin put on a work of his entitled *The Opera of Guffaws*. In the programme and in the subsequent published version, it is described as being based on 'John Gay's *Beggar's Opera*, and on some ideas from my son Jacopo.'[24] Acknowledgement was also made of the contribution of poets and rock singers including Allen Ginsburg, Patti Smith, Donovan and Frank Zappa. There was no reference to Bertolt Brecht or to *Threepenny Opera*. In fact, the project was initiated by the Berliner Ensemble who invited Dario to direct a new production of Brecht's play. Dario set to work in the spirit he had worked on Stravinsky, but when Brecht's heirs saw the modifications Dario intended to introduce, they recoiled in horror and refused him permission to make any use of Brechtian material for any production anywhere. Barbara Brecht later said that while she was happy to allow Fo freedom to adapt the script, objections were raised by the heirs of Kurt Weill, who objected to Fo's intention not to use his music.[25] Dario professed himself mystified by this elevation of a theatrical work into an untouchable sacred text, and devised a strategy to circumvent the legal veto. Brecht's play is itself a reworking of John Gay's original, but John Gay is dead and has no heirs to threaten recourse to law. Dario did what Brecht had done: he went back to Gay's *Beggar's Opera* and recast it in his own way. Or so he said, and no one could challenge him.

The work was first staged in Turin, before being staged in Milan the following year, and in Tubinga in 1984. It was not warmly received anywhere. Its interest for critics and theatre historians lies in Dario's discussion of his approach to translation and adaptation. He justified his reworking of the text by reference to Brecht's own theories, and went on to provide what reads like a manifesto for free adaptations, albeit based on a freedom he would not countenance with his own works when performed in other countries. 'In the first place, Brecht wrote it thinking of the period in which he lived, clearly dated between 1917 and 1920, and to the characters, the actions, the costumes of that moment; he was out to write a story linked to his own times. It seems to me right to do the same today.'[26]

In his introduction to the published version, Dario explained himself more fully. '... it seemed to me essential to set to work on Brecht's text with that open-minded irreverence Brecht had himself recommended. Another tricky piece of advice from Brecht was his repeated invitation to transfer the script into the space and time of the present, "especially since ours are times of tragic and desperate dejection" ... Certainly Brecht, if he were alive today and had to produce this play, would introduce into the script the tragically urgent problem of drugs, of kidnapping, of the internationalised, industrialised organisation of terrorism, of crime, of the robotic sex market, of widespread, worthless psychoanalysis, the mass media etc.' not to mention the question of the somewhat trivial level to which the political world has sunk ... everywhere.'

This was certainly the principle which guided Dario's own forays into the field of directing. With *Histoire du Soldat* for La Scala, Molière's *Le médecin malgré lui* for the Comédie Française or Rossini's *Il Barbiere di Siviglia* for the Pesaro Festival, he behaved not as a servant of the original text but as a creative adapter, free to reinterpret, rewrite and reorder, introducing mime and improvisation and impose his own vision. The resultant stage versions have produced in critics exactly the doubts and hesitations – or even the frustrated rage – which Dario himself has experienced over foreign adaptations or directorial interventions of his own work. It is hard to reconcile what he wrote about responsibilities towards original work vis à vis Brecht with what he expects in his own case. While as director or interpreter of the work of other playwrights he takes to himself the role of liberating contributor to the creative process, he expects his own directors and translators to be more faithful. This inconsistency may be brushed aside by reference to the superior claims of creative genius, but the further difficulty is that it is anything but clear that Dario's translators or directors would be doing his theatre justice by assuming the workaday role he requests of them. Dario's works are often, as he believed true drama ought to be, dull on the page.[27] Fo the actor best translates and enlivens Fo the author, but in his absence the job still requires to be done. Translation of Fo requires audience-centred techniques, which do not necessarily coincide with the author-centred translation he advocates for his own theatre, but not for those works he brings to the Italian stage from abroad.

CHAPTER 15

Separations and Reconciliations

In the 1980s, the hopeful revolutionaries of previous decades were no longer convinced they were marching in tune with history. They saw the Cold War at its height, Ronald Reagan in the White House, Mrs Thatcher in Downing Street, the Christian Democrats dominant in Italy with the Communist party in frustrated opposition and the extra-parliamentary Left dispirited. The new forces which would, for good or ill, convulse Italy at the end of the decade were hardly glimpsed. Umberto Bossi and his Lombard League were still the object of scornful jokes, the Milanese magistrates still did not dare inquire into the nefarious networks which linked politics and business and Silvio Berlusconi was still fully occupied with his commercial affairs.

The theatre of Dario and Franca continued to be dissident and satirical but was querulous rather than political in the more militant sense given to that word in the sixties. They performed once again in the grand, bourgeois venues they had previously spurned with such contempt. In theatre circles there was a certain gloom over the future, especially regarding politics in theatre, and Dario became embroiled in the polemics. His thinking was expressed in workshops and seminars collected and edited by Franca at the end of the decade as *Tricks of the Trade*. At a conference in Naples in 1986 to commemorate Eduardo, he was asked what was the future of the theatre. 'The story,' he replied.[1] Story-telling had been an element of his theatrical work since the earliest days, and was dominant in *Obscene Fables*, a series of three one-man narratives by Dario plus a reprise of *I Ulrike* by Franca. The monologues were presented first in Rome in summer 1980 as improvised pieces of work in progress, before being staged in early 1982 in Florence and Milan. The tales were reworked *fabliaux* of Franco/Provençal origin, originally told by a giullare and collected in an expensive academic volume by Rossana Busegan. As performer, this was Dario the native of Lake Maggiore dusting down the story-teller's craft he had learned as a boy, focusing on episodes of alternative history but discovering for the first time the liberating power of Eros. The core issue is not political liberation but, in the tones of a follower of Wilhelm Reich or Herbert Marcuse, of the liberation from suffocating complexes and individual repression. The personal is not political, but the personal is given a status it had not previously enjoyed.

The main innovation was the introduction of the erotic or the 'obscene' to a repertoire which would previously not have offended the most puritanical conscience. The language of the new pieces was too strong for Franca, who preferred greater linguistic sobriety, and was uncomfortable with coarseness of vocabulary. The works which make up *Fables* represent both continuity and a new development. In the introduction to one of the pieces, Dario satirised the PCI as well as the veteran DC politician, Amintore Fanfani, who had returned to government, but the monologues themselves deal with matters in the purely private sphere. Once again, Dario was operating inside tradition, but altering that tradition since by reviving pieces which had been performed by jesters and which survived only in oral literature, Dario remained faithful to the Gramscian division of culture into hegemonic and popular. The obscene, he believed, was also an instrument of liberation, from 'the idea of scandal imposed by the powerful as an act of terrorism'. He explained: 'the erotic obscene is used as a strongly liberating weapon. Today we might sum it up in a cry: the obscene is beautiful!'[2]

Beautiful was not the description people would instinctively have used for *The Tumult of Bologna*, a story based on an incident which had been neglected by official historians. 'Absolute censorship. And yet we are dealing with a stupendous page in our history. Stupendous yes, but the ingredient is the obscene.'[3]

The events concerned a siege in the late middle ages when the people of Bologna besieged papal forces holed up in the citadel of their city. Locked out, facing starvation, some defeatists spoke of giving up, but one man had the inspired idea of collecting all the human and animal shit available and catapulting it into the enclosure. Victory was guaranteed.

The other two tales were richly obscene in a more directly sexual sense, the one focussing on the vagina, given the nickname the 'butterfly mouse', and the second on the penis, given no nickname. *The Butterfly Mouse*, a tale of unexpected tenderness told with a wholly new lyricism, featured a simple man, Giavan Pietro, who falls on good times and in love almost simultaneously. Being simple-minded, he is easily gulled by the woman he loves and by a devious priest, Don Faina, who wants to keep the woman as his mistress even after marrying her off to Giavan Pietro. After the wedding ceremony, the woman persuades Giavan Pietro that she has left her 'butterfly mouse' in her mother's house, and sends him off through the forest to collect it, leaving her the opportunity to go to bed with her priest. The mother too dupes the unfortunate Giavan, who has to struggle back without the necessary implement, but his plight unexpectedly arouses the sympathy of his new wife, who tells him she has in her body all that is needed for their love-making. In his performance, Dario gave the best of himself as actor, reproducing every noise in the forest, every puff in the run through the woods, but the final twist, when the woman is moved to pity and affection by the spectacle of her deluded admirer, is one of the few occasions in Dario's theatre when human warmth for its own sake is allowed to appear.

The final story, *Lucius and the Ass*, a magical tale of a man turned into an ass when a spell goes wrong, is taken from Lucian of Samosata, not from the better known version by Apuleius. 'Anyone who knows the two versions will note the enormous difference in style and taste. Lucian satirises eroticism, but the other often descends into mere, gratuitous scurrility.' Dario suggests that the style of story-telling gives grounds for believing that the original author was a woman, and that the tale predates that of Lucian. 'The tale deals with a character stricken with fantasy phallocracy.' A man is converted into a donkey, which is then involved, to its evident delight, in various erotic adventures but when he resumes human shape he discovers that the woman who had been so taken by him in animal form has him thrown off her land. Dario had dusted down the story-teller's craft he had learned as a boy, focusing on episodes of alternative history but facing for the first time the possibility that the personal is all that remains.

Dario and Franca were still enveloped in a cloud of notoriety and viewed in certain quarters as dangerous individuals. They were dismayed when the Italian Ministry for Entertainment, who plainly had no grasp of the sense of the play, slapped a ban on a revival of *The Open Couple* forbidding access to the under-eighteens. The ban was lifted after protests. The State Department in Washington once again refused them a visa when, in 1983, they were invited to perform at Joseph Papp's free theatre in the Metropolitan Park in New York, but they spent a highly successful period in London, doing workshops and performances at the Riverside theatre.[4]

It was on this occasion that they met Mario Pirovano, an Italian then living in London but who was later to become almost the second son of the couple and certainly an invaluable collaborator. He had no knowledge of, and very little interest in, theatre when he went to see them perform, but they struck up a friendship. Franca invited him to join up with them, initially selling scripts and videos after shows. His interest in acting grew as a result of observing Dario and Franca on stage, but while he never received lessons, he did receive a mixture of encouragement and frank criticism. Once he performed Dario's *The First Miracle of the Child Jesus* for a group of young people visiting Alcatraz and was seen by Dario, who made approving comments, but Franca later saw him do excerpts from *Mistero buffo* in public and her response was for Mario such a 'terrible' experience that he offered to give up acting. But he persevered and has gone on to perform works from the Fo-Rame repertoire in English and Italian in many countries.

They were finally allowed into the USA the following year seemingly, or so they stated at a press conference, after the personal intervention of President Reagan, supposedly sympathetic to the plight of a fellow actor. This story was given widespread credence but it was one of Dario's pieces of fake news. He was astonished at the gullibility of the journalists. The visa was valid only for a period of six days and their movements restricted to New York alone. The occasion was the staging of *Accidental Death* in an adaptation by Richard Nelson, but the production itself, which had required the services of a literal translator, adaptor and of script doctors before being passed on to director and actor, was insensitively adapted and stylised. Jonathan Pryce played the part of the madman and although his performance was much admired, several reviewers wrote that he had made the piece a vehicle for his own talents. An especially trenchant review in *Village Voice* suggested that the process of transformation to suit American tastes and American expectations had made *Accidental Death* resemble a Neil Simon comedy. Another review attacked the production as representing the 'non accidental death of an author'. In an interview when he returned home, Dario spoke with his customary civility about Pryce's acting abilities, but lamented the absence of the 'aggressive passages', and their substitution by 'euphemistically innocuous material'.[5]

Franca went on her own to Quebec, and later they went together to a theatre festival in Havana where Franca performed some of her monologues. Springtime took them to Buenos Aires, where they received graphic proof that their power to shock was undimmed. In Argentina the military were in control and the church still a force in the land. Franca was due to perform some of her one-woman pieces and Dario *Mistero buffo* but even before the first performance, the theatre where they were to perform was the target for whistle-blowing, flag-waving and stone-throwing demonstrators. The so-called Mothers of Plaza de Mayo, who met each day to demand information on the 'desparecidos' expressed their support for them, but they were no match for the Archbishop of Buenos Aires who denounced *Mistero buffo* in the local press. Members of the Church Militant took him at his word and crowded into the theatre foyer, clutching pictures of the Sacred Heart of Jesus and kneeling in the doorways to recite decades of the rosary. Others made their way into the theatre itself, rising to their feet to scream in outrage each time the word 'pope' was mentioned. Some patrons had to be dragged forcibly from the stalls. This was unpleasant but bearable, but one evening a youth threw a tear-gas bomb at the stage, causing panic. Dario leapt from the stage to seize hold of him, as much to defend him from the police as to prevent him causing further havoc. Before the man was dragged off, Dario had time to note how young he was, and to conclude there and then that someone had put him up to it.

Edinburgh during the International Festival in August did not present the excitement of Argentina, but uninteresting times can be preferable. There were several productions of Dario's works being staged in the church halls, closes and masonic lodges which are pressed into service during the festival, and Dario toured them all to see what had been made of his writing. Having Dario or Franca in the audience can be a daunting experience for directors or performers. Dario himself was unlikely to be overtly dismissive in public, but Franca could be much more cutting. She did not suffer fools gladly, a Shakespearean euphemism which conceals a directness which can draw blood. At times, her recognition of shortcomings in the production of plays she had previously performed herself takes the form of an offer of private rehearsal sessions, which are physically taxing and psychologically draining even if dramatically enriching for the women who are the object of such attention, but on other occasions, she would rise majestically to her feet to issue loud and uncompromising denunciations.

Back in Italy, Dario and Franca set to work on *Almost by chance a Woman, Elisabeth,* a complex, multi-layered historical farce set in an imprecise land, half-way between Elizabethan England and contemporary Italy. Initially Franca had great reservations over the piece, and told a deeply offended Dario that while the play was an excellent essay on Shakespeare, it lacked stage rhythm and dramatic qualities. He went into a sulk, but did eventually re-write the work. Even then, Franca was never happy with the part of Queen Elizabeth, which she described as requiring the strength of an ox. In addition to giving expression to his highly idiosyncratic fascination with Shakespeare, Dario used the piece to discuss the birth of the modern state, to return to the theme of commitment and the intellectual and even to refer to the Moro kidnapping. He told an interviewer that it was 'a pamphlet, a theatre manifesto . . .

but also, I hope, comic'.[6] Much of the comedy was entrusted to Dario, who took on the mock-female role of Donnazza, a vulgar, quack beautician who babbles in a pseudo-popular idiom and trades in such eccentric beauty aids as bee stings which help the nipples stay erect. Elizabeth's urge to enhance her attractiveness is part female foible and part political stratagem, for she is facing a putsch led by her ex-lover, Essex, and numbering Southampton, Shakespeare's patron, as well as the Bard himself among the plotters. Dario's esteem for Shakespeare was boundless but he had little interest in the great universal poet who investigates subtle spheres of mind and emotion, and prefers to locate in Shakespeare a political commentator or even activist.

Shakespeare's participation in Essex's plot against the Queen is a factoid which Dario offers as the key to *Hamlet*. The relations between Elizabeth and Shakespeare were intended as the crux of the play, but it was also envisaged as a re-reading of *Hamlet*, which Dario believed was a depiction of Elizabeth's court. The tragedy of *Hamlet* is, in this view, a topsy-turvy depiction of the court, with the genders reversed so that Hamlet is none other than the Queen, who causes the madness and death of Essex as Hamlet did with Ophelia. However, there was so much bustle in the acting, and so many intercrossing threads in the writing that no one theme could ever command exclusive attention. Some lords loyal to the queen are kidnapped and, in a conscious parallel with the Moro case, Elizabeth maintains the hard line against entering into negotiation taken by the Italian Establishment, but the killing of Essex was also her own death as a woman, if not yet as queen. The burlesque elements in the plot, the echoes of *commedia dell'arte* and even of the Shakespearean fool in the part Dario wrote for himself ensured that the comedy was always amusing, but it was more soft-centred and less hard hitting than he had intended. Franca had a highly proprietorial relationship *Elizabeth*, as was clear when she once went to a student production on the Edinburgh Festival Fringe. The young student actress playing the main role was reduced to tears when Franca rose at the end of the first act to shout '*vergogna*'. There was scarcely any need for a command of Italian to grasp the sense, but she made Mario Pirovano translate her words, 'I do not recognise this play.'

This work was first performed in Riccione in 1984, and was quickly translated and performed in several countries. Dario received many requests to direct his plays in translation, and accepted such a request from Arturo Corso, who had appeared in many productions of his plays in Italy and who was then working with a Finnish company. In summer 1985, they arrived in Alcatraz, Jacopo's estate in Umbria. Dario was in overall charge of the production, with Corso as assistant and a Finnish director also helping in some unspecified capacity. As was invariably his custom, Dario found it necessary to rewrite as he went along, so the rehearsals were a confused, multi-linguistic babble of shouts, retakes, stops and starts, backtracks and instructions given and countermanded. It was a particularly hot summer and the strain proved too much for the unfortunate interpreter, whose stamina gave out and who collapsed on the set. She had to be carried from the camp on a stretcher, babbling incoherently in a mixture of Finnish and Italian. The hospital diagnosed her as suffering from 'non-specific stress', although her condition would appear to a non-medic extremely specific. She returned home, made a good recovery but shunned the theatre thereafter.

In October 1985, at the invitation of the Venice Biennale, Dario revisited history in a more personal way. He was now almost sixty, an age when successful men commonly take to composing memoirs as a hedge against mortality, but he was drawn to ordering his affairs, arranging his legacy, examining his origins and paying homage to his household gods in a different way. *Hellequin, Harlekin, Arlecchino*, a stage history of the Harlequin, was the first of a series of works which may be regarded as repayment of artistic debts, or as acts of deference to the authors, actors and even stage characters who populate his private pantheon. Molière, Ruzzante would receive similar veneration in future years, while Rossini, as previously Stravinsky, would be subjected to procrustean treatment to ensure that they too would fit into the niches in that pantheon reserved for them as revered predecessors or tillers of the same fields.

Following T S Eliot, it could be said that every great writer re-structures the past and creates from the chaos of inheritance a coherence termed tradition. Similarly, Harold Bloom has argued that every tradition is founded on a 'principle of selectivity', and not on some inevitable, given process. Dario had always lived inside tradition, and with the Harlequin show in Venice, he began a process of tracing his own, very personal, relations with each individual in the tradition he created for himself. If he had previously preferred the Middle Ages and had indicated the jester as his model, Harlequin was his twin and *commedia dell'arte* another source of inspiration. 'I have always played Harlequin, whether I wanted to or not. Even when not leaping about or doing somersaults, my characters have always been played in this style.'[7]

The Harlequin show could have been regarded as safely mainstream had he not aimed simultaneously to revise received wisdom on *commedia dell'arte*, which he believed had been neutered by theatre historians and contemporary directors. The surprise, or outrage, which greeted the production in some quarters was occasioned by the clash between the preconception that *commedia dell'arte* required an elegant, elaborately stylised display of delicately devised movement techniques, and Dario's belief that it should include a display of the clowning, horseplay, acrobatic tumbles and vulgarity associated with the popular tradition and with low farce. Some critics were disconcerted to discover that they were being offered a standard Fo piece rather than a more academic work on Harlequin in history. He decided not to wear the famous, long-nosed mask associated with the character, but chose to emphasise the continuity between the medieval jester and Harlequin. His beliefs and performance also indicated a break from the Harlequin as presented not only by Giorgio Strehler and the actor Moretti in the Piccolo's celebrated production of *Servant of Two Masters,* but also from Carlo Goldoni. Dario had limited regard for Goldoni and viewed the Harlequin of his comedies as naughty and mischievous but too bourgeois, while the Harlequin he admired was more primitive, crude and hard-edged, an anarchic force of nature who was domesticated by the Enlightenment.

Franca spent two months in 1985 in London attempting to learn English, but that was only part of the reason for her wish to get away. The relationship between her and Dario was going through a rocky patch occasioned mainly by arguments over Dario's affairs. She was also having trouble with the arm she had injured in a car crash in Genoa, and had planned to go to Ischia to rest and recuperate. At the last moment she changed her mind, and asked Mario Pirovano, who spoke excellent English, to accompany her. She rented a flat in Piccadilly, attended classes at a language school in the morning and went to the theatre in the evening. Dario's plays were now being performed regularly in Britain, with productions of *Elizabeth* and *Trumpets and Raspberries* both being performed in London about that time, so she spent some time overseeing the British end of the operation. Dario joined her over Easter, and Franca later described those two months as being 'absolutely the happiest two months of my life'.[8] She never did master English.

Meantime, there were moves afoot to persuade the American government to grant them a visa which would allow them to perform in the USA. Ron Jenkins, a circus clown turned academic, received from Harvard University a grant which would allow him to travel anywhere in the world to study theatre, and chose to spend his year observing Dario's theatre. He showed Robert Brustein, the celebrated critic and theatre historian, tapes of Dario's work, and together with Joel Schechter and Peter Sellers he arranged an invitation. The backing of a prestigious institution like Harvard University facilitated the grant of a visa. Jenkins also wondered whether the fact that Dario had a show running on Broadway made him heightened status with bureaucrats. 'With an investment of $500,000 in that production, Dario was automatically re-categorised from terrorist to businessman.'[9] It was agreed that Jenkins would appear as his on stage interpreter but since he had never done that kind of work before, Dario invited him to Brussels, where he was performing, to observe the techniques of stage translation. When he arrived, he discovered that Dario had decided to do the performance in French and dispense with the interpreter, but he asked Jenkins if he would like to accompany him to Vienna. Since Jenkins had no knowledge of German, this was of limited use, but he went anyway, and came away impressed by the need for a certain rhythm as much as for linguistic accuracy if Dario's improvised humour was to be communicated to an audience.

Arriving in America in May 1986, Dario and Franca embarked on a tour which took in Cambridge, Boston, New York, Washington and Baltimore. They appeared on successive nights, playing *Mistero buffo* and *Female Parts*. Dario was uncertain of the reception awaiting him from Americans but was quickly reassured. 'They can appreciate political satire,' he found, to his evident surprise. 'You can joke about them, about power, about society. I did not expect it, because in other countries, like Britain, irony on certain domestic problems simply does not work. They just don't laugh. In America, I brought up everything, Vietnam, Watergate, Black people, Italo-Americans, Republicans, veterans.' He discovered that it was possible to joke about death, since in a society of victors and vanquished, 'dying is like losing the game'. However, he also found there was 'a fear of sex, terrible prudery. They blushed'. There were two inviolable taboos, cancer and the American flag. Once, in his improvised prologue to the *Lazarus* sketch, he delivered a one-liner about the miniature place mat of the Stars and Stripes at each dinner he attended: 'just the right size for wiping the cutlery', he quipped but before he had spoken the line he felt the audience freeze. He did not repeat it.[10] One of Jenkins' tasks was to read the daily press to him, so he could incorporate into each evening's routine up to date gags about current affairs. On one occasion, Reagan opined that there was no hunger in America, only people who did not know where to find assistance. Dario retorted that the problem of the poor was that they did not know 'where the dustbins are placed'. This jibe was, to his surprise carried by the *New York Times*. For the rest of the tour, Reagan's words were put into the mouth of the Doge of Venice in *The Hunger of the Zanni* sketch.

Franca was accompanied by her sister, Pia, a theatre costumier, and her brother, Enrico, a theatre manager, both of whom were impressed by her progress and confidence in solo performance after a lifetime on stage with Dario. On the night before her opening at the Lincoln Center in New York, the whole troupe dined together. Enrico complained of feeling unwell and left early. The following morning he was found dead in his hotel. Franca was awakened by a call from the receptionist who announced casually that her brother had just died. The rest of the day was spent in the preparations for having the body flown home, but Franca was determined that, in the best traditions of the trade, the show must go on. She insisted that the news be withheld from the audience, and made only a veiled reference to it at the end when she was called back on stage by enthusiastic applause.

In August, after a brief tour in Denmark and Germany, Franca returned to the Edinburgh Festival Fringe with a programme consisting of *The Open Couple* and the monologues, *Medea* and *The Rape*. Although he was not performing himself, Dario accompanied her, and took the opportunity to see various shows, including Tilda Swinton in a one-woman performance at the Traverse of *Man to Man* by Manfred Karge, which features a woman who disguises herself as her dead husband to work as a crane driver. Dario did not speak English, but returned to the hotel that night in a state of excitement, fired by enthusiasm for an idea which had occurred to him while watching. At a party the following evening, he spoke of his developing idea with growing fervour, and in increasing volume. Franca, seated with her back to him, turned round repeatedly to tell him to be quiet as he was disturbing the other guests. Creativity is a mysterious phenomenon, and his listeners could not detect any connection between his ideas and the play which had supposedly inspired it. Suppose there is a woman in a flat, he told the group who gathered round him, making a video as her last testament to her ex-husband before she kills herself, but she is continually interrupted by phone calls from other women who are experiencing problems and undergoing suffering much like hers. Why would they be phoning, he wondered? A wrong number, obviously, but whose? He was initially unsure but began to devise the possible problems the women might be raising. By the following morning, the idea was even clearer, and over breakfast he began to write out notes. He had little paper and no patience with the idea of going to a shop to buy a notebook. He wrote furiously on napkins, talking as he wrote, the emerging script spilling off the napkins onto the white tablecloth. The management was magnanimous towards the demands of creativity. He left Edinburgh for Milan on a Friday, and phoned on Monday to say that the play, now entitled

An Ordinary Day, a gentle take-off of Michele Placido's celebrated film, *A Special Day,* when Hitler visited Mussolini in Rome, was fully written.

Rehearsals were completed in twelve days in autumn, and the new play, twinned with *The Open Couple,* opened in October as part of a double bill entitled *Female Parts.* The couple re-formed the Fo/Rame company they had disbanded in 1968, and sought re-admittance to ETI, the Italian Theatre Board, which they had abandoned the same year. They premiered in the Nuovo in Milan where Franca had last appeared in a variety show in 1952. The symbolism of the return to one of Milan's most stately, bourgeois theatres was laboured by several critics, who seemingly had not been aware of Dario's co-operation with La Scala. 'The days of the Palazzina Liberty, of the anoraks and of slogans are far-off now that Franca Rame is at the Nuovo, the most middle-class and traditional of the theatres in the city centre,' wrote the *Corriere della Sera.*[11] Even if *An Ordinary Day* did not arise from the life of Dario and Franca as directly as did *The Open Couple,* it is impossible to overlook the fact that it takes the fictional couple further down the same path. Now the separation has occurred and Giulia is seated in front of a camera, intent on suicide and recording last thoughts and memories which are transmitted onto a large video screen. The phone calls are the result of a confusion between her number and that of a phoney Japanese analyst who offers women in distress 'psycho-respiratory' cures based on Indonesian lore. The callers are other women oppressed by the misogyny to which they are exposed, or by the unmanageable problems of their married life. Some cases like that of the prostitute whose trade suffers when she develops a propensity for biting off the testicles of her clients have a surreal quality, but Giulia abandons her plans for suicide when she receives a call from one woman whose predicament is uncannily similar to hers. Dario's delight in incongruity and grotesque is kept in check as he traces Giulia's descent into panic and misery, and ascent into a state of determination which is still short of optimism. The ending is limp, but the play bounds along with Fo's zany momentum, even if it gives further evidence of a newer introspective tone and subdued, mellow mood.

Off the stage, relations between Dario and Franca were increasingly unsettled. Dario had had several affairs of greater or lesser levels of commitment. The annual gatherings at Alcatraz brought young women from all over Europe, and Dario had had brief encounters with several of them, even when Franca was housed in another residence on the estate. One participant at an event there recalls seeing Franca march along one morning to the cabin where Dario was resident, and throwing out the young lady who had passed the night with him. Newspapers carried reports of a more serious relationship with a young actress, Maria Passamonti, and some journalists speculated that she was about to replace Franca. Dario had been working with Passamonti on a book but the relationship seemed more than professional. The response of the press outraged him. 'It was the appalling behaviour of hyenas,' he complained.[12] The woman's parents in a village in the Marche were besieged by photographers and reporters, while Franca herself received phone calls from journalists anxious for her reaction. She became more and more offended and humiliated, and her lawyer, Giovanni Piscopo, said that on various occasions she requested him to draw up papers for a separation, but then backed off. She began to talk, but delicately, of relationships of her own. She told readers of *Marie Claire* that 'like Jean Cocteau' she considered any love affair between 'a man or a woman in their twilight and a younger person to be an act of turpitude', but she also spoke of a young actor who had fallen in love with her, and deprived himself of meals so as to buy her chocolates and flowers.[13]

Working relations were largely unimpaired, and the two continued living together. In any relationship of that duration and standing, there was much that could be entrusted, in every sphere, to habit and custom. Dario wrote and directed Franca in *The Kidnapping of Francesca*, which opened in Trieste at the end of 1986.[14] Dario and Franca insisted that nothing was to be read into the decision to give her name to the protagonist, a wealthy banker kidnapped while engaged on an adulterous liaison with a young employee of her company. The work was adapted catastrophically into English under the title, *Abducting Diana*, when the cult of Princess Diana was at its zenith.

302

However, the relationship between Dario and Franca was about to explode in headlines around the world. Dario went alone to Amsterdam in early 1987 to begin work on a production of Rossini's *Barber of Seville* for the Amsterdam Musiktheater. With the production itself, he extended his position as *enfant terrible* from theatre to opera. He viewed opera buffa as an offshoot of *commedia dell'arte,* and his production was notable for his inventiveness and for the sheer extravagance of the production. In his view, Figaro should be seen as 'a bourgeois Harlequin, a young man who could equally be a *Don Juan* or a *Tartuffe.* Don Bartolo is a Pantaloon, Don Basilio the usual know-all doctor or a Balanzone . . . with the whole of Spain or Italy possibly on stage or in the atmosphere. There are quotes from Goya, and an unequivocal Mediterranean air.'[15] The production was imbued with the witty panache which Dario brought to all productions and with the unruly exuberance which were part of his vision of *commedia dell'arte,* but the ingenuity, jocularity and inventiveness seemed to many critics simply an obstacle to the appreciation of the music. Perhaps Dario was more attracted by the Beaumarchais play on which the opera was based than by the opera itself. 'Fo will do anything,' wrote one reviewer, 'fly a kite, paddle a gondola, sit on a swing, toss a doll in a blanket, anything to distract his audience from Rossini.'[16]

While rehearsals were underway in Amsterdam, Franca was in Italy performing *The Kidnapping of Francesca* in Rome. She was invited in February to make what should have been a routine appearance on a Sunday afternoon TV chat-show, *Domenica In,* hosted by Raffaella Carrà. After performing an extract from the play, she sat down for the celebrity chatter which is a staple of such programmes, and Carrà asked about marriage in general, then about Franca's marriage and relations with Dario. Franca fended off this intrusive questioning, until in exasperation she burst out with the statement that the marriage between her and Dario was over. She referred vaguely to Dario's girls and to his evasiveness. What followed provided one of the most memorable moments ever recorded on Italian television, rivalling the couple's walk-out from *Canzonissima* decades before. The boundaries between private and public had long eroded in the life of Dario and

Franca, but now their life became theatre, or even soap opera. Viewers recalled Carrà turning pale and gawking in disbelief. 'Does he know?' she stuttered. Franca replied: 'No, but now that I have said it in front of your ten thousand viewers, he'll soon find out.' Carrà was not quite equal to the moment, and must have been later conscious of the bathos of her reply, 'In fact, my viewers come to ten million.' Franca was unmoved: 'So much the better. Dario will be informed more easily.'[17]

One of the ten million was Jacopo, now aged 31, who learned of what became known as the live divorce between his parents at the same time as the rest of Italy. Franca's sister Pia was another, and she told reporters she felt as though a 'tile had fallen on her head'. Dario remained in the dark. Messages were left for him in various parts of Amsterdam as Italian newsmen on the spot and his son at a distance struggled to reach him first. He was at the house of his Dutch interpreter, Franz Roth, and the two read the reports in the morning's paper. If he was surprised, so was Franca. She had had no prior intention of making this announcement, nor even any certainty that she wished to take this step. There was some ribald laughter in Italy over this couple who said in public things they were too shy to say in private, but tension had been high in the Fo/Rame household for some time and she was living in a state of personal anxiety and uncertainty. No set of intellectual beliefs, not even ones bound up under the heading 'women's liberation', were really of any emotional service to Franca at that time. The idea of separation had been on her mind, but the declaration was very much a spur-of-the-moment response to insistent questioning. Talking of the programme shortly afterwards, Franca herself said: 'You must understand what happened,' but it was far from clear that she understood herself. 'I had been invited onto the programme and was expecting questions about my work but – it was a bit funny – the presenter started with a barrage of personal questions. It was as though she was provoking me. Anyway, it just came out spontaneously. I told them – it's all over between me and Dario.'[18]

The news gave rise to a series of speculative, supposedly probing articles, some written in the obituary tone. Franca spoke of the humdrum life of any married couple after years together, of the poison of habit, of the lack of sparkle induced by familiarity, and also voiced the apocalyptic conclusion that 'marriage should be prohibited by law. Of course there is the will to sleep and waken up together, but then there comes the morning when you wake up and find that it is not working any more. It is the fault of life which grinds down relationships, of the fact that a man and a woman married for many years no longer make love, or if they do, make love two or three times a year ... At that point a relationship with people outwith the couple becomes indispensable. And then the troubles begin.'[19] In her case, however, the troubles had not begun with a normal sequence of familiarity-breeding-neglect, but with complex complaints of being under-appreciated in public, and of having to endure Dario's infidelities. Franca was hardly the ground-down, home-ridden housewife, and she had had her own affairs, but a sense of anger and humiliation was apparent in her statements. There was one image which recurred in several interviews, that male sexuality was like instant coffee.

> If there are a thousand women in the stalls, at least nine-hundred and ninety-nine are ready to faint if he looks at them ... What am I to do? If women go along with it, why not? It is well known that men, even the most intelligent, are ready on the instant, like Nescafé. It is the fate of every wife of a famous man. Every so often, someone asks me, how many women has Dario had? I would not know how to answer. I have not counted. Yes, sometimes, I have gone off my head. I have certainly suffered, but now, from the height of my years, I ask myself: Was the suffering worth while? I have a laugh to myself. I have put away the gifts they gave him.[20]

When apprised of the sutuation, Dario was contrite. He fully understood why Franca had taken this step, he was a swine to have forced her to it. 'The more I think about it, the more I am convinced that Franca was quite right to bring all this out into the open. Indeed, I admired her, I found in her that ability to give things a kick which I have always liked in her. At the end of the day, what Franca said was – I am fed up playing the wife who sees nothing and feels nothing, the cheery, dumb blonde who spends her time with stages and prisons, pretending not to notice that her husband is one enormous bastard.'[21] This interview was the beginning of a strange campaign which saw Dario publishing open letters to Franca asking for a reconciliation. He dispatched Franz Roth to Milan with a private message. Roth went into the green room in the theatre where Franca was performing, and watched her take the letter and tear it dramatically to pieces. She told Roth to inform Dario that she wanted nothing more to do with him and that if he wanted to return to Milan, he could sleep in the flat upstairs. Roth watched the show, and went backstage afterwards to find her on her knees, picking the pieces of the ripped letter out of the waste-paper basket and reassembling them on her dressing table. Two days later, when Roth was about to leave Milan, she called to say that it must be cold in Amsterdam, and that she had packed a case of warm clothes for Dario.

In newspapers and magazines, both made declarations of love and esteem in a profusion and with a frankness they had not used since the time of their courtship. Each was protective of the other. In April, he published in *Panorama* a list of his coming engagements, including the forthcoming *Tricks of the Trade* which had a section by Franca, but he wished that 'they could remain together and not only within the covers of a book.' In later years, although the story of their bizarre separation was one of the things which people remembered most clearly about them, Franca herself appeared to have erased the matter from her memory and would deny that they had ever left each other. 'I only said it because I was provoked by Carrà,' she declared.[22]

At the time, she considered going her own way professionally, and thought about setting up a company of her own. She circulated her various agents in Europe to see if they had any scripts on their books which would be suitable for a 57 year old actress, with wide experience of comic theatre, but willing to try her hand at anything. Nothing came of it. Dario stayed in Amsterdam for the period of the rehearsals and opening nights, but during that time, he phoned, Franca estimated, from five to seven times a day. When he returned to Milan, one of them did stay in the spacious attic flat which was part of their property, but they met for breakfast and continued life as usual. There had never really been any question of anything else. Franca was there at his side when Dario's mother died that spring.

CHAPTER 16

Debts And Homage

Tricks of the Trade,[1] published in Spring 1987 at the height of the public and private turmoil affecting Dario and Franca, remains Dario's major attempt to elucidate his ideas on popular theatre and to stake his own claim for inclusion in that tradition. The individual sections first saw the light as occasional writings and ad hoc contributions to a myriad of workshops and seminars held in various parts of the world from Jutland, London and Bogotà to the Teatro Argentina in Rome. Once again it was Franca who taped, deciphered, transcribed and edited the individual pieces for publication, guaranteeing their survival.

The Italian title, *The Actor's Mini-Manual,* gives, correctly enough, the impression of a pedagogic handbook, but its range is much wider. The focus on the actor rather than on the author is reflection of how Dario saw himself, but both figures receive consideration. Initially Dario toyed with the idea of giving the volume an anti-Diderot slant by entitling it *The Anti-paradox of the Actor* but he was persuaded this was too recondite. Since the work was never conceived as an organic treatise, anyone hoping for an equivalent of the writings of Stanislavsky or Brecht will be disappointed, but it is reasonable to regard the book as one of the component parts of the manifesto Dario never wrote. He makes fun of adversaries from past and present, pays homage to fellow spirits and thus clears the ground for some possible, more systematic definition of what constitutes 'popular theatre'. The refusal to be bound by too rigid a method is reflected in the structure of the book which is divided, in a parody of Boccaccio, into six 'days'. Included in the pages are discussions of the popular tradition from *commedia dell'arte* onwards, an account of the origins of the Harlequin, a demonstration of the problems of wearing masks on stage, an analysis of Greek tragedy, a proposal for the revival of the jeering monologues from Greek comedy, a polemical attack on Diderot, Jacques Lecoq and Louis Jouvet, a range of idiosyncratic judgements of Brecht, Chekhov, Shakespeare and Stanislavsky as well as accounts of individual workshops where dialogues were improvised and some of his own works dissected. The final section is Franca's contribution to discussions on women's theatre.

In the 1980s he treated questions on theatre, actors and dramatists with the same polemical passion as political issues. He had no sympathy with commercial theatre, with plays written and performed to function as a *digestivo*, but neither did he admire élite theatre-making, or anything which went under the name of experimentalism, avant-garde or theatre of research. On more than one occasion, he wondered whether those engaged in 'research' in small theatre clubs would ever have anything to show for their research, or why they rarely managed to break away from standard, mannered clichés. Equally, he showed little patience with politically driven theatre, even if he shared the political outlook of the producing company, if it was given to sermonising, to striking poses, and showed itself indifferent to seizing the audience's attention by entertainment or story-telling. For Dario, belief and conviction were essential, but they had to be founded on a clear idea of the totality of the theatrical experience. The indolence and reluctance of a new breed of actors to apply themselves with due diligence to mastering all aspects of theatre-making dismayed him. His generation had emerged from the war, and were excited by the prospects afforded them by the Liberation. Their ignorance was Socratic, based on the awareness that they were ignorant and had to acquire knowledge, an attitude far removed from the intellectual indifference he saw around him.

One essential element of Dario's poetics is his distinction between 'theatre' and dramatic literature. Those who produce the latter, including

Pier Paolo Pasolini, or who praise it, as does Benedetto Croce, are banished from his Eden. Approval of Brecht and his ideas of 'alienation' is guarded, but Dario subscribes wholeheartedly to a doubt Brecht once expressed on Shakespeare. The only problem, he wrote, was that his works were 'too beautiful on the page. It is his only defect, but a great one.' Fo shared the belief that a work of theatre, as distinct from a mere work of dramatic literature, should give limited pleasure when read, since its worth should be apparent only in performance. The actor-author, the linchpin of the Italian tradition of theatre, is his ideal. He encouraged actors to convert themselves into playwrights, but laid down demanding conditions. The dilettante could expect no kind words. The dramatist had to master the craft and not trust to instinct. A knowledge of history and tradition were indispensable, but so too was a deeper form of commitment. 'The moral problem is fundamental for the actor in particular. It is a guarantee of equilibrium and verve, a reserve of creativity, of life. If they said to me – "Is there anything to which you would never submit yourself?" I would reply, "to doing something in which I do not believe" . . . I wish to wage war on the jobbing actor, a greater affliction in theatre than any other calamity.'[2] Aged sixty-one, he was now conscious of generational differences, and complaints against his younger contemporaries began to appear with a certain frequency in his public statements. He fondly but pointedly recalled his own youthful apprenticeship in theatre when he dedicated himself to mastering every aspect of stagecraft from voice projection to lighting techniques.

Looking back over theatre history, Dario reversed conventional assessments and hierarchies, awarding pride of place to authors who worked in styles of theatre normally regarded as minor, or those performers more frequently regarded as purveyors of mere entertainment – clowns, variety artistes, farceurs and the nameless scribes of popular festivities of carnival exhibitions. His exemplars are as likely to come from Iran or Bali as from Slovenia or Sardinia, but all operate inside the boundaries of 'popular theatre'. To be worthy of that name, it is not sufficient to create accessible theatre or agit-prop. His ideal is theatre which has roots in history and society, which grows from the experience of one class and instinctively or consciously expresses the attitudes, humour and resentments of that class. The basic polarity was patrician versus popular, hegemonic versus subaltern, not didactic versus escapist. Fo's ideal was the combination of entertainment plus education; either one in isolation fell short of his notion of theatre. His supreme models came from carnival and characters associated with the carnival spirit – principally Harlequin and the jester. They displayed the impish or Puckish spirit but transcended it to give voice to the satiric, the tragic or the subversive.

Dario was never a critic *de métier*, and consistency was not one of his trademarks. On individual authors he would happily contradict himself according to the needs of the moment. There are, however, some constants. Ruzzante, the sixteenth century actor-author from Padua, is his alter ego and supreme model on whom he invariably wrote with passion and love. He always revered the Greeks, always venerated Molière and esteemed, somewhat idiosyncratically, Shakespeare and the Elizabethans. But remember, he said, to glance from these grand monuments at the more ramshackle tombs commemorating a motley crew who sang cruder songs, were more given to ribaldry, cavorted in the public squares, and were on the alert since they knew that at any moment, if the constabulary were sighted, they would have to pick up their jackets and run.

There is a Fo-land, situated somewhere between the Wasteland and Wonderland, and the sounds most frequently heard are the rage of indignant denunciation and the cackle of laughter. The Lord of Misrule is on the throne, and comedy is his servant, but the laughter is not necessarily the laughter of blasphemous derision. Laughter can be a response to elements normally identified as tragic. Dario was fond of attributing to Molière – and he might even have said it – the belief that tragedy was emotionally comforting but laughter defiant. Nothing characterises Dario's own thinking more clearly than the quest for a synthesis of laughter and tragedy. Laughter is the identifying mark of humanity. In laughter the human being becomes fully conscious of his own potential, of his individuality and of ability to assert his autonomy from convention and rule. 'Laughter denotes a critical awareness; it signifies imagination, intelligence and a rejection of all fanaticism.

In the scale of human evolution, we have first *homo sapiens,* then *homo faber* and then finally *homo ridens,* and this last is always the most difficult to subdue or make conform.'[3] In his youth, Fo had learned from Feydeau, but in depth of insight and subtlety of technique his farce had long since outstripped that of his old master.

Having overseen the publication of the book, Dario left for Boston to direct his 1959 play, *Archangels Do Not Play Pinball,* for the American Repertory Theatre. It was an odd choice. Perhaps he thought that the play which had set them on the road to success in Italy would do the same in America. If so, he was disappointed. His on-set rewriting and modifications to the original text created difficulties for the actors who found the demands put on them excessive. The revised work did not quite cohere, but his presence there gave a boost to the popularity of his work in the USA. Franca was with him in America, but she went to the West Coast on her own, and received the heightened appreciation invariably accorded her when she was able to appear in her own right.

Back home, they appeared together at a demonstration to oppose a decision by the Milan City Council to remove the plaque marking the spot at the police station where Pino Pinelli had fallen to his death. As part of the protest, Dario did a dramatised reading of *Accidental Death of an Anarchist.* The reactions from some critics read less like reviews than premature obituaries, for the actor if not yet for the man. 'Fo is a somewhat tired maestro, with an evermore detached look, who now rarely descends into the arena,' wrote Franco Quadri, a critic who had followed his career with sympathetic interest. When invited to retort, Dario, ever the gentleman, demurred gently but only to say that he had not lost the passion of other years but that he had acquired a technique which allowed him to work on stage without wearying himself.[4] Nevertheless, the impression was put about that the old ardour was spent and that since the 'Movement' had crumbled, Dario and Franca had been eclipsed.

In December 1987, journalists were preparing special supplements and documentaries to celebrate the twentieth anniversary of the student revolts in Paris in 1968, and saw Dario and Franca as belonging to a mood and culture which could be safely consigned to history. That month,

Dario was reminded that in an interview in April 1973, he had said that the revolution would come if they succeeded in 'managing the people's rage'. He agreed that he had been earlier 'guilty of ingenuousness' but added he had remained immune from the 'loss of irony' which had affected many of their contemporaries. Nevertheless, they were aware that the climate had changed profoundly. As Franca put it:

> For me today, doing theatre means above all speaking of people's lives. On the political level, there is a great deal of despair and aimlessness about. Some words like 'struggle' or 'commitment' make me shudder; I can't bring myself to pronounce them. It's not because things in Italy are getting better, in fact they're getting worse. There are two million unemployed now, and the only difference is that nobody wants to hear about them. But some ways of doing politics are over and done with, and there's no point in trying to revive them. But it is much easier to communicate if you talk to people about their existence, about everyday problems.[5]

Lest she be taken as one of the renegades now appearing on TV screens to deplore the errors of their youth and to express the hope that they could now settle to comfort and a career, Franca added that she was happy to have lived those years as she had, and would do it all again. John Osborne's *Angry Young Man* regretted that there were no 'great brave causes' for his generation. Dario and Franca had fought for their 'great brave cause', but saw those who had shared their beliefs deserting the field. If neither could any longer put trust in the certainties of previous decades, they at least would still ruffle feathers, but the days of danger were over. Drama would be confined to their activities in theatre.

They could still stir up controversy, as they did towards the end of 1987 when they appeared on successive weeks on a Sunday afternoon TV variety show. Franca performed her autobiographical monologue, *The Rape*, while Dario followed with *The Miracle of the Child Jesus*, based on an episode in the Apocryphal Gospels, which were arousing his curiosity. Although Franca's monologue had been seen many times in theatre, the TV performance aroused controversy, not about the outrage itself but about the appropriateness of showing such a work at prime

312

time. The Vatican followed with an attack on Dario for giving credence to a tale which was not part of canonical Scriptures. For most Italians the surprise was to discover that, after all the brouhaha surrounding the separation, they were back together. Franca's explanation was gnomic: 'for me, it's as though he was my father or mother. Maybe I was wrong to take it so badly, not to accept the inevitable contradictions of life as a couple. I have come to understand that in times like these, when you hardly have time to say hello to your friends, you cannot lose a relationship like ours; you cannot bankrupt an undertaking to which you have dedicated your whole life.'[6]

They were back on the screens early in 1988 with an eight-part series entitled *Forced Transmission*, which included many clips and extracts from work completed in previous years. Dario wrote a *Letter from China* at the time of the Tiananmen Square repression, a slightly melancholy corrective to what he had written years before on Mao. Unexpected corners of the world showed interest in their work. Companies in Sri Lanka found that the events chronicled in *Accidental Death of an Anarchist* paralleled experiences on an island divided by a long, internecine warfare. In 1989, Dario's production of *Barber of Seville* was presented in Rio de Janeiro, while both he and Franca toured the country with their own works. Later that year, he wrote a new farce, *The Pope and the Witch*, which opened in Novara in October with the two in the title roles. The witch encourages the Pope, who is plainly John Paul II and not some imaginary Pontiff, to swing in the air and to participate in various gags and escapades. He is then constrained by the witch's magic to rethink various dogmas, especially those relating to birth control, drug use and public policy towards addicts. Dario and Franca had been campaigning for years for the decriminalization of drug taking, and the question of the marketing and use of drugs is one of the core issues. John Paul II's name had been mentioned in several of Dario's plays, including the introduction to Boniface VIII, but comic treatment of him was gentle. Dario had a certain respect for him and he was not subjected to the savage satire unleashed on other people in positions of power who featured in his work. In spite of that, the play yet again caused scandal, but attracted more spectators in the 1989/90 season than any other production in Italy.

The following year, Dario was invited to direct Molière at the *Comédie Française*, an irresistible opportunity to repay accumulated debts to the greatest of comic playwrights. Typically, he chose two of the farces normally viewed as minor, *The Doctor in Spite of Himself* and *The Flying Doctor* and, as was his wont, set about restructuring them. Experts agreed that the extant texts were defective, and since they were based on the *commedia dell'arte* tradition, Dario considered he had full authority to digest and rework the plays in the style he knew best. Molière had been, he said, a friend of Domenico Biancolelli, the proto-Harlequin, and had himself played the part. For *The Flying Doctor*, Dario had the great good fortune to find an original script with a list of props, including a mysterious reference to a rope for which there was no obvious need. It was known that the same actor had played both doctor and the servant in Molière's original production, and that his entrances had at times been made via the window. Dario concluded that the entrances could have been effected, Tarzan-style, by leaping through a window, scaling down the rope to be met at the foot by an actor with one of two coats, a great coat for the doctor and a livery for the servant. Thus costumed, the actor could perform both roles. Dario was fortunate to find a French actor of considerable acrobatic ability, and he pressed into service an entire troupe of acrobats and trapeze artists. As rehearsals progressed, Dario decided that a flame-thrower was indispensable and was impressed when one of the cast said that he had done fire-eating as a student. The man gave a creditable performance but later admitted that he had never actually attempted the feat before. As usual, the demands made of actors were enormous, but Dario was repaid with intense loyalty. There were other curios in the production. The rediscovered script made reference to a sheep which Molière had apparently allowed to wander about on stage. Had he succeeded in taming a sheep, Dario wondered? For the modern production, they contented themselves with a dog in sheep's clothing. Molière received the approval of the King, while Dario had to make shift with a commendation from President Mitterand, who wrote a letter of appreciation.

In August two leading exponents of Italian theatre, the actor Vittorio Gassman and the director Giorgio Strehler, became embroiled in a polemical exchange of open letters and articles over the 'lack of any disturbing element' in Italian theatre.[7] Strehler wondered where was the sulphur in Gassman's productions, while Gassman replied accusing Strehler of refusing to take risks and of showing a preference for 'tried and tested scripts'. Gassman claimed to have expanded the range of popular theatre by staging Manzoni's *Adelchi*, a claim which aroused Dario's scoffing disbelief. He rejected the idea that *Adelchi* could be regarded as popular theatre, and added that Gassman too was immune to risk-taking, having staged Pasolini only when he was an accepted part of the theatrical canon. 'The classics have value only when you link them with the great struggles, with a denunciation of present day events,' Dario commented to a journalist,[8] but he took the opportunity to set out once again his reservations over the way theatre was produced and managed in modern Italy. His ideal remained a theatre which faced and confronted 'civil themes', as Vaclav Havel had done in Czechoslovakia. Issues requiring attention included 'the problem of the solitude of the elderly, of the impotence of the new poor, of mafia killings'. He dismissed both Gassman and Strehler for avoiding such topics, but his own choice showed the importance he now gave to the personal dimension, to old age as much as to the mafia.

He continued on his less travelled path, with no relaxation of the touring schedules. *Quiet, We're Falling* (1990) can be viewed as a turning point, even if not final, from political to social satire, a view accepted by Dario himself. While still offended by the conduct of politicians, he had come to believe that social problems had greater impact on the daily lives of ordinary people, so after making the circulation of drugs the core of *The Pope and the Witch*, he took the Aids epidemic as the subject of the new work, a farce set in a mental hospital. Riversi, played by Dario, is a sex-crazed engineer who wished to continue his career as a Don Juan but was aware of the health risks in an era when Aids was rampant. He is given to understand that an antidote to the contagion has been discovered in a mental hospital where the patients have been used as guinea pigs, but immunity can be gained only by having sex with one of them. The inmates include the unattractive wretched of the earth as well as financiers and businessmen, but there is one pretty woman (Franca Rame, obviously). However, she is unbalanced, believing she is Marie Curie and on the point of making revolutionary scientific discoveries. Riversi offers to help her if she will agree to sleep with him, but while she falls in love with him, he is cynically making use of her. The subsidiary characters and a massive electronic machine with protruding wires and cables, as well as orifices from which strange creatures emerge heighten the farce, while Dario offers the view that 'illness deserves respect. It's a tragedy, but the cynicism of certain kinds of conduct is an outrage'.[9]

Some new plays were now jointly signed by both Franca and Dario. In 1991, the couple produced a double bill of plays for Franca, for which she had done the original writing. As is common with her work, the protagonist of both plays is the mother-figure. In *Fat is Beautiful*, Mattea, engaged in a struggle to come to terms with desertion by her husband and the indifference of her daughter, has sunk into a state of chronic depression. In the second edition of the play, rewritten as a one-woman piece, her complaint is couched in edgy terms. She had been married for thirty years to her 'dear, quasi Nobel Winner of a husband' and that over time he had become 'important . . . oh so important! A monument! But a monument, as everybody knows, stands upright on a pedestal'.[10] To compensate for his desertion, she gorges herself with gargantuan quantities of food, becoming enormously obese, confined to bed and unable to walk. In this twilight world, a male voice speaks gentle, caressing words to her, but the words are pre-recorded, not spoken by a living man. A psychoanalyst, in an effort to raise her self-esteem, advises prostitution as a means of persuading her of her enduring attractiveness, but she finds comfort only with her virtual lover. Franca had to perform with padding around her middle, to make her appear obese. It was an acerbic comedy, relying on the comic-grotesque which Franca and Dario had employed for years, depicting a woman starved of affection, devoid of any sense of self-worth, but offering no hope of improvement of the female condition.

The inspiration *Heroin/Heroine* came from real events in Bologna, and the title expresses a grim pun between the two meanings of the one Italian word, *eroina*. Carla, the mother, has already seen two of her children die, one of a heroin overdose and the other of Aids. She declaims against an unseen God, and rages that her determination to save her third daughter, also an addict, has led her to lock the girl up at home, while she herself, having seen other addicts die from using contaminated substances, has turned to prostitution to raise the funds to buy pure, unadulterated, heroin for her daughter. Carla's hope is eventually to take her to Liverpool where, Dario believed after reading an article, enlightened detoxification and therapeutic policies were on offer. There are references to contemporary Italian politicians, such as Rosa Russo Jervolino, who had taken what Franca viewed as a reactionary line on sex education, but the other characters are identified only by symbolic names such as the blind man or the deaf mute, and emerge from some metaphysical dimension. The landscape is bleak, and the violence random, with shots fired by unknown assailants. The part she played permitted Franca to express herself as a dramatic, serious actor. The brutality of the plot caused upset and some theatres refused to accept a booking, but even critics who were doubtful about the work were impressed by Franca's performance. Beckettian in tone, it is the blackest play in the Fo/Rame canon, and has been unjustly neglected perhaps because it is too strong a challenge to a producer's idea of Fo-Rame theatre. Although Dario had collaborated fully in discussions, rewriting, directing and staging of *Heroin/Heroine* he had reservations about it, viewing it as too monotone, too unvaried, too consistently dark and lacking in episodes of irony or the leavening of comedy. When the possibility of reviving it was raised in later years, Dario was opposed to the idea and the proposal was dropped.

Dario was meantime engaged in writing an extended monologue, commissioned by the Expo in Seville, to mark the fifth centennial anniversary of the European discovery of America. The general theme was to be Christopher Columbus's exploits, although in the changed climate created by multi-culturalism and the heightened awareness of the impact of white men on the native American population, it was no longer acceptable simply to celebrate Columbus as hero. Even so, *Johan Padan Discovers America*[11] was judged dangerously iconoclastic by the Expo authorities, who rejected it. The premiere took place in the small northern Italian town of Trento in December 1991. Columbus himself was sidelined in favour of an anti-hero, whose forename is a corruption of the *zanni* character from *commedia dell'arte,* and whose surname is the adjective from the Padua region, the source of the dialect Fo employed in the work. Johan is the quintessential 'poor devil', whose lover is believed to be a witch, a misfortune which arouses the attention of the Inquisition in Venice. A scoundrel without principle or honour, intent on survival at any cost, he stows away on board a ship which he believes is making its way round the Italian coast, but which is actually bound for Seville. Here he meets up with Columbus, just returned from the Americas with a booty which the royal court judges insufficient. When he hears that the Inquisition is in pursuit, Johan joins Columbus's crew for the next voyage.

The tale itself has the dramatic momentum of a picaresque epic, featuring shipwrecks, battles, cannibalism, threats of execution and the encounter of Europeans and Indians with each other. From the early shipwreck off Santo Domingo through various captures and escapades, Johan is never at peace. His life is a whirlwind of unpredictable events. On mainland South America, he and his companions are first given hospitality by a tribe which then sells them to cannibals. Johan himself is saved from the pot because he has jaundice, uses the knowledge of astronomy he gained from his former lover to predict a hurricane and finds himself worshipped as a son of the moon. With the tribe now in his power, he uses his influence to persuade them to lead him to an encampment of Christians. Although his only thought is to escape back to Europe, he is obliged to teach them something of the mysteries of Christianity, from the Trinity to the relationship between Christ and Mary Magdalene.

The play has a Rabelaisian bawdiness and racy vigour which Dario in this later phase preferred to the bilious satire of his earlier work. Having read deeply in contemporary chronicles, he was impressed by an unknown history of the success of the Indios in campaigns and battles, and eschews all depiction of native Americans as either noble savages or victims. His main source was the work of Michele Da Cuneo, who also provided him with the pastiche dialect employed in *Johan*

Padan, or so Dario claims in the prologue, although Da Cuneo wrote in clear, standard Italian.[12] The synthetic dialect, inaccessible even to Italians, was an invention of Dario's, but the use of an impenetrable dialect caused spectators to focus on the actor's voice and body as it recreates storms, dances, horse-riding, wading though water, tramping through jungles, tending animals and attempting to make love in a hammock. The published text is accompanied by a translation into Italian by Franca, but is embellished by the designs and drawings which Dario used as an *aide-memoire* during performance.

While Dario was touring with *Johan Padan,* Franca was on the road with *Let's Talk About Women* but, as had happened in previous decades, she was refused permission to perform in theatres in, for example, Bolzano and Rovereto where the local parish priest was on the management committee. It was surprising that such power could still be exercised by the church, but two Italys were about to come into conflict. In an interview given while rehearsing *Quiet, We're Falling,* Dario repeated that he was tired of political satire and that his theatre would in the future be devoted more to social criticism. 'Secret services? Plots? Enough. These things no longer tempt us. The protagonists of our politics are such minor, minuscule, mediocre characters.'[13] It was an ill-chosen moment to be making a statement about loss of interest in politics, since the Italian political scene was about to be revolutionised and the mediocre characters swept aside. Although the newcomers on the political scene were hardly noble characters, at least as they were considered worthy of representation in Dario's theatre.

Italian politics, with its paradoxical combination of permanence and instability, has always bewildered foreign observers. Governments in the First Republic had short life spans, but the same parties remained in power in bewildering combinations, and the same politicians retained office years after their contemporaries in other countries had long since retired. This unstable permanence ended not as a result of the demonstrations on the street by the Left, nor of bombing campaigns by the Right, but principally by two events: the fall of the Berlin Wall in 1989 and the consequent collapse of the Communist parties in eastern Europe, and the emergence in 1992 of the *Clean Hands* anti-corruption drive headed by the Milanese magistrate, Antonio Di Pietro. The judges' initiatives revealed to Italian electors the full extent of industrial-political corruption behind the scenes in Rome, Milan and elsewhere. The parties which had dominated political life in the First Republic collapsed, and new forces and new figures assumed power, to be subjected by Dario to the same satirical derision as had their predecessors. Initially, particularly since the first of the new forces was Umberto Bossi's Lombard League, Milan rather than Rome occupied the front line. Commentators in Italy and abroad were disconcerted by the uncertainty of the League's basic programme as it wobbled between devolutionary, federalist and separatist demands, but if the ideology was imprecise and opportunistic, a constant factor was a quasi racist rhetoric and hostility initially to the poorer Mezzogiorno and later to immigrants. Dario was implacably opposed to the League from its inception and, like many left-wingers, found himself giving the Italian state the support he had withheld during the terrorist crisis. However, while Bossi was then and later subjected to contemptuous satirical remarks, he never received from Dario the same focused, satirical detestation accorded to Silvio Berlusconi and *Forza Italia!* After his 'descent onto the field', Berlusconi would become the principal object of scorn and satire over coming years.

The first move in the *Clean Hands* campaign occurred in February 1992 with the arrest in Milan on a charge of bribery of Mario Chiesa, a socialist functionary in charge of a rest home in the city. The campaign snowballed and soon the magistrates had uncovered the existence of what was dubbed *Tangentopoli* (Bribesville), a massive network of corruption which embraced the overlapping worlds of politics and industry. The Italian political system, which had remained impregnable when faced with the assaults of the 'Movement,' crumbled, taking with it the Christian Democrat, Socialist Republican and Social Democratic parties. Dario delighted in retelling tales of Socialist ex-Premier Bettino Craxi facing jeers and boos from outraged crowds. He recycled the title of an anti-corruption play from 1964, *Seventh Commandment: Thou Shalt Steal a Little Less,* but rewrote it and transformed it into a one woman show which Franca toured around Italy. She spoke the monologue from behind a lectern, with in the background huge photographs of politicians found guilty or facing charges, as the main prop. One banner displayed on stage read – 'Don't let the right hand know what the left is stealing.' The achievements of the magistrates, including Antonio di Pietro, who would later play another significant part in Franca's life, were celebrated.

When the first version of work had been staged twenty-five years earlier, the events recounted seemed as fantastic as episodes in *Gulliver's Travels*. What had been 'absurd episodes of speculation on bodies to be buried in the cemetery at Musocco,' explained Dario, were now similar to press reports as the misdeeds of politicians in every party came to light. 'We have discovered that we have been robbed of our script, without one lira in royalties being paid to us.' The monologue switched deftly between reportage and satire, but was shot through with an undercurrent of bitter indignation and spiced with comic force and imbued with the violence and scatological humour which Dario inherited from the medieval jesters. Chiesa had attempted to flush millions of lire down the toilet when the carabinieri arrived to arrest him, but in Dario's reworking of this scene, the flush mechanism failed to work and the toilet overflowed, leaving Chiesa drenched in urine and faeces. Di Pietro is shown having one of the accused in hospital injected with some substance to make him stop talking and revealing so many names, since otherwise the courts would be unable to cope with all the trials deriving from the revelations. One of the incidents incorporated into the script concerned a crooked device by which the consultant in one of most prestigious hospitals in Milan was chosen. Ten balls were put in a bag, each with a name, and the one picked out got the job. To make sure there were no mistakes, the ball of the person who had paid the required bribe was put in a refrigerator one hour previously. If the prime target was Tangentopoli and corruption in Italy, the play's focus widened when the Pope's elegant Mercedes was juxtaposed with images of starving children in Africa. The denunciation of inequality and injustice in other continents had not been abandoned.

Theatrical life on other fronts continued. *Dario Fo Meets Ruzzante*, premiered at the Spoleto festival in 1993, represented the repaying of

Dario's deepest debt. Angelo Beolco (1495/6-1542), known as Ruzzante from the peasant character he invented and played, was, like Dario, an actor-author. Ruzzante's theatre was rooted in contemporary history, providing the worm's eye view of the Renaissance Venice of Titian, Tintoretto and Bellini. His plays were precisely the hard-edged farces dealing with the tragic realities of hunger, sexual appetites, violence and the experience of warfare which Dario aspired to write. As originally conceived by Dario, the work was to be entitled *The Dialogues of Ruzzante*, with Dario directing a fifteen-strong cast drawn from the (private) Fo/Rame troupe and the (public) *Teatro degli Incamminati*, but even at this stage in his career, Dario still suffered the vexations of bureaucrats. A ministerial communiqué, circulated only when rehearsals were at an advanced stage, uncovered, or invented, an obscure law forbidding co-productions between public and private companies. The actors employed by the publicly funded company were required to withdraw, and the work was renamed and recast to include both Franca and Dario, who performed some individual pieces and provided the overall continuity and introductions. Ruzzante enthusiasts were appalled at the freedom Dario took with the original works, but it was a sell-out success with festival audiences, and he revived it in modified form two years later in Florence under the title *Fo Performs Ruzzante*. For the revival, the rest of the cast was eliminated and the show became a monologue, part performance and part lecture. Dario also incorporated a newly discovered one act play by Galileo, an admirer of Ruzzante.

One of the cast in Spoleto was Marina De Juli, who had been auditioned two years previously for *The Pope and the Witch*, but rejected then as too young for the part. Years later, she received a phone call and became from then until Franca's death an indispensable part of the company and the household. The number of people employed was growing, and in whatever capacity they were initially engaged, they often found themselves fulfilling multiple roles. Sometimes, they found their services contended between Dario and Franca. Marina and Franca became firm friends, so when the couple went touring with their own monologues after Spoleto, Marina went with Franca.

Marina had no real house of her own, and so moved in with the couple, even having her own room at the holiday home in Cesenatico. Franca oversaw Marina's development as actor in her own idiosyncratic way, not by giving lessons or notes, but inviting Marina to 'steal' from her, to observe from the wings, as Franca herself had done with her family. Any advice would be imparted while Franca was doing something else. For *All House, Bed and Board*, she initially got Marina to parrot the lines as she spoke them, although later Marina did these pieces in her own style, and played them together with other, more biographical sketches on Franca after her death.

Franca took the leading part in the next play Dario wrote, *Mamma! The Sans Culottes*, even though she was suffering from a recurrence of the devastating effects of her kidnapping and violation, and was experiencing a period of eating disorder which caused her to vomit all she ate. The play was described as a 'Feydeau-style mechanical farce,' set approximately in the days of the French Revolution but which pilloried corruption in the health service in contemporary Italy. Dario employed the brutal, quasi-cannibalistic humour he detected in Ruzzante and in Harlequinades for a scene where he played a vet who sits down for a meal whose principal dish was not a beef steak but a human being. His aim was to deride a complacent people who 'devoured themselves instead of rebelling', but the scene created problems for Franca who was to eat a plate of spaghetti. She decided to explain the root of her difficulties to the audience at the first night in Carrara, causing some people to weep, but in the event she found the confession and the performance therapeutic. She was at ease in the theatre, and her son Jacopo speculated that for her 'the stage was like a maternal womb'. Her recovery from the violence she had endured was slow, and perhaps never complete. Jacopo too still endured bouts of rage which were of their very nature ill-directed.

Franca encountered problems of a different order with her next work, given the saucy title, *Sex? Thank You! Don't Mind If I Do*, a monologue intended as a sex-instruction piece, based on a book written by her son Jacopo, *Zen and the Art of Screwing*.[14] The Ministry promptly stepped in to ban the work to under 18s. Outraged at this act of censorship,

Franca reverted to campaign mode, sending circulars to the Italian and foreign press. The Ministry prudently backed down and even issued a special edict to the effect that the work was 'imbued with maternal love', and could therefore be *recommended* to minors. Sex was good, decent, clean and could be made fun and an adjunct to love, provided men and, especially, women understood their bodies. It was hard to see what even the most myopic bureaucrat could have ever objected to. The work was a kind of guide to sex, offering instruction and assistance to those who lived in a state of ignorance, or who were afflicted with problems. This category included Jacopo himself, who was revealed to the world as having problems with premature ejaculation.

Franca spoke of difficulties of her own, so the work effectively smashed all barriers between private and the public. There were discussions of menopause, prostate problems, as well as of means of achieving orgasm – a word which previously Franca had found too indelicate to pronounce in public – including the location of the mythical G-point. The work was a further instance of the changed focus away from the directly political to the social, a shift which bemused some critics who were puzzled to find Franca putting on a show of this kind when Italy was facing so many political problems, but she replied that public life was 'so miserable, so self- parodying,' that she decided it was better 'to work on the positive, speak of the personal, try to propose a kind of new Humanism which speaks of the primary roots, of the relationship between man and woman'.[15]

May saw Dario travel to Denmark to conduct seminars with students, and then move to Amsterdam to organise an exhibition of his own work. Another exhibition was mounted in the cathedral in Bergamo. Dario produced another Rossini opera, *The Italian Girl in Algiers* for the 1994 Pesaro Festival. There was no let-up in his workload, and later that year he took the opera to Amsterdam. There were plans for a grand international tour taking in France, Germany, Britain and the USA in autumn 1995, in which Dario would perform *Johan Padan* and Franca her most recent piece, but these plans had to be abandoned when on 17 July 1995 at their summer house in Cesenatico, he suffered a stroke. He had been working long hours with his American translator, Ron

Jenkins, on the English-language subtitles for his plays, while also drafting a series of lectures for Florence. Jacopo was in the house at the time and he and Franca became concerned when Dario started complaining of severe headaches. In the evening, he began babbling incoherently, and then collapsed. The local doctor was summoned, and diagnosed a detached retina. He said Dario should be kept at home until the morning. Franca was unconvinced, and the following day packed Dario into the car and took him on a nightmare journey to Milan in the heat of mid-summer. He had in fact suffered a stroke. He was sick several times along the way, and doctors later told Franca the stress of the journey could have made him go into fibrillation or even suffer a second stroke. They arrived at the neurological unit in Milan, where he was put into intensive care.

Over time he made a remarkable recovery, but the stroke left its mark. The attack left no trace on his clarity of mind or speech, so he was eventually able to continue writing and performing, but under constraints. He initially lost 80% of his sight and his memory suffered. He had difficulties calling to mind the names of people or movements with whom he had worked all his life, while other times a name would come to him freely, only for him to forget it in the following sentence. He would remember scientific instead of everyday names or use odd circumlocutions, so was liable to say 'quick-moving fish in the Baltic Sea,' instead of cod.[16] Since his heartbeat was irregular, a lengthy period of convalescence was prescribed and the doctor advised long walks, but wracked by anxieties and desperate to get back to writing and acting, he was a poor patient. He resumed the work on a TV version of the lectures given in Florence, and started writing *The Peasants' Bible*, which he was due to deliver as a lecture in September at the Benevento Festival, for which the director, Maurizio Costanzo, had chosen *The Sacred and the Profane* as the theme. There was an audience of around 5000, and on the first evening Dario had a relapse. Franca did a longer version of her act, something which aroused adverse comment in some newspapers the following day. Dario went on stage but could not deliver the planned material, replacing it with another piece which was better known to him. The set-back had a deep effect on him and he considered giving up performing altogether, but Franca was concerned that if he did, he would have nothing to live for. She persuaded him to continue with the tour, whose next stop was Sicily.

With his impaired vision, reading and writing presented difficulties, but he had a special lens made, and had newspapers read to him so that he could keep abreast of current affairs. Rumours were spread, and *The Guardian* carried a report that he had gone blind. He issued a jocular denial: 'The Guardian came out with the headline: The blind Dario Fo will perform (with a dog). With a dog, with a dog. No, I wanted to be sincere. I did say I had a stroke. I spoke of the damage to my sight, an impairment in the visual field which has nonetheless made an extraordinary recovery, so much so that I have started working peacefully again. I paint, I write. That's it. The virtual Dario Fo, a media creation, lives his own life.'[17]

His ability to draw and sketch was not affected, and he resumed painting with a will. He executed some large canvases and covered pages with a series of designs, doodles and enlarged cartoons, some of which contained outlines of scripts, plots and speeches which were later used as prompts in future performance. Even though Franca had persuaded him to continue his career as actor, she was less convinced he had recovered as completely as he believed. In any case, he was now more dependent on her than ever. They developed a system whereby he wrote as best he could, in large lettering or sketches, leaving her to collect the pieces and type them in coherent form on the computer.

Something like normal life resumed. Dario celebrated his 70th birthday with a grand party at the *Lirico* in Milan. Being 70 years old was, he said, 'a surprise! Seventy years have gone by. Some people feel old at forty. I've had this great fortune: whenever I've wanted to pull in my oars, disembark at some port, go home and take off my shoes, the waves have always pushed me back out to the open sea.'[18] Artwork and exhibitions took up an increasing part of his time and energy and would continue to do so in the future. There were exhibitions in Copenhagen and Brescia and in July, Cesenatico, which had given Dario and Franca honorary citizenship, hosted a major exhibition, *Puppets with Rage and Feeling*, which would then be seen in various galleries around the world.

The Fos went back on the road, he performing scenes from *Mistero buffo* and she a pared down version of *Sex!* as part of the same bill in an effort to lessen the strain on Dario. The touring schedules required military precision. The two with their entourage arrived a day before performance so that Dario could settle, go for a walk and rest before going on stage. His prologues no longer had the up to date freshness which had been their distinguishing mark. His introduction to the sketch on *Pope Boniface* still used material relating to the attempted assassination of Pope John Paul II in 1981. On stage, there was little sign of any weakness or fatigue. The laughter of the audience acted as a transfusion of some life force, and made his rapport with the stalls seem once again fresh, but if he jumped and danced on the boards, as soon as the lights went down his energy drained.

Collaborating in this way, they produced a body of late work, starting with *The Peasants' Bible*, staged in September 1996, which was surprising both in volume and variety. A monologue on Leonardo's *Last Supper* went out on television, and Dario made a tentative, solo return to the stage in May the following year in Copenhagen, as part of a celebration of their work which included an exhibition of paintings, costumes and puppets. He insisted on arranging a new tour in Italy, and while on the road, the two were occupied with a new full-length play, *The Devil with Tits*. In this period, Franca performed in the evening, and rose early in the morning to type the previous day's work so that Dario could incorporate corrections or alterations to the script when he got up. This increased work load took its toll on her. During a stop in Udine, they were working on sections of the play where the female lead spoke in Neapolitan dialect. Franca was exhausted, and discovered that she had lost her command of Italian and could only speak in pure Neapolitan. The doctor diagnosed panic attacks and told her to suspend performances until she could regain her balance, and her command of standard Italian. *The Devil with Tits* was premiered in August 1997 in the Sicilian town of Messina, and played that summer in the Greek theatre in nearby Taormina. Dario agreed that he could not perform himself, so Giorgio Albertazzi appeared opposite Franca. The Milanese magistrates' *Clean Hands* campaign was still underway, so that although the play featured a judge conducting an enquiry into corruption at the time of the Counter-Reformation and the Inquisition, it was easy to see parallels with Antonio Di Pietro and the situation of contemporary Italy.[19]

Meantime, another legal case, further ramifications of the *Piazza Fontana* bombing which had dogged Dario since 1969, and which was the basis of *Accidental Death of an Anarchist*, returned unexpectedly to the headlines, causing Dario to take up cudgels against a further act of injustice. Some officers and magistrates had always viewed Adriano Sofri, one of the leading lights in *Lotta Continua*, as the principal suspect for the murder on 17 May 1972 of commissario Luigi Calabresi, held by many on the Left as responsible for the death of the anarchist Pinelli. In 1988 Sofri, together with Ovidio Bompressi and Giorgio Pietrostefani, two other ex-members of the same organisation, were arrested and charged with the murder of Calabresi. The news caused consternation, not least because Sofri, like many other sixties revolutionaries, had in the intervening years become a writer and journalist, a supporter and apologist for Bettino Craxi's moderate, reformist brand of socialism and a well-connected figure in the most elegant salons of Milan and Rome. His case became a *cause célèbre*, taken up by writers and intellectuals including Vincenzo Consolo, Umberto Eco, Dacia Maraini and the historian Carlo Ginzburg. Some were motivated by friendship, but others were moved to indignation by what seemed to them as one of the most outrageous miscarriages of justice in twentieth-century Italy.

Assessments of Calabresi the man and his motives have varied enormously, so that he now seems a Pirandellian character, elusive and unknowable in himself, with different personalities imposed on him by others. Two Popes have referred to him as a man of faith, almost a martyr, and the process of beatification was initiated under Pope John Paul II. His widow published a moving book on his personal qualities,[20] while the director Marco Tullio Giordana gave a very positive portrait of him in his 2011 film, *Romanzo di una strage* (Novel of a Massacre). His son became editor first of *La Stampa* and later of *La Repubblica*, and has always, unsurprisingly, proclaimed his father's innocence. Others have continued to portray Calabresi as a torturer and even as a murderer, responsible for the death in custody of the anarchist, Pino Pinelli. Dario wavered in his assessment of the man, and ended by describing him as a victim of one of the more sinister mysteries of twentieth-century Italian political life.

Dario and Franca remained fully involved over the coming years, but it will be convenient to summarise the main events here. The judicial history of the Sofri case has been a disgrace to Italian justice. There were seven trials in nine years. In the first in Milan, 2 May 1990, Sofri, Pietrostefani and Bompressi were condemned to 22 years, and Marino to 11 years. This was upheld by the Court of Appeal the following year, but over-ruled by the Court of Cassation in October 1992 because of defects 'of form'. The case was referred back to the initial court, who found all the accused not guilty, but this verdict was in its turn reversed by the Cassation for the same reason as before. The case came back before the Appeal Court in 1995, which this time found the three guilty and sentenced them again to 22 years, but acquitted Marino. Finally on 22 January 1997, the Cassation confirmed the finding and sentence of the Appeal Court. Sofri and Pietrostefani were found guilty of being the instigators, and Bompressi the actual killer. The men finally began a 22 year sentence in 1998, only to be released for yet another trial the following year. In 2000, Sofri, Bompressi and Pietrostefani were again found guilty, although this time on grounds of moral responsibility, and Sofri sent back to continue his sentence. The other two had gone into hiding.

It transpired that for the first trial the *carabinieri* relied on the testimony of an informer, Leonardo Marino, who had also been in *Lotta Continua* in the seventies but who in the eighties was under police investigation for alleged criminal activity. Marino was himself accused of having driven the vehicle at the time of the killing, although contemporary eye-witnesses all agreed that the driver was a woman. According to police accounts Marino only made his confession on 20 July 1988, but it transpired that he had been in touch with the *carabinieri* since 2 July. The accounts given by Marino in the course of the various trials were contradictory on many details, and differed from the accounts provided by eye-witnesses. He suggested, for instance, that he had been overwhelmed by an onrush of guilt, especially after a conversation with a Salesian priest. In the witness box, the priest denied having ever set eyes on him.

Although his involvement in the Sofri campaign was altruistic and humanitarian, Dario found himself retracing his own steps through the 'years of lead' as the Italians called them, and drawing up balance sheets. Franca wrote of the dismay both experienced when they saw 'comrades' from the days of militant campaigns appear on television as government lawyers or representatives of multinational corporations. The Sofri case made them wonder whether much had changed in the 'system'. Power resided where it always had and behaved as it always did, but Dario and Franca stood where they had always stood. They had never changed, even if the days of 'struggle' were over.

CHAPTER 17

The Actor Vindicated

In early 1997, a television company came up with a bright idea for a series to be called *Roma-Milano*. The formula was simple: engage a couple of instantly recognisable celebrities who have never previously met, put them in a car furnished with three cameras, set them on the autostrada between Milan and Rome and film their every word and gesture. On the assumption that they would hold entertainingly clashing views about television and society, Dario Fo and Ambra Angiolini, a teenage singer and TV personality, were chosen to inaugurate the series. The date for the filming was fixed as 9 October 1997, which was, by chance, also the date scheduled for the announcement of the winner of the Nobel Prize for Literature. Rome had been buzzing with rumours over Dario's nomination. He played down his prospects, but the risk of missing a big story was too great so the car containing Dario and Ambra was tailed by a task force of press vehicles.

Near Orvieto, there was a commotion. A journalist from *La Repubblica* got the news and made frantic but unsuccessful signals to attract Dario's attention. Eventually, he scribbled out a message on a piece on cardboard and held it up to the window. It read – 'You've won the Nobel Prize!' Since Dario could not drive, Ambra was at the wheel and she stopped at the first service area, where champagne was produced. Some children in the vicinity restored a sense of measure. They rushed over for an autograph, not of the new Nobel laureate, but of Ambra. Surrounded by journalists and TV lights Dario had to make an on-the-spot declaration. 'I'm terrified,' was his first response, 'I'd had some vague hint, but I'd put my chances at no more than ten per cent.' The reporters crowded round him but his first wish was to contact Franca, since 'a good half of the prize is hers'. Ambra, clearly gifted with sense of irony that Fo must have appreciated, explained to puzzled passers-by, 'he has won the Nobel Prize and I'm signing autographs.' Dario did a series of immediate radio interviews by phone but, ever the professional, got back into the car to finish the journey to Milan and the programme.

Meantime a Swedish journalist phoned Franca, who was alone in the flat in Milan making the bed, and screamed, 'it's him, it's him', before breaking down. Franca too burst into tears, and had little time to compose herself before the phone started ringing from around the world as the news media everywhere sought her first reaction. The day before in Rome, *Communist Refoundation* led by Fausto Bertinotti voted with the Right to bring down the moderately Leftist coalition headed by Romano Prodi, whose government Dario and Franca supported. The two events shared headlines round the world the following day. Internationally, a creative Italy was juxtaposed to a political Italy whose ways were judged simply incomprehensible. Franca was dismayed by the vote in Parliament so when a journalist from *Liberazione* called her for a quote, she was told, 'my dear girl, the first thing is to berate Bertinotti.'

The Swedish Royal Academy's official citation stated that Dario Fo

emulates the jesters of the Middle Ages in scourging authority and upholding the dignity of the downtrodden. For many years, Fo has been performed all over the world, perhaps more than any other contemporary dramatist, and his influence has been considerable. He if anyone merits the description of jester in the true meaning of the word. With a blend of laughter and gravity he opens our eyes to abuses and injustices in society, and also to the wider historical perspective in which they can be placed. Fo is an extremely serious satirist with a multifaceted oeuvre. His independence and clear-sightedness have led him to take great risks, whose consequences he has been made to feel while at the same time experiencing a deep response from the most varied quarters.

The citation also identified the 'non-institutional tradition' as vital to his development, explaining that 'commedia dell'arte and such twentieth century writers as Mayakovsky and Brecht had provided him with important impulses'. Dario himself took delight in the term 'jester,' telling La Repubblica: 'I am pleased with this prize because it is the vindication of the actor, and because it is given to a jester and not to a man of letters.' In Italy, every expression of delight over the award was balanced by an equal and opposing expression of gawking disbelief, outrage, curmudgeonly envy or partisan gracelessness. The politicians, unsurprisingly, divided along party lines. Gianfranco Fini, leader of the neo-Fascist National Alliance, spluttered that the whole business was a disgrace. 'I can't understand the motivation for this prize. What has Fo given to Italian or world literature?' Others on the Right took the opportunity to revive the issue of Dario's membership of the Salò militia. 'The first veteran of Mussolini's Republic to be celebrated by the highest honour for Literature' ran the headline in Il Giornale. The Vatican's daily, L'Osservatore Romano was equally hostile. 'Fo is Italy's sixth Nobel prize winner after Carducci, Deledda, Pirandello, Quasimodo and Montale; after such wealth, a jester' it wrote, shaking its patrician head. Whatever the Academy thought, the term 'jester' was no compliment in the eyes of the Vatican. 'Swedish Mystery' was a common headline, but others were more vicious: 'In the place of Ezra Pound, another repubblichino,' the first page of Il Giornale stated. Silvio Berlusconi limited himself to a brusque – no comment. The mayor of Milan declared himself unable to deliver congratulations in person because of a prior commitment to attend a fashion parade.

Many representatives from the world of culture and the arts found it equally hard to be magnanimous. There had been a widespread feeling that it was 'Italy's turn' for the Nobel, and one man who had set his heart on receiving the prize was the poet, Mario Luzi. Florence had even prepared a reception for him. When the press phoned him, he attempted an Olympian disdain: 'I am glad for this new acquisition and knowledge offered us. As an author I do not know him. I have never read him. I cannot give an appreciation.' It was a hard pose to sustain, and his next comment had the spareness and purity of poetry: 'All I have to say is I've got a pain in the balls.' Rita Levi Montalcini, who had herself won the Nobel for medicine in 1989, was asked for a reaction but claimed never to have heard of Dario Fo and not even to know if he was Italian. Reactions among theatre people were mixed. Franco Zeffirelli said he had always viewed Fo as a genius, the actor Carmelo Bene said he was outraged, and Giorgio Strehler's comment was scarcely categorisable: 'We are honoured as Europeans and actors. This more and more 'virtual' world needs a grand, vitalising chuckle.'

Alongside personal spleen, the announcement gave rise to a more serious debate about theatre and literature, about the properties of playwriting in itself and the kind of writing that should be eligible for the world's supreme literature award. From Peru, Mario Vargas Llosa added his voice to the dissent, wondering whether Fo's writings were of a quality to merit that level of recognition. Not everyone in Italy was able to detect the 'vitality and range' that so impressed the 'Immortals' in Stockholm. Giulio Ferroni, author of a much admired *History of Italian Literature*, was left perplexed, and returned to a familiar refrain – 'I have a high regard for Fo the actor, but where is the literature?' he asked. Dario had many prestigious defenders, including the novelists Dacia Maraini and Vincenzo Consolo, as well as Umberto Eco, who stated unequivocally that Fo deserved the prize for his manifold achievements.

> I am delighted by the fact that they gave the prize to an author who does not belong to the traditional academic world. What I find impressive is his enormous popularity abroad. For us in Italy it is very difficult to separate the power of Fo as a theatrical character from the scripts he writes. We are mistaken if we allow ourselves to be conditioned by the character, great as it is. His plays are of great importance in our literature.

These debates over Dario Fo had been rumbling on for years in Italy. Political judgements and personal rancour aside, there had always been a certain perplexity over his rank as writer. Is Fo an actor who writes rather than a writer who acts? Are his scripts merely what *commedia dell'arte* performers would have termed a *canovaccio*, in other words an outline script or a pretext, often a very flimsy pretext, for a display of his improvisational skills and bravura as actor? Have the scripts he has produced any depth and vitality independent of his on stage presence, or are they a fraud perpetrated on a gullible theatre public but easily exposed by the more alert reading public? Is theatre, especially theatre of the sort Dario wrote, really literature?

The debate was rendered more complex in Dario's case by the lack of critical instruments adequate for judging a playwright of his particular stamp. He claims to be a popular playwright, so the question could be reformulated to ask whether a comparison between Fo and George Bernard Shaw or Luigi Pirandello, two other Nobel prize winning playwrights, is of any greater worth than a comparison of, say, Conan Doyle and Dostoevsky? The latter both wrote novels, but the genres in which they operated and thus the critical criteria to be applied are wholly different. What answer can be given to a questioner who asks if an igloo is better than an adobe, or a whale stronger than a lion? An adobe is of little value in the Arctic, and a whale would be weak on land. Dario walks what were conventionally considered the lesser trodden paths of the Western tradition, ignored by theatre historians. The distance between writing and performance is in his case minimal. In his theatre, the offer of enjoyment has the same importance as weighing ideas, or more precisely, the one is a means to attaining the other.

There is a further problem. There are words, and hence concepts, which are untranslatable in themselves and comprehensible only after explanation. One such term is *canovaccio*, a term which has sense only inside the exclusively Italian tradition of *commedia dell'arte,* and which can be in a historical sense a term of approbation or in a more modern sense a term of belittlement, suggesting that the author was incapable of producing a fully rounded script. Dario's plays may be similar to traditional *canovacci*, and he himself has embraced or rejected the term when in different moods. At times he was irritated by the dismissiveness implicit in its use, at others he has said that Shakespeare's plays were *canovacci*, and that all theatre scripts were *canovacci*, so let's get on with it. Dario does not beguile academic critics by inviting their participation in the erudite dissection of psychic wounds or existential dilemmas exposed by his works. He has no interest in investigating fractured psyches, in portraying the plight of the human animal in a world made barren by the death of God or in delving into the adequacy of language for communicating emotional or spiritual predicaments. There is no subtext to be uncovered, no hidden ambiguities to be revealed, no delicate psychology of character to be probed, no curiosities of flawed personality to be dissected and analysed, no alternative world of the fantasy to be contemplated. Further, he does not construct a philosophy, as does Pirandello, offer a social portrait of a bourgeoisie in thrall to a claustrophobic malaise, as does Ibsen, look askance at a regime in terminal decline, like Chekhov. Critics will search in vain for the metaphysical dimension constructed by fellow farceurs like Beckett or Ionesco. Nor does his theatre display, unlike that of Artaud or early Strindberg, neurotic symptoms of the creative mind which could be taken as a warped illumination of the senseless world in which men and women have their daily being. Dario stands with the buskers at the theatre door, singing and joking about matters of importance to the queues seeking admission to the gods. But how important is a busker?

When one journalist put to him the apocalyptic scenario that the award marked the end of literature as such, he politely distinguished between the standards needed in theatre and those required of literature. Traditional theatre, he said, had never relied entirely on the written text. 'Improvisation has always been important, and then there is what we could call the lesson of Molière. The actor who wrote was always taken as a fool. In the case of Molière, the word was put about that he couldn't have written his own works. This prize is a vindication of poor Molière as well.' [1]

While Fo's satire addressed the issues of the day, his theatre stood on tradition. He spoke of himself as the actor-author, the central figure in Italian tradition, and revelled in the description 'jester' that had appeared in the official commendation, always insisting that his writing was in the theatrical mainstream. His farce can be fully appreciated only if seen robustly outside the context created by his more respected contemporaries. As a performer, he could have gambled and pirouetted in the amphitheatres alongside the Atellan farceurs, the medieval *giullari* or the late Renaissance Harlequins. It is odd and inconsistent that the Harlequin of times past is now an object of reverential study but a Harlequin of today like Dario is treated with condescension. His theatre speaks to and of the needs of the powerless in a world they do not control, while he looks towards utopian horizons, and invites his audiences to join in liberating laughter at the spectacle of dishonesty and power. His real success can be gauged by the way he made theatre dangerous again. His Stockholm speech touched on the perils faced by performers in other times, but he too was the object of official harassment and persecution. He was hounded not by harmless critics, but by censors, politicians, magistrates, police and, ultimately, by terrorists in cahoots with ministries.

The citation also recognised that Dario fashioned theatre as a public arena where values, mainly but not exclusively political values, could be aired and discussed. He was the first to attempt to weld seriousness of purpose onto the supposedly light-weight genre which is farce, and he is not to blame if followers allowed that style to degenerate into lumpen didacticism. His comedy, or farce, has an underlay of a seriousness which tragedy struggles to attain for a contemporary audience. Like Molière and Ruzzante, he lacked refinement of taste and was wholly free of the urge to conform to canons of aesthetics sanctioned by the bien-pensant salons of his age. Like his illustrious predecessors, his wish was to create an upside-down world in which it is normal to flay the practices of those who wield power in the hope that these practices will be shown as preposterous, perpetrated by people who, whatever status they have arrogated to themselves, are themselves ridiculous. 'Oh, the world is so so beautiful / if you look at it hanging from your feet,' in the words of a song in *He Had Two Pistols and Black and White Eyes*. 'This award will be first time an actor has shaken a king's hand,' he said.

With the authoritative backing of the Swedish Academy, he could now reiterate his deepest held conviction that theatre writing was an independent branch of literature, different in kind from novel writing or poetry, with distinct merits and qualities but of equal dignity. It could not afford to be fey and meandering. Any verbal magic had to be subordinate to action and incorporated in a vivid whole. The names he produced to back up his claims for the autonomy of theatre writing were Ruzzante, Shakespeare and, above all, Molière. The debate about his own scripts could and should be rephrased so that it becomes not a writing-versus-performance dispute but recognition that writing-plus-performance, or writing with a view to performance, provides the only standard by which drama can be judged. When it was put to him the great playwrights were also littérateurs, he replied:

> Those who reason in this way show that they have never understood what theatre is. These gentlemen who go into ecstasies over the reading of Shakespeare forget that his scripts too were *canovacci*. 'The word is the theatre', said Shakespeare. And I believe that this Nobel Prize is indeed a recognition of the value of the word on the stage. The word can become written only after it has been used, after it has been chewed many times on the set. That's the way it was for many famous authors. Half of what we know of Ruzzante was printed only after his death. The scripts of Molière were *canovacci* until some traditional authors encouraged him to have them published.[2]

There would be little point in attempting to trace the Shakespearean quotation. Nor is it clear how it coheres with his other assertion that one of the most important aspects of his break with conventional theatre in 1968 was liberation from the slavery of the script. 'We rejected the law according to which "the script is theatre." We put a bomb under its bum,' he said then. For Dario theatre was the word made flesh. Many of his opponents would have agreed that he had a unique ability to give life even to banal words and would have conceded him any theatrical prize he coveted, but they contended that the world's supreme literary prize should be based on qualities of the page alone. Dario saw the prize principally as giving new but overdue dignity to the totality of page plus stage.

The 1997 award plainly recognised the value of the spoken rather than the purely written word, but the combination was what counted. 'Pirandello was an extraordinary dramatist, but he never went on stage. I did. And so this prize sounds like an extraordinary vindication of the all-round man of theatre.'[3] Dario did not have a high opinion of Pirandello, whom he regarded as boring, and although his 1997 judgement seemed at the time relatively generous, it contained the subtle reminder that he had not performed his own work. Dario, and in this he was at the heart of the Italian tradition, esteemed above all the actor-author.

But that raised other questions. Shaw, Pirandello, Beckett and other previous theatrical winners of the Nobel Prize restricted themselves to writing. The malicious question put in regard to Dario was – to what extent was the success of his theatre due to his skill as an actor, which no one called into question, and to what extent was it due to his ability as writer? His theatre involved elements which could not be relayed on the page, like improvisation, so what did this have to do with literature? This question had dogged Dario all his life. When Mayor Albertini was finally spurred into recognising Dario's achievement, he suggested that he might like to write a show for Milan. Dario retorted that he had done exactly that, and it was running at the Carcano, but he went to point out to Albertini that the prize had been awarded to him as writer, not as actor. Actor or author? Fo claimed the prize in both guises, but also believed they were inseparable.

The second and more intractable problem for critics was that Dario worked in the field of popular theatre, a genre pundits were unequipped to confront. Few of them, excepting Umberto Eco, who was warm in his appreciation of Dario, had the critical vocabulary or the intellectual tools to judge popular literature with any discrimination. Their training, their thinking, their tastes and their preferences were all in the field of the great western tradition and to its established names. A kind of theatre, popular theatre, which spoke its mind without ambiguity, which aimed to entertain as well as debate, which was clowning and rumbustious, which was often direct in its appeal and unsubtle in its styles was not one to which they were accustomed. Jocularity and vulgarity could be accepted in Martial or Rabelais, but in a modern actor-author? These debates over Dario Fo had been rumbling on for years in Italy, but it is curious to find them voiced so noisily and polemically in the land of Antonio Gramsci, the writer-philosopher who first made the distinction between hegemonic and popular literature and who had insisted on the need in Italy for a national-popular literature. Critics who were sympathetic in principle to Gramsci's line of thought were paradoxically often the most hostile to Fo, whose break with bourgeois theatre in 1968 was both political and theatrical. From the days of his early one-act plays, he had held that farce was 'a noble genre' which he wanted to rehabilitate, but his farces were not the intellectually respectable farces of Ionesco and Beckett.

Dario found himself at odds with friends and admirers who feared he risked becoming the lost leader. The question put on the Left was not whether he was worthy of the Nobel, but whether the Nobel was worthy of him. Establishments had always tamed their opponents by distributing baubles or giving them ribbons to stick in their coat, and how could Dario Fo, the anarcho-marxist-subversive-utopian radical justify taking from the King's hand a bagatelle sponsored by a dealer in dynamite? The example of Jean-Paul Sartre, who refused the offer of the Nobel, was used as a reproach, but Dario had in fact never entertained for a moment the possibility of turning down the award. Referring to Sartre, he said, 'those were other times. Dreadful things were taking place. There was a clear conflict between culture, our "culture" and the bourgeoisie. These were the years of the great conflicts. The Vietnam war was getting under way and America was still fearsome. Sartre's gesture was part of this all out struggle.'[4]

In spite of that reassurance, right up until the last moment the Swedish authorities were fearful that Dario would 'do a Sartre on them', or pull some trick to show that his compliance had been part of some elaborate hoax. They could have set their minds at rest. He was enchanted at the honour, and threw himself into discussions on appropriate dress and fashion needs with the enthusiasm of a young dandy. One of Italy's most prestigious dress designers, Gianfranco Ferré, designed the formal wear both he and Franca would require. Initially Franca declared she would be unable to go to Stockholm, since she had a touring schedule with *The Devil with Tits* and the show must go on, but Dario declared he would not go without her. He hired a private jet to fly her from Genoa.

All intellectual problems aside, the preparation of the official Nobel Lecture presented difficulties for a man who had not been able to write in the normal way since his stroke. The new laureate is expected to make a formal speech on literature and life, and to facilitate translation, the Academy requests that the lecture be in their hands at least three weeks before delivery. Nothing arrived by the due date, and they were even more disconcerted when a mere three days before the due day the fax machine spilled out three pages of coloured, fanciful drawings and doodles. It confirmed their worst fears that they had been duped. There followed days of anxiety until Dario emerged from the plane, bringing with him the other pages of his speech, in a similar style and almost completely unfurnished with any conventional text which could be distributed to the world's media. It transpired that the drawings, with a few words in capitals, were his prompts. He forgot to bring a tie, which etiquette requires for the ceremonial delivery of the speech and had to borrow one in Stockholm. The speech was performed rather than delivered in the bravura style Fo habitually employed on stage, but it did respect traditional requirements of such occasions. Yeats, Camus, Shaw and Beckett had used the occasion to give a statement of the basic poetics which informed their work, and those among the elegantly dressed audience in the surprisingly dingy rooms of the Swedish Academy who could see beyond the idiosyncrasy of style, would have recognised that Dario's speech had a similar aim. The speech was a mini-manifesto, a statement of belief in the aims and nature of theatre.

The imposing Latin title, *Contra Jugulatores Obloquentes*, (Against Jesters of Irreverent Speech), was taken from the law passed in 1221 by the Holy Roman Emperor and King of Sicily, Frederick II. The speech was a carefully structured venture in literary autobiography, opening with a heretical examination of passages from history, continuing with homage to acknowledged masters, known and unknown, who had contributed to Dario's formation as writer and ending with a denunciation of injustices perpetrated in his own day. The recipe was the same as in many of his plays: laughter with anger, farce with denunciation, history and topicality, and always theatre as the universal fulcrum. He paid homage to the *fabulatori* from his home village on the shores of Lake Maggiore, from whom he had learned the techniques of story-telling and the value of irony. 'We laughed, but, but . . . we stopped to appreciate the irony.' The approach was illustrated by the tale of Caldé, a village on the lake which the inhabitants were advised to leave since it was slipping into the water. Being a stubborn folk, they declined to move, and were still there when the village was finally submerged. To this day, the people of Caldé can be seen going about their business between the houses and churches, still refusing to acknowledge that the water is over their heads.

If he owed a great deal to the *fabulatori*, he was indebted also to such predecessors as Ruzzante, Shakespeare and Molière, and his praise of them was equally fulsome: 'Ruzzante remains too little known, but this man who lived seventy years before Shakespeare is the greatest playwright of the Italian Renaissance. Together with Molière, he is my master.' In the course of his speech, Dario performed an extract from Ruzzante and a poem by Mayakovsky. He somewhat spoiled the effect the following day by admitting that he had made up the poem on the spot, but suggested that Mayakovsky would have been pleased with it. No doubt he would.

Having established his line of tradition, he repeated his belief in the indispensable topicality of theatre, genuine theatre today. 'A theatre which does not talk of its own time has no right to exist,' he said, before referring to the slaughter by Islamist fundamentalists of a group of intellectuals in Sivas, in Turkey, raising the question of genetic engineering, and returning to the case of Adriano Sofri and his colleagues languishing in jail in Italy. On more than one occasion, he said the Nobel would be dedicated to Sofri, Pietrostefani and Bompressi, unjustly imprisoned in Italy.

Dario also focused on the nature of laughter. There was nothing in his self-prompts which dealt with this question, so the analysis was improvised on the spot. Although his delivery aroused guffaws, the subject of laughter had become as serious for him as it had been for Bergson. While never denying the value of laughter as relaxation, he also saw it in more transcendental terms. 'The ancients regarded the moment when man laughs as the moment he comes to awareness of his own humanity. In the South of Italy, during a baby's first forty days, everyone speaks in funny, clowning voices so as to make it laugh. A baby's first smile is viewed as the birth of intelligence, or even as the moment of the infusion of the soul. Laughter is sacred.' The sacred was assuming a central place in his later life.

The following day he filled the city's Dramaten Theatre for what was billed as a dialogue with Swedish actors and public, but which turned out to be another one-man performance. No one paid much heed to a figure who stood silently in the doorway and who put no questions, but he was Ingmar Bergman, who had previously held seminars for actors on Fo's drama and acting methods. Those who stood alongside him said he laughed uproariously during Dario's exhibition in a way not typical of him. On leaving he told a local journalist they had been in the presence of a genius. To Dario's regret, the two did not meet.

On this occasion, Dario spoke at length about the nature of the political and moral commitment required of the actor. Acting is a vocation whose mission consists not only of providing a celebration of living, but also of spreading awareness of social reality. The actor, or writer, must not allow himself to become a mere professional or a master of technique, capable of arousing any reaction by acquired skill, nor can he allow himself the indulgence of objectivity. His obligation is to temper his capacity for arousing indignation, hilarity or rage by a willed decision to direct these emotions towards a cause which is worthwhile. The luxury of moral neutrality cannot be justified in the actor, a point which has kept Fo at odds with his friend and one-time master, Jacques Lecoq. He told his audience he had recently visited Lecoq in Spain, and found what he had found each time he watched young actors trained by the Lecoq method – a total command of mime and gesticulation, an enviable expertise in technique, a perfection of agility and acrobatics, but no sense of any greater finality. 'Lecoq teaches his actors to walk, stand, use their hands, impersonate, hold their breath and deliver a joke, to talk endlessly but to say nothing.' Lecoq's method, he said, encourages performers to exist in a political and historical vacuum and take no responsibility for the effects they create. For Dario the impact created by performance is central, and to exemplify his point, he acted out a scene from Ruzzante of a soldier escaping from battle, and another from *commedia dell'arte* involving the Magnifico and Harlequin from the point of view of both parties. The Magnifico was overseeing the preparation of a table for a banquet, watching as the waiters came in and out with dishes of greater and greater opulence, casually carrying on a conversation with a famished Harlequin, whose attention was so taken by the procession of dishes that he was incapable of concentrating on his master's words. Dario was devastatingly amusing in both roles, but emphasised that the failure to choose between them is dangerous and morally indefensible. The sketch of the poor devil can be made pitilessly humorous, hunger can be portrayed as amusing greed, the offhand cynicism of the uppercrust can be the stuff of brittle comedy, but in discussing the responsibilities of actors, Fo was motivated by the same, wary moralism as Einstein on the duties of scientists.

There was no laughter at the official ceremonial itself in the grand Stockholm Concert Hall on 10 December. Dario paraded on stage with due solemnity in a line with the other Laureates, dressed in the evening attire which was de rigueur, the first time he had worn such dress since 1958, and then in one of his early one-act farces. The Royal Stockholm Philharmonic Orchestra plays a piece of suitable music as each Laureate is introduced, and while the others were introduced by stately pieces from Berlioz or Mahler, Dario was introduced by the playful music of Stravinsky's *Circus Polka for a Young Elephant*. There was nothing anarchic or Harlequinesque about him that day. He came forward to receive the medal from King Gustav of Sweden, and made the regulation triple bow to the king, the Academy and the audience. At the official dinner that evening, he was seated beside King Gustav, who, according to an account Dario gave to Stefano Benni, spoke for two hours on the joys of deer-hunting.[5]

However, in an interview Dario himself gave a more appreciative view of the king. The Fos were invited to a private dinner the night before the ceremony, and while the king confessed he had never seen any of Dario's plays, he promised to do so soon. The discussion turned to the idea of justice implemented by Gustav III but inspired by Cesare Beccaria, and on how the same monarch had received permission from the Pope to acquire 200 Roman statues which still stood in a gallery in the royal palace. 'This king is very youthful, not only in appearance but in spirit in the verve with which he expresses himself. He is someone who will never grow old, and Queen Silvia is the same. They are open to every type of artistic exression.'[6]

At least that evening Dario took on the role of the courtier, but he was to employ his new status for different purposes.

CHAPTER 18

"My Teeming Brain"

In a poignant sonnet, John Keats spoke of his fear of dying before his pen had 'gleaned' all the ideas in his 'teeming brain', and before he had set them out in 'high piled books'. These words could be applied to Dario Fo as in the years following the Nobel award he engaged in his own race against time, reducing his assistants to impatience or worse while he struggled to produce his own high piled books, to give expression to the ideas and convictions which demanded to be stated. He pushed himself, not always wisely, into new territory in which he had not previously demonstrated mastery, so a new Dario Fo, endowed with enhanced status, emerged. He did little new work for theatre, even if performance remained a need for him, but turned his mind and imagination in new directions. To some extent, this new persona was thrust upon him.

In 1933, one year before he was awarded the Nobel Prize and three years before his death, Luigi Pirandello wrote a wry, introspective, unquestionably autobiographical play, *When You Are Somebody* which addressed the perils and discontents of fame. The central character is identified only as 'Somebody' and the dialogue spoken by him is indicated in the script not by a name but by a series of asterisks. Having won the Nobel Prize, Dario too unquestionably became 'somebody', a public intellectual in today's terms, facing the problems and relishing the challenges accompanying this status. It might have been better had he also shown what Keats called 'negative capability', a quality 'when man is capable of being in uncertainties, mysteries and doubts', and not endowed with firm convictions in every field. Dario had long been accustomed to fame and universal recognition, but there was now attributed to him a new prestige, as well as the status of 'celebrity'. Despite this honour and the grudging respect it bestowed, Dario's critics remained strident.

Following the award of the Nobel Prize, Dario and Franca were accorded the respect that accompanies celebrity. They were regular recipients of honours, prizes and awards in Italy and abroad. Both he and Franca were given honorary citizenship of many Italian towns, including Pieve Emanuele, Cesenatico and Riolo Terme, while Franca alone was granted this honour in Palermo and Dario in Sartirana Lomellina, where his mother was born. He was also given the gold medal by the Centro Pio Manzú, while Franca received in Spain the Leon Felipe Prize for Human Rights. The Province of Milan awarded her a Gold Medal of Recognition for her work with prisoners and drug addicts. In subsequent years, the couple received jointly or singly honorary degrees from several prestigious universities including Athens, Westminster, Sorbonne, Harvard, Brussels and Santiago de Chile. They had theatres named after them and festivals organised in their honour; were awarded literary and theatrical prizes, were the subject of retrospectives, were invited to many countries to give lectures or make personal appearances and received many medals and plaques in gold. To their embarrassment, they were the subject of academic conferences, the most grandiloquently titled of which was held in Athens in 2000 with the title *From Aristophanes to Dario Fo*. They found the doors of Italy's RAI and other TV studios thrown open to them, and were also contacted regularly by the international media to make pronouncements on a range of topics on which they had no special knowledge. Perhaps most astonishingly of all, after decades in which parish priests had refused them the use of church premises and the Vatican had pronounced anathemas against them, Dario, particularly in his view, because of his four plays featuring St Francis of Assisi, received a commendation from the Catholic press in Italy for keeping theological debate alive and for treating religious topics more seriously than was done by many overtly Catholic authors.

There was another factor at play. The work created by strong creative spirits in their later years when they face the facts of mortality frequently has a unique, enigmatic, haunting or taunting character of its own, showing a restlessness of mind and imagination which pushes artists and thinkers beyond acknowledged limits. The late work of Michelangelo, Titian, Rembrandt and of Beethoven not to mention Ibsen and Pirandello has always aroused a response of exhilarated excitement in sensitive critics. Dario deserves to be included in that category of artist whose energy does not diminish with age, whose passion is unspent, whose creativity is unimpaired and perhaps even enhanced, whose curiosity is still keen and whose interest in the manners, mores and ethics of life lose nothing of their sharpness. In his later work he aimed to probe the wellsprings of human life – the irrational, the sacred, the religious, the sexual and even the obscene – more deeply than he had done before. He chose the path less travelled, moving into a fresh poetic and political space, avoiding pedantry but assuming a didactic role as disseminator of knowledge whose honourable goal was to deepen general consciousness and rearrange the lumber cluttering the mental universe, his own as well as that of others. His views were expressed in art, in fiction, in criticism and in treatises, but no longer in original works of theatre. He produced a series of lavishly illustrated works on art history, a field he had studied in his youth but had neglected for decades, and also ventured into biology and ecology where he was at best a dilettante, and where the spirit in which his research was carried out and conveyed can on occasions be defined as Puckish rather than rigorously scholarly. At the same time, he resumed his painting with a vigour, dedication and inventiveness he had not shown for that art since his youth. And he formed new alliances in politics.

Dario displayed that greater seriousness of mind described by Montaigne as one of the positive facets of human ageing and one that can carelessly be mistaken for the acquisition of wisdom. Quotations which appear in the introduction to a book on Boccaccio, the first from the Fool in *King Lear* and the second from Herodotus, are instructive. He invariably quotes from memory, making it hard to find the original, if there is an original. In lines quoted from *King Lear*, the king questions why he had fallen into a trap of his own making, causing the Fool to aver that he had lived his life in too much haste and had failed to savour 'the sublime imbecility of youth.' This might be a reference to the Fool's words in Act II scene I to Lear, 'thou shouldst not have been old till thou hadst been wise', but it might not. In the other citation from Herodotus, describing the flight from Halicarnassus, he wondered why human beings consider only the things which bring success, satisfaction and pleasure, while burying too quickly all that has produced despair and was linked to a deep sense of failure. Dario himself commented that 'good and bad luck take each other by the hand like two sisters. If we divide them and exalt only those things which it is convenient to consider, we reduce ourselves to empty beings like forgotten bagpipes.'[1] Dario was determined to make people face the things that are inconvenient.

It would have been easy, with advancing years and considering the debilitating effects of the stroke he had suffered, for Dario to retire to a life of gilded and respected ease, but he could not avoid controversy. He frequently referred with uncomprehending disbelief to Shakespeare's withdrawal from the London stage to his birth place of Stratford upon Avon when *The Tempest* had shown that he was still at the height of his powers. Actors die on stage, he said, adducing the example of Molière and leaving the impression that he himself hoped to meet his end that way. In spite of the testimony of all the Bard's biographers, he refused to believe that Shakespeare did in fact retire unbidden. 'There must have been other forces at work,' he said darkly.

He promised a book on Shakespeare, who intrigued him more and more but on whom his views can be best described as fascination tempered by idiosyncrasy. Not being a critic *de métier*, his criticism of playwrights is essentially egocentric. He examines them from his own point of view, taking from them what he needs and tending to remake them in his own image. He searched in Shakespeare for signs of political dissidence, for dissatisfaction with the Elizabethan or Stuart monarchy, for opposition to the power structure and the prevailing status quo and clung to the belief that Shakespeare and his company were persecuted in England precisely because they were players. He had read somewhere that one of the first acts of King James on arrival in London was to expel Shakespeare from the city, and remained sceptical when told that the company in fact performed in court and were given by the new monarch the title The King's Men. Conversely he was delighted when he learned that Queen Elizabeth had stated, 'Richard II is me,' fearful that the fate of the deposed monarch in Shakespeare's play was what her adversaries had in mind for her. Dario was encouraged by the notion that Shakespeare might have been numbered among such adversaries, and that he and his company may have been supporters of the Essex rebellion. He always viewed *Measure for Measure* as a parable on puritanical Jacobean England, and wrote that the duel between Laertes and Hamlet and the multiple deaths that follow from it are an allegory. 'What is the allegory underlying that slaughter? It is clear. All the rulers in Denmark (but in all truth, the allusion is to the Kingdom of England) deserve to be killed, cancelled from history.'[2] Hostility to authority is the position he expected actors and playwrights to demonstrate in their work. Molière and the actors of *commedia dell'arte* in Paris provided him with an ideal in this respect.

It is tempting to compare him at home in Milan to an alchemist-scholar of other times, seated at his desk, surrounded by assistants, doing sketches for paintings, turning out books and filmed material which face, with levity, wit and varying degrees of profundity, intriguing problems of life and art. Dario was not cut out to conform to the image of an obliging celebrity and he exploited his new status to make pronouncements in fields where he was at best an observer. His detestation of today's meagre cultural diet of football, tabloid misinformation and TV spectaculars was profound. He adopted a viewpoint akin to Nietzsche's on the benefits of, or even necessity for, an aesthetic vision permeating life. The Italian press were in the habit of referring to him as 'the Nobel' without further qualification. He was certainly able to address a wider audience and irritate more people after the award, which conferred on him an authority he had not previously enjoyed in Italy. An enormous quantity of books, five in one year, poured out, many dealing with topics which might have been adumbrated in previous years, but only tangentially. If he wrote little for the theatre, his books were conceived for circulation by all media – publication, performance, exhibition and perhaps TV. Books produced in this latter period had titles such as *Dario and God, Darwin, Jesus and Women, The Apocalypse Postponed, The Obscene is Sacred*, among others. He found new collaborators anxious to help in all these activities, writing, TV appearances and artwork. He also did a televised *History of Theatre*, authored or co-authored six novels and saw his work celebrated in many art exhibitions around Italy and abroad. Future critics will debate which phase of his life and creativity represented his most significant contribution to Italian theatre, art, politics, society or culture, but it is beyond doubt that, in his post-Nobel work there was no diminution of his energies or closure of his interests. He himself suggested that in his final phase he did his most important work.

The Fo home became an atelier, with secretaries, researchers and clerks peopling the offices and rooms, helping in the way apprentices assisted, one must assume, in the *bottega* of some late Renaissance artist. Dario's monograph on Leonardo's *Last Supper* was illustrated by two sketches by him showing Verrocchio's workshop where Leonardo was sent to learn his trade. The first carries the caption *Verrocchio magister* and shows two men preparing paint in a large canister, two apprentices examining a canvas while another is seated at a table staring at blocks of wood. The second shows a male model on a pedestal, a figure named as Leonardo contemplating a huge canvas, while others named as Perugino, Botticelli, Lorenzo di Credi and Pollaiuolo are perched on a scaffold with brushes in their hands near the same canvas.[3] If the structures are different, the same level of activity surrounded Dario. The intensity of work took a toll on his assistants and the turnover among them was high.

The phenomenon of broadcasting would have astonished even the most prescient of alchemists, but Dario knew how to make full use of it alongside the traditional printed word. In a 'lecture-performance' genre he devised, ideas are processed from the printed book to stage performance and on to the screen. In this format, he has, in addition to the work on the *Last Supper*, written and 'performed' – this being a more precise term than 'lectured' – histories on the Cathedral in Modena and on the city of Ravenna as well as on such Renaissance masters as Giotto, Correggio, Caravaggio, Mantegna, Raphael, and Michelangelo.

It is not possible to subject to critical examination all the works produced after the Nobel award, but their number and range is impressive. Franca's role in this explosion of productivity, apart from the political activity which saw her elected to the Senate in Rome, is important. On the cover of most of the recent volumes of this period, she is credited either as co-author or as editor. This is in one sense unremarkable but is a recognition not always previously afforded her for her contribution to the output of the couple. Her health was often frail and she was confined to bed for long periods, but she too produced books and plays and continued touring. She also spent hours in front of the computer screen typing, correcting, transcribing, even translating (as in the case of the dialect in the work on Boccaccio) and producing versions of earlier works, *Accidental Death of an Anarchist*, for example, which will be as definitive as any Fo-Rame work can be. She was also credited with editing the transformation of *Can't Pay? Won't Pay!* to *Low Pay? Won't Pay!*, updated in the light of the 2008 economic crisis. It was Franca who prepared new editions complete with video of such other work as *Ruzzante* and *Arlecchino*, which came out in 2011 and 2012 respectively as volume and video.[4]

Only those who are 'somebody' are permitted to write an auto-biography, and Dario's autobiographical work, *My First Seven Years (plus a few more)* was published in 2002.[5] The choice of timescale is based on the principle supposedly enunciated by Bruno Bettelheim that developments in a human being's first seven years are decisive and formative although, as the words in brackets indicate, the book stretches the range of years to include an account of his wartime experiences. In 2004, together with the actor Giorgio Albertazzi Dario prepared for television *Il teatro in Italia*, a history of theatre which was left uncompleted when RAI decided to broadcast the programme after midnight. This work is wider in scope than the title suggests and opens with an analysis of Greek theatre, moving on to Roman writers and actors, and then examining *commedia dell'arte* and Renaissance authors. Since the programmes were an invitation to deepen appreciation and enjoyment, critical content was not high. Discussion took in theatre sites as well as acting styles, and it is a matter for regret that the series was broken off.

Love and the Guffaw contains five tales of utopian dreamers, heretics or transgressives. The first is Héloise, who recounts from her place of banishment in Argenteuil the story of her forbidden love for Abélard, while another is Mainfreda of the Milanese noble family, the Visconti, who renounced her position in society and took the veil but was disturbed by the low esteem in which women were held by the church. 'A woman is worth exactly as much as a man, so we women in this community are not willing to submit neither to husband or priest.'[6] Exactly as he had done with political topics, Dario searched history for examples of women's suppression, and made stories from his research.

He had also been invited over the years to direct opera. He was attracted to Rossini, and worked on several occasions at the Rossini Festival in Pesaro, the composer's home town. *La Gazzetta* was produced at the Festival in 2001, *Il Viaggio a Reims* in Helsinki in 2003 and later in Genoa, and a new production of *The Barber of Seville* in 2008. 'I directed it in such a way as to bring out the humour, joy and amusement. Indeed these elements were fundamental,' he said. These productions were controversial and offended many conventional music and opera critics, since Dario re-imagined and re-created these works in his own idiosyncratic style, focusing more on acting and scenery than on music. His main aim was to present Rossini as belonging to the tradition of *commedia dell'arte*. Some critics were accommodating in their response. Watching Dario take command of every aspect of production, a dazzled journalist in *Sipario* observed: 'There is no lack of actor-directors, but they stage the works of other writers; nor of author-directors; nor of actor-authors, but I have no recollection of actor-designers, much less of actor-playwright-director-designer-costumiers ...'[7]

Religious and quasi-religious issues came to interest and perplex him. His was not the well trodden path from atheism in youth to belief in age, but the view of religion expressed in these years was respectful but certainly not devotional. Perhaps only Dario could twine together religious and erotic elements, as he did in two books published in

2010, *The Peasants' Bible* and *The Obscene is Sacred*. The first is a scrutiny of popular culture, a recurrent theme all his life, specifically of the social-political vision inherent in the popular beliefs and cults related to Christianity. It can be regarded as a development of the thinking which produced *Mistero buffo*, but was directly inspired by an invitation he received from the canons of St Paul's in Rome to prepare a lecture-performance to celebrate and publicise the Bible of the French King Charles the Bald which is in their possession. In the event, the performance was premiered in Benevento in 1996, but Fo continued working on the idea over the years, coming across bibles of different sorts with "stories in opposition to official Bibles, stories which derive from written and oral tradition in every region of Italy". The quest for popular alternatives to conventional tradition, which Gramsci termed the hegemonic line, was Dario's search for the Holy Grail. He spent much of his life searching, and then embellishing, making accessible and at times inventing, aspects of a culture, a people's culture, which he was convinced existed underground and which had been ignored, perhaps systematically, by the protectors and exponents of the dominant cultural and political tradition. Undermining the one was a means of subverting the other. Popular culture is to be located in the by-ways of religious celebrations, in the writings, hymns, feasts and cults which had been written out of history and were now denied official recognition but which had been an intrinsic element of popular devotion. As he wrote of the peasants' bible:

> (It is) moving to witness the affectionate attitude of God towards every creature, especially towards peasants. Splendid is the image of God which peasants have. Peasants never think of reducing God to the level of man, not even if that man is an emperor, or of raising themselves to the level of God. For them God is immense, vague and infinitely great, stretched out on the seas or on the mountains. He rolls on the clouds and every so often peeps out to see his creation. 'Oh what a beautiful universe I have set up! Look, what a masterpiece that animal is! And that one too! A horse! How lovely a horse is!'

354

This God, as Fo reports from a study of the peasants' beliefs, is the opposite of the Manichean divinity. He does not recognise the distinction between the spiritual and material dimensions, and this allows peasants to spurn any notion that material things or beings are in some way inferior. Dario writes on their behalf that

> God is in a jug of wine or in the lamb that they are slaughtering. The peasants have always been eating God. They love and they curse him. They are sure that God is goodness but also in part evil, that he is the father of the angels but also a near relative of the devils, that he is life but is also death.[8]

The God of the peasantry can also be female, as the lavish illustrations in the book, assert. The cover shows a naked woman, the Great Mother, with a torch and a dove in each of her raised hands and two goats sucking her breasts. The chapters, sketches in the performance version, begin with the story, unrecorded in Genesis, of the creation of the pig, and then retell many of the dramatic incidents narrated in the Old and New Testaments, such as Adam and Eve, Cain and Abel, Sodom and Gomorrah as well as such later episodes as the Slaughter of the Innocents and the scene of Mary standing under the cross on which her son is being crucified.

If the sacred was a new interest, the erotic, if not exactly the obscene, had always figured in Dario's creativity, but it is viewed from a fresh angle in *The Obscene is Sacred*.[9] He had always had the insight and artistic flair to bring implausible opposites into arresting juxtaposition, thus displaying unconsidered truths about both, but he does not quite pull it off in this work. In spite of the grand title, this is not a treatise of the sort Walter Benjamin might have attempted, and the two poles of the antithesis are never quite reconciled in a wholly convincing synthesis. Once again, sections of the book were performed as monologues, and once again, the published version was embellished by copious, original illustrations, many of which are sexually explicit, raunchy, or voluptuous, featuring naked females or couples in positions of joyous, uninhibited intimacy. No man has less of the pinched, repressed puritan in his make-up, so erotic humour is everywhere in evidence: some cartoons are inspired by classical works, others original creations of Dario's imagination: some are basic line drawings and others elaborately worked, colourful paintings. St Ambrose is also there due to his intention to establish a unisex religious community, although the women are in this case modestly clad. St Francis, who was a recurring presence in Fo's mind, was pressed into service since before his conversion he had loved women and 'dedicated to them love ballads in Provençal'. None are extant.

Dario was half way through *The Obscene is Sacred* before clarifying that the topic he wished to examine was that of 'language and behaviour in regard to the erotic'. In fact the range is much wider. The opening sections do consider in detail various words, in dialect and the national language, for the sexual organs. The obscene, he asserts, is part of routine consciousness, and only the censorious power of church and state had suppressed the rumbustiously liberated language used by the people to describe sexual activity. Dario's treatment of the theme is free of all gravitas or solemnity, but as with his Nobel Prize speech, under the surface there lurks a seriousness of purpose. Only at a very late stage does the sacred come into play, and even then somewhat summarily. Dario refers to an unnamed American researcher who had found that in the Orient the spot where some act of violence occurred could be cleansed by rituals involving groups of people, clowns and 'comic elephants' who recount humorous tales and perform 'obscene acts and fictitious violence'. In the Christian tradition, he refers to liturgical acts, the *Exultet* and *Risus Paschalis*, once performed in church at Easter, and which could reach a climax with singing and dancing, but at times, he says, these practices got out of hand and so were suppressed. An illustration on a red background featuring naked couples in positions powerfully suggests a loss of composure and clarifies the reason for the clerical veto.

His politics widened to take in overtly anti-politics or populism as well as green issues. He produced four book-length interviews with the journalist Giuseppina Manin, where he is permitted to appear as the sage and seer.[10] The first, *The World According to Fo*, is a discussion on his life in the theatre, and was followed by *The Town of the Comic*

Mysteries, a series of sketches on Italian public life in the satirical vein. The characters featured were mainly politicians from the First Republic, with Berlusconi as undisputed protagonist.

To this list of publications, which is incomplete, could be added works of a generally scientific interest, where the science is viewed from the perspective of a moralist. *The Apocalypse Postponed,* is an ecological tract while the DVD *God is Black,* originally delivered at the Museum of Natural History in Milan on Evolution Day, 2011, takes a sideways look at Darwinism, who was the subject of his last book. In *God is Black,* evolution is viewed idiosyncratically and the central topic is the appearance of human life in Africa, with the twist that since *homo sapiens* first emerged in Africa and since man is made in the likeness of God, God must be black. The lecture moves beyond biology to reprise ideas advanced elsewhere on the coming ecological catastrophe when resources run out, and concludes with the hope of a return to an original, gentler matriarchy. One of the highlights was Dario's delighted reply to a young boy who asked, 'How do you become primitive?' He was unsure, but thought it a valid aspiration.

CHAPTER 19

The Artist and Art Historian

'I am a professional painter and a dilettante playwright,' Dario enjoyed saying, and the light witticism was not a total bluff. 'I have been painting ever since I was a boy,' he said when interviewed before the opening of an exhibition of his work in Pontedera in 2010. 'I began before learning how to form numbers. I was quite good, a little phenomenon,' he added cheerfully.[1]

It was art and not theatre that he studied at the Brera, so it might seem paradoxical to suggest that his dedication to art, art criticism and art history from the late 1990s onwards represented a change of course. It was certainly a reordering of priorities, partly as a response to problems with his eyesight after his stroke. This new dedication to art took the double form of an outburst of personal creative activity and the production of works on artists and art history. He had never stopped painting, but in previous decades his artwork mainly took the form of designs for sets and costumes in theatre. It had been different in the heightened cultural frenzy of Milan in the period following the Liberation, when his intellectual focus was on artistic not theatrical activity: 'I knew De Chirico, I was in contact with Carlo Carrà, as well as with Ennio Morlotti, Emilio Tadini, Bruno Cassinari, Cesare Peverelli, Alik Cavaliere. I also met Remo Brindisi and many others later.' Once travel in Europe became possible after the war, he made a visit to Paris which was highly influential for his intellectual and cultural development. He said he got to know Léger 'quite well', was dazzled by the Impressionists and even more strongly by Chagall, in whose honour he helped organise an exhibition in 2015.

Two assertions he made in a revealing interview in 1984 are important for the work he undertook in the late twentieth and early twenty-first centuries: firstly, that he was 'passionate about the Renaissance, not only the Italian Renaissance but also the Spanish Renaissance. I studied the Flemish and French Great Masters', and secondly that he had 'always had a predilection for representational art'.[2] This predilection was evident in his own work from the beginning, while his statement of love for Renaissance artists determined the choice of artist he would celebrate in the period under discussion in various formats – as performance pieces, in TV programmes and in books.

Emilio Tadini himself a distinguished artist, called attention to Dario's visual sense, both in theatre and in painting.

> Dario Fo's theatre has been, and continues to be, distinguished by his extraordinary capacity to see: it is enhanced, we might say, by his extraordinary ability to make figures, to create figures, to arrange sense and meaning in figures – more precisely, to uncover sense and meaning in the figures.[3]

His capacity to see had been impaired by his stroke, but he retained an astonishing visual memory. Tadini identified a further 'ability to see the unexpected in already famous painters', together with a formidable critical intellect which was under-written by love and erudition. These qualities would form the basis of all his writings on art.

As with theatre, Dario's habitat is tradition, and his instincts are popularising, but whereas in theatre history he was drawn to the marginal figures – the jester, the Harlequin, the clown – in art history he focused on the recognised old masters. The purpose of his criticism is illumination, the main driving force is admiration and the central ambition a desire to share the pleasure he had experienced. When writing of the artists of the Renaissance, Dario addressed himself to an audience traditionally excluded from the appreciation and enjoyment of such art by the restrictive language employed by scholars and experts.

He brought a fresh eye and a new perspective to his critical writing on such artists as Leonardo, Mantegna or Caravaggio, and while he was no debunker, he believed that he detected in many of their works a disenchanted, satirical view of the powerful and wealthy who had given the original commission, and that this approach had been concealed by the more or less systematic mystification of generations of critics.

His writings in this period indicate a new scale of human and humanist values, a wider vision of the individual and society, founded on the recognition that political engagement and cultural values taken together are the twin requisites of civilisation, in any epoch. He had already moved from zeal for the purely political to an involvement in social causes, but now his thinking showed his awareness of the need for the deepening and dissemination of cultural and artistic values. His critical style could be described as erudite populism. He made use of political categories and judgements, but not in the style of Marxist critics of earlier generations. His objective was to lay bare the workings of the hierarchies of power in art production, but he was not out to present cultural products merely as self-serving, hegemonic dressing created to allow the powers that be to justify or embellish both the sordid substructure and the glitzy superstructure of society. For Dario the ethical, aesthetic and philosophical complex of values which go under the name 'culture' was principally a force which enhanced life and represented a higher value in itself. He deplored the fall in educational standards and the coarsening of culture, especially popular culture, in contemporary society, so when discussing Michelangelo in his lecture-show, he contrasted the view of education and culture of contemporary rulers with the current situation: 'in the sixteenth century even despots understood the importance of a cultured citizenry, and knew that an ignorant population is something negative. They also understood the value of knowledge to the individual citizen, even if that involved the risk of them wanting to participate in government.'[4] More than once, he compared the presence at the unveiling of works of art in Florence or Rome to the crowds who now flocked to football stadiums, or the willingness of princes and dukes to gather artists in their courts in Urbino, Mantua or Ferrara to the keenness of contemporary

European plutocrats to purchase footballers for the teams they owned. As a democrat and a utopian, Dario was motivated by a desire to share all that was good. He was not moving into the field of high art as it was commonly understood, but was intent on indicating the presence of the popular even among the old masters commonly identified, in the division of cultural spheres authorised by Antonio Gramsci, as belonging to the hegemonic tradition.

At the promptings of a group of art students from the school of mosaics in Ravenna who turned up in 1998 at his holiday home in Cesenatico, Dario became engrossed in the history of Ravenna. Doing some location work, he went to the Basilica of Sant'Apollinare in Classe where he saw a bearded Christ, who he was convinced was a figure from one of the apocryphal gospels. These gospels had been on the fringes of his mind for some time, but this discovery heightened his commitment to the subject in hand and to the apocryphal gospels themselves. The outcome, far surpassing the modest request made by the students, was a TV documentary and a book on history of Ravenna,[5] the first of a series of works which would take the form of book, performance and programme. The period covered goes from the foundation of Ravenna until the arrival of the Longobards in Italy in the sixth century. If it is popular history, written in a conversational, relaxed, whimsical, playful, accessible and occasionally comic style, it is founded on scholarship and knowledge and is not in any sense a spoof or attempt to demythologise the history of this city. The director was Felice Cappa, who had already done some filming with Dario, and who was to introduce him to the world of the video and television documentary. The final programme, Cappa insists, was structured with a carefully worked out storyboard, with Dario at various spots in the city associated with episodes in the colourful history of Ravenna when it was capital of the western half of the Roman Empire.

The book has the appearance of a graphic novel, with original illustrations by Dario of arresting scenes and characters in the history, such as a bright painting of the journey to Africa of the future Empress Theodora with her rich merchant husband, pen drawings of Belisarius on horseback or of the love-making of Galla Placidia and Attila, as well as re-elaborations by Dario of the Ravenna mosaics or other classical works. These artworks, neither kitsch nor pastiche, are part of the narrative, an alternative history of Ravenna and Constantinople. Dario does not take any post-modern, relativist view of historical fact. There is nothing invented in a chronicle which includes discussion of the construction of the aqueduct by Trajan, the biography of Galla Placidia, the explanation of the Arian heresy, a detailed account of imperial family jealousies and the tormented relations of Theodora and the Emperor Justinian. Granted Dario's own outlook, he provides history seen in the class terms Gramsci would have recognised. Theodora is presented both as a proto-feminist who made her own way in life, working first as a prostitute but later, as empress, closing brothels and locking the women in convents. She also closed theatres, Dario writes, bringing to an end a rich tradition. Justinian is not the codifier of laws who earns himself a place in Dante's Paradiso, but a mass murderer and psychopath. The positive hero of the piece is the Ostrogoth Totila, who recruited an army of slaves and peasants and redistributed land, believing that every man will fight more tenaciously in defence of his own fields than those of a distant ruler. An original illustration by Dario on the battle of Caprara where Totila was finally defeated by the imperial army under Narses, a eunuch of Armenian origin who rose to become a general in the army of Byzantium and who pacified Italy in the interests of the Eastern Emperors, carries the caption, with words attributed to Narses himself – 'But why do they insist? They are now defeated, but they fight not for king but for their lands.' Fo's Totila was a successor of Spartacus, a liberator of peasants and proletarians. In a sign of changed times, the volume received the commendation of the Cardinal Archbishop of the city.

The following year, the Ministry for Culture was keen to find some suitable means of celebrating the unveiling of Leonardo's *Last Supper* after extensive restoration work. Felice Cappa put forward Dario's name to RAI and the idea was taken up with alacrity by the Minister, Giovanna Melandri, who was American by birth but Italian by upbringing and active in the Left Democrats. Dario accepted the invitation enthusiastically and quickly became obsessed with the work.

He studied the various critical texts on Leonardo and spent a week in the lab of Pinin Brambilla Barcilon, the restoration project leader, who had dedicated 21 years to the project, four times as long as Leonardo had taken for the creation of the original. The restoration work drew heavy criticism in some quarters for its undue boldness and for producing changes in colours and tones, but Dario, like Melandri, was broadly supportive.

He brought his own gifts as incisive narrator to the project.[6] As with his Nobel Prize speech a few years before, beneath the lightness, there was a critical method and an aesthetic. The tone was off-hand, light, jaunty and jovial, totally devoid of any dry-as-dust gravitas or solemnity. He relied on the classical description given by Giorgio Vasari in his contemporary history of Leonardo's modus operandi, especially Vasari's account of the construction of special scaffolding which allowed Leonardo to work at the level of the faces and to make Christ's right eye the ideal centre of the painting. Dario recalled visiting the monastery refectory and listening to guides, some learned, some ill-informed, but all focusing either on individual figures or on the grouping of the apostles into three, a number taken to be significant, perhaps in homage to the Trinity or to cabbalistic writings. Dario did not dissent and was happy to pay homage to the deep religious sense underlying the painting and to discard all notion that Leonardo was a sceptic or even a cynical atheist, but his own critical focus was on the overall design. In aesthetic terms, he drew attention to the general geometric perspective, the painting's qualities, the dynamism, the sense of theatrical movement in the arrangement of the figures, the choreography of the hands, clothes and even shoes glimpsed under the table.

The introduction to the published volume is largely biographical and historical, without any attempt at the kind of analysis of the artist's psyche of the type favoured by Freud. He was intrigued by two coincidences, that Leonardo was born in the same year as Savonarola, and that he was illegitimate, like Ruzzante, Fo's favourite actor-author. The Church ensured that illegitimate children were barred from attending institutions of learning, and Dario speculated that such exclusion may have encouraged in Leonardo independence of thought and a preference for experimentation. He pondered other aspects of Leonardo's biography, for instance his friendship with Machiavelli which may have fostered the growth of the democratic spirit, for Dario's Machiavelli is not the amoral worshipper of naked power, but primarily a republican democratic.

Democratic Leonardo may have been, but Dario was also intrigued by the contradictions in his beliefs, at least as they appear to modern eyes. He was a courtier and servant of princes, who introduced himself to Ludovico Sforza, Duke of Milan, as skilled in the creation of weaponry, and only incidentally as an artist. In his notebooks, Leonardo demonstrated a deeply religious, humane spirit, moved by the wonder of creation, describing man as indeed the measure of all things, and as such a creature of beauty whom it would be a crime to destroy, yet Leonardo had no compunction in developing armaments of great sophistication. Dario comments, 'Italy may be called the cradle of the Renaissance, but it was also called the land of the dead because of the great number of corpses scattered all over the land.' Dario was never the pure historian, but preferred to move backwards and forwards from the past to the present, so his speculation about the mentality that allowed Leonardo and other artists such as Verrocchio to devote their genius to developing weaponry borrowed more recent vocabulary of 'weapons of mass destruction'.

His treatment of Leonardo, and of the other artists about whom he wrote, was embellished by sketches and paintings of his own. One illustrates the use as target practice of a statue of Francesco Sforza sculpted by Leonardo but treated with disdain by soldiers, an event recorded by Vasari. Dario expatiated on other works by Leonardo, showing his own visual acuteness but also the quirkiness of outlook which will mark all his art criticism. On *The Adoration of the Magi*, he drew attention to the dark areas behind the central scene of the Mother and Child surrounded by kneeling visitors, where battles are still underway and women and children flee in terror. 'Peace to men of good will,' he wrote, had not been established. His curiosity, or sense of mischief, was also aroused by a scarcely visible incident where an angel with a long horn is plainly blowing raucously into the ear of a fellow angel who is not grateful for the attention. This is not art criticism as it is commonly practised, and indeed his work drew the scorn of academic historians, but they were not his intended audience.

The most significant and engaging work of this period was probably a history of the cathedral in Modena, a subject which provided the ideal vehicle for the expression of Dario's views of art and history. The work took the form of a televised lecture-performance on the architecture and history of the building and its relations with the city.[7] Not all churchmen in Italy had changed their views of Dario, and the local church reacted to the announcement of the intended programme by organising novenas and public recitations of the rosary, inspired by the fear that Dario would provide a blasphemous, Marxist or atheist interpretation of the pious work of medieval artisans. Paradoxically had they had a deeper knowledge of the mixture of the sacred and secular in medieval, ecclesiastical architecture, they could have spared themselves the trouble.

Dario invited those who attended the spectacle, which was given in the open air outside the cathedral on an extemporised stage with two giant screens on either side of him, to read the architecture as they would read a book. Since the book was medieval, the language would be as unfamiliar as the *Divine Comedy,* but Dario acted as decoder and populariser, spicing his performance-lecture with jokes about contemporary politics and ironic allusions to the present day. Berlusconi could never be too far away. Discussing a carving of the Flood, he remarked: 'In the days of Noah, the Eternal Father saw that the world was not to his liking, that there were men in government who made laws in their own interest, and he decided to send the Flood. We can only hope that he doesn't have the same idea today.' Absent was all irony on Christian belief, nor did Dario use the sacred architecture as a pretext for superficial jokes on the naivety of primitive styles of representational art, as Renaissance art historians like Vasari were wont to do. At one point, having just discussed the protection God gave to Cain after his murder of his brother, he digressed into a philippic against violence, but stopped the crowd from applauding. 'I prefer your astonishment. That's the right reaction.'

Behind the professionalism of the skilled performer, there lies genuine erudition. When dealing with history, whether political, architectural or artistic, Dario is never a bluffer. He may offend experts, his style of delivery may be more appropriate to the entertainer than the meticulous lecturer, but he deals in facts which have been researched and checked. The cathedral was constructed between 1099 and 1117, a time of conflict between Church and Empire over the question of investitures, an issue recounted without the leaven of humour. St Augustine wrote that ecclesiastical art should aim to be the *libri idiotarum,* the books of the illiterate, and medieval architecture, to whatever phase it is attributed, is an encyclopaedia. The decorative range in Modena stretches well beyond what would nowadays be regarded as pious art, and it is this aspect that Dario enjoyed revealing, perhaps because it confirms what he already believed about medieval culture and what he had discussed when staging *Mistero buffo.* He delighted in highlighting the fact that where it would have been normal for the name of the lord or bishop who commissioned the work to appear on the walls, in Modena it is the architect, Lanfranco, who is celebrated by a plaque on an outside wall. In Dario's interpretation, the Duomo of Modena is a work of popular art, expressing the culture, lay as well as religious, of its time but speaking to people of all ages. He drew special attention to the façade decorated with a riot of foliage, gargoyles, mythical or fantastic beasts. He pointed out how the knights of King Arthur feature on the exterior walls alongside Adam and Eve and how *homo selvaticus* finds a place near a twin-bodied but single-headed deer which may represent the dual nature of Christ. There are even erotic carvings of women with generous breasts fully exposed, representing, in Titian's terms, *amor profano,* not *amor sacro.* The erotic in art was another subject to which Fo was dedicating greater attention.

The entrée into the world of television, and the success of the programmes themselves sharpened Dario's appetite and he was keen to continue with documentaries on artists. Plainly, the works on the great Renaissance masters themselves required a different approach, but once again there was nothing of the dilettante in his treatment of Caravaggio, Mantegna, Michelangelo, Correggio, Giotto, or Raphael, each the subject of TV documentary, a performance-lecture and a handsomely illustrated volume. There is no trace of objectivity or neutrality in his approach to these artists, and neither are these talks or books the products of Fo the satirist, except when he implies, subtly, parallels with contemporary society or when he speaks of outrages in history, but such moments are paralleled by passages of lyrical intensity and expressions of delicacy of feeling. Dario's motivation is love of the painters whose works he surveys, and he evinces a surprising level of reverence, evident, for instance, in his discussion of music, of tones of light and shade, of colours of flesh in Caravaggio's *Rest on the Flight into Egypt*, or in Correggio's *The Assumption of the Virgin* in the cathedral in Parma. These are works which he found awesome, and Dario's style in writing and voice expresses his admiration.

The first subject was Caravaggio, whom Dario had first encountered in 1948 when he was still a student, at an exhibition in the Palazzo Reale in Milan, where he would later exhibit his own work. The occasion for the programme was an 'impossible exhibition' in Naples in 2003 when the curators, having abandoned all hope of receiving the works of Caravaggio on loan from the galleries which owned them, organised an exhibition of originals alongside acknowledged forgeries, copies and electronic reproductions. While he was engaged on research on Caravaggio, Dario took time off to go with Franca to Scotland to present his autobiography at the Edinburgh Book Festival. They brought with them copious reproductions of Caravaggio, as well as photocopies of excerpts from various works of criticism or history which they spread over the floor of their hotel room, to the dismay of the staff. Dario was driven around the city to see the castle, the New Town, Holyroodhouse, the cathedral of St Giles and other sights in Scotland's capital, but his attention was elsewhere. Accounts of the history of Parliament House were listened to with courtesy, but would be followed, disconcertingly, not by requests for elaboration but by a monologue on the Knights of St John of Malta, thoughts on Caravaggio's time in Sicily or of the dynastic divisions in Rome in the late sixteenth century.

Dario shows no sympathy with conventional, dramatic portraits of the *'artiste maudit'*, preferring to see Caravaggio in the context of his troubled age, so that even the infamous killing of a rival after a game of tennis was, in his view, more probably the result of a political dispute than an act of anger. In more strictly artistic terms, he dismisses those who held that Caravaggio had painted directly on to canvas with no preparatory sketches, and to support his case quotes Carlo Carrà: 'Whoever invented this tale of extempore creation? Michelangelo da Merisi (Caravaggio), like his Florentine namesake, was a man who confronted a canvas with everything already in his head and fully imagined.'[8] Armed with Carrà's authority, Dario rebuts facile notions of Caravaggio's supposedly instinctive style, and emphasises the professional artisanship in each of the individual paintings, as well as the painstaking preparatory work needed to give form to the philosophical-theological thought. While many scholars conceal trite thought by the employment of complex, technical vocabulary, Dario employs every-day speech to ensure maximum diffusion of his analysis.

He is content to act as unassuming gallery guide as well as informative critic. He subjects *The Deposition* to a detailed, professional examination, illustrating his analysis with the aid of sketches of his own. Although his illustrations are never pastiches, additional figures or colour tones unknown to Renaissance artists are included. In this case, he superimposed geometrical lines to establish Caravaggio as 'an authentic mechanic, a scientist of painting'. He will also go blithely beyond limits which a professional critic would observe. In his discussion of *St Matthew and the Angel*, he underlines the presence of the 'compass and the set square, which he employed for his geometrical developments', but then goes on to interpret the precise message being delivered by the angel. The saint should 'liberate himself from theological science so as to make the simple doctrine of the humble and poor of spirit his own'. Criticism of this sort is ipso facto non-conformist, and is dictated by a wish to draw out the popular roots he believes are evident even in the works of the great masters. He is forthright in his expressions of contempt for professional art historians, even those of the acknowledged stature of Roberto Longhi or of the historical authority of Giorgio Vasari, both of whom he convicts of the capital crime of mystification, and thus of having betrayed the intention and vision of the artist. Dario's narrative is based on the belief that he is releasing Caravaggio and other artists from layers of misunderstanding, and presenting them in their true light.

His personal or even idiosyncratic approach was most apparent in his highlighting the satire, irony and even sarcasm he detected in the attitude and outlook of the painters themselves, particularly so in the case of Mantegna, the subject of, perhaps, the finest of his studies.[9] He has disparaging comments for previous critics of the artist, noting that 'the dominant tendency is to look at art for art's sake and not at its different levels; the art of satire, of mockery, or overturning the logic of power, this was not to be studied'.[10] It was precisely this aspect that Dario set out to bring to the fore. He recorded his surprise and pleasure in noting that 'all the great artists of every age reserve considerable space in their own works for satirical irony and poetic humour', a tendency he observed in Leonardo, Dante, Giotto. In Mantegna, he found these elements particularly in *The Triumphs of Caesar,* a series of works commissioned by Francesco II to celebrate his victory over the French at Fornovo. Mantegna devoted more than twenty years to these canvases, and Dario subverts the normal reading by switching the focus from the protagonists to the minor figures. While seemingly fulfilling the commission given by the ruling Gonzaga family, Mantegna made, in Dario's view, the procession a revelation of the horrors of war, of the emptiness of pomp and of the pettiness of power. One example will suffice. In one canvas, *The Senators,* he draws attention to a boy squeezed between 'the buttocks of an obese minister and the belly of a young assistant'. What is his function? 'A singular motion of sarcastic and at the same time poetic fun which we will learn to uncover and appreciate as we look at the nine works in the series.'

The same critical tools are applied to Michelangelo, Raphael and later Correggio. Dario judges Raphael's early works 'elegant and delicate', but writes that after he moved to Florence he was influenced by what he observed in Florentine painters and sculptors, specifically 'stories of dramas and festive occasions but also the force of ideas, the indignation against injustice, the violence of those who exercise power, the rage and despairing commitment to see the world change'.[11] The

369

study of Michelangelo contains vivid accounts of his rivalry with Leonardo, as well as beautiful accounts of the Sistine Chapel.[12] His delight in Correggio seems inspired principally by his admiration for his technical expertise, for instance, in the light and delicate depiction of the Madonna, in the cupola of Parma cathedral, as she is assumed into heaven.[13] In the case of all three artists, he demands respect for the composition of the figures in the canvas and reverence for the artists' beliefs. He shows an eye for the telling but overlooked detail in his carefully argued but subversive quest to reveal the 'true' artist previously concealed by academic misinterpretation.

A projected programme on Giotto was dogged by problems with church and state. Together with Cappa, he made five visits in 2008 to the Scrovegni Chapel in Padua where the artist completed in 1305 his celebrated cycle of frescoes of divine history and of the lives of Christ and the Virgin Mary, but the chapel was not used for the final broadcast. Problems with the authorities in Assisi were of a different nature. Visits to churches in Trastevere in Rome convinced Dario that the frescoes on the life of St Francis in the basilica in Assisi were not the work of Giotto but of the relatively unknown Pietro Cavallini and his assistants, one of whom might have been Giotto. He initially wished to broadcast his performance-lecture in front of the basilica in Assisi but a change in church law meant that jurisdiction over the Franciscan order passed from the Pope to the local bishop, who disapproved of the project and who, motivated by a fear of heresy but also by a worry about the impact on Assisi's tourist trade, denied permission to film in the basilica's precincts. Progress was stymied, until Jacopo came up with the idea of switching the venue to Perugia, and the final programme was filmed in part there and in part in front of Santa Croce in Florence. Dario viewed Giotto's frescoes as 'a mystical, political, and ideological battleground', and detected in them 'a painting, a reading against established power'.[14] Giotto was in this view a dissident and a rebel against the power used by the Church to impose an interpretation of the Bible which contradicted the social teaching of Christ.

The programme on Giotto went out at roughly the same time as a televised show, shot by the same Cappa-Fo team, in Abano Terme to celebrate the opening of a museum of the work of the Sartori family of mask-makers. Since Dario, in disagreement with Vasari, found in Giotto the elegance of Greek art, he was also able to note in both the craft of the Sartori and in the art of the medieval painter a common poetic, a return to myth and to tradition, to the Greeks and to *commedia dell'arte*. The accompanying volume was given the significant title, *Giotto or not Giotto*.[15] There were no further TV programmes on art history for a number of years, but Dario continued to publish historical or critical work.

Saint Ambrose and the Invention of Milan was published in 2009 and broadcast later.[16] A more fully written work, it was in essence a mixture of biographical and historical study and, but since it also contained passages of invented dialogue, it comes close to being a historical novel of the type Dario was to produce a few years later. Dario writes that he would have preferred to give the performance version in front of the basilica of St Ambrose or of St Laurence, but in the event it was presented and televised in the Piccolo theatre. As portrayed here, Ambrose is not an object of worship but as a secular figure who exercised power in the late Roman Empire. Dario tells of his surprise firstly when he discovers that Ambrose owes his rise to prominence to the influential friends he had made, and secondly when he finds no evidence of any conversion or change of heart once he devoted himself to the church. 'How am I to get along with this easy-going "accumulator of offices" who does not show the slightest sign of any crisis of conscience as he intrigues with certain dubious local figures? Is this a Saint?' he asks. He contents himself with the judgement that Ambrose was the man who made Milan what it had become, for better and for worse.

In addition to producing these critical and historical books, Dario devoted much more time to his own painting. There have been many exhibitions of his work in Italy and abroad, but although it has been reproduced in several richly illustrated catalogues, the fact that Dario Fo is a painter as well as writer still comes as a surprise to many.[17] His art has yet to receive the focused criticism it deserves, and the brief discussion here is no substitute.

In the autobiographical *My First Seven Years*, he claims to have started painting when still at primary school in his home town of

Valtravaglia. The first painting he remembers doing was a copy of a portrait of Cavour, a work which caught the attention of his teacher, who encouraged him. He also recalls occasions when he was invited to paint the portraits of schoolmates or townspeople, including his teacher, as well as the daughters of the mayor and the mistress of a gangland boss. 'More than one enthusiastic parent repaid me with gifts, some with cash.' The earliest canvases of any artist are normally given the heading 'juvenilia,' but already at the age of 16, for example in a self-portrait in pencil and water colour dated 1942, Dario showed a remarkable sureness of touch. There are three self-portraits dating from 1942-49, all showing a serious, unsmiling youth looking out challengingly at the viewer. The most introspective is the 1948 oil painting, in which face and shoulders are shown against a light blue background. It would be easy for the professional critic to isolate echoes of Picasso, Gauguin, Chagall or De Kooning in such early work, but whether reproducing landscapes around Lake Maggiore, painting female nudes or executing cartoons of scenes from Tolstoy, the freshness of eye, the clarity of line, the boldness of colour, the impeccable pictorial resolution and fidelity of representation are characteristics which shine through.

Early on he won prizes and his work was accepted for exhibitions, but it was 1984 before he had his first solo exhibition, *Theatre in the Eye,* in Riccione. With many additions and alterations, this exhibition toured galleries around the world, to be succeeded by *Puppets with Rage and Feeling,* first seen in Cesenatico in 1998. The following year Milan hosted a joint exhibition of designs by Fo and Fellini, and there were other exhibitions which focused on sketches and drawings done as preparation for productions. In 2010, the town of Pontedera mounted a large-scale retrospective exhibition, including puppets, tapestries, working sketches as well as canvases from his youth. Finally in January 2012, the Palazzo Reale in Milan was home to what must be the definitive exhibition, *Painted Gags and Sniggers* with over four hundred works covering the whole range of his output – paintings, sketches, costumes, *papier maché* sculptures, masks, puppets, photography as well as videos. He received a singular honour in 2015 when the Italian Ministry for Culture established in Verona a gallery dedicated exclusively to the display of his work. No Italian artist had ever before received such recognition from the state.

Early contact with innovation and experimentation elsewhere was blocked by Fascism, but his visit to Paris after the Liberation opened a new world to him. He was deeply moved by Picasso, Léger and Chagall, but had already been fully involved in the debates on realism and neo-realism in 1940s Milan. He was part of that democratic movement which found expression in the periodical *Realismo* and sought to ensure that art maintained a dialogue with the tastes of ordinary people and did not appeal only to a small circle of aesthetes. Significantly, Dario used only such elements of cubism as could be reconciled with figurative art. At this time, he produced some delightful still lives and landscapes reminiscent in execution of the work of the *Macchiaioli*, Tuscan contemporaries of the French Impressionists. He has said that he was unsure whether he should devote his energies to art or to theatre, and if his theatre has been conditioned by his painter's eye, his artwork, and not only that which began life as preparatory work for productions, is dramatic in conception and execution. The sense of motion in his canvases is one of their most remarkable features.

Dario's canvases display a wide diversity of styles and subjects, as is to be expected of any artist who has been active over a span of fifty years, but an exuberance of imagination is a constant characteristic and delight. Compilers of catalogues and curators of exhibitions divide his work into various styles and categories: his early "free works," sketches for particular plays (which were often fully painted works of art),[18] designs for the productions of Rossini operas, illustrations for his art history books, re-working of classical canvases, portraits of Franca, works inspired by his love for Greek civilisation, and political works. The early work was given a careful finish, while much of the work in his middle years is evidently more hurried. He came close to many trends and schools, and was influenced at differing times by many artists without ever throwing in his lot with any one and without losing his own individuality. Christopher Cairns draws attention to Dario's 'visual language based on an artistic culture (which is itself grounded) on the study of the great artists of European painting'.[19] The engagement of Fo with the European tradition, both in theatre and in art, is striking. He redid some classical work for his art criticism, while the influence of such painters of Léger and Picasso in their cubist periods are evident in the portrait, known as *The Typist*, of a figure seated amidst an assortment of unrelated shapes. At times Dario's strokes are understated, at times they have a strength which causes them to explode in riotous vigour.

His most active period dates from the late 1990s. After his stroke, damage to his eyesight was a real impairment but he retained his ability to paint, to create figures, to reproduce and re-imagine the works of other artists. He relaxed when he sat down in front of a canvas, and his staff remarked that this was the time when it was most possible to discuss day to day business with him. By any standards, he was extremely prolific. Rodriguez Amaya imagines the mixture of disbelief and wonder with which some future cataloguer or museum keeper will pull out from various cases:

> ... at random some of the thousands of sheets of paper and cartoons bristling with polychrome images. There will suddenly come to life blue minotaurs, cloth puppets, fierce monsters, damsels in gilded peplums, groups of lovers under dark colonnades, ironical putti staring out of windows, metaphysical citadels, elaborate codices, ships raising anchor, prancing horses, portraits of the eternal muse.[20]

He returned to the female nude all throughout his life. In Dario's treatment of this theme, the body is king, or queen, so these canvases do not portray some aesthetically distant or stylised female body, but flesh and blood women, young, alluring and sexy. The female nude is not exactly an unfamiliar figure in western art, but Fo's nudes, both the static portraits painted as a young student or those drawn for theatre works of later years, are unusually sensual and lusty.

Dario's later works may create headaches for future purchasers and curators over attribution. The Fos already owned the attic in the large condominium in Corso di Porta Romana where they lived and it became both a workshop and store room for piles of paintings. He also bought another flat in the same building, initially used as an office for the theatre company but later pressed into service as a studio. The house itself became a workplace, with a variable number of staff, few of whom had totally defined roles. Some were essentially secretaries or clerks, others were mainly actors who lent a hand in administration, and others again graduates from art schools and assistants to Dario in his artistic work. The workplace and work practices were like those in the studio of a Renaissance artist, where apprentices learned the trade and carried out work under instruction from the master, with the result that disputes have arisen over attribution to, for example, Mantegna himself, studio of Mantegna or school of Mantegna. None of Dario's artistic assistants were apprentices. All had either studied at an art school or had acquired experience as artists in their own right, but they operated in the communal style of a Renaissance *bottega*. Typically, Dario would initiate the project with his own ideas, normally sketch the overall design or structure, supervise, correct, criticise, add some strokes and debate colour schemes, something made necessary by his uncertain eyesight.

Jessica Borroni was with Dario from 2010. As is common enough with aspiring artists, to make ends meet she worked in a bar frequented by another of Dario's assistants. He encouraged her to send a CV to Franca, who attended to all household matters. She was called for interview, and recalls being initially terrified of Dario, who was then 83, although she later developed a close relationship with him. He put her to work on a huge canvas needed for a performance of *Mistero buffo* in the Greek Theatre in Taormina. Her work plainly impressed him, for she was invited to join the staff, once again as general factotum as much as artistic assistant. While others worked on Monday to Friday, she was there seven days a week, since Dario permitted himself no rest. She recalls him as being demanding in his standards, with certain quirks, particularly over the depiction of legs in paintings. 'The ideas were always his. Some came to him in dreams, so I would arrive in the morning to find a bundle of scribbles or drawings which we put together in a small scale before transferring onto canvas. He was meticulous about proportions but left decisions over colour to me,' she said. She was also responsible for cataloguing the paintings, and found that the total from around the year 2010 until his death came to 2008.

For the last major retrospective, *Painted Gags and Sniggers* in the Palazzo Reale in 2012, he was assisted by students from the Academy. He sketched outlines in pencil and told them which colours he wanted. While the erotic charge is still to the forefront, other works were more explicitly political. *Disembarkation at Lampedusa* is an overtly didactic piece on the tragedy of North Africans trying to reach Europe and dying while making the crossing, while a canvas alongside it carried the ironic words, *A Human Welcome is Synonymous with Democracy*. A painting of the bridge over the Straits of Messina, a project proposed by Berlusconi, recalls Bosch's *Tower of Babel*, while *A Quiet Evening in the Dragon's Home* has some nude girls dancing a "bunga-bunga" around Berlusconi. If there is some evidence of Christian symbolism, for example in the canvas depicting a kiss between Christ and Mary Magdalene or scenes from the life of St Francis, Dario was always inspired more strongly by the Greeks or medieval epics. *Sequence of Loves,* inspired by Ovid, gives his sensuality full expression, while the whirlpool of movement and the range of coloured figures in various poses in *The Rape of Europa* shows Dario combining his most thoughtful moods with unrestrained imaginative force.

CHAPTER 20

Renewal and Reaction in Italy

Even if he was engrossed by art and art history, a man of Dario's stamp of mind was hardly likely to turn his back on politics. The post-tremors resulting from the Milan magistrates' *Clean Hands* campaign which revealed the scale of the political-industrial corruption scandal dubbed 'Bribesville' were still being felt. The First Republic collapsed, the Christian Democrat, Socialist, Social Democratic, Republicans and Liberal parties had already dissolved and were followed in November 1999 by the Communist party when its leader Achille Occhetto announced in Bologna that the party's historical role was ended. The main component became the Democrats of the Left, but other factions split off.

There was no vacuum. New forces appeared, the first being the Lombard League led by Umberto Bossi which emerged on Dario's own doorstep. Silvio Berlusconi 'came onto the field', as he put it, with *Forza Italia* in 1994. The new party topped the polls in the general election later that year, meaning that Berlusconi became Prime Minister. Dario was implacably opposed to both forces, and found himself in the paradoxical position expressing his loathing of the League's racism by giving the Italian state the support he had withheld during the terrorist crisis. During a demonstration on 20 September 1997 in Piazza Duomo in Milan, the scene of the great trade union and Leftist demonstrations in the sixties, he was to be seen on the platform singing, admittedly with ironic comments, the Italian national anthem and waving the tricolour vigorously in the face of League hecklers. At this stage, Dario gave allegiance to no party or movement.

Franca continued to tour *Seventh Commandment: Thou Shalt Steal a little Less, No.2* as a gesture of support for the magistrates' anti-corruption campaign, which was now attracting criticism. A work of bitter indignation spiced with comic force, it was enthusiastically received and if it will not enter the catalogue of works likely to outlast the authors, the sarcastic tone chimed in with the public mood.

Dario staged his final work on the Sofri case in 1998, when the legal process seemed to be finally exhausted – in fact there were several more rounds to come – and the men committed to prison. *Marino Free! Marino Innocent!* can hardly be subjected to normal critical scrutiny.[1] Dario relied on pages of drawings as well as on slides and diagrams of the murder scene to aid him through the lecture-cum-performance, but he subjected the hapless Marino and the judges to a barrage of ridicule, anger and scorn, all based on rational argument of a force worthy of Voltaire in the Calas affair. It is not surprising that the historian Carlo Ginzburg, an expert on witchcraft, concluded that the 'logic which led to the condemnation of the three men is that of the witch trials'.[2] The mysteries in this case were as deep and troubling as ever. The conviction of the three men was based on the testimony of one informer, Leonardo Marino, who had also been in *Lotta Continua* in the 1970s, and who claimed to have been the driver of the car which carried Calabresi's assassins. The accounts given by Marino in the course of the various trials were contradictory on many details, and differed from the accounts provided by eye-witnesses. In spite of his collaboration with the prosecution, Marino had ended up in jail as co-conspirator, so Dario's play is a sardonic defence of his innocence and an advocacy of his claim for immediate release on the grounds that if Marino can been shown to be a liar, his evidence against himself as well as against the others is unreliable. Marino was represented by a little puppet which sat on Dario's knee, and which, according to the stage directions, 'will be animated, interrogated, caressed an even slapped' in mock encouragement or irritation during the performance.

378

The purpose of the monologue, Dario tells his spectators, is 'to recount the follies, the absurdities, the lies invented by Marino, by the judges and the carabinieri'. His mathematics were precise. The total number of 'lies, absurd declarations or egregious errors came to 120'. The work combines forensic skill with expressions of outrage, interspersed with episodes of pantomime clowning, although at times there was no need of creative farce, since the words of Marino and the judges were beyond satire. The work was shown on RAI2 on 17 March 1998. The broadcasts aroused public protests, but alas! literature and drama, as poets and playwrights have discovered from the days of the Spanish Civil War, have limited use as instruments of politics. Sofri remained in prison, and was released only in 2012 on completion of his sentence.

Environmental issues and the ethics of scientific research now gripped Dario's attention. In a televised debate with other Nobel laureates, he attacked the amoral cynicism of some scientists in their indifference to the ends which their research served. He branded them 'people for whom there is no difference between a plutonium bomb and a machine for cleansing the polluted deposits in the sea'. He was unhappy with the statement of an American Nobel laureate who complained about US government cuts in funding for military research, believing that this would have a detrimental knock-on effect on all scientific research. Here Dario found himself on the same side as Pope John Paul II, whose 'proclamations against war and against murderous experimentation on human beings are sacrosanct'.[3] The two never met, but tended to see eye to eye on many issues.

Over the following years, Dario invited controversy by venturing further into green politics, and expressing opinions on such disparate subjects as global warming, bio-engineering, GM crops and other problems created by modern science, medicine and technology. Current trends dismayed him, and the prospect of human cloning in particular shocked him. News of the cloning of Dolly the sheep in a laboratory in Edinburgh, the city where the tale of Dr Jekyll and Mr Hyde was conceived, horrified him. Already in his Nobel Prize speech he had voiced his distaste for the attempts of an American researcher to produce a humanoid clone without a brain to provide a source of spare parts in transplant surgery, and he now gave speeches, appeared before committees, wrote books and did lecture-performances on his fears for a future dominated by big industry and backed by scientists devoid of humanist philosophy and unchecked by ethical considerations.

In February 1998, he accepted an invitation from a specialist committee of the European Parliament in Strasbourg to give evidence, which he then published in a pamphlet entitled *To Oppose the Copyright of Genes, There is no Need to be a Genus* (sic). His specific objection was to a directive approved by the Parliament which allowed the copyrighting of human organs. 'I called it the Frankenstein pig-brother operation,' he declared shortly afterwards. What began life as a scientific paper, even if one not couched in conventional academic jargon, became a performance piece, *The Pig-Man and the Man-Pig*, performed in Lugano in May.[4] The title referred to the fact that some medical researchers had attempted to implant embryos into pigs, and the script itself included a typically grotesque twist. A sow has ovaries implanted in her womb, and begins to show pre-humanoid tendencies, including the ability to say 'Mamma and Papa'. Dario had a photo-montage made of him with pig's trotters instead of feet.

With no background in science, he was aware he was on thin ice and risked being made to appear an opponent of research, so he went out of his way to deny being a Luddite opposed to all scientific experimentation but only to the unethical misuse and application of scientific discoveries. At a conference, *Ten Nobel Prize-Winners for the Future*, he delivered a widely reported philippic against genetic manipulation in which he invoked Leonardo da Vinci who wrote in his notebooks that there were certain findings he would not publish for fear of the damage they might cause. One scientist wrote to the *Corriere della Sera* asking if Dario believed that anyone who received an international award has the automatic right to deliver opinions on all topics, and asking him not to misuse his gifts as entertainer and satirist to stir up public opinion against research in delicate areas.[5] Dario replied that he had the same right to attack genetic engineering as he had had to attack nuclear technology, and that his concerns were shared by scientists.

He became increasingly outspoken on global warming, pollution, the over-exploitation of the planet's resources and the future prospects for a planet where human life had been rendered unsustainable by the human destruction of the ecology. He was viewed in some quarters as a trespasser in areas of which he had no knowledge, in others as a prophet of doom, but making use of his familiar weapons – humour, irony, wit and a feeling for the absurd – he set out on a mission to warn humanity of the fate that many environmentalists feared lay ahead. *The Apocalypse Postponed or Welcome Catastrophe!*, a work which he performed around Italy before publication in book form in 2008, exemplifies his approach.[6] The cover illustration shows a grotesque Moloch with several mouths, each one devouring a baby. In his fable, the saving cataclysm for humanity arrives when the oil reserves are exhausted, cars, buses and trains can no longer run, a blackout affects the world's great population centres and modern mass media cease to function. However, this vision is not dystopian. Civilisation does not collapse into the war of all against all which Thomas Hobbes argued was the natural condition of pre-political humankind, but a gentler order emerges as human beings alter their way of living and, significantly, rediscover older values and ways of life. Regrettably, not all the established authorities are equal to the challenge. The Pope, for instance, fails to capitalise on the opportunity the crisis offers for returning to the beliefs of St Francis of Assisi, whose teachings were of growing interest to Dario, as was the cultural and political life of the medieval city-states of northern and central Italy. This reliance on St Francis and the city-states reinforced a new outlook in Dario best defined as anarcho-utopianism. In one sense the ideas he was expressing at this time are a logical development of the ideology to which he had always adhered, the rejection of competition and repression, the core canons of capitalism. He had always believed that the official, hegemonic culture supported the political power of the privileged, and had sought all his life for the forgotten, popular culture which could be employed for reform, but his thinking had shifted at least in emphasis. The prevailing political order, he believed, required reformation not on Marxist lines but on spontaneous, willing cooperation between human beings and on a quest for harmony with nature. The coming environmental cataclysm could be headed off by the construction of a new, fairer, greener society. The alternative is an apocalypse.

St Francis of Assisi and Silvio Berlusconi make strange and unexpected bedfellows, but from the turn of the century these two figures and the values they represent stand out, like the church spire and the municipal tower in an Italian medieval hill town, as the most prominent, symbolic presences in the mind, imagination and conscience of Dario Fo. They make a perfect Manichean pairing, good and evil, the devil and the angel, the aspirational ideal and the pernicious reality.

Dario's main works on these two contrasting figures are *Francis The Holy Jester* on the one hand and *The Twin-Headed Anomaly* on the other.[7] His detestation of Berlusconi is hardly a surprise, but the emerging cult of St Francis requires more consideration. Dario always declared himself an atheist, and was always an adversary of the church as institution, while Francis was a Catholic saint who never wavered in his allegiance to the church, although the power, pomp and wealth of the church aroused Francis's ire as much as Dario's. The secular image of Francis has been reshaped for every generation: as a representative of social virtues, as a man imbued with democratic attributes, as a defender of the dispossessed, as an early ecologist, as a lover of animals and nature, as an adversary of hierarchy, as an opponent of power, including ecclesiastical power, and above all a preacher of love and gentleness, perhaps even a pacifist. Arnold Toynbee, in the closing section of his monumental *A Study of History*, defined him as the greatest man in the West, and admired his ideal of the harmonisation of spiritual and temporal values. Dario created his own Francis as enthusiastically as had Victorian religious sceptics like Renan or Matthew Arnold, even if his Francis had little in common with theirs. He saw him as a revolutionary, a dissident, an independent, a free spirit, an egalitarian, an opponent of privilege, an environmentalist, a lover of nature and of animals, an apostle of peace but also, more unexpectedly, as a holy man. Dario used St Francis to denounce the distortions of the gospel which he saw inscribed in current Christian practice and teaching.

It is hard to avoid the conclusion that at this period, Dario's absorption in religious themes was rooted in instincts deeper than the historical or sociological. He was disturbed by the crassness of popular culture and by the cult of purely materialistic values in contemporary society. A new interest in the spiritual and transcendental is evident, and drew him, secularist though he was, to a quasi-religious dimension of life. The Bolognese Catholic daily, *L'Avvenire,* in an unexpectedly favourable review of the monologue on Francis, wrote that 'the wrath of Fo against the Church has more than anything else revealed that his relationship with the Church cannot be eliminated'.[8] The use of the word 'Church' in the second part of the sentence is mistaken, since his enduring relationship was with religious belief, not with the Church as such. St Francis expressed all that Dario most admired in the Christian tradition. If Francis was viewed in his own time as an *alter Christus,* Dario too admired the teaching of Christ as it was set out in the gospels, not as it was embodied by the contemporary church. Francis was attacked as heterodox because he wished a return to the basic evangelic teaching on poverty. Dario was of a similar mind, although he looked not only to the canonical gospels of Matthew, Mark, Luke and John, but also to the more radical, apocryphal gospels which he researched. The first manifestation of this interest in the apocrypha was the early one-act play, *Jesus' First Miracle* (1977), a simple narrative of the infant Christ creating a bird out of clay. The tone was respectful and could not have disturbed a believer, except that the episode was not recounted in the canonical four gospels.

Francis was also the first Italian poet and described himself as a jester, God's jester, which gave Dario the title of his one-man play in celebration of him. Controversy surrounds Dario's view of the jester or *giullare,*[9] a title he applied to himself. Dario was keen to emphasise Francis's theatrical qualities:

> . . . in the days of Francis, to define oneself a *giullare,* even if in the service of God was a deeply provocative act, close to 'blasphemy' . . .
> He knew the techniques, the trade and the absolute rules of the jester's profession. We know from a great number of historians

that the holy 'jester' did not ever deliver sermons in accordance
with ecclesiastical conventions . . .

He was impressed by one detail recounted by Francis's earliest
biographer, Tommaso da Celano, who wrote that his public addresses,
even to the Pope, were delivered as a performance employing mime,
movement and gestures of his whole body as well as words. Dario's
style of acting had always been physical, and at the first performance
on the saint in a cloister in Spoleto as part of the *Festival of the Two
Worlds*, he declaimed, danced, jumped, pranced and gesticulated
against a backdrop decorated with scenes, painted by himself, from the
life of the saint. After his stroke, Dario was unsure of his memory, so
Franca hovered in the wings as prompter, not merely suggesting lines
but intervening in a more homely way to advise him to cover up against
the cold as night fell. The fourth wall had long since been beaten down.

One other aspect of Francis's life which appealed to Dario the
story-teller was the abundance of colourful, compelling narratives
and anecdotes associated with the saint. There were to be four major
versions of *Francis the Holy Jester*, and the number of scenes in Dario's
play grew as the work developed. The language used in performance,
but not in the introductions, is an invented mixture of dialects and
onomatopoeic sounds. Early scenes recount the youth of Francis,
including his demolition of towers built for warfare, his apprenticeship
as stone-mason in the reconstructing of the same towers for peaceful
purposes, his imprisonment after a war, his spiritual crisis, conversion
to the religious life and his difficulties with papal authorities over the
recognition of his new order. The performance closed with a rendition
of Francis's poem *The Canticle of the Creatures* in pseudo-Gregorian
chant.

One scene in particular caused controversy with a Franciscan
historian, Tommaso Toschi, doubting its historical authenticity. It was
Dario's belief, backed up by reference to historical sources but denied
by the friar,[10] that in Bologna Francis delivered a harangue calling for
an end to a war between the city and Imola. No record of the actual
words remains, so Fo invented his own version in which the saint

384

ironically, wittily and satirically pretends to exalt war and the death and destruction which are part of armed conflict. In an evident reference to recent history, Dario's Francis tells his hearers:

> ... there was the war against the Albigensians and the heretical Cathars. Many of you went on this most holy war in obedience to our Holy Pope Innocent who put himself at the head of this just and fearsome crusade ... after this butchery ... many men among you, courageous and religious people, set off for the Holy Land, to war against the infidel.

History is never purely history with Dario Fo and listeners in late 1999 needed no reminding of the wars in Iraq and Afghanistan. The tale of Francis and the wolf of Gubbio is well known and appears in an early work, *The Little Flowers of St Francis*. Dario subtly alters the direction of the tale to make it a questioning of human aggression and double-dealing rather than a story of the miraculous taming of a ferocious animal. With the remarkable vocal range he displays in all his monologues, he alternated between the part of the saint and that of the wolf, speaking the wolf's lines in a gravelly voice. The tale is narrated in the style of a children's story, with a talking wolf justifying its ferocity by referring to the nature with which it was born. Francis remonstrates jovially with the beast: 'Hey, that's a good one, that story about nature! With an excuse like that everybody's got a free pass. He can steal, kill, cheat and it's all down to nature.' When a settlement has been reached between Francis, the wolf and the people of Gubbio, Francis sets off. Dario inserts a new episode in which villainous monks set their dogs on Francis, but he is rescued by the wolf which had come looking for him to beg to be released from the agreement. The people of Gubbio have been treating him badly, he complains, and feeding him inedible food. The danger, in other words, arises from the incivility of human beings, not the violent instincts of animals. Francis concludes: 'I threw myself whole-heartedly into teaching animals to be good people and now I've got to educate men to become good animals!' Dario's Francis is a revolutionary who debates the much repeated question over whether it is necessary to change individuals to produce a new society, or change society to improve individuals. Francis, and Dario, are convinced it is necessary to change both culture and individual behaviour.

With few exceptions, the Catholic world greeted the work enthusiastically as evidence of the emergence of a 'new' Fo. The Jesuit monthly, *Civiltà cattolica* suggested that he had been touched by "divine grace", and a columnist wondered if as Dario was playing St Francis, the saint in heaven had not taken the opportunity to 'to take possession of his soul'.[11] *L'Avvenire* also ended decades of polemics with Fo by writing that he was 'one of the few Italian (and non-Italian) writers to speak of Jesus Christ with a sincerity . . . which it is hard to find in a Catholic or so-called Catholic, writer'. This was wishful thinking, since Dario had not undergone a conversion, even if the vision underlying this work was evidence of a shift in emphasis and outlook.

Dario and Franca took part in the Year of Commemoration for the victims of the terrorist campaign. In December 1999, on the thirtieth anniversary of the bombing in Piazza Fontana, they organised the Caravan of Truth and Memory, which saw them hire a train which set out from Brescia, where there was a ceremony of remembrance for the eight people killed by a neo-Fascist group in 1974, to Milan for a march proceeded by a band which escorted them to Piazza Fontana. The following day, the train proceeded to Bologna, Florence and Rome, cities which had seen terrorist outrages. At each stop, they unfurled drapes designed by Dario with the help of students in Art Schools around Italy. In Rome a delegation, including Dario and Franca, was received in the Quirinal Palace by President Carlo Azeglio Ciampi, who promised that they would be reimbursed for the cost of the hire of the train, although this did not actually happen. Not all who had been activists in the days of militant campaigns wished to remember, and Franca wrote of her dismay on seeing former comrades appear on television as lawyers or PR representatives for multinational corporations.

If the response to the monologue on St Francis had been favourable, there was no comparable generosity of response following the production of works focusing on the business and political career of Silvio Berlusconi. It was 2001 before Dario produced a work, uncompromisingly entitled *The Big Liar,* with Berlusconi at the centre.

He then pressed the surreal work of Alfred Jarry into service for a polemical denunciation of Berlusconi entitled *Ubu Roi-Ubu Bas* (2002). In a pamphlet accompanying a reissue of the work, he backed up his scorn for his target by referring to St Francis and to the figure of the *giullare*-jester. When replying to French journalists on restrictions on liberty of expression in Italy, Berlusconi had said 'his persecutors were nothing but a gang of *provocateurs*', and defined them as 'clowns and buffoons'. Such a remark was an obvious provocation to Dario:

> Who are the clowns and the buffoons? Let us be clear that clowns, buffoons and jesters are all part of the same group. St Francis, talking about himself and his free-wheeling tirades, used to say, 'I'm a jester in the service of God!' I don't believe that Francis, defining himself in that way, intended to insult himself![12]

Once again, in moral and political terms, Francis is a reproach to the supposedly Catholic Berlusconi, while in terms of literary technique the idealisation of Francis was the reverse side of the satirical caricature of Berlusconi. Dario defined *Ubu Roi-Ubu Bas* as an oration in the style of Ruzzante, supposedly retelling the plot of Jarry's surreal masterpiece, but updated and sub-titled *From Bribesville to the Irresistible Rise of Ubu Bas*. 'It's just a story,' he repeated as a refrain in the course of a comic, ironic monologue detailing the problems of the fictional Ubu with the law, and his skill in cutting a path through obstacles put in his way, however feebly, by legislators. Ubu's career was hampered, or facilitated, by unresolved questions over the separation of powers, as had that of Berlusconi, who commanded a great media empire which gave him control of TV channels as well as of magazines and newspapers, while at the same time leading a political party and becoming the country's Prime Minister. The following year Dario produced a sequel, *Ubu Bas Goes to War*, a work which referenced the Afghan and Iraqi wars.[13]

Meantime Dario and Franca were at work on *The Twin-Headed Anomaly*, with open rehearsals in Bagnacavallo, the pretty town in Emilia where Byron entrusted his daughter to an order of nuns and where she died. The couple planned a nation-wide tour starting from the Piccolo in Milan, but even before the official opening, they encountered obstacles created by the new political climate. In October 2003, Sergio Escobar, temporary director of the Piccolo, wrote in the *Corriere della Sera* that he was having difficulties with the theatre's board of management over staging the work. No one in the theatre had actually read the script, which was still a work in progress, but it was being whispered that it might, just possibly, you know, be unwise, ill-advised, tactless, undiplomatic to accept such a politically sensitive work at this time. Perhaps Dario could be persuaded to submit the work to the theatre management for prior approval by more discreet spirits? The article caused a storm in the press, with most columnists focusing on questions of the limits and acceptability of satire. The real issue was a return of censorship which had been officially abolished years previously.

The tour went ahead but when it was underway, Senator Marcello Dell'Utri, Berlusconi's right hand man both in business and politics, raised a legal action against Dario and Franca, claiming he had been defamed and demanding in damages the enormous sum of one million euros. The couple regarded the action as an attempt to intimidate them and to bring pressure on theatres where they had made bookings. While the court hearing was still pending, there occurred an event which was more grotesque and absurd than anything even Dario could have invented. The play had been accepted for transmission on a network of local and satellite channels on 27 March, but Dell'Utri issued a threat to the companies involved, the chief of which was Planet, an associate of Sky. Planet initially bowed to the pressure and agreed to withdraw from the deal but then reached the incredible compromise that the play would be televised but without sound, meaning that a style of performances not seen since the invention of the talkies went on air on Italian TV in the 21st century. The actors could be seen on screen moving and talking, but the audience could not hear a word. What made the ban more unbelievable was the fact that the play had been on tour in Italy for almost a year, and its contents reported and discussed by reviewers and columnists. If any proof was needed of the power of the mass media, Senator Dell'Utri provided it. He was indifferent to theatre, but apprehensive of the power of the television.

A few days later, after public protests and a series of incredulous or mocking articles, the company changed its mind and the play went out in the standard way. After delays, the case came to court where Dell'Utri's action was dismissed.

As had happened with earlier plays by Dario, notably *Accidental Death of an Anarchist,* the play was rewritten during the run to take in new developments or revelations. One such was the Parmalat affair, a scandal that engulfed the Parma-based milk-processing firm owned by the Tanzi family, who were also sponsors of Formula One racing cars and owners of the city's football team. They had previously been regarded as examples of financial probity and business acumen, but in 2003 a hole in its accounts of some €14 billion was uncovered. Enquiries revealed links with shadowy offshore companies and brought to light a series of interlinked frauds involving European and American banks, developments which provided Dario with the opportunity to embellish his script with jibes on financial-political intrigue. The core of *The Twin-Headed Anomaly* remained the satirical assault on the emergence of Berlusconi in politics, and of the consequences of *berlusconismo,* the Italian version of late capitalism, on society. While not Dario's most accomplished or imaginative work of satire, it gave a dystopian view of a society in decline, corrupted by a culture and an ethic which was the reverse of that preached by St Francis. The play was always a work in progress, but it was also paradoxically a kind of Selected Works by Fo, incorporating many comic devices which he had used over the years – *grammelot,* the use of the dwarf figure as in *The Kidnapping of Fanfani,* the transfer of brains and bodies as in *Trumpets and Raspberries,* the use of electrotherapy treatment, the double ending as in *Accidental Death* and others.

The lead character was a director, played by Dario, who plans to make a satirical film on Berlusconi and signs up an actress, played by Franca. Berlusconi himself is busy entertaining Vladimir Putin in Sicily, where they are attacked by a criminal gang, leaving the two men alive but badly injured and requiring complex surgery. All does not go well, and in the course of the operation part of Putin's brain and memory is implanted into Berlusconi, but since Berlusconi's own memory has completely failed, his wife Veronica has to help him recall past activities – including the means employed to build up his business empire Fininvest, the dubious source of the funding for Milano 2, (the housing estate on the outskirts of Milan whose financing had always been controversial), his relations with Socialist leader Bettino Craxi who helped him resolve an impasse when the High Court had ruled illegal his ownership of national TV networks, and his membership of P2, the mysterious, high-powered Masonic Lodge whose covert political programme was curiously similar to Berlusconi's policies in government. However, since the reconstructed Berlusconi has the brains of Putin, the joint character threatens to implement pseudo-Marxist policies, including the repeal of the laws he had passed in his own favour, a proposal which terrifies his sycophantic allies who have recourse to further electro-therapy treatment to bring him back to what he was.

In part due to the controversy surrounding it, the play was a great success and the run in the Piccolo in January 2004 was a sell-out. The critical reception was more mixed. The complex structure, in which Dario and Franca play themselves, then Berlusconi and his wife and finally the director and actor, did not always work in dramatic terms. The play was a bitter, outraged denunciation of one man, one situation, one abuse of power in one age in one country, Italy.

Dario used similar situations and ironic devices to lambast Berlusconi in the series of episodes which make up *The Land of the Comic Mysteries*, another of the works co-authored with Giuseppina Manin.[14] The key to the situation is that Berlusconi, after visiting the tomb in the grounds of Arcore, the villa he had designed for himself, goes missing. On his reappearance, he declares to an incredulous public that he had been kidnapped by devils and taken on a Dantean journey to hell where he met up with other figures from recent Italian political history. Berlusconi is disbelieved and is locked up in jail, where he passes the time explaining to other inmates the stories he had heard in the underworld about the scandals which rocked political life in Italy from World War II onwards. He does not complain of his main misfortune in life, that of being a contemporary of Dario Fo.

CHAPTER 21

Acting Politicians

Increasing frustration with contemporary politics and politicians led Dario to abandon mockery from the sidelines and enter the fray personally. The first issues were green and in autumn 2000, he and Franca were to be found advocating the use of rape-seed oil instead of petrol as fuel on public transport. He gave grudging support to a campaign in Milan to have twelve car-free Sundays a year, even if he believed the measure to be inadequate. 'The truth is that they (such measures) touch interests which are too great, starting with Seven Sisters of the oil industry. There needs to be greater information.'[1] Later that month, both were among the promoters of an anti-pollution, 'Clean Air' referendum which they hoped would be held the following spring. Around this time, Dario let it be known that he was contemplating putting his name forward as candidate of the Centre-Left alliance for mayor of Milan. Predictably, the initiative caused controversy and dissension at a time when the unity of the Left was precarious, and by January he had decided to withdraw, saying enigmatically, 'I am not a bumpy wheel, nor a Don Quixote sent into the fray by someone who then poisons his steed.' Franca, however, was given the position as leading figure in the list of candidates for the group *Miracolo a Milano* but was not elected. Gabriele Albertini, representing the Pole of Freedoms coalition headed by Berlusconi was elected mayor. Dario's ambitions were put on hold.

In December 2005, Dario and Franca travelled to London to attend a rally against the Iraq War which was to feature a one-act monologue of his, *Peace Mum*. The event was somewhat chaotic, and Dario's name was inserted among the speakers only at the last minute. He was given an unannounced and unpublicised slot during the lunch break, and his speech was interrupted by one of the organisers, a strange little English woman who stood in front of the podium, smiling inanely and making chopping motions with one hand to indicate that Dario should cut his contribution to a maximum of a few minutes. However, if he drew few listeners at that moment, his work held the audience in the evening when *Peace Mum* was performed by the celebrated English actress, Frances De La Tour. This brief work was based on a letter written by the American anti-war activist, Cindy Sheehan, to President George W. Bush. Sheehan's son had been killed in Iraq, and she had gone to camp outside Bush's home in Texas demanding the opportunity to speak to him in person. She travelled to London to attend the demonstration, and met Dario there. In Turin later that month, Franca performed the piece at a demonstration of activists in the *No TAV* movement set up to voice opposition to the construction of a high-speed railway line along the Susa valley towards Turin and Lyons. One of the participants at the rally was Beppe Grillo, a comedian who was emerging as a leading figure in all anti-government protest movements, and whose stance increasingly attracted Dario's support.

While in London, Dario met the mayor, Ken Livingstone, and was immediately impressed by the fact that he had travelled to the hotel by subway, not in an official car, which he had sold. 'A mayor must use public schools, public transport and public hospitals,' Livingstone told him. Dario was particularly interested in the congestion charge Livingstone had introduced as a means of reducing traffic pollution in the city. He was also moved by the fact that Livingstone and other campaigners had used the English title of Dario's play *Can't Pay? Won't Pay!* as a slogan against the hated poll tax introduced years before by Mrs Thatcher. Livingstone told him he had seen all of Dario's plays in translation, so amicable relations were quickly established. Dario had already decided to stand for Mayor of Milan in 2006, and Livingstone accepted an invitation to go to Milan to offer support.

The main points of the abortive 2001 platform – traffic, corruption, pollution, bureaucracy, urban planning and city cleansing – re-appeared in the manifesto for the primaries which would select a candidate to represent the Left's broad, disputatious coalition, the Union. The manifesto, in Dario's distinctive style, was a glossy pamphlet with a self-portrait on the cover and illustrations inside of the incumbent's proposed building plans, of an orator denouncing Berlusconi while balloons listing his alleged crimes swirled around, of St Francis in front of a crumbling church in Milan and of the homeless huddled around a brazier. From the outset, Dario forthrightly rejected the conventional belief that only an appeal to the centre ground would win over the electorate. *Waken up, Milan, It's Late*, it announced on the front, while the first page carried a poem declaring, *I am no moderate!*

If you're looking for a moderate, beware of voting for me
Because you're taking a risk with me!
Do you really want a moderate mayor?
The moderate is strong with the weak and weak with the strong.
The moderate pretends to resolve problems without facing them.
The moderate turns a blind eye to building speculation.
The moderate chases tenants from homes in the centre
And then resells those houses to speculative magnates.
The moderate transforms the suburb into a ghetto.
The moderate accepts one school for the rich and one for the poor.
The moderate saddens the city, cheers at skyscrapers
Where there is no sign of children playing and people cycling.

For all this rhetoric, the manifesto and campaign were not some sort of Dadaist joke. Dario did give free range to his utopian visions but his manifesto was detailed, specific, well researched and not limited to grandiloquent statements of intent. He gathered together groups of experts and consulted widely. The campaign was addressed, as he put it, to people who wanted to hear the story suppressed by the media in the age of Berlusconi, and was conducted in a mixture of conventional and eccentric methods. He told a correspondent from *The Times* that

Milan needed a revolution, and when asked if writers should enter politics, he pointed to Machiavelli and Leonardo as precedents, and to dramatists in ancient Athens.[2] He hired a bus which on one occasion went to *Piazza della Scala* where groups of refugees from Eritrea were protesting in the cold of winter against the failure of the Council to give them shelter. There was a debate underway in the Council Chambers on this question, and some councillors alleged that shelter had been offered but refused by the asylum seekers, who preferred to pose for the TV camera. 'Liar, shame' Dario shouted from the public gallery.

The attacks on the incumbent mayor were relentless, as were the sharply pointed satirical barbs aimed at Berlusconi to whom he expressed gratitude for 'the most beneficial of lessons. From him I learned what tax havens in holiday islands are, and where real capital, earned in strange and dark ways, can be transferred into fantasy banks ...' The central policy points were control of gas emissions, reduction of pollution, the shift in energy use and improvement in housing. Other policies, such as one based on the experiences of London and Helsinki, advocated the construction of car parks on the outskirts to encourage people to travel inside the city by public transport, which would be free. He wanted to bring public facilities back into public ownership, attacked planning catastrophes in three key areas of the city, and promised new housing policies to be arrived at after discussion with the inhabitants themselves.

Ken Livingstone came for the main rally, held in the Mazdapalace on 21 January, an event which left him stunned. It attracted some 7,000 spectators and was a unique mixture of political meeting, rock concert, clown show, party, dance exhibition and musical. Interspersed with political speeches by Ken Livingstone and Fausto Bertinotti, leader of Communist Refoundation, were songs by Enzo Jannacci, performances by bands and rock groups, and a lecture-performance by Dario entitled *If only You Knew How Strange it is to Love One Other in Milan*. It was all to no avail. The primaries took place a week later and Dario's rival, the ex-prefect Bruno Ferrante, won with 67.6% of the vote against Dario's 23.3%. Dario gave Ferrante his full support in the campaign itself, but in the event he lost to Berlusconi's candidate, Letizia Moratti.

Dario's candidature was followed by Franca's venture into public life. She was recovering from an extended period of ill health but when a general election was called for April, she was invited to stand for the Senate as an independent in the lists of *Italy of Values (IdV)*, a Centre-Left party founded in 1998 by Antonio Di Pietro, the ex-magistrate who had spearheaded the anti-corruption campaign. As the high-sounding name suggests, its main aim was the ethical reform of public life in Italy. The invitation to Franca was promoted by Leoluca Orlando, now a colleague of Di Pietro and ex-mayor of Palermo, who had long admired her work and had granted her honorary citizenship of the city in recognition of her activities for the disadvantaged. Franca, who was now 77, initially hesitated, and Dario too was doubtful, worried that the strain and the constant travelling would be too much for her, especially in view of her uncertain health. She took soundings among her friends, while her son Jacopo did an online consultation, and the consensus was that she should accept the nomination. As is possible under electoral law in Italy, she headed the party's list of candidates in six regions, Veneto, Piedmont, Lombardy, Tuscany, Emilia-Romagna and Umbria. Her decision caused some annoyance in the ranks of Communist Refoundation, which had been Dario's main supporter in his mayoral campaign, but Franca replied simply that the *IdV* was a party of the Left adding, 'I am standing for Di Pietro's party because he has blown the system up in the air and made Italians smile.'[3] The desire to blow up the system would be used to explain support for Beppe Grillo and his movement.

Jacopo prepared colourful, striking leaflets which established the main points of Franca's campaign. Some carried personal commitments – 'I will use my salary as senator to raise awareness of state waste. An end to throwing public money out the window!' Another was a powerful call for a reform of the law on rape – 'No excuse for rape.' Franca's appeal to women voters was conveyed by a cartoon with a balloon coming out her mouth with the words, 'Women of Italy show courage! Seek your own representation. A woman for women.' Underneath there was an attractive rhyme, *Se di questa Italia sei stanca / il 9 aprile vota per Franca* (If you're tired of this Italy / On 9 April vote for Franca.) The main antagonist was Silvio Berlusconi, depicted in posters in convict uniform, or dressed as Putin, or announcing – 'In the last 10 years, I've made €10b. How did you get on?'

In speeches, Franca denounced Berlusconi, both for the personal laws he had introduced to defend his own interests and for the neo-liberal, anti-Welfare policies his government had implemented. The alienation of Italians from the state and its representatives, together with the cynicism which resulted from it, seemed to her to flow from institutional injustice and to represent a danger to democracy. As Dario had done, she proposed a strong programme of radical reforms. Perhaps the distinctive feature of her campaign was her vociferous outrage at the waste of public resources, evidenced in the inefficient administrative structures of the state, the useless expenditure of national income on grandiose but worthless schemes, the sheer incompetence, or worse, of bureaucratic practice, the tolerance of tax evasion and the ineffectiveness of a court system which allowed wealthy criminals to escape justice. She proposed a more energetic drive against financial waste, fraud and the privileges enjoyed by those who were elected supposedly as servants of the people – all factors she and Dario had exposed and denounced in their theatre. She promised to use her salary as a senator to finance campaigns for reform. Support for the anti-war movement too was a central theme in her candidacy. She declared herself in favour of bringing back the soldiers from Iraq, although this stance would create some tactical problems for her later. Her platform included a drive to revive the anti-corruption 'Clean Hands' campaign which was losing strength, encouragement for the movement to increase the numbers of women in elected positions and greater funding for the protection of the environment. After the initial excitement had subsided, she found it hard to get her voice heard, so she took paid advertisements in newspapers.

Plainly her appeal resonated with voters, because on 9 April she was elected with over 500,000 votes in the Piedmont constituency. 'I found myself elected without having lifted a finger,' she wrote in her autobiography,[4] although she later put it even more strongly when she said she had done all she could so as *not* to be elected. The Centre-

Left recorded a victory and Romano Prodi, for whom Franca felt a high degree of personal affinity, became Prime Minister.

The victory was exhilarating for her supporters; but for Franca herself the result itself was to prove the high point in what was to be a bitter personal experience. She remained a senator only until January 2008, but almost from her arrival in Palazzo Madama she was telling journalists that she was tired, disillusioned, exasperated and unhappy. 'I felt like an eighteen-year old bride married off to a man she does not love,' was the colourful expression quoted in several newspapers. Her early days made her feel as though she had been 'catapulted into Uganda, without knowing the language, without knowing where to go or who to talk to'.[5] She was plainly disoriented in the Roman Senate, and her later memoirs read like a report written by an anthropologist studying the ways of an exotic and not particularly sympathetic tribe in some foreign land of which he knows little. Not even in retrospect could she reconcile herself to the time in the Senate, which she described as 'the refrigerator of feelings. Never a smile in that building, and solitude you cannot imagine. Nineteen months of imprisonment, the worst in my life.'[6]

Franca published two accounts of her life as a Senator, one in the final pages of the episodic autobiographical work which is credited as being co-authored with Dario, *An Improvised Life*, the other in the more reflective *Flight from the Senate*, which she was credited as having written by herself.[7] The image on the cover, designed by Dario, shows a disconcerted Franca seated uncomfortably on an old-style bicycle with flowers in baskets before and behind her. Her hands are in the air, and the bicycle is free-wheeling. Dario used this book as the basis for a theatrical monologue which he performed all over Italy in her honour after her death. In whatever form, it was the work of a deeply disappointed and disenchanted woman. Although she could face audiences of thousands with tranquility, she was intimidated by the solemn impersonality of the Senate, the hollowness of the rituals, and by details like the routine salutes of the guards whose greetings etiquette did not allow her to return. She reported being unable to sleep the night before her initiation into the Senate and wandering about

Rome in the early hours until she found herself in front of the Senate building, Palazzo Madama:

> Leaning on a wall facing it, I observe the palace with a feeling of emptiness in my stomach. Maybe I am hungry. I have not found a bar open. My God, I really have to go in there. What's waiting for me? I am really agitated.[8]

In the following days, she found herself bursting into tears outside the *Teatro Argentina*, wondering if she was in the company of a tribe of Indians in the Rockies or had fallen down the rabbit hole like Alice in Wonderland. She was deeply offended by the refusal of parliamentarians, especially women whom she had previously known and to whom she had shown kindliness and friendliness, to acknowledge her presence. The fact that she would have to meet face to face politicians like Marcello Dell'Utri, who had sued her and Dario, or Giulio Andreotti, whom they had satirised and derided decade after decade, dismayed her. Curiously, these two men both behaved with courtesy. Dell'Utri made himself known to her, asking her if she recognised him, and whispered that she need have no worry about the one million euros he was seeking as damages for the injury to his reputation. She replied that they were not at all worried, as she was sure the case would fail. 'I have many lawyers,' was his delphic reply. Andreotti displayed the personal touch towards her, albeit in his characteristically patrician and condescending manner. He was chair of a meeting Franca had to attend, and when he saw her he greeted her with the words, '*Piccina*, your smile illuminates the senate.' Piccina means approximately 'little girl,' but was seemingly spoken with warmth not disdain, thereby throwing Franca off guard for the moment. She rallied and tried to engage him in conversation about the kidnap of Aldo Moro and why the Christian Democrat government had refused to enter negotiations with the Red Brigades for the release of their president. Andreotti replied it would have undermined the state to have given equal dignity to the *Brigate Rosse*, and when Franca objected that they could have saved the life of a human being, his reply was to stretch out his arms.

She was not exactly an ingenue and had witnessed bitter ideological struggles, double dealings, deception and mendacity between rival groups in the late 1960s with the companies, *Nuova Scena* and *La Comune*, but if her earlier experiences had stripped her of any trace of innocence, she entered the Senate with the candour and determination of mind and outlook which were among her most attractive characteristics. They were severely tested. The procedures of the legislature seemed to her more farcical than anything she and Dario had ever devised. She compared the situation in parliament to the plot of Ben Jonson's satirical comedy, *Bartholomew Fair*, where, she said, 'there was no difference between normality and madness'.[9] The exposure to party politics with all the infighting, compromise, tangled negotiations, conflicts dictated by self-interest or naked ambition rather than principle appalled her. Her words are a record of humiliations, of disappointment and frustration and of deceits perpetrated on her. On one occasion some 374 amendments to a Bill were proposed in her name, but with her signature forged. Another disappointment was with the conduct of her colleagues towards their own employees. Enquiries revealed that it was the custom of members to engage their assistants without giving them proper contracts and without passing on to them the full amount made available by Parliament. Franca did not make herself popular with Deputies and Senators when she revealed these practices and other abuses of privileges, such as subsidised visits to the hair dressers, cheap meals, coffees or the overuse of official cars or planes.

It was less than a month before she was embroiled in her first public controversy. Francesco Storace had been Minister for Health under Berlusconi until he was forced to resign when implicated, although later acquitted, in a scandal over alleged misappropriation of public funds. She was quoted in the press as saying that she would have liked to tell Storace, 'cross your arms so you can get used to handcuffs.' These remarks would have been greeted with laughter in theatre, but she was now a parliamentary deputy and found herself arraigned in the national press for a lapse in style. It would not be the last time she made personal, ironic criticism nor the last time she would find the whole establishment lined up against this outsider.

There was no shortage of other issues to arouse her scorn. She was enraged when during a debate on the massacre of Italian soldiers in Iraq, some Senators failed to behave with due gravitas and were seen laughing and joking. However, she had not alienated everyone, and somewhat to her dismay discovered she was proposed for the office of President of the Republic. Voting is carried out by a specially convened college of all Deputies and Senators together with a selection of representatives of city and regional councils. At the first round of voting on 9 May, she received 24 votes, more than any other woman candidate, but a low enough vote to let her off the hook.

She had an early mishap when she pressed the wrong button on a vote on a tax measure, but she remained determined to make a difference and to implement the policies she had advocated. She failed with a motion to reduce the expenses provided to political parties, but issued a blog which attracted many followers and which drew attention to practices followed across party lines. A motion on refinancing the Italian mission in Afghanistan presented her with a moral challenge of a different, deeper order. Franca had campaigned in favour of withdrawing the Italian forces from the country, but any defeat of the motion was likely to lead to the resignation of Prime Minister Romano Prodi and the return to power of Berlusconi. She was faced with a dilemma concerning the clash between moral ideals and political reality expressed centuries before by Machiavelli in the pithy statement that he thought differently when he was in the piazza from when he was in the Palace. In the palace, including *Palazzo Madama*, the Deputy had to debate with herself over how power should be wielded, to what end it should be used and how its various outcomes could be reconciled. In the context of this vote, every course of action entailed dangers and every move was unacceptable in its own way. She could not justify voting for the continuing presence of Nato forces in Afghanistan, but nor could she face the consequences of casting her vote in a way which would bring down the government. Her instincts were to vote with her conscience, but she received messages, from Dario and Jacopo among others, urging her to vote in a way that would keep Berlusconi out. She considered resigning. At the time, she was suffering from a badly sprained ankle and had some difficulty walking. Some malicious articles appeared suggesting that this temporary disability might provide her with a convenient excuse for absenting herself for the vote. In the event, she turned up, took the long view and voted for the renewal of the financing, thus ensuring that Prodi stayed in power – and that the Italian military presence in Afghanistan was maintained.[10]

Her energies were not exclusively taken up on party business. She organised conferences on reducing waste and on reforming electoral services, introduced bills on such subjects as excluding from office civil servants who had been found guilty of crimes, and on improving health facilities for soldiers injured in service. With some other Senators, she drew up and presented in press advertisements a manifesto containing what became known as the 'Ten Laws to Change Italy.'[11] The proposals covered such topics as making property seized from the mafia available for socially useful projects, making it easier for citizens to obtain redress when victims of crime and recognising the responsibility of companies for accidents at work. None of them became law, while Franca herself received anonymous death threats, although she was used to that. Her presence in the Senate seemed to her increasingly futile, and in January 2008 she wrote to the President of the Senate announcing her intention to resign and explaining at length her dissatisfaction. The Prodi government fell in May. Franca gave her entire salary to a variety of bodies from the Centre for Research into Tumours to the Milan Prosecutor's Office. The latter used the money to buy 20 computers.

Even after her resignation, there was no reduction of her public activities, particularly those involving the struggle against organised crime, against violence on women or against racism. She also campaigned for reform of the drug laws and of prison conditions. At the same time, she was editing volumes which were published under both their names, such as *The Obscene is Sacred* or *Correggio Who Painted Suspended in the Heavens*. In January 2012, she addressed an open letter to Mario Monti, the economist and ex-EU Commissioner who had become head of the 'technocratic' government in 2011. In it, she expressed general support for his endeavours but chided him for his failure to introduce reforms to reduce waste, and urged him to introduce greater equity in sharing the burden of remedying the Italian economy after the financial crisis of 2008.

Now that she was no longer an elected representative, both she and Dario were free to move closer to Beppe Grillo and his style of politicking. He had given Dario and Franca his full support in their campaigns, and the two men were clearly soul-mates. Grillo too had started his career as a satirical comic, and both had a cast of mind which made them constitutionally ill at ease with the prevailing power structures of society, probably of any society. The alliance with Grillo brought out the central traits of Dario's enduring mindset. Rather than a systematic Marxist, he was a permanent outsider or dissident, like St Francis or Vladimir Mayakovsky, a book of whose writings he once edited.[12] He is best described as a utopian anarchist, intolerant of injustice but incapable of accepting the discipline of any political organisation. For that reason, he was most at home with ill-regulated groupings, like those that flourished after May 1968, or in associations of men like Grillo. Perhaps Grillo would have remained in the same category had he lived in a pre-internet age, or had he not encountered Gianroberto Casaleggio, whose views of the potential of the internet and the computer were messianic. Grillo's attacks on corruption in public life grew more and more strident over the years, and on 8 September 2007, to protest at the current state of Italian politics and politicians, he organised a demonstration, called uncompromisingly *Vaffa Day*, from the vulgar but common yell – *vaffanculo*, stick it up your arse. Grillo's populist movement became the focal point for growing disgust with politicians and the politics Italian-style, especially among the young. He appeared with increasing frequency alongside Dario and Franca at demonstrations or in shows, for example at Forlì in 2009, to oppose plans to increase energy production even at the cost of destroying the countryside.

Having grown exasperated with the limitations of protest movements, in 2009 Grillo founded the *MoVimento 5 Stelle*, the 5 Star Movement, where the five stars have nothing to do with excellence ratings but stand for the central issues on which the party intended to campaign – Water, Environment, Transport, Connectivity and Development. Baffled pundits found the term anti-politics or populism a convenient description for the new body, although it was an inadequate tag. The Movement put up candidates in regional elections, gaining considerable success, and when a general election was called for 2013, the new party was well placed to make big gains. Dario gave speeches in support at several meetings, but he was at the time in a state of deep exasperation and depression, judging by a wide-ranging interview he gave to *Euronews*.[13] His hopes for renewal with the 'Clean Hands' campaign had been disappointed and he declared that Italian politics were in a state of degeneracy which was moral as much as political. 'If there isn't a system which is strong, solid, and based primarily on culture and knowledge, which instills equality, freedom and justice in the collective consciousness, then everything collapses.' Not surprisingly, he identified Berlusconi as the principal source of his country's ills:

> Just yesterday I did a satirical performance based on Buster Keaton. It was about a statue in a large room, and all around there are characters trying to prop it up. They move in all directions, they go in and out, they try to support it with mechanical devices to keep it balanced. But the statue falls and is on the verge of breaking. They stand it back up and it's OK again. It comes back, but each time it's closer to the abyss.

The fault with the condition of contemporary society lay with 'the banks mostly, and the big entrepreneurs. All those who hold the reins, or "the play within the play," who – through the media, television and in other ways – make every effort to ensure that the people accept the conditions they find themselves in.' He repeated to his interviewer the inadequacy of moderation he had voiced in his mayoral campaign. Moderates may well wear 'the mask of a good person,' but it is 'really a trap. They appear nice and gentle in their mannerisms and gestures; they never let go, they never have fun, they never play, or dance.' They stay in a corner and decline to come forward, he said, summing up his views. This was not his way, especially now that Grillo and his movement seemed to offer a vehicle for change.

His main contribution to the campaign was his co-authorship of a book which took the form of a Platonic dialogue and whose speakers were Dario, Grillo and Casaleggio. The three were engaged on an imaginary journey across Greece towards Athens, home of Periclean or direct democracy. No need to labour the symbolism. The title *The Cricket Always Sings at Dusk: Dialogue on Italy and the 5 Star Movement* was based on a rather heavy pun on the name of Grillo, the Italian for 'cricket.'[14] The ideas debated are in the tradition of European utopian or millenarian literature, in line with works by Thomas More or Tommaso Campanella, even if firmly rooted in the age of the computer and internet. 'The 5 Star Movement exists thanks to the net,' declared Grillo. Dario was not of the wi-fi generation, but agreed that if the Movement's aims were realised 'the whole system is up in the air . . . from being a representative democracy the Italian state will become a direct democracy'. Casaleggio was recognised as the guru of the computer age, and his ideas on the revolutionary potential of the internet intrigued many, including American electioneering agents who had no sympathy with his ideology. 'The destruction of the planet is at a good point,' he said, which meant that 'it is necessary to find alternatives to this model of civilisation'. All three agreed that the apocalypse could not be postponed indefinitely since resources, not only oil, were near to exhaustion, but the problems they wished to face were only superficially political-industrial corruption and the inequities of late capitalism but really others which lay deeper, including 'the law which is not applied, workers who die, work itself as blackmail and the reduction of people into slavery'. In Casaleggio's analysis, all these problems 'at the end of the day come back to the question of money which has taken over all other aspects of life'. His solution was that 'no-one should possess more than . . . 3 or 4 million euros,' but he felt obliged to underline that this was 'not a Franciscan but a political point'. References to St Francis recur throughout the dialogue, and it was a bit of bad luck for Casaleggio that he complained that there had never been a Pope called Francis only a couple of months before the election to the Papacy of the Argentinian Cardinal Bergoglio, who took the name . . . Francis.

The collaboration and cooperative discussion between the three men cannot conceal differences. All three were united in disgust with the present system and with the parties and personalities who held power in it, and all were motivated by open-hearted optimism and idealism. The split, handled amiably, concerns the means to be adopted and the potential of the computer and the internet. For Grillo and Casaleggio, the new technology of the digital age promised wholly new opportunities which could empower people even in unlikely areas such as personal health problems. More fundamentally, for the twin seers the computer age could also enable the formation of new non-parties where leaders are dispensable and people can be consulted on all questions. This would make for the creation of the new community, new governing system and new culture and civilisation all three believed necessary for the survival of the species. In Casaleggio's vision, the computer was the equivalent of the philosopher's stone for alchemists, capable of transforming the base material of traditional political rule into the rosy future of which millenarians had dreamed. Unsurprisingly Dario, while intrigued, remained sceptical about matters in which he was unversed, and suggested to the other two that while they enthused about a virtual online community and its implications for a new democracy, they should not neglect the value of face-to-face communities. He was also dubious when they informed him that he would shortly not be able to rely on expertise of the sort he found in bookshops, since 'in a short time, bookshops will no longer be those to which you are accustomed. They will change and may well disappear altogether.' While they drew their inspiration from the new technology and its value in the future, he turned, as he had always done, to history. His contributions to the discussions contained stories of Charlemagne and of St Francis, as well as discussions of Jacques Le Goff's theories of the invention of Purgatory, of the force of the Italian city-states, or how a group of 'irregular warriors' had resisted Federico Barbarossa. An irregular warrior seems an ideal description for Dario himself in politics.

The election results were a major triumph for the 5 Star Movement, which became the third party in the Chamber of Deputies. In April, during the parliamentary debates over the choice of the new President of the Republic, Grillo, who was not himself a Deputy, had some of the party members propose Dario for the office. He declined the offer, so it will never be known how events would have developed had Pope Francis and President Fo been in power at the same time.

CHAPTER 22

Franca Rame: Love and Death

To many observers, it was strange that the Nobel Prize was not jointly awarded to Dario and Franca, as it had been to Marie and Pierre Curie. Dario himself recognised the strength of this argument, and said as much in his official address in Stockholm. One page of his prompts contained a sketch, based on Raphael's *Lady with a Unicorn*, of Franca holding a friendly animal which may have been a unicorn, but without a horn. It was an affectionate portrait, and the following page depicted a male, arms outstretched, standing upright on the back of a female who was crouched on all fours, an ironic depiction of Franca's wistful statement that she was accustomed to being the pedestal supporting the great man. Dario's caption over the drawing reads, 'I am in training', although the wording leaves it unclear who is undergoing the training, Dario or Franca. There is no such ambiguity to the words at the foot of the page, 'Without her, I would not have won.'

The authorship of the comedy *The Devil with Tits* she was touring at the time of the announcement of the award is attributed to 'Dario Fo, with the collaboration of Franca Rame,' and the play is dedicated to her. The question of her overall contribution to the writing of the couple's theatre is complex and will be debated as long as their work is deemed worthy of performance. Both have made contradictory statements, some times claiming more credit than was probably due and at others modestly giving all praise to the other. Each did work that can be unambiguously viewed as his or hers, but it is not easy to determine how much of the theatrical work, especially in the early days, was jointly authored even if the only name on the cover was Dario's. The case is nowhere near as extreme as with Bertolt Brecht and Margarete Steffin, where it is now believed that she was the creator of much that has been attributed to him. Part of the dilemma concerning Dario and Franca arises in part from the way their works were produced. Writing may have started in the classical way with Dario, or sometimes Franca, seated at a desk, but it was then read and debated, sometimes acrimoniously, with the other. Changes could be made then and would continue to be made in rehearsal, during the run and even at the end of the tour. The actual performances could vary from night to night, partly in response to outside events and partly to moments of improvised inspiration. It was Franca who collated all these scattered writes and rewrites to prepare a version for publication.

The two cooperated on all fronts personally and professionally, so that at times the one was genuinely unsure in retrospect of how much credit the other was due. Franca was scarcely a suppressed female, but Dario had by far the more vigorous imagination, so my own belief is that he does deserve credit for the bulk of the work they did in the various phases of their lives together. But at what point did constructive criticism made by Franca of an early version of a play by Dario become an act of co-creativity? It seemed to me that the plays began as Dario's but ended as Franca's, but it has to be added that in her last interview with me, she declined to accept that view:

> This is not fair. There are scripts which are all Dario's. I intervene at the moment of the 'audit,' if I can put it that way. The difficulty lies in establishing the collaboration between us. What happens ? Dario sits down to write a play, he hands every page he writes to me, and generally I found myself in the position of making criticisms or at least of giving him some suggestions. At the beginning I did not have the authority I later gained with the passing of time, above all with *He had Two Pistols and White and Black Eyes*. That was a work where, when I read it, I felt it did not work ... we went

on stage at the Odeon in Milan. The play was a success but not the success we expected . . . I remember when we were in the green room, Dario handed me the script and said, 'Make the cuts you suggested.'[1]

The change in authority and authorship – two closely related words – occurred over the years, particularly with the rise of feminism. There were works which were unquestionably hers alone but, however counter-intuitive it may appear, these were not the monologues on the condition of women which she performed from the 1970s onwards. In her account, she suggested to Dario ideas and situations to dramatise the condition of women and these were then given full theatrical form by him. These were then discussed and tried out, so to whom should authorship be credited? Moreover, in his oration at her funeral, Dario announced that her part in the authorship of the plays was greater than had been admitted, and even suggested that he might have denied this fact out of jealousy. He also said that she was the real author of *The Open Couple* (1983), something both of them had previously denied. This account certainly conflicts with a version he gave to me once in Edinburgh when he said he had written the play during a tense period in their relationship, but had not really intended it for performance. It was given a private reading to a close circle of friends including Carlo Barsotti, who was then based in Sweden and who had produced several of Fo's plays in translations by his Swedish wife, Anna. He asked permission to stage it in Stockholm, and only after its success there did Dario think of presenting it in Milan. Franca took the principal part in a play, a comedy which shows the male character's delight and his wife's dismay at the opportunities afforded by the anti-bourgeois concept of the 'open couple,' until she turns the tables by taking a lover. The work was considered too outrageous for the Italian Ministry and young people under 18 years of age were banned from attending.

Franca worked and published on her own later in her career, and in retrospect the lack of full recognition seems to have irked her. In 1999, she gave Giuseppina Manin an interesting interview which revealed more of the couple's private life than she was normally prepared to divulge. It was published under a title chosen by the sub-editors, *How Tiring to Live Under the Shadow of Fo*,[2] and in it Franca gave vent to her feelings on a variety of items, domestic, personal and authorial. At home, the couple had decided that it was politically incorrect to employ a servant, but she found herself living with 'two men: a disorderly son and a husband whose mother even used to put on his socks. One day I got fed up and pinned a notice on the wall of the living room; from today on, anyone who wishes to eat or to have his shirts ironed can do it himself.' She had to add that 'to avoid chaos, I had to put my principles to one side and hire a fantastic Filipino maid'. These domestic arrangements are interesting enough, although they did have trouble with later Filipinos who were less fantastic. Domestic servants of various nationalities became a fixture in the Fo-Rame household, which became increasingly crowded as secretaries and assistants were taken on to help with an increasingly heavy work load. The Fo house in Milan, as more than one journalist noted, was in a state of permanent creative disorder.

All during her time in the Senate, Franca supervised the task of putting all the works, including successive edits, on-line, but she also continued humanitarian work, giving well paid and rewarding work to prisoners. She identified inmates capable of the uploading of their joint archive onto a website where all reviews, interviews and successive drafts of the plays were made available. She also attended to correspondence, taking bookings, looking after management tasks and overseeing the final editing needed before a play could be viewed as suitable for publication. Dario was happy with this arrangement, and rarely dissented. *Fai tu* (You do it), were the words she said she heard most frequently from him. The implication was that he would trust her totally, but also that he felt he need not concern himself unduly with mundane matters. She also issued a regular blog. In the same interview, Franca moved on to her role as archivist, defining it as 'my real profession', and future producers and researchers will be in her debt, and her debt alone. Advances in technology made this task easier and in the years following the award of the Nobel Prize she spent much time seated in front of a computer, editing their work. It was she who made available for publication the revised version of *Can't Pay? Won't Pay!*, which became *Low Pay? Don't Pay!*, and gave *Accidental Death* its final form.

Of greater interest is another statement made under the heading *Author* in the same interview. On an earlier occasion, Franca had denied herself a role in the composition of the scripts,[3] saying that Dario was the writer in the house, but in conversation with Manin she said that 'of the one hundred plays written by Dario, we wrote half of them together. I am his consultant, a thankless role. It is necessary to tell the truth.'[4] Perhaps there is no simple truth. Perhaps their collaboration was so close that it is not possible to identify individual contribution. The principal creative contribution and impulse in the vast majority of cases was Dario's, but that does not mean that Franca's part is to be downplayed or that at times she does not deserve to be viewed as author. Authorship is acknowledged in differing ways in the volumes which were to make up their Collected Works, published by Einaudi. The series ends in 1998 with volume XIII when the company was bought over by Berlusconi, causing the couple to break off dealings with them. Later works were published elsewhere. The first twelve volumes were published as *Le commedie di Dario Fo*, although for volume XI and XII, the title page carried the rubric, 'edited by Franca Rame.' Volume XIII was issued under the title *Le commedie di Dario Fo e Franca Rame* and included the double bill, *Fat is Beautiful* and *Heroine/Heroin*. When these two works were initially published together by Kaos Edizioni in 1991, the title was *Let's Talk About Women*, with Franca Rame's name alone on the cover. However, both she and Dario were identified as joint authors in an inside page, suggesting that the publishers too were confused. In fact, Franca not only performed the principal part but was also main author of *Fat is Beautiful* and was certainly sole author of *Heroin/Heroine*. That year, in reply to an interviewer who asked how she felt about writing a work on her own, 'I think I've succeeded in expressing the concepts I wanted to. I can die happy, don't you agree?'[5] On the authorship of *Fat is Beautiful*, she later explained the procedure: 'The script was written by me. After that, Dario came along and added his touch of genius.'[6]

That gnomic statement is probably as close to the truth as we are likely to get. The creative process is easier to follow for these two plays since the comments and successive versions are available on the Fo-Rame website. The works had undergone the customary process of joint discussion, comment, writing, rewriting and final modification in rehearsal, but it is clear that in these cases the original inspiration and first version was Franca's. In her final interview, she again expressed the wish that her contribution be recognised, this time employing feminist idiom:

> I bear no rancour towards Dario, because at the basis of everything there's my biggest failing – that of having no ambition. It's not that Dario ever thought, 'Franca will provide me with ideas and I'll look smart!' No, that never crossed his mind. If I hadn't been his wife, if I'd been somebody else, he would of necessity have had to put my name too as author. Einaudi published numerous scripts by Dario all edited by me, and initially there was not even the acknowledgement 'edited by Franca Rame.' When I asked Roberto Cerati for an explanation, he said, 'We just never thought of it.' The problem is that I am the *wife*, and a wife sometimes is a piece of domestic furniture.[7]

In addition to writing and acting, Franca continued her humanitarian endeavours on several fronts. The Nobel Prize money amounted to a massive 1,650,000,000 lire, and the Fos decided to establish what they called the Nobel for the Disabled to distribute the entire sum to handicapped people and to organisations dedicated to working with them. Franca dedicated herself energetically to the task and managed to persuade Volkswagen to contribute vehicles. The takings from shows which the Fos produced, as well as from sales of prints and sketches by Dario, were also donated to the cause. Requests were invited from deserving causes, but in this sad and tainted world some applications turned out to be fraudulent or completely bogus. A committee was set up to examine requests, and an accountant, Luciano Silva, was appointed to head the organisation. Silva seemed a man of the utmost integrity, and gained the trust of his colleagues. When the organisation was fully functional, some well publicised events were arranged and donations made to several charities, with the gift of equipment, machines and Volkswagen mini-buses being particularly appreciated.

Regrettably, by mid 2004, Franca began to have suspicions that there was something awry in the administration of the fund, and that some moneys were being embezzled. Investigations revealed that a large sum had been paid from an account which had been closed some years previously, and suspicion fell on Silva. A pattern of systematic fraud was uncovered, and advertisements were placed in national newspapers to announce that he had been dismissed and no longer represented the committee. When the case went to court in September 2006, it was revealed that the missing sum amounted to almost €400,000. A further hearing took place in May 2007, and on this occasion Dario and Franca took advantage of the provision of Italian law which permits injured parties to be represented directly. Silva's lawyers proposed a deal which would have seen him repay €50,000 and serve a sentence of one year and four months. Discussions over repayment were inconclusive and the case adjourned until July when the court was told that Silva did not have the money to make reparation. In November, he was sentenced to two and half years' imprisonment and to a repayment of €200,000, although this penalty could be implemented only after further civil action. The court also ordered payment of €20,000 in damages to the bank. In a statement, Dario said he was satisfied with the outcome, although puzzled that the bank was recognised as an injured party. Franca's health suffered from the stress of the lengthy, wounding proceedings, and she had to receive medical treatment and cancel some performances. She and Dario had behaved with great generosity and magnanimity, but had been cheated. So too had the disabled they had attempted to assist.

Meantime, Franca was defendant in a case brought against her by Roberto Castelli, a member of the Northern League and Minister for Justice in the coalition government headed by Silvio Berlusconi. In 2002, the minister had expressed bewilderment over a hunger strike by prisoners, since in his view 'prison is comparable to a five-star hotel'. This statement outraged Franca, who had been campaigning for years for prison reform, and in a demonstration outside the Regina Coeli prison in Rome, she called the minister 'un pirla,' a term of abuse which could be rendered in English as 'prick,' but which, like its English equivalent, has transmogrified into a generic insult. Castelli, obviously a sensitive soul, claimed that the term was defamatory and raised an action for damages of €100,000. The case was settled in July 2005, with a symbolic award of €3,000. The judge noted that the word 'pirla' was a dialect word and that its use had not been reported in all the media covering the event.

Franca served in the Senate, as has been already described, from 2006 to 2008, after which she and Dario went on tour with some scenes from *Mistero buffo*. She had never completely left off her other work, and assisted Dario in his performances, ensuring that he did not exert himself unduly and aiding as prompt when his memory failed. She also participated fully in writing and editing volumes on Boccaccio (2011) and Picasso (2012). In both cases, she was recognised as 'editor', and as translator of dialect passages in Boccaccio.[8] The Picasso book was an act of homage, lavishly illustrated and transformed for performance, but the Boccaccio volume was a more substantial piece of work.

A renewed interest in story-telling and in the erotic was bound to lead Dario to Giovanni Boccaccio, Italy's most renowned teller of tales and one who was not averse to narratives with a high erotic content, but Dario (and Franca?) present a more feminised Boccaccio than is common. The title A *Revised and Incorrect Boccaccio* contains an untranslatable pun on the word *scorretto* which can mean both 'uncorrected' as well 'inappropriate', and the work as a whole is a personal reconsideration of a writer whom Dario had earlier dismissed as reactionary. In the new evaluation, Boccaccio is presented and celebrated as a short-story writer of genius and as a neglected humanist thinker, and also a man who had advocated living life to the full. Many of his protagonists had luxuriated fully in all the opportunities life offered the rebellious, hedonist young, even in the midst of the calamity of the plague which drove his story-tellers from Florence in the first place. In the *Decameron*, Dario detects that combination of the tragic and the farcical which was his personal ideal in drama, but which was, he writes, a revolutionary innovation which made possible the emergence of *commedia dell'arte* and which influenced Shakespeare. Dario is not given to cautious or measured judgements.

> Briefly, without this free alteration of the balance of narrative, we would not have had the advantage of the great revolution of *commedia dell'arte* and, following from that, of the extraordinary renovation of all European theatre starting with the Elizabethans; led by Shakespeare.[9]

Dario provides both a guide to Boccaccio and a retelling of many of the tales from a new perspective. He begins with the story of Ginevra, which provided one element of the plot of Shakespeare's *Cymbeline*, although the Bard did not exactly 'translate' it, as is suggested. The ending of the tale, where in the court of the Sultan Ginevra pardons the husband who had commissioned a friend to kill her in vengeance for an adultery she had not committed, did not satisfy Dario any more than it had pleased Bernard Shaw. Quoting Shaw as justification for his alterations to the ending, Dario has Ginevra say that she would prefer to remain as a concubine in the Sultan's court rather than return to the marital home. This is a liberation of a sort, and Ginevra is not the first female in Dario's work for whom prostitution, or concubinage, represents an act of self-determination.

Dario permits himself considerable leeway in his retelling of some of the other thirteen tales he narrates, but they are all recounted with brio and panache. Among the qualities he praises in Boccaccio is his willingness to condemn himself as a plagiarist or even an outright thief of stories created by other writers, a crime of which Dario himself was often cheerfully guilty. He uses the first story on Day One to deplore the growth of the banking industry in early Renaissance Italy, but he emphasises throughout the high position Boccaccio gives to women, either as narrator or protagonist. 'One of the great achievements of Boccaccio is to have given prime place ... to the female world, making women often absolute interpreters of the story-performance.'

In this period, Franca did more writing of her own than ever before, producing her autobiography, *An Improvised Life*, and the memoir on her experiences in the Senate. Her health continued to be poor, and she required greater and greater medical assistance. Late in 2012, she suffered what was described as a minor stroke, which left her even more badly weakened. She had to spend more time resting, although she was always willing, probably more than was wise, to offer help when requested. I met her in her home in February to do a book-length interview, which turned out to be the last interview she was able to give. Her voice had no longer the vivacity of other times and she was visibly enfeebled. When asked if she had any unfulfilled ambitions in theatre, she replied, 'Perhaps now the real aspiration is to rest.' She died on 29 May 2013, with Dario and Jacopo at her bedside. After her death, Dario locked the door of her room, and sat alone beside the body for some forty minutes until the undertakers arrived, when he came out and sat down to begin preparing for the funeral and dictating articles in her memory.

Tolstoy writes that all happy marriages are happy in the same way but unhappy marriages are unhappy in their own unique style. These are moving, much quoted words, but most marriages are neither wholly happy nor wholly unhappy. Dario and Franca were locked in a relationship of mutual dependence and affection. While it is true that Franca broke off the relationship in public on the Raffaella Carrà show, she later rewrote history and denied that they had ever been apart. She was deeply unhappy during the period when Dario was having multiple affairs, and those who frequented their house recall times when they would not speak for weeks, and when Dario would cower in the bathroom making phone calls supposedly in private but within Franca's hearing. She kept trunks with letters and presents sent by enamoured admirers, whom Franca described as turning up with their knickers in their hand. But she did not adhere to vows of conjugal fidelity, and had her own affairs, most publicly with Nanni Ricordi.

However, theirs was a love story, certainly no sugar candy romance or tale of *la vie en rose*, but a story of regard and affection interspersed with argumentation, moments of aversion, anger, bitterness, then reconciliation, patching up and normality. What makes them distinct was that they lived a personal and a professional life simultaneously.

Without Franca, had she not been there to give form and permanency to work which became theirs, Dario might have enjoyed contemporary fame, but he would have dropped out of history like the old Harlequins. In the last years, Jessica Borroni, who shared their life, says that Franca was behind everything that Dario did – the work on Maria Callas, on Darwin, the novels, and the performance-lectures. After his stroke, she would be there in the wings, and would even call him off stage when she feared he was putting his health at risk.

Franca's death was marked by respectful obituaries in newspapers all round the world, recognising her achievements as actress, writer, political activist, feminist and campaigner against social injustice. Her coffin was covered in a red drape and her funeral ceremony held in the open outside the Piccolo Teatro in Milan. Mourners waved red flags and sang songs from the days of the Resistance. In his panegyric, Dario told a story which he said Franca had adapted from an apocryphal version of the Book of Genesis. Eve preceded Adam, and when God spoke to them He offered them the chance to choose to eat the fruit of one of two trees, the first of which would guarantee immortality but the other would bring wisdom undermined by doubt, as well as love together with the certainty of death. She preferred the chance of finding love, even if it meant mortality and death.

CHAPTER 23

The Sadness of the Clown:
Life without Franca

Franca, who had well founded doubts about Dario's financial nous, left everything of hers to Jacopo, but Dario was more than amply provided for. After the funeral, he resumed writing and painting more intensely than ever, but, as Mario Pirovano recalls, it was still performance he preferred. 'He wrote then presented his work. He had a sense that he had not a moment to lose, so there was an acceleration in his work rhythms. He had accumulated stories, ideas, concepts, but had little time for research.' He needed people around him. On a typical day, he would rise early and go straight to his office, skipping breakfast. Mario brought in the newspapers, which he would read to him. The staff turned up at nine, assisting according to their allotted task with writing to his dictation, reading passages from books he required to hear, photocopying or doing artwork under his general supervision. Jacopo was there more frequently now and took his mother's role in general management of contracts, translation and also sale of the canvases; Michela Casiere and Jessica Borroni attended to the painting, while Mario became engaged on every front. The number of assistants grew, with a domestic staff engaged for cleaning and cooking. Lunch was served at 1.00pm, after which Dario retired for a rest. The afternoon proceeded in the same way, but visitors, including actors, stage designers, photographers, translators and young artists from many countries turned up, announced or unannounced. Visitors were disconcerted at the level of activity at his home in Milan, but in spite of his energy, Dario was prone to the normal ills of age, so a nurse came to live in the house, guaranteeing round the clock care and ensuring that he took his regular doses of medicine.

He carried on as he had done before Franca died, largely because there is no alternative given to human beings in such circumstances. He missed her sorely, and mourned her deeply. Keeping the memory of her alive and supporting the causes she had worked for became one of the mainsprings of his life and purpose. Once when asked how he coped with old age, he replied that it would all have been so much easier if Franca had been at his side. 'I dream of her. She comes back to me, the last time just a couple of days ago. She gives me advice, even if from a distance.'[1]

He was hardly a recluse. The status as prophet or oracle was thrust upon him, even if his views would then be subject in some quarters to derisive rebuttal. He complained that while the *New York Times,* for example, would call and begin with an apology and a promise not to take more than a few minutes of his time, a local paper in Sicily would peremptorily demand his attention for half an hour or more. He was quoted worldwide when in 2015, to his gratification, the post-coup regime in Turkey banned his work together with that of Chekhov and Shakespeare.

There was no let-up in the output of articles for the press, in his touring, his appearances on television shows or in his general political activity. He held the established press in contempt and found an alternative for his articles on Italian politics and other subjects in a new, independent newspaper, *Il Fatto Quotidiano.* He continued to hold three times a year in Alcatraz the seminars on acting he and Franca had previously conducted together. His political activity was now wholly focused on Grillo and his 5 Star Movement. He gave speeches in public with the same frequency as ever, championing human rights, attacking the new governing establishment but retaining his freedom to be critical of the parties and people he supported. One of the causes which engaged his attention was the treatment of immigrants fleeing from poverty or war. He was appalled by the loss of life in the Mediterranean where many refugees making the crossing from North Africa in improvised, overcrowded boats were drowned. Some were saved by Italian coast guards, but in spite of the efforts of various charities and official bodies, the survivors had to endure dreadful conditions. Dario phoned the mayor of Lampedusa, where many immigrants ended up, to offer to provide tents at his own expense, but he was told she could not accept them because the police were dealing with the situation which meant it was outwith her jurisdiction. When he protested at this bureaucratic inhumanity, she outdid satire by replying simply, 'we are in Italy.' She was flayed for her trouble in the next day's press, and the matter was resolved. Changes in the law to ease the plight of illegal immigrants were proposed and supported by some elected representatives of the 5 Star Movement, but to Dario's dismay these deputies were then publicly disowned by Grillo. Dario expressed his disagreement with the party leader in public, and repeated his view that, all humanitarian considerations aside, immigration was good for the Italian economy.[2]

Autumn 2013 saw Dario in Genoa for the first stop on a tour with a theatrical version of Franca's book on her experiences in the Senate. He took the opportunity to visit Marassi prison where builders with the assistance of the prisoners had constructed a theatre on an empty space inside the prison walls. While happy to applaud the scheme, he used the inaugural event to condemn the prison system as one of the fifty plagues of Italy. In the same city in December, he appeared on a platform with Grillo for his third *Vaffa Day*. His official theme was culture and the position of working people, but he ranged widely, delivering a rebuke to the Left-wing parties for their tardiness in denouncing the escape of gases from an industrial complex in Taranto, reiterating his objections to the plan to build a tunnel for the high speed train in the Val di Susa and once again calling for action to alleviate the condition of refugees. However, a fellow satirist, Vauro Senesi, a friend who had taken part in many campaigns with him, took exception to his views, or perhaps to the company in which he expounded them and wrote an open letter inviting Dario to 'get down from the stage'.

The reply he received showed that Dario, although he wrote in tones of hurt incomprehension over a lost soulmate, still had a command of acerbic sharpness when offended. He wondered why Vauro had neglected all the other themes raised in his speech and on which they had campaigned together, and why he had fixed especially on one phrase used by Grillo. Jeering at the coalition government in Rome, Grillo had raised his voice, as he was wont to do, to yell from Genoa to the capital, 'You're all dead, corpses.' Vauro, somewhat stretching the point, detected in this an echo of the Fascist worship of death, and invited Dario to dissociate himself from it. In reply, Dario gave him a lesson on the ferocity and offensiveness intrinsic to satire, referring to scenes from Lucian of Samosata, from Dante and from *Hamlet,* where death is portrayed with savagery. He promised not to reproach Vauro if he was heard supporting some cause, even in dubious company, by 'recounting stories packed with irony, for that is our job as clowns'.[3]

The clown was given another outing when *A Clown's Going to Bury You All*, co-authored with Giuseppina Manin, was published.[4] Although ill at ease with the neo-liberal beliefs and practices implemented in Italy as elsewhere, he adopted a wry, sceptical but tentatively sanguine attitude towards the possibility of the emergence of a new Italy. Could the country be stumbling towards a cultural revolution comparable to 1948 or 1968? Dario had lived through the climate of hope in those moments, and was with one side of his brain in the grips of one of those moods of optimism, however cautious, to which he was prone, but with the other side of his brain, he sounded dismayed when he thought back to the crushing of the high hopes that had swirled around him and his circle twice in his life, firstly after the Liberation and then in the excitement of the post-1968 movement. The victories won then had been undone, the culture was now more toxic, the laughter more forced and hollow, the feeling of despair more deep-seated. This interview-book gave him the opportunity to repeat that the irritant whose jibes and provocations might produce the pearl of change was Beppe Grillo, the clown of the title, even if Manin treats this hope with some scepticism. Dario suggests that Grillo is 'like a character from one of my comedies, a surrealist visionary whose imagination and jokes have at least had the merit of awakening the sleeping country'. Dario is incapable of writing in any style other than the ironic, so any hope, however desperate it is, is based on the belief that Italy after putting up with scandals and corruption year after year, may finally be close to some final but cleansing catastrophe. The country is in his view precariously balanced between the longing for change, even revolutionary change, and a yearning for order and stability. The aspiration towards a more orderly version of the status quo was evident in the overarching governing coalition of Left and Right headed by Prime Minister Enrico Letta, but perhaps below the surface the old order may be tottering and new forces stirring, as shown by the 163 deputies elected for the 5 Star Movement:

> In fact, 163 Martians have landed in Parliament . . . And they don't have little green aerials on their heads. They are young, nice, some with degrees, a bit unsure, highly excited. They're all somewhat stunned by their sudden, bumpy landing in another world, but they're determined to stun the natives in the place, the ones seated on the public seats that have put down thousand-year old roots, who consider that court to be their property. In other words, they're the real UFOs, scruffy in appearance but underneath fearsome and insidious. No sci-fi film had ever imagined anything like this. Never mind Spielberg, the man of the moment is Beppe Grillo.

In spite of the hopes he placed in Grillo, Dario was puzzled and saddened by the turn events had taken, especially as regards the environment. He began to sound like a quasi-religious visionary without a properly defined creed. Ever the utopian optimist, or the anarchic dissident, he was most at home with political mischief makers, like Grillo. He feared, as he declared in tracts like *The Apocalypse Postponed,* that humankind's disregard for nature and his own habitat would, if left unchecked, lead to catastrophe. Grillo offered some hope as did, however incongruous the pairing, the man who occupied the throne of St Peter, and behind him St Francis, whose name the Pope had taken. Dario now preferred to advocate change of culture rather than purely political upheaval, so the gentle teaching of the Poor Man of Assisi was as useful as anything in Marx, Lenin or Darwin.

It was not easy to establish a stable partnership with such a flamboyant, unreliable gadfly. Grillo enjoyed being provocative, issued blogs and posts on the spur of the moment and was given to ranting at great length on public platforms with the risk of losing control. Dario had never joined a party, unlike Franca who had been for a short time in the Communist Party. He was as little suited to the discipline of party membership as was Groucho Marx of belonging to a club, but he remained of the view that the 5 Star Movement, warts and all, represented the best vehicle for radical change in Italy. This meant that he received regular calls from journalists anxious to find out if the latest outburst from Grillo had finally made him lose patience. He remained relaxed when asked for his reaction when Grillo raised his index finger gesture to a female journalist, and replied that he had been provoked by the lies written in the press. In February 2014, in response to the introduction by the government of a guillotine to restrict discussion on important measures, some 5 Star deputies in the Chamber stormed the chair of the speaker, who was female, shouting sexist slogans as they did so. Dario called them to order and invited them to respond to objectionable measures with irony and imagination. On another occasion, he advised Grillo, who was known to be considering an anti-EU coalition with UKIP in the European parliament and was seen dining with Nigel Farage, to proceed with caution, but his reaction was remarkably mild. He admitted he knew little about Farage, and his experience in Italy led him to be sceptical about information picked up only in the press. 'I trust Grillo and Casaleggio, but Farage has different values,' he said.[5]

In late 2013 and early 2014, Dario was engaged on a tour with Franca's *Flight from the Senate*. Readings from her book were interspersed with stand-up comedy and improvised routines in which Dario extended his wife's acid portraits of politicians with satirical routines and barbs of his own. Although the book was mainly concerned with Franca's time as Senator, it also covered her campaigns against drugs, her anti-war activity and her involvement with groups which offered assistance to refugees. While the tour was still at the planning stage, there was an odd and unexpected hitch when the Vatican authorities revoked a booking Dario had made to appear in Rome at the *Auditorium della Conciliazione*, a theatre owned by the Church. He protested, pointing out that he and Franca had previously performed in that venue and wondering how far down the reforms introduced by Pope Francis had percolated. The episode did him no harm, since it gave the show wide publicity and several Roman theatres offered him their premises. He used the occasion to wonder aloud if he, a known admirer of the Pope, was being used by dark forces inside the Curia to obstruct Francis's reform agenda.

As he travelled around Italy, he gave his support to other causes in the places he visited. In January, he visited Padua, where he called a press conference to express concern over the precarious state of the Scrovegni Chapel, home of Giotto's masterpieces and subject of one of his TV programmes, but now in danger from the humidity levels. Everyone agreed about the risks, but there was no consensus on what was to be done, leaving Dario worrying that the immobility of the City Council and its unwillingness to heed expert advice would lead to disaster. The vice-mayor, Ivo Rossi, turned up uninvited at the press conference to offer the reassuring news that the matter was in hand, and to invite Dario to plant a tree in a street dedicated to Nobel Prize winners, but unfortunately he had neglected to bring the tree.

In Bologna in February, Dario opened with a rewritten, revised version of his play on St Francis of Assisi, fifteen years after the first production, all proceeds going to the charity, *Terra Madre*, set up by Carlo Petrini, also founder of *Slow Food*, to help alleviate poverty in Africa. Dario's devotion to the two Francises, the pope and the saint, seemed to overlap, with life imitating art and art struggling to keep pace with life. His admiration for Pope Francis was such that he rewrote *Francis The Holy Jester* with the Pope in mind, since the Argentinian Francis seemed to Dario to embody all that he valued and admired in Francis of Assisi. Like the saint, the Pope was in Dario's eyes a man of renewal, showing scant respect for established ways, demonstrating a bold willingness to stand up to the powerful, giving concrete expression to his love of the poor and his detestation of poverty, prepared to go any distance to secure peace and, whether dealing with politicians or cardinals in the curia, determined to avoid the easy way out. He reacted with annoyance to any attack on the Pope, so having heard sly slights uttered by certain Italian intellectuals, he inserted a special scene in his defence at the performance in June at the Roman Arena in Verona. He underlined that he himself remained 'an atheist, a Marxist-Leninist and a Darwinist,' but he invited His Holiness to come and see a performance. Alas, the invitation was not taken up. However, on 22 June, RAI broadcast the play, the first of Dario's works to be screened in seven years.

There were other figures besides Grillo and the Pope who occupied Dario's mind. Matteo Renzi, previously Mayor of Florence, ousted Letta to become Prime Minister and leader of the Democratic Party. For many, not only on the Left, Renzi was viewed as the last hope of Italy, the only politician with the strength to oppose Berlusconi, the only leader capable of bringing union to the fractious Left and of introducing the reforms needed to help the country resolve the economic problems created by its chronic debt and the demands made by the EU. This was not Dario's assessment. Renzi's rise to power gave him no cause for hope, and he satirised him as mercilessly as he had done Christian Democrat leaders in the 70s and 80s, or Berlusconi in the 90s. In Dario's eyes, Renzi, himself a Catholic, was in part a new breed of Christian Democrat, and in part the incarnation of a new breed of technocratic, pragmatic politician, bereft of vision, ideology or moral principle. The proof of this for Dario was his general indifference to the plight of working people who had borne the brunt of the austerity programme imposed after the great financial crash of 2008. Renzi's openness towards Berlusconi, and his willingness to accept his support for electoral reform, dismayed him further, so much so that at times he found it difficult to refer to him by name. 'Deaths at work follow one after the other. The regime, exactly as it did yesterday, silences dissent. Look at the attitude of that Tuscan towards the working class. A horrible, pitiless, shameless attitude. He wants to cancel workers, sweep them away.'[6] There was no need to identify the Tuscan.

New targets for his satire did not cause him to forget the older one. The news came that Berlusconi, who was known to have constructed a private mausoleum in the gardens of his villa near Milan, had had it extended and was even installing central heating. This titbit was too good an opportunity for Dario to miss. He wondered if Berlusconi, who was appearing in the dock in various courts in Italy, saw himself as a latter day Viking King. He fantasised, but it may have been more than a fantasy, that Berlusconi wished to be surrounded in death as in life by attendants, courtiers, servants, assorted flatterers and dancing girls performing 'bunga-bunga' turns. Perhaps the place was being kept heated because Berlusconi believed he would only be hibernating until resuscitation.

Meantime, Dario emerged as being in every sense on the side of the angels, or at least of the saints and their representatives on earth. His lecture-performance on St Ambrose, patron saint of Milan, had been published as a book and given as a performance at the Piccolo in 2009, but the date set for its transmission on television, 7 December 2014, was deliberately chosen to clash with the worldly, non-spiritual celebration of the saint's feast in a concert in La Scala to which all the great and good, or at least the fashionable and the powerful, of the city were invited. The official evening was rounded off with a sumptuous banquet to which the inner élite was invited. Dario addressed another audience, telling the Milanese what manner of man their patron saint was. In January 2015, he gave an interview to a Catholic newspaper, which after lambasting him in previous years for his blasphemy and disrespect for the clergy and the church now treated him with respect. The theme was Pope Francis, and the enlightened papal attitude on many topics of the day on which Dario and the Pope saw eye to eye. 'I am a fanatic for St Francis. I have written four plays on him, have conducted studies on him and have been close to the greatest European researchers on his life, I have found in the Pope not only someone who says the same things as Francis but in the same language. He has understood that it is possible to say stupendous things while speaking with humility.'[7]

That same month, he wrote a more secular article which was vintage Fo in its use of Aristophanes to provide a lens or a distorting mirror through which a very modern scandal in Rome could be examined. The occasion was the interception by the Italian police of a phone call between the head of a perfectly legal co-operative business, Salvatore Buzzi, and a mafia boss, Massimo Carminati, who was heard boasting of his ability to make money from the immigrant community. Carminati made the claim that he and his like inhabit middle earth and from that vantage point control Rome. In his response, Dario feigned admiration for the culture of the mafia man who knew about Tolkien and the territory known as 'middle earth', but then pushes the fiction further back, to the creation of the imaginary Cloud-cuckoo-land in Aristophanes' comedy *The Birds*. In Dario's summary, life in Athens had been made intolerable by corruption and the contrast between the poverty of the many and the wealth of the few, causing some citizens to decide to emigrate, but where to? Sicily is considered and rejected, but they hear of the mystic land beyond the clouds where the gods ensure that peace and harmony reign. Reaching the heavens requires the construction of wings to allow the would-be emigrants to fly, but when they reach the desired land they find the birds complaining that the gods are every bit as depraved and self-seeking as the aristocracy of Greece. Dario was so enraptured of Greek theatre that his delight in retelling the plot and outlining the wonders of ancient stage machinery made him lose the original impulse to point the parallels between then and now. But perhaps it needed no more underlining than his own evident disillusion with the society he inhabited.[8]

CHAPTER 24

The Emerging Novelist?

'Actors denied I was an author and authors did the same. You are nothing more than an actor dressed up as an author,' he reported being told, but he was able to add, 'I remained outside every category and I managed very well. I have had a stupendous life.'[1] There was one new category to be added. At the age of 88 he published his first novel. In all, he would produce six, two co-authored, all works that can be labelled historical fiction, even if the time frame was in some cases recent. The volumes spontaneously raise some questions, such as – what level of imaginative manipulation should historical research undergo before the book is regarded as a work of fiction? Or even that old question so beloved of the more pedantic literary theorists – what is a novel?

When he started writing the first of these, given the arresting title *The Pope's Daughter*, he did not plan it as a work of fiction, but said it developed in that way. The image on the cover is an adaption of a portrait by Bartolommeo Veneto of a young woman, taken by many critics to be Lucrezia Borgia, and one of many illustrations by Dario in the book.[2] She is at her most alluring, staring boldly at the viewer, reddish, artfully curled hair falling over her shoulder, one breast tauntingly exposed. Lucrezia was the daughter of Pope Alexander VI, and the impulse to write her story was Dario's disgust with an international TV blockbuster, *The Borgias*, directed by Neil Jordan and with a high profile cast including Jeremy Irons as Pope, Holliday Grainger as Lucrezia, and Steven Berkoff and Derek Jacobi in minor roles. He considered the TV series in general and the depiction of Lucrezia in particular as up-market porn, and undertook on a course of reading and research to establish her rightful persona. There is no shortage of books of every kind on the Borgia dynasty, from the classic biography by Ferdinand Gregorovius to a dynastic history by Alexandre Dumas which Dario considered 'stupendous'. His first reading was John Ford's Elizabethan tragedy, *'Tis pity She's a Whore*, although critics are divided on whether or not that work is inspired by Lucrezia's life.

If there is near unanimity in the assessment of the Borgia pope, Alexander VI, and his son, Machiavelli's hero and model prince, Cesare Borgia, few characters have divided historical opinion as deeply as Lucrezia. For some, she was a woman devoid of all humanity and morality, she-devil, murderer, poisoner, nymphomaniac psychopath who casually slaughtered her lovers when they were no longer of any interest, a sexual predator guilty of incestuous love affairs. Dante Gabriel Rossetti provided the classic portrait of her in this guise, depicting her washing her hands to free herself of guilt after administering poison to her innocent husband, Duke Alfonso, while an image in a mirror shows her father keeping Alfonso on his feet not out of humanity but to ensure that the poison permeates every part of his body. Lucrezia does not emerge much better from Donizetti's opera. The alternative view sees her as a saintly, oppressed, wronged woman, used and abused as a political pawn by male power at its most savage and satanic as exercised by her unscrupulous, deeply corrupt father and brother.

Dario was largely of the latter view. His reading convinced him that Lucrezia was a humane, courageous, highly cultured figure, misrepresented by historians. He saw her as a lover of art and an excellent, enlightened ruler of a city-state in an age when women were considered to be incapable of exercising power. He furnished his novel with footnotes giving validity to historical incident, but he also freely invented dialogue and, far from being the invisible novelist, intervenes with his own comments as he goes along. His first complaint with other works on Lucrezia and on the Borgia family in general was that she was viewed in isolation, not in the context of the corrupt state of the church in Renaissance Italy, reference to which allows him to make comparisons with the reforming zeal of Pope Francis. Other revolutionary figures from the time, such as Copernicus, are introduced, but the latter's dialogue with the Pope does not concern the geocentric or heliocentric universe, but the self-interested obstacles posed by the curia and cardinals to the reform of the church proposed by the Pope. Is this Pope Alexander VI or Francis?

By the age of twelve, Lucrezia was aware of her parentage and found herself betrothed to the widowed Giovanni Sforza, Lord of Pesaro, a man more than twice her age and one whom she did not know and certainly could not love. When her husband had served his purpose, the marriage was dissolved by order of the Pope, and she was remarried to Alfonso, Prince of Salerno, who in Dario's account she genuinely loved. When the Borgia alliances changed he was murdered, irrespective of Lucrezia's feelings. Given governorship of Spoleto, she showed herself both an excellent civil ruler as well as an able military commander. She was paired with a second Alfonso, ruler of Ferrara, one of the great centres of Renaissance poetry. Already an educated, cultured and perspicacious woman before her arrival at Ferrara, she brought to the court the greatest Humanist philosophers and writers. Here too she embarked on one of her many love affairs, with Pietro Bembo, himself one of the most distinguished poets and neo-platonic thinkers of the sixteenth century. The letters they exchanged are extant and Byron described them as 'the prettiest love letters in the world.'[3] She bore seven or eight children and died in childbirth.

Dario's purpose is to underline her resistance to the powers that wished to treat a mere female as a pawn, and her drive to take control of her own destiny and to build on her native abilities. The volume, which is more history than fiction and is not notably different in style and aesthetic from the volume on St Ambrose, follows Lucrezia's life without unexpected twists, but with vividly presented scenes. Unsurprisingly the dialogue is bright and lively, which made the transfer to the stage straightforward, but performance had been envisioned from the outset. The premiere was held in the castle in Nepi which Lucrezia's father had refortified and refurbished for her when he was still a cardinal and presented to her when he became Pope. Here she found refuge after Cesare Borgia had the first Alfonso assassinated.

More or less simultaneously, Dario turned his attention to Maria Callas in a work he chose not to call a novel. In his account, he and Franca 'thought of enhancing their series of essays and theatrical accounts by describing the lives of celebrated personages in novel form, alternating them with texts dealing with historical events . . . We dedicated the last two stories to two celebrated female figures, Lucrezia Borgia and Maria Callas.'⁴ Dario had first met Callas in his twenties during his days at the Brera academy. He was earning extra cash by helping erect the scenery when a woman walked on to the stage. When she started singing, the young men climbed down to sit enraptured in the wings and listen to Maria Callas rehearse Bellini's *Norma*. Later in life, she had a flat in Milan, where Dario got to know her better. She and Franca shared the same dress designer.

The projected work was given the provisional title *A Forgotten Callas*, and was being co-written with Franca as a playscript but was unfinished at her death. He revised and rewrote it as a biographical portrait, once again presented in three forms, the book entitled *Dario Fo Paints Maria Callas*, an exhibition of paintings and performance. There were three performers on stage, identified as Dario, Actor (the narrator), and Actress (Maria Callas). The performance version included excerpts from her operas, while images by Dario were projected onto a screen behind the performers. The exhibition was held in Verona, and all the works on display were bought up by one admirer for his own gallery, following which the Minister for Culture established in an ex-granary in the same city a public gallery exclusively for Dario's works.

The book and the paintings were produced at a speed and intensity which was typical of those years. Dario could be found in one room dictating the text to a young man, while in an adjoining room two young artists, Jessica Borroni and Chiara Porro, were working on a highly erotic depiction of a naked Callas as Venus, with little men clambering over her body. Seemingly, this image had come to Dario in a dream. In the book, the image is altered and she is shown in a recumbent pose, with one man seated on a breast, another dangling from her hair and others paddling around her on little boats. The reference is not now to the goddess but to *Gulliver's Travels*. The dialogue has her report on a dream in which she, who notoriously had problems with her weight, lies naked on a beach while her fellow actors and singers tuck into a sumptuous meal in a restaurant nearby. The beach is in Lilliput, the little men who surround her are not ogling her but simply walking over and around her. 'A pleasant dream,' pronounces the character Dario, to which the Actress retorts, 'Pleasant but anguished, so much so that after the dream, I burst into desperate tears.' She suffered early humiliation when she found the doors of opera houses in America closed to her. Even when she had attained international fame, she endured further, extremely public, humiliation at the hands of Aristotle Onassis who after a long relationship abruptly and callously abandoned her for Jacqueline Kennedy. Dario compared her to Medea, but the tone of the piece is celebratory rather than tragic.

The urge to pass on his experience was strong, and in September he helped the students at the Milan Drama College stage *The Story of Qu*, inspired by stories of the Chinese writer, Lu Xun set in the early days of Chinese revolution. Dario played his part with his face covered by a cage of the sort which people in ancient China were compelled to wear if guilty of having offended the powers that be. He was no longer keen on long journeys by plane, but in November he was in Stuttgart for the opening of an exhibition of his work and a performance of *God Is Black*, a work which had first been performed in Milan in 2011.[5] It was more than a revival. The concept of evolution was yet another subject which piqued his curiosity and became a dominant interest which would lead him to produce a book on Darwin.

There was one more book before 2014 was out, the novel *Ciulla, the Great Miscreant*,[6] co-authored with Piero Sciotto, a singer-songwriter and actor who had worked with Dario and Franca as performer and administrator since the 1970s. Sciotto is Sicilian and introduced Dario to the figure of Paolo Ciulla, failed architect, aspiring artist, political agitator, anarchist, gentleman crook endowed with just enough generosity towards the poor to make him a plausible candidate as a Robin Hood figure, and forger of genius, perhaps 'the greatest forger in Italian history.' He was also gay, which made life awkward in the nineteenth century, but he was a survivor and an opportunist. In spite of the dual authorship and the interest arising at the urging of Sciotto, Ciulla drew a high level of solidarity from Dario and may be the character with whom he most fully identified. Ciulla's anarchist convictions, his status as artist, his zeal as political activist, his position as social outsider, his utopian aspirations make him an alter ego of Dario Fo. In the novel, he is described as a *fabulatore,* the term for the teller of tales Dario had known as a youth on Lago Maggiore, and whose influence on him he repeatedly emphasised. Ciulla attempted to 'earn some money to add to his bursary by telling satirical stories in restaurants on speculation in the building trade and on political theft', just as Dario had done.

When he came back into Dario's life, Sciotto gave a colourful description of life at home:

> We worked on the book at a distance. It would have been impossible to work elbow to elbow. Dario divides his time between thousands of the most varied tasks – painting above all, which fills in his days and takes up the dead moments between one activity and another. Then, apart from our novel, there's the other writing he was engaged on, other novels and the revision of *The Holy Jester Francis.* Not to mention the productions on tour in Italy and Europe, Franca's *The Flight from the Senate,* for instance. And then there was the TV work, the endless meetings and interviews on a wide variety of subjects. In other words, Dario does not spare himself. He never stops. He was always the same, but even more when Franca was not there with him. Collaborating with Dario, in the sense of working together, is never an easy business. His presence is so strong and overwhelming that it makes life difficult for anyone who wants to establish an equal relationship. A vain hope![7]

Sicilian history is dotted with men like Ciulla, normally celebrated in song and legend in spite of, or perhaps because of, being bandits, but mainly for their prowess in besting the system. The qualities that made him admired in Sicily are those which made him appeal to Dario and Piero, and the portrait is benevolent and largely uncritical. As they discussed the project, they were struck by connections revealed between Ciulla's biography and present-day conditions, as Piero explained: 'leaving aside the mythical, legendary aspect of the story, in reconstructing the events we immediately had the sensation that we were working on a political script, as though we had discovered the DNA of modern Italy.' The historical novel is rarely only about history. The landmarks that rose to the surface, as mentioned in the preface, are the depressingly familiar phenomena of 'organised crime and corruption. The much flaunted innovations concern only the *techniques* of application. Nothing else. This story has been repeated in various forms for 150 years. It has not ended and who knows when it will end?'

They fixed on an acceptable division of labour. 'Dario devoted himself to the reconstruction, imaginative at times, of the life of Paolo Ciulla. I attempted to document his life in a historical context. We both of us threw ourselves into the study of the history of Italy from Re-Unification to Fascism.' Little is known about Ciulla's private life, and in the book he emerges as an anti-hero, almost at times as Dario's rogue twin. Both men displayed a tendency to view society as being awry, both possessed a wayward wit and displayed anarchic behaviour and disrespect for authority. The historical background, in this case post-Risorgimento Italy already home to banking scandals and political malfeasance, is carefully sketched out to explain the context within which Ciulla's life unfolds. That life was not lacking in colour and incident. After failing to make his way in Italy, he left for South America, where he was confined for years in a mental hospital in Argentina, a period he used to perfect the printing skills he put to gainful use as a forger on his return to Italy. He was discovered by the police by pure chance, and his trial became one of the *causes célèbres* of Italy in the turbulent Twenties. Detailed legal records and journalistic accounts survive and they provide the bulk of the latter half of the book. Ciulla tested the judge's patience with mischievous comments from the dock. He ended up in jail, but his irreverence won him a place in the pantheon of popular heroes.

Dario was now producing books as though from a mass production line. In January 2015, another historical novel was published, set at the opposite end of Europe, in eighteenth-century Denmark. *There is a Mad King in Denmark* was authored by Dario alone, although Jacopo is credited with sparking his interest in the subject.[8] The characters and theme are those which provided the plot for the acclaimed Danish film, *A Royal Affair,* directed by Nikolai Arcel and released in 2012, although there is no reference to the film in the book. Both focus on the lives and policies of King Christian VII of Denmark and his son, Frederick, although Dario's novel covers a slightly longer time span.

Christian had intermittent periods of insanity and of lucidity, and in his clearer moments showed an awareness that there was something rotten in the state of Denmark. The ideas disseminated by the Enlightenment philosophers offered a way forward. It is not clear whether he reached this conclusion on his own or at the promptings of his English Queen, Caroline Matilda, and of his private physician, the German Johann Friedrich Struensee, but both certainly encouraged him in his policies of innovation and reform. Struensee's admiration for the thoughts of Jean Jacques Rousseau was no secret. The king and the physician developed a deep friendship, which led to the king appointing Struensee Chief Minister of his government. Together they embarked on a far-reaching reform programme, including banning torture, releasing the peasants from burdens laid on them by their lords, introducing freedom of the press and ordering the liberation of slaves in the Danish empire. These policies outraged the conservative nobility, particularly the Queen Mother, Juliana Maria of Brunswick-Lüneburg, a figure who has all the ingrained malice, even more strongly portrayed in the film than in the book, of the wicked stepmother of fairy-tale. She was the second wife of Christian's father and had the additional motivation of wishing to see her son eventually succeed to the throne instead of Prince Frederick. A personal motif, the blossoming love of Struensee and Queen Caroline Matilda, complicates life in the palace even further and threatens to bring vengeful repercussions, although not from the king. One of the symptoms of Christian's psychological disturbance is that having fallen in love with his wife on their first meeting and having made her pregnant with Frederick, he loses interest in her. He views the growing intimacy between his wife and friend with equanimity, and is even happy to encourage Struensee to provide his wife with the affection he can no longer give her. This love affair is central to the plot of the film and provides some erotic scenes, but while it is recounted in Dario's novel, it does not have the same prominence. However, this novel is one of the few times in his career as writer that he attempts to endow his characters with an emotional life. He may have shown elsewhere a desire to enquire into eros and the erotic, but the interest was abstract and societal, not conveyed in the personal lives of his characters. In *There is a Mad King in Denmark*, there are moments where he describes with lyrical touches the joy of romantic union and physical contact between a loving couple, but this is not the leitmotif of the plot. This dimension is not Dario's forte.

The novel is mildly didactic in intent, as had been the story of Paolo Ciulla, and Dario's interest is in society and reforming ideas. His involvement with eighteenth-century Denmark and the cult of reason and moderation that were part of the Enlightenment is deep and genuine, but it is never hard to glimpse contemporary Italy behind the Danish façade. The narrative and the authorial voice of this first part have greater assurance than in *The Pope's Daughter*, and there is little sign of the overt, sometimes intrusive or heavy irony of the sort employed elsewhere. This is a more soberly written work, produced by an author who recounts the eighteenth century, its culture and behaviour with a lightness of touch which carries echoes of Italo Calvino. Irony in this case springs from the tone of disbelief and incredulity which is intrinsic to the narrative itself and which seems demanded by a sane response to the unfolding events. Nor are the illustrations to the novel the exuberant, riotous sketches which had embellished other works in this period, but restrained, highly professional full-length or head-and-shoulders portraits of the chief players, framed and finished in the style visible on the walls of eighteenth-century mansions all over Europe. They resemble the work of a master forger.

This may be his most complete and satisfactory work in this genre, but he produced another three. *A Man Burned Alive* retells, with the assistance of the man's daughter, the story of a Kosovan immigrant who was indeed murdered by his Italian employer after having the temerity to demand a salary and his rights as a worker. *Of Gypsy Race* recounts the tragedy of Johann Tollman, a German boxer who aspired to represent his country at the Amsterdam Olympics, but who was on account of his race barred by law. He turned professional, and was denied the title of national champion in spite of having won the decisive bout. He actually fought in the German army in World War II, but under the Nazis the Sinti suffered the same fate as the Jews and Johann eventually died in a concentration camp. For his final novel, Dario recycled a title, *Almost by Chance a Woman,* he had used for a play on Queen Elizabeth I, but this time his subject was Queen Christina of Sweden, who ruled in the days of the wars of religion. She may have been lesbian and certainly chose to dress as a man, but perhaps this was a means of asserting her right to rule. A highly cultured woman, she invited philosophers such as Descartes to Stockholm, but she herself converted to Catholicism and moved to Rome, where she is buried.

It may not be the central point of the novel, but it is noticeable that Dario showed sympathy for the travails of age, for even his physical energy was failing. Not so his intellectual energy. In this late flowering, the topics he faced included Renaissance Italy, Fascist Italy, Nazi Germany, opera, Enlightenment Denmark, contemporary racism and a Swedish monarch.

CHAPTER 25

At Odds with God and Darwin

In his final years, Dario found himself impelled to come to terms with God and Charles Darwin, although his encounter with God was comedy and that with Darwin serious drama. In some senses, the one is the distaff side of the other. If he remained engaged with the politics of the community as well as with art and theatre, he was also drawn to reflect on the opening and closing of life in a style which might in another age have been described as a search for the numinous, the transcendent or even the religious, but his was a totally secular vision. His search was that of an unrepentant atheist who had been educated as a boy in the Christian ethics of charity and love, who accepted as an adult the emptiness of the heavens but who in age could no longer prevent himself from wondering about a dimension of life beyond the material and the social.

He was not engaged in a quest for a unifying theory of theories. Dario's mind was a crowded place, with unrelated ideas crashing into one another. All his projects at this time took the final form of book, exhibition and performance, and before his tussle with the Divine and Evolution, there were three main initiatives, on widely differing subjects, which engaged the Fo studio in 2015. *More Tricks of the Trade* was presented as a sequel to the earlier *Tricks of the Trade,* but while the first work was a collection of random workshops and talks given in various venues and collated by Franca, the new work was conceived as a whole and had as much unity and coherence as Dario's restless mind was capable of imposing on any subject. It is best viewed as a mixture of manifesto and autobiography of his life in theatre, richly illustrated with new paintings and then transformed into a stage work. The illustrations on *Mistero buffo* were subsequently displayed in an exhibition mounted at Pavia, and they then formed yet another book.[1] The autobiographical chapters go back to his debut days with the one-act farces in the 1950s and his important meetings with the director Giorgio Strehler at the Piccolo. More unexpectedly, he tells of an encounter in Berlin with Samuel Beckett while the latter was supervising the lighting and set construction for a production of *Endgame,* an example was used by Dario to demonstrate to actors, directors and authors the need to be fully conversant with every aspect of theatre, not merely their own sector. He goes into some detail on the days of terrorism in Milan which were the background to his own *Accidental Death of an Anarchist,* and discourses at length on the production of *The People's War in Chile,* a play inspired by the overthrow of Salvador Allende and which included the fiction that a coup d'etat was taking place in Italy while the production was on stage, an episode which caused havoc among the audience. The history of the occupation of Palazzo Liberty, his clashes with the Milan City Council and contemporary difficulties with magistrates and police even after the abolition of censorship are important chapters in his theatre history, as are his accounts of his approach to staging *grammelot* in Paris and to directing Stravinsky's *Histoire du Soldat* at La Scala. He never did provide a wholly systematic treatment of his ideas of popular theatre, but he returned again to the subject to make it clear that he intended it as class-based theatre which combined political fire with entertainment and eschewed overt preaching.

Those around him, especially Jacopo, goaded him to share their interests and obsessions, and looked to him to give the final shape to their projects. Jacopo came across the story of the Seminole Indians, natives of Florida, whose culture was, they believed, peace-loving, whose power structure was matriarchal and who had never had any truck with slavery. He arranged a conference in Perugia in 2010 to examine their way of life and involved Dario in the research over the following years. The outcome was a book, *The Forbidden History of America*, written by Dario with the collaboration of nine others and whose publication in late 2015 was accompanied, as was then usual, by an art exhibition and a touring theatrical work.[2] The book features such unusual, strong characters as Alexander McGillivray, a chieftain of partly Scottish origin who managed to become leader of a confederation of tribes, or John Horse, a black, former slave who led his followers from a plantation to unite with the Seminole. In spite of their pacifist inclinations, the tribe had fought off the British, Spanish and incomer Americans and had never surrendered nor signed any treaty with the Washington government. The paintings included some powerful individual portraits as well as some colourful scenes of agriculture and warfare. The history of the tribe has that touch of idyllic utopianism which could not fail to appeal to Dario, especially since it allowed him, as he had done with the novels on Lucrezia and Queen Christina, to challenge accepted myths, this time on Red Indians as depicted in Hollywood films. The Seminole eventually made their peace with modern America, although Dario's disappointment is almost tangible as he recounts their problems with drugs and the wealth they accumulated through establishing betting casinos. They are also owners of the international chain of Hard Rock Cafés.

The book was published in November and in the same month he was in Brescia for the opening of an exhibition commissioned by the city's gallery and featuring work from the Russian years of Marc Chagall, together with works of Dario's executed as an act of homage to the artist. There were thirty-five works on loan from St Petersburg together with original works by Dario, who also wrote the discursive text for the catalogue and the script for a monologue which went on in the municipal theatre.[3] It was an act of love, for Dario had first seen Chagall's work in Paris when he was in his twenties and was struck by similarities between Chagall's art and that of the contemporary Italian 'metaphysical' school which included some of his masters such as Carlo Carrà. He was also taken by the lightness of touch, the harmony and the delight in colour he detected in Chagall. In his presentation of the exhibition, Dario emphasised that his own new canvases were not an imitation or a copy of the Russian master, but a continuation of his work, representing an attempt to draw and paint as Chagall might have done had he survived. 'I pushed on, I put myself in his mind,' he said.

The approach of his 90th birthday on 24 March 2016 was the occasion for an outpouring of public praise, the organisation of conferences and exhibitions, journalistic and academic retrospectives and for a general summing up, although he himself was engrossed in the various tasks in hand and looked back only when invited to do so by interviewers. Harvard hosted a commemorative event, but while he had travelled there in the past, on this occasion he was only able to send a greeting by skype, a modern device he did not enjoy using. Milan made a late bid to become the home of the enormous archive which had been built up by Franca, and which included all his writings and re-edits as well as his canvases, backdrops and papier maché sculptures, but the decision had already been made to house everything in Verona. The gallery was officially opened by the Minister for Culture on Dario's birthday. Meanwhile, moves were underway in Edinburgh to organise a Fo-Fest which would include the first exhibition of his paintings in the UK. This event was scheduled to include a personal appearance by Dario at the Lyceum for a discussion with the audience based on the *New Tricks of the Trade*. The project ran into various difficulties, exacerbated by his ill health, particularly over the choice of works to be displayed. It was planned as a retrospective and this idea was encouraged by the administrators in Verona who were happy to lend works, since the newly opened gallery was about to close to allow restructuring and extensions, but Dario himself vetoed the plan since he wanted to be fully involved in the definitive lay-out of his gallery. The exhibition in Edinburgh went ahead in October in a much reduced format, and was accompanied by seminars and a much applauded performance of *Francis the Holy Jester* by Mario Pirovano.

Dario's health was declining, but he could not reconcile himself to the infirmities of age and insisted on continuing with new work and with public appearances. The performances which were intrinsic to his ongoing project were done mainly in small theatres in the towns where the exhibitions were mounted, but he still appeared before huge crowds with scenes from *Mistero buffo* which had been in his repertoire since the 1970s. He was required to take medicines and drugs, and perhaps they were the reason why he was occasionally prey to hallucinations which caused him to see his canvases moving. 'Ninety seems a crazy age to be, I have still ideas to proceed with, and I get indignant.' He explained to one interviewer that 'life surprises me, often negatively,' adding that he was delighted to have his faculties intact and his lucidity unimpaired. 'I have some loss of memory for certain facts or situations, I cannot remember names but I have produced so much and have never been so passionate or enjoyed myself so much as in these times.' His happiness was diminished only by his consciousness of living in a world of the 'walking dead. A man who does not participate in the life of his community, who keeps himself apart is a dead man walking. There are so many people, including young people, who struggle to get by. This is a society which does not give you stimuli. Seeing people who allow themselves to be bought, who lick other people's boots, who accept any mortification just to keep themselves afloat – that's how people die, because they are wedded to the obvious, the banal.[14]

Dario had some years previously informed the bemused world that 'the obscene is sacred', and ever since *Mistero buffo,* with its sketches on *The Marriage Feast at Cana* or the *Raising of Lazarus,* and the later monologues on St Francis, he had been drawn to the sacred or the religious, more powerfully so with advancing years. He always insisted that only the cultural outgrowth of religious practice interested him. In 2007, he had published *Jesus and Women*, a large, sprawling album which relies on the apocryphal gospels.[5] The original inspiration for this work derived from a visit Dario and Franca made to Barcelona to perform in the *teatre grec*. The group on stage before them were gypsy singers who sang that 'Christ was undoubtedly a gypsy', and that he 'snapped his fingers and danced'. No one was able to identify the author of this number which probably belonged to folklore, but discussions and research led the couple to reconsider the role of women in the life of Christ and to mount in this book an attack on institutional or religious-based misogyny.

He returned in his own idiosyncratic style to the theme of the sacred, the divine and the spiritual with *Dario and God*, another book-length interview with Giuseppina Manin.[6] The title does not indicate some Augustinian conversion. He dismisses in the opening lines any notion that God might exist, and regards His existence as an invention of human genius, adding that God is made in the image and likeness of man. Being asked how he viewed God, he replied, 'As a talented madman. Obsessive and brutal, ironic and touchy. The greatest of story-tellers, a phenomenal con-man. Certainly an egocentric of the "me me me and nobody else" type. In addition, vengeful and contradictory. Someone who says he loves you but the moment you upset him, he unleashes the angelic hordes on you.'

It is an intriguing book, blasphemous in some eyes but laced with willing respect for belief and believers. Dario draws generously on the apocryphal gospels to devise an alternative evangelical story and create a new Christ who gave greater prominence and power to women, who may have been married to Mary Magdalene, who during the private first thirty years of his life performed miracles to please his companions, who may have had a secret pact with Judas – himself author of an apocryphal gospel – and who after his entombment descended into hell to close it down. Dario's quotations and use of sources was always haphazard, and certainly here he gives his imagination free rein.

However, there is a deeper layer and a more personal quest in the book, a humanist probe into a zone of the mysterious, the inexplicable and even the uncanny. He demonstrates the state of mind of other creative geniuses, such as Ibsen with *When We Dead Awaken* or Pirandello with his late myths such as *Lazarus*, when they struggle to accept that the world around them is all there is, that the intensity of their creative vision is no guard against the common lot of humankind. The chapter entitled *Mors mea, vita mea* (My Death, My Life) has Dario expatiating on the suddenness and absoluteness of death. When Manin challenges him, 'Then nothing, nothing other than nothingness?' he replies:

> We are dust. Dust and Water. Full stop. That's what reason tells me. But then ... Imagination, fantasy, craziness give me other

443

visions. What can I say? I hope to be surprised. Already some marvels that I cannot explain happen to me. For me, who believes in logic and science, certain sensations are really hard to accept, and yet, that's the way it is. Alongside me I am often aware of some 'active presences' which help me resolve doubts or problems. When I am in a muddle and have no idea of how to get out of it, I instinctively cry out: Franca, help! And shortly afterwards, there's the unexpected answer.

There was no let-up in his touring programme. In May he was in Padua performing *Mistero buffo,* as well as part of the *Story of a Tiger.* He explained to the audience that in China 'to have a tiger is a figurative way of displaying strength of will'. It was a quality he was showing in abundance. On 3 June, he was on a platform in Rome supporting Virginia Raggi, the 5 Star candidate for mayor. All this activity took its toll. After the performance in Padua, in spite of the entreaties of his entourage, he stayed around signing books and chatting to the audience until three o'clock in the morning. He lost his voice for days, and finally contracted laryngitis with the result that a sell-out event in Rome planned for 21 June had to be postponed. Thousands turned up for the rescheduled performance at the vast, open air auditorium on 1 August, and his full-hearted exertions meant that his voice completely went. He retired to his second home in Cesenatico hoping that the sea air would help him recover. He carried on painting, and involving himself in planned exhibitions. The first on Darwin opened in Cesenatico and Dario, Jacopo and Mario Pirovano escorted parties of school children around the exhibition. It was scheduled to move to Biella in October.

He moved back to Milan, and carried on painting every day. He knew he was ill, but was keen to honour his promises to Edinburgh and Biella. It was in these circumstances, that the book on Darwin was published. Even if after receiving the Nobel Prize he had written and spoken on bio-engineering and ethical aspects of other scientific topics, to find Dario Fo tackling this subject is as implausible as finding a tract by Shakespeare on astronomy. In a letter to the mayor of Biella, written when he still hoped to be present at the opening, he said that his interest was awakened by an incident in 2009, the bi-centenary of Darwin's birth, when a 'group of reactionary hooligans' gathered to throw stones and break windows at the Museum of Natural History in Milan. The mayor of Milan, the same Letizia Moratti who had emerged victorious after the campaign when Dario had been a candidate, cut the subsidy to the museum. A director wrote to invite Dario to prepare a theatrical work on evolution as part of a campaign against reaction and ignorance, and promised to put the resources of the museum and the university at his disposal. The first result was the already mentioned 'God is Black,' but Dario's interest was whetted and he continued to work on evolution with a group of researchers.

It took some time before he found the best approach, but he eventually decided to develop the story of a character. He began with paintings, and abandoned the story he had initially in mind. *Darwin: But Are We Monkeys on the Father's or the Mother's Side?* is hardly a primer but it is also a somewhat tired work.[7] Although he originally intended to address an adult audience, Dario discovered that his most enthusiastic readers were among the young. In style, with extended sections of invented dialogue, the new book, the last he produced, is not noticeably different from others categorised as novels. There are anecdotes on moments in the life of Darwin, passages on the intelligence of animals and their sense of beauty, on politics, digressions on the Seminole as well as on Dario's revered grandfather, Bristin. He was intrigued by some of Darwin's less well known works, such as *On the Fertilisation of Orchids*, or *On the Expression of Emotions in Humans and Animals*, which for Dario establish a kind of continuity in creation. The illustrations, especially those of flying fish or of the *Beagle* in full sail, are done with crisp lines and controlled colours, while the dialogues are lively and sharply pointed, none more so than that with the captain of the *Beagle* who, as a pious Anglican, was horrified at Darwin's denial of the biblical account of the seven days of creation.

This rebuttal of Genesis was, 150 years after the publication of *On the Origin of Species*, Dario's central issue and the proof of the secular vision. The first chapter is dedicated to his tardy discovery after the fall of Fascism that the account of creation given in Genesis was not exact, and that the first humans did not live on the banks of the Tigris and the Euphrates but in Africa. So what remained? He searched in Darwin for ultimate philosophical and scientific explanations of what makes human beings what they are and what makes nature what it is. The history of evolution is retold by Dario in the style he had employed to retell the story of the gospels or ancient myths, as a teller of tales. He ends with an account of a creature which Darwin does not discuss, the flying fish, telling their story not in scientific terms but in the style of a fairy tale, with the fish assembling to discuss ow to escaper predators, and concluding that the ideal way is to grow wings.

Jacopo speculated his immersion in the writings of Darwin gave Dario renewed strength and will, but not for long. He had to submit to being taken to hospital, but had no wish to stop working even there. Jacopo and others of his closest friends and assistants turned up every day, and on more than one occasion, had to intervene when he got out of bed, started dressing and announced he was going home. The story of his illness was kept out of the newspapers, in part because the family were worried about the impact of the news on his sister, Bianca. He kept in touch with Biella by phone and sent apologies to Edinburgh. He was painting the day before he died, on 13 October 2016. The official cause of death was respiratory disease.

'I do not fear death,' he had stated earlier than year. 'My motto is to make people laugh. I dialogue with myself about it. I do not believe in paradise. I am a rigorous atheist. I love life.'

Endnotes

Chapter 1

1 Dario Fo, *Il paese dei mezarat: i miei primi sette anni (e qualcuno in più)*, Milano, Feltrinelli, 2002, 7. English translation, *My First Seven Years (Plus a Few More)*, translated by Joseph Farrell, London, Methuen, 2006.

2 Unpublished article, 1960 (?), quoted by Lanfranco Binni, *Attento te . . .!*, Verona, Bertani, 1975, 193.

3 Pina Rota Fo, *Il paese della rane*, Turin, Einaudi, 1978, 21-2.

4 Pina Rota Fo, cit. 10.

5 Quoted in *Fabulazzo*, edited by Lorenzo Ruggieri, Milan, Kaos, 1992, 52.

6 *My First Seven Years*, 73.

7 *La Repubblica*, 14 August 1996.

8 Pina Rota Fo, cit, 92.

9 Enzo Colombo and Orlando Piraccini (editors), *Pupazzi con rabbia e sentimento*, Milan, Scheiwiller, 1998, 16.

10 *Fabulazzo*, 27.

11 Interview with Dario Fo, in *Corriere della Sera*, 2 July 1993.

12 Unpublished article, 1960 (?), quoted by Lanfranco Binni, *Attento te . . .!*, Verona, Bertani, 1975, 193.

13 Lanfranco Binni, cit, 194.

14 Italo Calvino, *The Path to the Spiders' Nests*, London, Jonathan Cape, 1998, 22.

15 Pina Rota, cit, 107.

16 Documents preserved as folders 21 and 25 in the Fo-Rame Archive. Some sections are reproduced in Claudio Meldolesi, *Su un comico in rivolta*, Roma, Bulzoni, 1978, pp.18-20.

17 Chiara Valentini, *La storia di Dario Fo*, Milan, Feltrinelli, 1977, 24.

18 *My First Seven Years*, cit, 177-183.

19 Roberto Vivarelli, *La fine di una stagione*, Milan, Il Mulino, 2000; interview in *Corriere della Sera*, 6 November 2000, 17.

20 *My First Seven Years*, cit, 195-7.

21 Articolo firmato A.C.P. in *Espresso*, 23 ottobre 1997.

22 *Corriere*, cit.

23 Dario Fo, *Ballate e canzoni*, Rome, Newton Compton, 1976, 140.

24 Primo Levi, *Conversazioni e interviste 1963-87*, edited by Marco Belpoliti, Turin, Einaudi, 1997.

25 Quoted by David Ward, in *Antifascisms*, Cranbury, NJ, Associated University Presses, 1996, 165.

26 Bianca Fo, *La ringhiera dei miei vent'anni*, Turin, Einaudi, 1981, 11.

27 Claudio Meldolesi, cit, 33.

28 Interview with Pietro Landi, in *Dario Fo: il teatro nell'occhio*, Florence, Casa Usher, 1984, 17.

29 Dario Fo and Franca Rame, translated by Joseph Farrell, *More Tricks of the Trade*, London, Methuen, 2016, 14-15.

30 Pietro Landi, cit, 18.

Chapter 2

1 *My First Seven Years*, cit,.155.

2 Franco Parenti, *Di me stesso*, in pamphlet entitled 'Franco Parenti', Rome, Armando Curcio editore, 1981, 30.

3 Bianca Fo Garambois, cit, 64.

4 For information on her life, and the experiences of her family, I am grateful to Franca Rame for a long interview she gave me in 1998. She also allowed me to see pages of an autobiography which years later became *Una vita all'improvviso*, Parma, Guanda, 2009. I am also grateful to Professor Ferruccio Marotti of the University of Rome for letting me watch a video of an interview he had recorded with Franca.

5 Serena Anderlini, 'Franca Rame: Her Life and Works', in *Theater*, Winter, 1985, 34.

6 Fabulazzo, cit, 72

7 *Una vita all'improvviso*, cit, 92-3.

8 Interview in *Donna*, April 1991.

Chapter 3

1 Enzo Jannacci, *Canzoni*, Roma, Lato Side, 1980, 66.

2 Private interview with Enzo Jannacci, in Udine, January 2000.

3 Interview of Dario Fo with Marco Mangiarotti, in *Doppiovu*, February 1978.

4 Umberto Eco, in *'Sipario'*, December, 1963, p.29

5 *'Dario Fo Explains'*, interview with Luigi Ballerini and Giuseppe Risso, in Drama Review, March '77, p.36.

6 Interview with Enzo Magri, in *Fabulazzo*, cit, p.40.

7 Jacques Lecoq, *Le corps poétique*, Paris, Actes Sud-papiers, 1997, 6-8.

8 Chiara Valentini, cit, 45.

9 Dario Fo, *Manuale minimo dell'attore*, Milano, Einaudi, 1987, 235-6.

10 *Fabulazzo*, cit, p.22.

11 *Il Giorno*, 27 May 1958.

Chapter 4

1 Miriam Mafai, *Il sorpasso*, Milan, Mondadori, 1997, 50.

2 Dario Fo and Franca Rame, translated by Joseph Farrell, *More Tricks of the Trade*, London, Methuen, 2016, 58,

3 Miriam Mafai, cit.56.

4 Bent Holm, *Dario Fo's Bourgeois Period: Carnival and Criticism*, in *Dario Fo: Stage, Text, and Tradition*, edited by Joseph Farrell and Antonio Scuderi, Southern Illinois University Press, 2000.

5 Erminia Artese, *Dario Fo parla di Dario Fo*, Cosenza, Lerici, 1977, 40.

6 Paolo Puppa, *Il teatro di Dario Fo*, Venice, Marsili, 1978.

7 *My First Seven Years*, cit, 139-141.

8 *Sipario*, no.164, September, 1959, 37.

9 Dario Fo, *Aveva due pistole e occhi bianchi e neri*, in Commedie, volume 1, Turin, Einaudi, 1966, 97.

10 Franca Rame and Dario Fo, *Una vita all'impovviso*, Parma, Guanda, 2009, 119.

11 Dario Fo, *Ballate e canzoni*, Rome, Newton Compton, 1976. p.49.

12 *Ballate e canzoni*, cit, p.50, and the episode recounted in Chiara Valentini, cit, 80.

13 This analysis is made by Paolo Puppa, op cit, and by Bent Holm.

14 *Le commedie di Dario Fo*, vol 2, 207.

15 *Le commedie*, cit, 214.

16 Dario Fo, *Tricks of the Trade*, cit, 22/3.

17 *Le commedie*, cit, 246.

18 I am grateful to the late Nanni Ricordi for his recollections of this period. I have also made use of the history of the NCI by Cesare Bermani, *Una storia cantata*, Milan, Jaca Book, 1997.

19 Bermani, cit, 87.

20 Quoted in Bermani, cit, 87.

21 Ceare Bermani, *Il nuovo canzoniere italiano dal 1962 al 1968*, Milan, Mazzotta, 1978, 17.

22 Lanfranco Binni, *Dario Fo*, Florence, La Nuova Italia, 1977, 44.

23 Michele L Straniero, *Giullari & Fo*, Rome, Lato Side, 1978.

Endnotes

Chapter 5

1   Gianfranco Manfredi, introduction to Enzo Jannacci, cit, 30.

2   Dario Fo, *Tricks of the Trade*, cit.,171/2.

3   David L Hirst, *Giorgio Strehler*, Cambridge University Press, 1987, 14.

4   Dario Fo, *Le commedie di Dario Fo*, volume 1, 1966, 26.

5   From interview in *Liberation*, 9 January 1974, quoted by Lanfranco Binni, *Attento te . . .!*, Verona, Bertani, 1975, 227.

6   Dario Fo, lecture on Popular Theatre. Quoted by Lanfranco Binni, cit., 147.

7   Binni, cit.,146.

8   Valentini, cit, p106.

9   Franceschi's speech is quoted in *Giullari & Fo*, cit. 150.

10 *Giullari & Fo*, cit, 151.

11 Philip Willem, *Puppet Masters*, London, Constable,1991.

12 Michele L Straniero, cit, 44.

13 Dario Fo con Luigi Allegri, *Dialogo provocatorio sul comico, il tragico e la ragione*, Bari, Laterza, 140-1.

14 Dario Fo, op. cit. 94.

15 Dario Fo & Franca Rame, *Nuovo manuale minimo dell'attore*, Milano, Chiarelettere, 2015, pp107-120.

Chapter 6

1   Quoted by Lanfranco Binni, op. cit. 263.

2   Dario Fo, *Fabulazzo*, cit. 76.

3   Among the many works on the Piazza Fontana bombing and the subsequent court cases, the following are particularly relevant: Camilla Cederna, *Pinelli: una finestra sulla strage*, Milano, Il Saggiatore, 2004: Adriano Sofri, *La notte che Pinelli*, Palermo, Sellerio, 2009; Adriano Sofri, a cura di, *Il malore attivo dell'anarchico Pinelli*, Palermo, Sellerio, 1996.

4   For the testimony of the family, see Mario Calabresi, *Spingendo la notte piú in là*, Milan, Mondadori, 2007, and the interview with Gemma Calabresi, "Il valore della speranza", in *A onor del vero*, Trento, Il Margine, 2012.

5   Dario Fo, *Compagni senza censura*, Milan, Mazzotta, 1973, volume 2, 189.

6   Dario Fo, introduction to the third edition of *Bang! Bang! Who's There? The Police!* Verona, Bertani, 1974.

7   Dario Fo and Luigi Allegri, op.cit. 149/150.

8   Interview with Gianni Giolo, in *Il Lombardo*, 8 September 1973.

9   These dates and figures are taken from Tullio Barbato, *Il terrorismo in Italian*, Milan, Editrice Bibliografica, 1980.

10 *L'Europeo*, 16 February 1981.

11 *L'Europeo*, 3 June 1980.

12 *L'Europeo*, cit.

13 Franca Rame, in *Non parlarmi degli archi parlami delle tue galere*, Milan, F.R. edizioni, 1984, 133-4.

14 Alberto Franceschini, *Mara, Renato e io*, Milan, Mondadori, 143-4.

Chapter 7

1   *Il Giorno*, 21 February 1973.

2   Dario Fo, *Il Boccaccio riveduto e scorretto*, Parma, Guanda, 2011, 16.

3   Interview with Natalia Aspesi, *Corriere della Sera*, 15 February 1988.

4   Jacopo Fo, private interview, May 2017

5   Based on interview of Franca with me, and with Natalia Aspesi, cit.

6   Translation by Gillian Hanna, in Dario Fo and Franca Rame, *A Woman Alone & Other Plays*, London, Methuen, 1991, 86.

7   Article in *La Repubblica*, 11 February 1998.

8   Natalia Aspesi, cit.

9   Introduction to *Ci ragiono e canto 3*, Verona, Bertani, 1973, 7.

10 Interview with Gianni Giolo, *Il Lombardo*, 8 September 1973.

11 Franca Rame, cit, p.XI-XII.

12 Epilogue to volume quoted, 89.

13 The document in quoted in full in Lanfranco Binni, cit. 67-84.

14 Op cit,,85-96.

15 Franca Rame, Introduction to *Le commedie di Dario Fo*, volume, 111, Turin, Einaudi,1975, XI.

16 *Avanguardia Operaia*, 26 October 1973.

17 *Avanguardia Operaia*, 19 October 1973.

18 Quoted by Chiara Valentini, cit, 147.

19 Dario Fo in Artese, op. cit. 124/5.

20 This account is based on Chiara Valentini, *Panorama*, 22 November 1973, and *More Tricks of the Trade*, cit, *129-157*.

21 Dario Fo, *Guerra del popolo in Cile*, Verona, Bertani, 1974.

22 Franca Rame in *Il teatro politico di Dario Fo*, cit. p.148.

23 *Panorama*, 22 November 1973.

Chapter 8

1 Colette Godard, *Le Monde*, 12 December, 1973.

2 *More Tricks of the Trade*, cit, 160-1.

3 *More Tricks*, cit, 169.

4 Corriere della Sera, 7 September 1975.

5 Autobiographical writing by Franca Rame. Unpublished in that form.

6 Lanfranco Binni, cit, 1975, pp.127–175, provides a detailed account of this conference, with verbatim reports of Fo's speeches.

7 Binni, cit. 137-8.

8 Binni, cit, 153.

9 Dario Fo, in a note to the first edition of *Non si paga, non si paga!*, Milan, 1974.

10 Paolo Prato, *Tradition, Exoticism, Cosmopolitanism in Italian Popular Music (1950s-1980s)*, Differentia 2 (1988), p212

11 *Non si paga, Non si paga!* cit, .4

12 *Non si paga, Non si paga!* In Le commedie di Dario Fo, volume XII, Turin, Einaudi, 1998, 11. The quotation is taken from the version revised for the 1980 production.

13 Dario Fo, translated by Joseph Farrell, *Low Pay? Won't Pay!* London, Methuen, 2010.

Chapter 9

1 Interview with Paolo Calcagna, in *Corriere d'Informazione*, February 1975.

2 Op cit.

3 Panorama, 12 June 1975, 144.

4 Panorama, cit, 147.

5 Franco Quadri, *La politica del regista*, Milan, Edizioni il Formichiere, 219.

6 *Il Manifesto*, 29 June 1975.

7 Philip Short, *Mao: A Life*, London, Hodder and Stoughton, 1999; Jonathan Spence, *Mao*, London, Weidenfeld, 1999.

8 *Corriere d'Informazione*, 6 September 1975.

9 *Il Mondo*, 25 September 1975.

10 *Espresso*, 25 September, 1975.

11 Interview in *La Gazzetta Sportiva*, February 1986.

12 Panorama, 25 September 1975.

13 Conference proceedings published in Lanfranco Binni, *Dario Fo*, cit, 83.

14 Op. cit, 87.

15 *Corriere d'Informazione*, cit.

16 *L'Espresso*, cit.

17 *L'Espresso*, cit.

18 Article in *L'Espresso*, republished in *Fabulazzo*, cit, pp301-3.

Chapter 10

1 Giorgio Bocca, *Il caso 7 Aprile*, Milan, Feltrinelli, 1980, 97/8.

2 Tullio Barbato, *Il terrorismo in Italia*, Milan, Editrice Biblioteca, 1980, p.123.

3 Quotes from an article by Guido Passalacqua, in *La Repubblica*, 1 April 1976.

4 Wladimiro Greco, in *Il Giorno*, 15 April 1976.

5 Dario Fo, in *L'Espresso*, December, 1975.

6 *Le commedie di Dario Fo*, edited by Franca Rame, Turin, Einaudi, 1998, 87.

7 Tullio Barbato, cit. 126.

8 Carlo Brusati, *Corriere d'Informazione*, 28 April 1976.

9 Dario Fo, *La Marjuana della madre è la più bella*, Verona, Bertani editore, 1976.

10 Interview in *Fronte Popolare*, 22 February 1976.

11 *La Marijuana*, cit, 116.

12 Tullio Barbato, cit, 117.

13 Grant Amyot, *The Italian Communist Party*, London, Croom Helm, 1981, 208.

14 Corriere d'Informazione, 26 July 1976.

15 The articles by Abruzzese and Fo, as well as contributions by other directors such as Mario Missiroli, appeared in *Rinascita*, nos 42, 43, 44, October, 1976. Fo's article was republished in *Fabulazzo*, cit, 275-280.

16 Corrado Stajano, article in *Ill Messaggero*, 12 October 1976.

Chapter 11

1 Corrado Stajano, *Il Messaggero*, 12 November 1976.

2 *Radiocorriere*, 6 November 1976.

3 Interview with Ettore Mo, *Corriere della Sera*, 22 April 1977.

4 Antonio Scuderi, *Dario Fo and Popular Performance*, Ottawa, Legas, 1998, 68-77.

5 *La Repubblica*, 24 April 1977.

6 *La Repubblica*. cit.

7 *Panorama*, 26 April 1977.

8 *La Repubblica*, 26 April 1977.

9 *Panorama*, cit.

10 *La Repubblica*, 26 April 1977.

11 *Milano Sera*, 26 April 1977

12 *Panorama*, cit.

13 *Milano Sera*, cit.

14 Luigi Accattoli, *La Repubblica*, 28 April 1977.

Chapter 12

1 *Il teatro politico di Dario Fo*, Milan, Mazzotta, 1977.

2 *Noi Donne*, 13 March 1977.

3 *Il teatro politico*, cit, p.144.

4 Chiara Valentini, *Panorama*, March 1977.

5 *La Sicilia*, 6 March 1979.

6 Natalia Ginzburg, in *Corriere della Sera*, 10 May 1977.

7 "Contaminated Art", interview with Matthew Fleury, in *Bomb*, 1985; quoted in *Fabulazzo*, cit.

8 Interview with Marisa Fumagalli, *Noi Donne*,16 April 1977.

9 Interview with me in *The Scotsman*, 28 August 1986.

10 Serena Anderlini, "Franca Rame: Her Life and Work," in *Theater Studies*, Winter, 1985, p.34.

11 Interview with Rosella Simone, in *Marie Claire*, August 1988.

12 Franca Rame and Dario Fo, edited by Stuart Hood, *A Woman Alone and Other Plays*, London, Methuen, 1991.

13 This point is made by the historian Anna Rossi-Doria, quoted by Paul Ginsborg, *A History of Contemporary Italy*, London, Penguin, 1990, p.368.

14 Anderlini, cit, p.39.

15 *Brescia Oggi*, cit.

16 Rosella Simone, cit.

Chapter 13

1 *La Repubblica*, 24 April 1977.

2 Quoted in *Fabulazzo*, cit, 208-9.

3 Quoted in *Fabulazzo*, cit, 209-214.

4 *Corriere della Sera*, 29 September 1977.

5 Eugenio Scalfari, *La Repubblica*, 15 September 1977.

6 Dario Fo, *Storia della tigre*, Milan, edizioni F R La Comune, 1980, 6.

7 Interview in *Il Manifesto*, republished in *Fabulazzo*, cit, 298.

8 Bent Holm, *Fo, the Story-Teller*, lecture delivered at University of Copenhagen, 12 December 1997. I am grateful to Bent for providing me with a translation of his talk.

9 Interview in *Bolero Teletutto*, 18 January 1988.

10 Alberto Franceschini, *Mara, Renato e io*, Milan, Mondadori, 1996, 161.

11 Interview with Roberto Sciubba, in *L'Europeo*.

12 Interview in *L'Europeo*, 19 January, 1981.

13 *L'Europeo*, cit.

14 In *Fabulazzo*, cit, 174-189.

15 *Corriere della Sera*, 5 April 1979.

16 *Panorama*, 14 March 1978.

17 Fo provided a detailed account of the rehearsal and production process in *More Tricks of the Trade*, cit, chapter 11.

18 *Corriere*, cit.

19 *L'Espresso*, 14 October 1978.

20 Dario Fo, in *Panorama*, 7 March 1978.

21 Interview in *Ottobre*, 22 February 1979.

22 Dario Fo, *La Storia di un Soldato*, Milan, Electa, 1979, 22.

23 Marta Morazzoni, in *Il Sipario*, January, 1979.

24 *Corriere*, cit.

Chapter 14

1   *Il Giorno*, 27 January 1979; Dario gave later accounts of these days in *My First Seven Years*, chapters 22-24.

2   *Gente*, 4 March 1978.

3   *Il Giorno*, 28 January 1979.

4   Indro Montanelli, *Il Giornale*, cit in http://archivio.francarame.it

5   *Il Nord*, 8 January 1979. All articles relating to the case are now available on-line at http://archivio.francarame.it

6   *Il Nord*, 1 February 1979.

7   *Il Nord*, 22 February 1979.

8   Roberto Vivarelli, *La fine di una stagione*, Bologna, Il Mulino: interview with Dario in *Corriere della Sera*, 6 November 2000.

9   *My First Seven Years*, chapters 22-24

10 Interview with Silvia Truzzi in *Il Fatto Quotidiano*, 24 January, 2016

11 Anna Pensotti, interview with Franca Rame, *Oggi*, January 1980

12 Lalla Mori, interview, *L'occhio*, January, 1980.

13 Cristina Maza, interview, *Bolero Teletutto*, 18 January 1980.

14 Pensotti, *Oggi*, cit.

15 Mori, *L'occhio*, cit.

16 Interview with Truzzi, cit.

17 Theodore Zeldin, *An Intimate History of Humanity*, London, Sinclair-Stevenson, 1994, p.233.

18 Mori, cit.

19 *La Repubblica*, 11 March 1987.

20 This information is based on a discussion with Dario Fo in Edinburgh in 1984.

21 Franca Rame in interview with me, *The Scotsman*, 28 August 1986.

22 Interview with Ferdinando Scianna, *L'Europeo*, 19 January 1981.

23 *Sipario*, August-September, 1985, quoted by David L. Hirst, op. cit., p.74 (translation mine).

24 Dario Fo, *L'opera dello sghignazzo*, Milan, Edizioni La Comune, 1982, p.5.

25 Private interview with me.

26 *La Stampa*, 23 luglio 1981.

27 *Tricks of the Trade*, cit, p.92.

Chapter 15

1   Quoted by Anna Maria Mori, *La Repubblica*, 3 ottobre 1986.

2   Dario Fo, *Fabulazzo osceno*, Milan, Edizioni La Comune, 1982, P. 5.

3   *Fabulazzo osceno*, cit, p.8

4   *Dario Fo and Franca Rame Theatre Workshops at the Riverside Studios*, London, Red Notes. 1983

5   *Oggi*, 5 December 1984.

6   Interview with Ugo Volli, *La Repubblica*, 6 December, 1984.

7   *Il vole*, (in flight magazine of Alitalia), November, 1985, p.35.

8   Interview in *Marie Claire, August 1988*

9   Private interview with Ron Jenkins.

10 Interview in *Panorama*, 17 August 1986.

11 Renato Palazzi in *Corriere della Sera*, 17 October 1986.

12 *Il Messaggero*, 16 aprile 1987.

13 *Marie Claire*, August 1988.

14 Dario Fo, *Il ratto della Francesca*, Milan, Edizioni La Comune, 1986.

15 Interview in *Il Messaggero*, 16 April 1987.

16 Gerald Larner, *The Guardian*, 26 March 1987.

17 Dialogue reported verbatim in Carlo Verdelli, 'Sono solo nozze di Rame,' in *Epoca*, 16 February 1987.

18 Interview with me, in *Plays and Players*, June, 1987.

19 *Panorama*, 15 February 1987.

20 *Corriere della Sera*, 11 March 1987.

21 *Panorama*, cit.

22 *Non e' tempo di nostalgia*, cit, p75.

Chapter 16

1   Dario Fo, *Manuale minimo dell'attore*, Turin, Einaudi, 1987; *Tricks of the Trade*, (translated by Joseph Farrell), London, Methuen, 1991.

2   Interview on *Tricks of the Trade* in *Il Messaggero*, 16 April 1987.

3   *Tricks*, cit, p.109.

4   Interview in *Panorama*, 20 December, 1987.

5   *Panorama*, cit.

6   *Panorama*, cit.

7   *Il Corriere della Sera,* 24 agosto 1990; *La Repubblica,* 25 August 1990.

8   *La Repubblica,* 28 August1990

9   Interview with Fo, *La Repubblica,* 9 November 1990.

10   *Le commedie di Dario Fo e Franca Rame,* Turin, Einaudi, 1998, p.54

11   Dario Fo, *Johan Padan a la Descoverta de le Americhe,* Florence, Giunti, 1992.

12   Antonio Scuderi, *Dario Fo and Popular Performance,* New York, Legas, 1998, pp.42-3.

13   *La Repubblica,* 9 November 1990.

14   Jacopo Fo, *Lo Zen e l'arte di scopare,* Bussolengo, Demetra, 1995. The playscript is given as an appendix.

15   *Il resto del Carlino,* 19 November 1994.

16   *La Stampa,* 25 October 1996.

17   *Panorama,* 5 December 1996

18   Ibid.

19   Dario Fo, edited by Franca Rame, *Il diavolo con le zinne,* Turin, Einaudi, 1998; English version translated by Ed Emery as *The Devil with Tits,* London, Faber, 2000

20   Gemma Capra, *Mio marito il commissario Calabresi,* Rome, Edizioni Paoline, 1990.

Chapter 17

1   *La Repubblica,* 10 October 1997

2   Chiara Valentini, *Espresso,* 23 October 1997, p.80.

3   *Il Corriere della Sera,* 10 October 1997.

4   *La Repubblica,* cit.

5   Stefano Benni, *Introduzione a Pupazzi con rabbia e sentimento,* Milano, Libri Scheiwiller, 1998.

6   *Il Corriere della Sera,* 12 December1997.

Chapter 18

1   Dario Fo, edited by Franca Rame, *Il Boccaccio riveduto e scorretto,* Parma, Guanda, 2011, p.8

2   *Il Fatto Quotidiano,* 7 December 2013.

3   Dario Fo, *Lezione sul cenacolo di Leonardo,* San Lazzaro di Savena, Nuovi Mondi edizioni, 2001, p.33. Second edition, revised and extended, Modena, Franco Cosimo Panini, 2007.

4   Dario Fo, *Hellequi Harlekin Arlekin Arlecchino,* edited and translated by Franca Rame, Turin, Einaudi, 2011. Dario Fo and Franca Rame, *Ruzzante,* Turin, Einaudi, 2012.

5   Dario Fo, *Il paese dei mezarat: i miei primi sette anni(e qualcuno in più),* Milan, Feltrinelli, 2992; English translation by Joseph Farrell, *My First Seven Years (plus a few more),* London, Methuen, 2005.

6   Dario Fo, *L'amore e lo sghignazzo,* Parma, Guanda, 2007, p.64.

7   Domenico Manzella, quoted by Christopher Cairns in *Dario Fo e la "pittura scenica",* Naples, Edizioni Scientifiche Italiane, 2000, p. 131

8   Dario Fo, *La Bibbia dei villani,* Parma, Guanda, 2010, pp 11, 14.

9   Dario Fo, *L'osceno è sacro,* Parma, Guanda, 2010.

10   The four are *Il mondo secondo Fo* (2007), *Il paese dei misteri buffi* (2012), *Un Clown vi seppellirà* (2013), *Dario e Dio* (2016). Manin authored the posthumous *Ho visto un Fo* (2017). All published by Guanda, Milan.

Chapter 19

1   Interview with Dario Fo, *Il Tirreno,* 17 April 2010.

2   Interview with Dario Fo by Paolo Landi, in *Il teatro dell'occhio,* Firenze, La Casa usher, 1985, p.20.

3   Emilio Tadini, *Quelle figure da non perdere d'occhio,* in *Il teatro dell'occhio,* cit., p.10

4   Interview with Dario Fo, *L'Arena,* 28 August 2007.

5   Dario Fo, *La vera Storia di Ravenna,* Modena, Franco Cosimo Panini, 1999.

6   The programme was broadcast on 27 May 1999. The full text with illustrations by Fo was published as *Lezione sul Cenacolo di Leonardo,* San Lazzaro di Savena, Nuovi Mondi, 2001: second edition, revised, Modena, Franco Cosimo Panini, 2007.

7   Dario Fo, *Il tempio degli uomini liberi: il Duomo di Modena,* Modena, Franco Cosimo Panini, 2004.

8   Dario Fo, *Caravaggio al tempo di Caravaggio,* Modena, Franco Cosimo Panini, 2005, p 30

9   Dario Fo, *Il Mantegna impossibile,* Modena, Franco Cosimo Panini, 2006, p12.

10 Interview in *La Gazzetta di Mantova*, 4 July 2006

11 Dario Fo, *Bello Figliolo che tu sei Raffaello*, Modena, Franco Cosimo Panini, 2006, p60.

12 Dario Fo, *Tegno nelle Mane Occhi e Orecchi, Michelagniolo*, Modena, Franco Cosimo Panini, 2007.

13 Dario Fo, *Correggio che dipingeva appeso in cielo*, Modena, Franco Cosimo Panini, 2010.

14 Intervista in *Il Corriere del Veneto*, 20 February 2005

15 Dario Fo, *Giotto o non Giotto*, Modena, Franco Cosimo Panini, 2010.

16 Dario Fo, edited by Franca Rame and Giselda Palombi, *Sant'Ambrogio e l'invenzione di Milano*, Turin, Einaudi, 2009.

17 The major catalogue-books are: *Il teatro dell'occhio*, cit.:Dario Fo, *Pupazzi con rabbia e sentimento*, Milan, Libri Schweiller, 1998: Federico Fellini e Dario Fo, *Disegni geniali*, Milan, Mazzotta, 1999: Dario Fo e Franca Rame, edited by Luciano Silva, *Una vita per l'arte, L'arte per una vita*, Milan, Elle Esse, 2002: *Pupazzi con rabbia e sentimento: la vita e l'arte di Dario Fo e Franca Rame*, Edizioni Festival Sete Sòis Sete Luas, 2010: Dario Fo a Milano, *Lazzi sberleffi dipinti*, Milan, Mazzotta, 2012.

18 Christopher Cairns, *Dario Fo e la "pittura scenica": arte teatro regie 1977-1997*, Naples, Edizioni Scientifiche Italiane, 2000.

19 Christoper Cairns, op. cit., p28.

20 Fabio Rodriguez Amaya, *Un artista completo: Dario Fo tra impegno, ludus e creatività*, in *Una vita per l'arte, L'arte per una vita*, cit.

Chapter 20

1 Dario Fo, *Marino libero! Marino innocente!*, Turin, Einaudi, 1998.

2 Carlo Ginzburg, translated by Anthony Shugar, *The Judge and the Historian*, London, Verso, 1999, 8.

3 *La Repubblica*, 13 December 1997.

4 *Il Corriere del Ticino*, 27 May 1998.

5 *Il Corriere della Sera*, 15 December 1998.

6 Dario Fo, *L'apocalisse rimandata*, Parma, Guanda, 2008.

7 Dario Fo, *Lu santo jullàre Francesco*, Turin, Einaudi, 1999; *L'anomalo bicefalo*, supplement to the periodical, MicroMega, 2/2004

8 *L'Avvenire*, 10 July 1999.

9 Antonio Scuderi, *Unmasking the Holy Jester Dario Fo*, in Theatre Journal, 2003, pp. 275–90,

10 *Il Corriere della Sera*, 2 agosto 1999.

11 *La Repubblica*, 17 September 1999

12 Dario Fo, *Ubu Roi – Ubu bas*, distributed with La Repubblica, January, 2010.

13 The two talks were issued on a DVD with *La Repubblica*, January 2010.

14 Dario Fo & Giuseppina Manin, *Il paese dei misteri buffi*, Parma, Guanda, 2012

Chapter 21

1 *Il Corriere della Sera*, 10 June 2000.

2 *The Times*, 24 January 2006.

3 *La Stampa*, 28 February 2006.

4 Franca Rame – Dario Fo, *Una vita all'improvvisa*, Parma, Guanda, 2009, p.279.

5 *Libero*, 29 May 2006.

6 *Espresso*, 17 January 2013.

7 *Una vita all'improvvisa*, cit. In fuga dal senato, Milan, Chiarelettere, 2013.

8 *In fuga dal senato*, cit., p.22.

9 *Espresso*, cit, p.286.

10 *Il Corriere della Sera*, 23 July 2006.

11 *La Repubblica*, 15 July 2007.

12 Vladimir Majakovskij, *Messaggi ai posteri selezionati e condivisi da Dario Fo*, Rome, Editori Riuniti, 1994.

13 Interview, 21 February 2013, *What Took Centuries to create in Italy was Degraded in a Very Short Time*. Euronews website, Retrieved January 2015.

14 Dario Fo, Gianroberto Casaleggio, Beppe Grillo, *Il grillo canta sempre al tramonto: dialogo sull'Italia e il movimento 5 Stelle*, Milan, Chiarelettere, 2013.

Chapter 22

1 Franca Rame with Joseph Farrell, *Non è tempo di nostalgia*, Pisa, Della Porta editori, 2013, pp81-2.

ENDNOTES

2   Interview with Giuseppina Manin, *Corriere della Sera*, 8 December 1999.

3   Interview with me, in *The Scotsman,*, 28 August 1986.

4   Manin, cit.

5   Interview with Franca in *L'Unità*, 26 November 1991.

6   *Non è tempo di nostalgia*, cit., pp94-97.

7   *Non è tempo di nostalgia*, cit., p87.

8   Dario Fo, *Picasso Desnudo*, Parma, Guanda, 2012.

9   *Boccacio*, cit, p16.

Chapter 23

1   *Il Fatto Quotidiano*, 23 November 2014.

2   *La Stampa, 10 December 2013*

3   *Il Fatto Quotidiano*, 7 December, 2013.

4   Dario Fo and Giuseppina Manin *Un clown vi seppellirà*, Parma, Guanda, 2013.

5   *Il Fatto Quotidiano*, 2 June 2014.

6   *Il Fatto Quotidiano*, cit.

7   *L'Avvenire*, 4 January 2015.

8   *Il Fatto Quotidiano*, 6 January 2015.

Chapter 24

1   *Il Fatto Quotidiano*, 23 November 2014.

2   Dario Fo, *La figlia del Papa*, Milan, Chiarelettere, 2014.

3   Lucrezia Borgia & Pietro Bembo, translated by Hugh Shankland, *The Prettiest Love Letters in the World*, London, Collins Harvill, 1987.

4   *Dario Fo dipinge Maria Callas*, 2014, Milan, Skira, p.15.

5   Dario Fo, edited by Franca Rame and Felice Cappa, *"Dio è nero!"* Milan, Raffaello Cortina, 2001.

6   Dario Fo and Piero Sciotto, *Ciulla, il grande malfattore*, Parma, Guanda, 2014.

7   Private communication from Piero Sciotto, 30 January 2015.

8   Dario Fo, *C'è un re pazzo in Danimarca*, Milan, Chiarelettere, 2015.

Chapter 25

1   Dario Fo e Franca Rame, *Nuovo manuale minimo dell'attore*, Milano, Chiarelettere, 2015; translated by Joseph Farrell as *New Tricks of the Trade*, London, Methuen, 2016. Dario Fo, *Mistero buffo a colori*, Milano, Skira, 2016.

2   Dario Fo et al, *Storia proibita dell'America*, Milan, Guanda, 2015.

3   Dario Fo, *Omaggio a Marc Chagall*, Milan, Giunti, 2016.

4   Interview in *Gazzetta del Sud*, 24 March 2016.

5   Dario Fo, *Gesú e le donne*, Milan, Rizzoli, 2007.

6   Dario Fo e Giuseppina Manin, *Dario e Dio*, Milan, Guanda, 2016.

7   Dario Fo, *Darwin: Ma siamo scimmie da parte di padre o di madre?* Milan, Chiarelettere, 2016.

Index